HANDBOOK FOR THE COLLEGE AND UNIVERSITY CAREER CENTER

HANDBOOK FOR THE COLLEGE AND UNIVERSITY CAREER CENTER

Edwin L. Herr, Jack R. Rayman, and Jeffrey W. Garis

The Greenwood Educators' Reference Collection

GREENWOOD PRESS
Westport, Connecticut • London

Library of Congress Cataloging-in-Publication Data

Herr, Edwin L.
　　Handbook for the college and university career center / Edwin L.
Herr, Jack R. Rayman, and Jeffrey W. Garis.
　　　　p.　　cm.—(Greenwood educators' reference collection, ISSN
1056-2192)
　　Includes bibliographical references and index.
　　ISBN 0-313-28148-3
　　1. College placement services—United States—Management.
2. College placement services—United States.　3. Employment
agencies—United States—Management.　4. Employment agencies—United
States.　5. College students—Vocational guidance—United States.
I. Rayman, Jack R.　II. Garis, Jeffrey.　III. Title.　IV. Series.
LB2343.5.H47 1993
378.1′9425—dc20　　　　　92-21360

British Library Cataloguing in Publication Data is available.

Library of Congress Catalog Card Number: 92-21360
ISBN: 0-313-28148-3
ISSN: 1056-2192

First published in 1993

Greenwood Press, 88 Post Road West, Westport, CT 06881
An imprint of Greenwood Publishing Group, Inc.

Printed in the United States of America

The paper used in this book complies with the
Permanent Paper Standard issued by the National
Information Standards Organization (Z39.48-1984).

10　9　8　7　6　5　4　3　2　1

Contents

Illustrations

TABLES

Preface

In contemporary American higher education, there are continuing questions, among others, about mission and purpose, the diversity of persons being served, and the effectiveness with which this is being achieved, as well as the implications for the content and services offered by higher education institutions as they continue to implement national goals of democratization of access to the collegiate experience. Within the array of issues related to the purpose or mission of higher education in a time of dramatic change in the political, economic, and social challenges being confronted by the nation, there continue to be questions about whether the collegiate experience should focus on education for its own sake or education as preparation for more instrumental ends: citizenship and work. This reference book focuses on the latter: the rise of career centers in American higher education and the increasing comprehensiveness of their goals both to facilitate the career development of students and to provide direct assistance in the placement of students into specific jobs following graduation. As the ensuing chapters portray, both of these goals are complex in their possibilities, planning, and management of personnel and resources, as well as in their implementation.

Career centers are unique entities in higher educational institutions because they stand astride two cultures: academe and the corporate world of employment. They must be credible to both cultures in their goals, credentials, and services offered. They must respond to and reflect the values of the academic culture as they foster the career development of students; they must respond to and reflect the values of the corporate culture as they help match the placement or employment needs of students with the human capital needs of diverse corporate organizations.

As this reference discusses, career centers in collegiate environments have been evolving in the United States since late in the nineteenth century. In historical terms, their goals and structures have continued to unfold from early and relatively narrow institutional commitments concerned with providing formal mechanisms through which students can be placed into employment. Career centers are now and will be increasingly concerned as well with developing the antecedents to such placement: exploratory processes, career planning, linkage of academic majors to career paths, job search strategies, and so on.

This professional reference contends that both the career development process and the placement event need to be tailored to the career development needs shared by all college students as well as those that are unique to subpopulations of the student population defined by such variables as age, ethnicity, race, gender, national origin, and other factors that may require special attention (e.g., disability). The balances of student diversity will vary dramatically by institutions of different purpose and geography. Regardless, the characteristics of the student population to be served or other possible constituent client groups of the career center (e.g., alumni, college or university employers) are key factors in organizing the career center's services and staff.

The reference also describes the models of career centers now extant. It discusses the advantages and disadvantages of centralized and decentralized approaches to the provision of career services within different types and sizes of collegiate institutions. It emphasizes the necessary connections between the mission of an institution, the scope and implementation of the career center, and the interaction among career center staff, academic departments, and other student affairs units.

The premises, issues, and purposes on which the content of the reference rests are discussed in ten chapters. These chapters span a range of topics, including the evolution of the career center; career needs of students; planning for, and management of, the career center; career center services; building and maintaining a career library; the use of technology in the career centers; working with governmental, corporate, and nonprofit employers; coordination of graduate assistants, interns, and peer counselors; and future trends in the development of career centers. Virtually all of these topics will be relevant to career centers located in either small colleges or large multiversities. If there is a bias in the reference, it is probably toward the planning and management of career centers in larger institutions because of the complexity that is added to the structures, staffing, and communications located within the large university. Even so, however, the major issues affecting career centers remain the same regardless of size, location, or institutional purpose.

In writing a professional reference that attempts to combine scholarship and pragmatic or practical approaches in one volume, there are compromises to be made. Since this book is entitled a "handbook," we have focused its content on the practical and generalizable rather than the abstract and philosophical. We have tried to provide a context for thinking about the importance of career centers and how they have gotten to their present level of development, but we have primarily focused on our accumulated experience in attempting to plan, staff, implement, and manage career centers. We hope that the content balance we have provided is useful to our readers.

Since authors are always products of their own training and experience as well as the personal lens they use to filter and synthesize the relevant and existing professional literature, we want to acknowledge our indebtedness to the persons who have shaped our professional identities, who have offered us their advice and insights, who have permitted us to quote their work, or who have shared their work with us through the professional literature. There are too many such persons to identify by name here, but we are confident that they know who they are, and we thank them.

Finally, we express our personal debts to our wives and children for bearing with us and being supportive while we have worked on this book. We appreciate their patience and love.

Edwin L. Herr
Jack R. Rayman
Jeffrey W. Garis

1

The Evolution of the University Career Center: Contemporary Trends and Models

Since the recorded beginnings of higher education, the responsibilities of colleges and universities for helping students prepare for and make the transition to paid employment have been the subject of debate. In the early centuries of higher education in Europe and the United States, "career services" were essentially confined to how a professor or a don advocated for or mentored a student prodigy as part of his induction into a profession. This was primarily a male activity, an old boy's network, by which a faculty member would speak in behalf of a student to persons of importance who might employ him as a favor to, or out of respect for, the professor. Such activation of the professor's network of friends and acquaintances typically arose at about the time of the student's graduation from college or a university. As such, the transition from higher education to the world of employment was seen as a "placement" event, a rite de passage, in which the student underwent a metamorphosis from student to professional, from late adolescent to adult, under the tutelage and sponsorship of his or her principal professor.

Through time, placement of students into the workplace and professions for which they prepared in colleges and universities became less an act of mentoring or advocacy or networking at the level of individual professors and increasingly a centralized role of a college or university to be implemented for all students, not only those fortunate enough to have a personal advocate.

THE RISE OF PLACEMENT OFFICES

The early prototypes for such placement offices have been identified as the Oxford University Committee on Appointments, created in England in 1899 (Wrenn, 1951), and, in the United States, the office established by Yale University in 1919 (Teal & Herrick, 1962) to provide vocational guidance to students and to match them with employment positions during the academic year, the summer months, and after graduation. From these prototypical efforts and through the influence of the emerging vocational guidance movement being pioneered by the concepts of Frank Parsons in the early 1900's, as well as the growing interest of student and employers for such services, employment offices or placement bureaus rapidly appeared on campuses throughout the nation. Often, these offices were combined efforts of faculty and other college and university student personnel officials working together with alumni to identify employment opportunities and match students to them (Lorick, 1987).

In 1924, the first professional organization devoted to placement in the United States was established in Chicago. Originally called the National Association of Appointments Secretaries, using the British notion of *appointment secretary* as equivalent to the American term *placement director*, this organization changed its name to the National Association of Placement and Personnel Offices in 1928, and during the 1930's the name of the organization was changed again to that of the American College Personnel Association (Shingleton & Fitzpatrick, 1985).

As placement offices arose as part of the infrastructure of a college or university, they tended to be independent of counseling centers and other manifestations of student affairs, student personnel services, or student development. Student placement was linked to business, to economics, to employment, not to psychology, emotions, and personal development. Placement was a process by which the student's training, abilities, and preferences could be matched to the requirements of commerce, of industry, and of the professions.

Early in the current century, as colleges and universities increasingly incorporated student personnel services, student affairs, or student services as a series of student support activities parallel to the instructional or academic dimensions of university life, counseling centers and placement offices often became separate elements of such student support activities. Counseling centers and placement offices have typically functioned in most collegiate models as independent entities under the supervision of different student services or academic administrators and located in distinct sites on campus.

Counseling and Placement Functions: Independent or Integrated

In such contexts, the counseling office was responsible for career planning and other self- and career explorations while the placement office was focused on the specific skills (e.g., interviewing and résumé work) associated with the job search process. In these models, placement offices tended to be concerned with matching students and jobs, using traits (individual abilities, preferences, attitudes) and factors (job requirements, performance demands of occupations) as the content. The time frame in which such matching activities occurred tended to be limited to the weeks and months immediately before the student graduated. In contrast, counseling centers were more likely to be process- and clinically oriented, concerned with students' development or the remediation of emotional or academic distress at any time during the students' college career (McLaughlin, 1973; Kroll & Rentz, 1988).

Currently, there is no single type of counseling center or career development and placement center. Each of these evolve from different institutional histories. In some cases, college and university counseling centers embrace the full range of career services; in others, they have essentially none. Indeed, some colleges and universities offer virtually no counseling or career planning services. As evidence of the diversity, Whitely, Mahaffey, and Geer (1987) surveyed some 1,770 four-year institutions. From the 963 institutions responding, they developed a typology of counseling centers by doing a cluster analysis of counseling center characteristics. The five major types of centers they found include:

1. Macrocenter—broad range of services, including career and personal counseling, testing, and special functions such as training and consultation with limited advising (21%).
2. Career planning and placement—career-oriented services with minimal counseling and other functions (16%).
3. Counseling orientation—similar to macrocenters except with fewer career services (29%).
4. General-level service—broader functions, including some "dean of students"-type functions, more services to more students than a conventional counseling center (20%).
5. Minimal service—characterized by providing only minimal services in all areas (15%).

By extrapolating from these data, it is possible to suggest that counseling centers per se vary dramatically in whether they embrace career services or whether, if present on campus, career services are likely to be offered outside the counseling center.

Regardless of the actual location of career services on a campus, it is clear that beginning in the late 1950's and early 1960's, the disparity in function between counseling centers and placement offices took a new direction (Kroll & Rentz, 1988). The career-planning process activities that had been a part of the counseling center tended to be pulled out of such organizations and combined with the activities formerly associated with the placement office. In essence, in many colleges and universities, an organizational entity frequently known as the career planning and placement office or career development and placement center or service was formed (Bishop, 1966). Thus, the college or university's commitment to placement of students was no longer seen only as an event or a limited matching activity by which employers seeking students with certain majors or other characteristics could be effectively brought together at the end of the student's college career. Rather, it was increasingly assumed that the placement event needed to be viewed as the end of a process of career development that involved knowledge, exploratory activities, the development of skills, career planning, the choice of a major as an intermediate career decision, and other learning that began before entrance to college and continued through diverse learning in higher education and that ultimately brought the student to the activity called placement: the culmination of the student's career development in college or a university. A further assumption was that deliberate programs of intervention in a student's career development throughout the college years would increase the likelihood that the student would arrive at the point of placement knowing about his or her preferences, values, abilities, opportunities; ready to make a commitment to a job search; and having the skills to do so. Combining the career-planning activities formerly located in counseling centers and the job search activities of the placement office into one entity, which by 1991 was most commonly called career planning and placement or, in a second place, career services (College Placement Council, 1991), gave the career development of students a holistic and developmental perspective, which suggested that career development was not a peripheral and limited mission of higher education but that it was central to it and gave many students purpose in their pursuit of subject, disciplinary, or technical knowledge.

In the evolution from a limited placement or brokering role to a career development role, colleges and universities have used many forms of intervention in behalf of career development and placement. The remaining chapters in this reference deal with specific career development and placement processes. For the purposes of this chapter, only the broad outlines of the activities of college and university career centers are identified.

PERSPECTIVES ON THE FUNCTIONS OF CAREER CENTERS

It would be inaccurate to contend that all colleges and universities have abandoned a placement approach as their only commitment to career services. Similarly, it would be inaccurate to suggest that colleges and universities that have developed a comprehensive career center or career development and placement service have embraced the same services delivered in the same way. Such assertions would deny both the complexity and the diversity of institutions of higher education in the United States. There are, nevertheless, perspectives that can be useful in describing the current status of such activities or in providing rationale for their more integrated organization.

From the perspective of the broad goals to be met in the development of career services in higher education, Herr and Cramer (1988) have argued that in a truly comprehensive program provision will be made to achieve the following:

- Assistance in the selection of a major field of study
- Assistance in self-assessment and self-analysis
- Assistance in understanding the world of work
- Assistance in decision making

- Assistance in meeting the unique needs of various subpopulations
- Assistance with access to the world of work

While for purposes of planning, these are useful goals to be achieved through career services, the further question is what mechanisms need to be included in career services to address the goals cited above or others. Some perspectives on this matter follow.

Hale (1974), for example, has proposed some useful descriptions of the types of career services that should be available on a campus. In his view, these services should include career advising, career counseling, and career planning. The first, career advising, is academic advisement by a faculty member who helps students translate career choices into educational goals and programs and helps them relate academic majors to likely career opportunities. Career counseling includes psychological procedures used to assist students with self-evaluation as well as assessment and understanding of their capabilities and interests. Career planning is the process of helping students relate the outcomes of self-evaluation to information currently available about the world of work. Emphases here would involve decision-making about specific occupations or corporations in which to seek employment and might include the acquisition of skills pertinent to job seeking, résumé preparation, and interviewing behavior. As these emphases are engaged by students, they blend with some of the skill aspects of placement.

Hale (1974) also contends that the career services he described should be at the center of an integrated, coordinated career system that is composed of five elements: (1) a structured and comprehensive universitywide program of career education; (2) a central agency offering career information, career counseling, and career planning and placement in a one-stop service for students and academic advisers; (3) a cadre of specially qualified and prepared academic advisers selected from among faculty of the many subject disciples; (4) a central administrator in academic affairs who can devote full-time to the supervision and coordination of the career education, counseling, and academic advisement system; and (5) a commission on academic advising and counseling (for advising and coordinating functions).

CAS Standards and Guidelines

The comprehensive, articulated delivery of services that Hale proposed in 1974 is similar in spirit and in design to what exists in the early 1990's in many major higher education institutions. It is also similar to the prospectives advocated by the Council for the Advancement of Standards (CAS) for Student Services/Development Programs. The council is a consortium of 21 professional associations in higher education that collectively devised and published *Standards and Guidelines* (Council for the Advancement of Standards, 1986), a document that recommends criteria for evaluating some 16 components of student services in colleges and universities. One of these major components is career planning and placement. In significantly abridged form the *Standards and Guidelines* suggests the following:

Mission. Career planning is a developmental process that must be fostered during the entire period of a student's involvement with the institution. The primary purpose of career planning and placement must be to aid students in developing, evaluating, and effectively initiating and implementing career plans.

Program. Career planning and placement services must offer the following programs:

1. Career counseling, which assists the students at any time to:
   - analyze interests, aptitudes, abilities, previous work experience, personal traits, and desired life-style to promote awareness of the interrelationship between self-knowledge and career choice;
   - obtain occupational information, including, where possible, exploratory experiences such as cooperative education, internships, externships, and summer and part-time jobs;
   - make reasoned, well-informed career choices that are not based on race/sex stereotypes; and
   - set short-range and long-range goals.
2. Placement counseling and referral, which assist the student to:
   - clarify objectives and establish goals;
   - explore the full range of life and work possibilities, including graduate and professional preparation;
   - prepare for the job search or further study;
   - present oneself effectively as a candidate for employment or further study; and
   - make the transition from education to the world of work.
3. Student employment, including part-time, vacation, and experiential education programs that assist students in obtaining work experiences, financial resources, and/or the opportunity for academic credit.

Organization and Administration. Career planning should be integrated with placement. Career planning and placement may be offered by a separate student services unit and may be offered by other student services or institutional units such as counseling centers, financial aid offices, and academic departments.

Human Resources. Professional staff members must be skilled in career planning, placement, and counseling and must have the ability to function effectively with students, faculty, administrators, and employers.

Funding. Funds should be provided for adequate career/employment information and for the preparation and maintenance of student placement credentials.

Facilities. Space for at least the following is recommended: reception area, staff offices, a private office for the unit head, interview and counseling rooms that allow privacy, employer lounge, student registration and sign-up area, career resource center, office equipment, bulletin boards, work areas, storage, filing, and rooms for group meetings and conferences.

Campus and Community Relations. The career planning and placement service must:

- develop job opportunities on a continuing basis from a variety of employers;
- provide all employers the opportunity to consider candidates for employment;
- maximize students' exposure to employers through a variety of programs;
- collect information on occupational trends and employers' needs;
- encourage dialogue among employers, faculty, and administration concerning job needs and trends;
- encourage employers to recognize career planning and placement services through public acknowledgment and/or other avenues of support;
- develop a working relationship that encourages the academic administration and faculty to maximize and give support to an effective program for students and graduates;
- promote better understanding between the institution and employers of the relationship of curricula and other activities to the career needs of, and opportunities for, students; and
- promote a systematic flow of information to faculty members and students from alumni concerning their academic preparation and employment experiences.

Ethics.

- Referral of an employed graduate to another employer must be preceded by that person's request for referral.
- Career-planning and placement office personnel must use their best efforts to ensure that the student's selection of a career or a graduate school is protected from improper influence by faculty, administrators, placement staff, and employers.
- Conditions of employment and salary offers made to an individual by an employer must not be divulged in a personally identifiable form by career-planning and placement office staff members.
- Unless permission is given by the student, information disclosed in individual counseling sessions, as well as information contained in records, must remain confidential.

These sorts of criteria are deceptively innocent at first glance; in fact, however, each presents a potentially volatile activity. For instance, the seemingly naive statement that career planning and placement should "provide all employers the opportunity to consider candidates for employment" gives no hint of the spirited debates and occasional confrontations that occur on campuses when organizations try to recruit that bar the employment of homosexuals or represent activities loathsome to some (e.g., the military, industries that manufacture weaponry, businesses that trade with nations such as South Africa, and so on).

The standards and guidelines proposed by the Council of the Advancement of Standards for Student Services/Development Programs go significantly beyond arguing for a career center in colleges and universities as an isolated organizational entity. Rather, these standards and guidelines suggest that career services need to be interdependent with other student services as well as with academic units in the higher education institution. While there needs to be a facility with space to administer and coordinate career services, these services should reach into all aspects of the experiences of students and be comprehensive in their availability.

That career services in contemporary colleges and universities are becoming more comprehensive is attested to by a variety of research studies, as well as the annual reports of many career services. For example, by 1978, Koehn's survey of career programs in higher education in California indicated a broadening of the roles of these programs beyond placement. Credit-bearing career planning courses were offered at over 40 percent of the schools. Skills identification, values clarification, speakers on the content of particular occupational fields, and emphases on developing job search skills were common activities at every institution.

Reviews of Career Services Offered

In 1982, Goodson attempted to determine how comprehensive career services were in institutions with more than 2,000 students. His data collection consisted of a questionnaire sent to the director of career services in colleges and universities in all 50 states and the District of Columbia. The questionnaire asked the director to assess his or her offerings in six areas felt to be necessary to meet career guidance objectives at institutions of higher eduction. The areas were career counseling, career workshops and seminars, career classes, interest inventories, other services such as career libraries, and program evaluations. Goodson found that of the 98 institutions responding, 15 had all six elements, 40 had five elements, and 28 had four elements. All but two of the institutions offered career counseling (usually on an individual basis), 88 offered interest inventories (some 38 different types were listed), 72 offered other career services, 63 offered career classes, and 30 had evaluations of developmental programs (usually based on student attitudes about the career help they received). The most commonly offered workshops and seminars dealt with placement, career exploration, or career planning. Career classes, usually given for credit, tended to emphasize career exploration and development and career planning and decision making.

In 1979, Reardon, Zunker, and Dyal surveyed 302 colleges and universities and found that the larger the institution, the more varied the career services. By frequency and diversity, the career-planning programs and services found in this survey included the following:

1. Occupational Information
2. Résumé Preparation
3. Interview Preparation
4. Educational Information

5. Individual Assessment Information
6. Referral (Campus)
7. Referral (Community)
8. Self-Help Materials
9. Group Career Counseling
10. Faculty Consultation
11. Testing
12. Resource Speakers
13. Advising Undeclared Majors
14. Decision-Making Training
15. Multimedia Materials
16. Academic Advising
17. Orientation
18. Mini-Career Courses
19. Study Skills
20. Special Women's Programs
21. Staff In-Service Training
22. Assertiveness Training
23. Career-Planning Course (Credit)
24. Career-Planning Course (No Credit)
25. Card Catalog
26. Job Simulation
27. Employability Skills Training
28. Curriculum Infusion of Career Materials
29. High School Visitation
30. Faculty In-Service Training
31. Computer-Assisted Guidance

In one sense, the rank order of these career services is less important than the diversity they reflect. Clearly, certain services, for example, computer-assisted career guidance, have become much more frequently used in college and university career centers in the past decade. So, too, have multimedia materials, minicourses on careers, and self-help materials. Trends since the study of Reardon, Zunker, and Dyal in 1979 can be seen in a recent major study of services offered by career-planning and placement centers done by the College Placement Council in January and February 1991. There were 823 respondents, permitting an update of the surveys previously done by the council in 1975, 1981, and 1987. Table 1.1 portrays these most recent data. In general, this table shows a decrease ''in the percentage of offices offering placement of graduates into full-time employment, placement

Table 1.1

Services Offered Through Career Planning and Placement Center

	Percent of Respondents			
	1975	1981	1987	1991
Career counseling	89.0	96.0	94.1	94.2
Occupational and employer information library	92.0	91.0	93.6	93.7
Placement of graduates into full-time employment	96.0	95.0	96.8	93.4
Campus interviewing	96.0	95.0	96.5	91.6
Placement of students into summer and part-time employment	81.0	83.0	87.0	83.2
Placement of alumni	87.0	90.0	88.9	82.7
Credential service	79.0	81.0	76.4	71.9
Resume referral	–	64.0	74.2	71.6
Cooperative education, intern, experiential program	26.0	49.0	53.7	62.8
Resume booklets	–	62.0	56.3	56.3
Vocational testing	31.0	51.0	53.2	52.1
Computerized candidate data base	–	–	–	48.2
Career planning or employment readiness course	–	30.0	32.1	31.6
Academic counseling	30.0	37.0	33.0	28.7
Dropout prevention and counseling	22.0	26.0	19.9	16.2

Source: College Placement Council (July 1991). 1991 Career Planning & Placement Survey. Special Report. *Spotlight*, the Council, Bethlehem, PA.

of students into summer and part-time employment, placement of alumni, campus interviewing, credential service, and resume referral. . . . The greatest increase overall was in cooperative education, intern, or other experiental programs. . . . About 90 percent of these respondents to the current survey reported using personal computers, up from slightly more than 80 percent in 1987'' (p. 5).

The essential point in these studies is the diversity and growth in comprehensiveness of the forms of delivery of career services in colleges and universities. This comprehensiveness of such services is also affirmed by Herr (1989), who has observed that in addition to individual career counseling of students, there are at least ten categories of providing career guidance in higher education. These services include:

1. Infusing academic subject matter systematically with information pertinent to career development (e.g., how the academic content is used in solving particular kinds of programs in work settings, the relationship between academic majors and the occupations in which graduates are employed).

2. Providing specific credit courses that have personal development and career information components (e.g., course content dealing with self-assessment, career evaluation, career planning, decision making).

3. Use of external resources (e.g., speakers, field trips, internships, and so on) in classes, in dormitories, and in clubs or Greek organizations to provide direct communication of career-related information.

4. Integrating placement and transfer processes in support of career planning.

5. Opportunities for work-study/cooperative education with career information incorporated.

6. Decentralized counseling using academic departments as the location for counselors who, among other responsibilities, coordinate the career and academic advisement of faculty.

7. Seminars on college life and educational and career planning.

8. Personal assistance groups or group counseling focused upon self-awareness and career planning.

9. Human potential seminars.

10. Use of interactive, computer-based guidance systems.

Being a bit more precise, Herr (1989) suggests that colleges and universities have used four major approaches to deliver career services: (1) courses, workshops, and seminars that offer structured group experiences in support of career planning; (2) group counseling activities that are generally less structured and that emphasize broader, more affective aspects of human and career development; (3) individual counseling opportunities that accentuate diverse theoretical orientations applied to career concerns; and (4) placement programs that culminate the career planning and decision-making process and facilitate the students' transition to paid employment.

The Tailoring of Career Services to Constituents

Increasingly, colleges and universities are attempting to adapt their career services to the needs of emerging or special populations. For example, as suggested in many studies and reports, a major change on many campuses today is the large influx of so-called nontraditional students. In reality this term usually means returning adult students, those older than traditional college students.

Broch and Davis (1987), among others, have argued that career services are one of the areas in which adult students need different emphases than do traditional college students. For example, career services for traditional college students typically focus on initial career choice; career services for adult students may need to focus on career change. At Virginia Commonwealth University, where Broch and Davis are employed in the career-planning and placement office, services have been adopted and new programs developed to meet the needs of adult students and alumni. For example, in deference to the schedule of adult students or alumni, evening hours are available for career counseling or participation in evening group counseling sessions. Computer software programs are available that are designed specifically for use by adults and that incorporate the opportunity to assess present skills and relate these to occupational selection processes. A special section in the Career Resource Center is devoted exclusively to books and pamphlets that concentrate on career-related topics for adults, for example, general adult career issues, career changers, adult career planning, and reentry.

Heppner and Olson (1982) have reported that the Career Planning and Placement Center of the University of Missouri-Columbia has also modified its services to accommodate adult students more fully. Among such modifications were evening hours and the hiring of older peer counselors. These staff members are required to be knowledgeable about the process of returning to school or changing careers, local business, job-keeping skills, time and money management, the psychological implications of underemployment, counseling adult women, organizational patterns of companies and organizations, major adult development theories, and assessment tools of special relevance to adults.

REASONS FOR THE EVOLUTION OF PLACEMENT TO CAREER SERVICES

It would oversimplify the matter to suggest that any one reason is dominant in explaining the movement from a limited placement or brokering function at the end of the collegiate experience that focused on matching graduating seniors with existing job opportunities to career services that are more comprehensive in goals, process-oriented, concerned with educating students to choose as well as with their job search per se, and developmentally connected to all phases and components of the collegiate experience. There are, however, several factors that deserve mention as motivators of the transition in collegiate career services.

Factors Stimulating Career Services

One of these factors is inherent in the changes of mission and in the characteristics of student populations served by higher education in this century. Higher education in the United States is a huge enterprise that includes some 3,500 institutions varying dramatically in size, purpose, cost, resources, and other characteristics. While some of the idealist stereotypes of small colleges that focused on a narrow range of liberal arts studies designed to prepare highly selected and intellectually gifted graduates for several major professional activities—law, medicine, teaching, ministry—in an intimate and personal environment may still be true in some cases, it is certainly not true for all. In this century, the number of students attending college has grown dramatically, and the size of many institutions has followed. The number of Americans enrolled in either two-year or four-year postsecondary and higher educational institutions now approximates 5 percent of the total population. In 1990, some 13.2 million students were enrolled in higher education; of these about 8.3 million were enrolled in four-year institutions and 4.9 million were in two-year institutions. About 11.5 million were undergraduates, 1.5 were graduate students, and approximately 0.2 million were pursuing first professional degrees. In 1990 about 1 million bachelor's degrees were awarded (The Department Chair, 1990).

Since World War II and the educational benefits provided by the GI Bill, American higher education has become increasingly democratized and open to all population segments. College enrollment is no longer confined to the children of privilege but has increasingly become open to larger proportions of the youth population. For example, in 1988, of the 2,780,000 high school graduates in the United States, almost 1,600,000 or some 58.8 percent of these persons entered college. Many of these persons did so through open admissions policies that gave them access to college in spite of low test scores or poor high school achievement. Others entered college because of some major governmental or institutional program of financial support through grants and loans that allowed persons who, before the 1950's or 1960's, would have been unlikely to be able seriously to consider bearing the financial costs of college. At the same time that larger proportions of the youth population are entering college, so, too, are adults returning to college because of the need to update skills, gain new skills, or otherwise become more competitive in an economy where formal academic credentials have replaced experience as the criterion for occupational entry or mobility in many sectors. Many, if not most, of these persons are in college because of career motivations of some sort.

As the composition of college students has changed in ethnicity, socioeconomic level, academic preparation, proportion of the population enrolled in higher education, and reasons for being in college, higher education institutions have also responded in a variety of ways. As suggested above, many colleges have gotten bigger. They offer a greater diversity of courses, majors, and technical specialties; class sizes have increased; and levels of personal interaction and knowledge between faculty and students have diminished. Certainly these trends are not true in all institutions, but where they are true, it is likely that the development of a complex and diverse program of career services has evolved to address the multiple needs for help with educational and occupational choices, with career planning, and with connecting the collegiate experience to the employment or educational options beyond college.

To illustrate the multiplicity of needs for just one of many functions provided by a major university career center, Table 1.2 indicates the reasons, by number and percentage, for which clients at Pennsylvania State University sought career counseling in 1989–1990 (Career Development and Placement Services, Penn State University, 1990).

Embedded in the first set of factors of the size and diversity of both institutions and student populations is the growing visibility of research studies that show the importance of help with career planning to large numbers, if not the majority, of college students. While Chapter 2 will explore this matter in some depth, selected studies will make the point here. For example, in one study of the academic, career, and personal needs of 1,625 students at the University of Georgia (Weissburg, Berenten, Cote, Cravey, & Heath, 1982), career development needs were experienced by a greater percentage of students than experienced either academic or personal needs. Over 80 percent of the students

Table 1.2
Reasons Clients Sought Intake Counseling

	Summer	Fall	Spring	Total
Choice of major/career	91(18%)	590(27%)	471(22%)	1,152(24%)
Occupational information	29(6%)	137(6%)	109(5%)	275(6%)
Job search	108(21%)	315(15%)	350(16%)	773(16%)
Résumé preparation	94(18%)	555(26%)	800(37%)	1,449(30%)
Cover letter preparation	41(8%)	111(5%)	215(10%)	367(8%)
Interview request from review	35(7%)	301(14%)	139(6%)	476(10%)
Internship/summer job search	6(1%)	118(5%)	142(7%)	266(6%)
Graduate/professional school admissions	7(1%)	64(3%)	50(2%)	121 (3%)

wanted to explore job opportunities related to their majors and to obtain work experience in a career area; 77 percent desired to develop job-seeking skills; 72 percent wanted to learn how to prepare for their careers; over half said that they wanted to explore their career interests, values, and abilities, to obtain information, to talk to a career counselor about career plans, and to learn how occupations can affect their future life. As other studies cited in Chapter 2 will show, such findings for students are not isolated to one institution but tend to be reflected in studies spanning the collegiate spectrum.

A second example suggests that the importance of career services is not confined to students in four-year colleges and universities. Healy and Reilly (1989) studied the career needs of 1,540 women and 1,386 men from ten community colleges in California. They divided the student sample by age and gender and assessed their career needs across the following categories: (1) knowing more about their interests and abilities, (2) understanding/deciding on career goals, (3) becoming more certain of career plans, (4) exploring careers related to interests and abilities, (5) selecting courses relevant to career goals, and (6) developing job-finding skills. They found that all age cohorts from 17 to 19 through 41 to 50 and both sexes reported at least minor needs in each category, with major needs more likely among younger students. The lowest needs for the older students were in deciding upon career goals, becoming more certain of plans, and obtaining jobs. While their highest needs were in exploring jobs related to talents and interests and in selecting courses related to goals, women of all ages reported more need to become certain about their career plans, and men reported a greater need for obtaining a job. In essence, the two examples cited here at the community college level and at the university level make clear that students in higher education, younger as well as returning adults, across the spectrum of postsecondary institutions—two-year, four-year, technical, graduate, and professional schools—declare their need for career guidance and career counseling, for comprehensive career services as a central aspect of their collegiate experience.

A third major factor motivating the evolution from placement to career development emphases in the career services provided by colleges and universities has to do with the changes in theory that have occurred since the last century. Wherever placement, occupational, or vocational guidance services were originally offered—public schools, community agencies, higher education—such services were primarily committed to a trait and factor or matching model. The conceptual frame of reference for such a model was that of individual differences or differential psychology. In essence, the emphasis was on predicting occupational success or compatibility from an individual's test scores prior to entry into the labor market. A primary strategy was seeking to match the aptitude for performance or the occupational interests of those seeking employment to the requirements of available options, always attempting to maximize the compatibility or fit between the two. Whatever vocational guidance an individual received tended to occur at one point in the life of the individual, that is, either at entry into the labor force from high school or college or when an occupational choice or adjustment to work was not positive in an individual's life and he or she was fired or otherwise in need of a job change. In either of these situations, providing "vocational guidance" as an event at one point in life seemed appropriate because individual traits were primarily seen as static and unchanging, certainly after adolescence. Against such a context, a placement, matching, or brokering view of limited career services in higher education made sense. In functional terms, professional staff in placement offices engaged in such activities as soliciting jobs, registering students, scheduling employer interviews, matching students and employers, and keeping records of job placements (Blaska & Schmidt, 1977).

During the 1950s and proceeding to the current time, an additional conceptual perspective began to influence the provision of vocational or occupational guidance, regardless of setting. Indeed, in the 1960s the term *career guidance* or *career counseling* began to be preferred to the earlier terms *vocational* or *occupational guidance* or *counseling* to symbolize some of the shifting perspectives on how career behavior is influenced and how it changes over time. While matching, brokering, or placement continued to have a role in career services, they were increasingly seen as the end point or only one aspect of a dynamic process of learnings and self-concept development that needed to precede placement. The latter stressed the need for career services to focus on helping students develop self-acceptance and self-understanding as the base to which educational and occupational alternatives could then be related. As career development was seen as an ongoing process of combining understandings, experiences, commitments, values, and skills into a process of forging and integrating the many facets of personal identity—self, family, educational, occupational—with career maturity or career adaptability, the process of decision making increasingly came to be seen as the mechanism by which the individual translated his or her self-concept into action through choices made. Some observers were keying in on the growing awareness that there are specific stages in the developmental process that lead to securing employment (Super, 1957). Others were suggesting that persons needed to be educated to choose (McDaniel, 1968) and implying that the progression toward employment was comprised of a series of tasks, knowledge, and skills that need to be assessed and facilitated by career services in a process that spans the years of schooling or higher education. Thus, what students need is longitudinal and developmental, a process that aids one in acquiring knowledge, attitudes, and skills through which one can develop the behaviors necessary to cope with decision points, including choice of a major or placement into a job or occupation, to acquire a career identity, or to develop career maturity and adaptability. When collegiate career services are designed to facilitate such processes, they become comprehensive in their impact on the individual, educative, intended to maximize growth rather than repair deficits, and concerned about delivering services in concert with a whole range of possibilities in the environment—through academic courses and departments, in residence life, by making academic advising more career-relevant, through specialized individual and group counseling, seminars and workshops, and the use of role models and other resources, as well as the use of various forms of career technology (e.g., computerized career guidance systems). In these cases the career development and placement center models and plans in accordance with a developmental process of self-awareness or assessment, exploration, decision making, preparation, and employment (Kroll & Rentz, 1988) that constitutes both a rationale for, and the content of, career services that are not confined to a placement, matching, or brokering function in isolation from the aspects of career development that precede such an event.

THE LOCATION OF THE CAREER CENTER ON CAMPUS: CENTRALIZED OR DECENTRALIZED

As college and university career centers have taken on expanded roles in the last several decades, continuous questions arise about their integration with the rest of the university community and, indeed, the model and location of the center that should be advanced in a particular institution. These are not trivial matters. They affect the stature of the program and the support it is likely to receive. In this chapter, we have briefly explored some of the historical antecedents to current perspectives on career centers in colleges and universities, factors related to the evolution of career services from the limited placement, brokering, or matching function to the expanded role captured in such titles as career planning or career development and placement service. We also identified the types of delivery systems and services contemporary career centers offer.

What has been implicit in this chapter is the need for planning, for leadership, for administrative support, and for effective communication to students, faculty, employers, and others about the significance and the availability of career services in a particular college or university. Subsequent chapters deal with each of these topics in an expanded fashion.

In this section, the positioning or location of the career center is examined. Regardless of the particular model of career and placement services used in a specific higher education institution, the position occupied by this center in the hierarchial organizations of the university becomes critical. Following that issue, whether to centralize or decentralize such services becomes relevant.

Position of the Career Center in the Organizational Hierarchy

It is likely that the position of the career center in the hierarchy of the college or university is a function of several factors: the credibility of the leader of the career center, the communication to central administration of the contribution that the career center can and does make to the mission or goals of the institution, and the clarity of planning of the career center and its services. While these are obviously interactive matters, they are each worthy of brief and separate attention.

Leadership. The authors of this reference believe that it is essential that the director of the career center/service for a college or university be academically trained in counseling and career psychology. Certainly in a research-oriented university, the leader of the career center needs to have academic and research credentials that give credibility with faculty members and academic departments. Holding rank in an academic department, occasionally teaching in it, and engaging in periodic scholarly activity are important symbols of the director's credibility and commitment to the process valued in an academic environment.

However, beyond the academic credentials important to the leaders of the career center are management style and vision. Shingleton and Fitzpatrick (1985) contend that the management style of the leader of a career development and placement center is closer to that needed in business than that needed in an academic department. Such differences in leadership needs are obviously not absolute in one setting or the other, but, in the case of the career center, the leader must attend to and manage a set of performance expectations for staff related to student placement rates, by the number of students seen in various career guidance and counseling settings—individually and in groups, by employer interviews on campus, and by related matters that are not abstract or ethereal. These are specific indicators of the status of outcomes that are the lifeblood of the program and the data from which new resources to support the center's operations are likely to flow.

The management style of the career center leader must also emphasize effective communication to the various constituencies of importance to the center. These obviously include students, alumni, and current faculty and staff. But, as important, the career center leader must have direct communication access to the president, vice presidents, deans, and department heads. Communication contacts at this level suggest that the positioning of the career center and, obviously, the director of the center must be such that the center is not so isolated or low in the organizational hierarchy that communications from it are layered in bureaucracy or that the leader of the center is so constricted by persons above him or her that necessary communications are delayed, distorted, or discouraged.

A major role of the leader of the career center must be educating the central administration about the significance of the career center in meeting the needs of students and in advancing other university goals (e.g., public relations, acquiring development funds, gaining external credibility). Such a role requires the constant pursuit by the director of demonstrated results that are respected by administrators, by faculty, and by corporate representatives and other employers.

The credibility of the career center director, results-based management, and effective communication about the significance of the career center's contributions to the university are ultimately interactive with both the vision for the center and the clarity of planning facilitated by the leader. This requires the career center's director to know the institution, the products (students) and their competencies from different colleges or university sectors, and the characteristics of the markets (recruiters) into which these students will move. Planning of the center must aggressively integrate institutional history, the products, and the markets for students that the career center must both accommodate and educate. This involves not only the services to be provided and the performance standards expected but the public relations strategies to be employed with students, faculty, employers, central administrators, politicians, and other community, state, and national contacts.

The Model to Be Used

The precise model of career centers or of the delivery of career services to be used is, in one sense, less important than what has just been argued for, the need for the career center and its leadership to be positioned high enough in the organizational hierarchy of the institution that it can communicate easily and effectively about resource needs, results, its availability of services, and the promise of center activities to a wide range of constituents. Once such positioning occurs, then, whether or not a centralized or decentralized model of the career center is used becomes a planning function related to institutional history and structure.

Centralized/Decentralized Models

A *centralized career development and placement program* is housed in a specifically identified office whose director has responsibility for all career services offered by a college or university. Thus, each of the career-related contacts and commitments of the college or university for recruitment of students by employers, career-planning courses and workshops, career counseling of students, outreach to other university sectors—faculty, departments, counseling center, residence life, and so on—would be coordinated by, and the responsibility of, this office.

Weber (1982) surveyed 1,265 career planning and placement offices in the United States. From the 754 responses he received, he estimated that 80 percent of the offices were centralized by 1981. He also reported that use of the term *placement* alone in the office title decreased from 32 percent of the offices in 1975 to 13 percent in 1981. In a more recent study of 823 career planning and placement offices (College Placement Council, 1991), the trend toward centralized operations seems to have continued to increase. In this survey, 87 percent of the offices responding indicated that they were centralized, while 13 percent reported they were decentralized. These figures compare with previous College Placement Council surveys in 1975, 1981, and 1987 that reported 80 percent, 80.4 percent and 85 percents, respectively.

A *decentralized program*, in contrast, is one where there is not a director who has central control of all career services in an institution. Instead, in a decentralized model separate colleges, departments, programs, or other administrative entities within an institution assume independent responsibility for career services pertinent to their area of content or interest. In essence, each entity has its own staff, budget, program of services, and rationale.

A variation on this theme that does not meet all of the criteria for a decentralized model but is illustrative of some of the model's emphases has been reported at the University of Rhode Island (Bartel, 1984). Essentially linked to what is a centralized career services model on the main campus, the University of Rhode Island also has a separate College of Continuing Education campus, which serves primarily adult students who tend to be enrolled in extension courses to upgrade their skills, retrain for a new career, or prepare to enter or reenter the work force. Career and life planning tends to be central to the needs of this group but is not always available in the comprehensive ways important to adult populations. The career staff of the University of Rhode Island decided that rather than provide a special emphasis for adults within their Central Career Services Center, they would provide a comprehensive career services program at the separate campus occupied by the College of Continuing Education. The decision was to provide administrative oversight, a professional counselor, and three adult peer counselors in a satellite career services program away from the centralized career center but capable of offering a comprehensive program for the adult students involved and including individual career counseling, support group for career changes, career development course, self-assessment workshop, résumé-writing workshop, job search strategy workshop, interviewing skills workshop, career topic symposium series, and a career forum.

While this program might more accurately fit under the combined centralized-decentralized model discussed next, it has been included here to illustrate that career services can ensue at different locations on a campus that are geographically removed from each other, with separate administrative authority, and dealing with student populations that differ in some significant way by discipline, by age, or by other characteristics.

There are also *combined models of career services*, where there is both centralized leadership and decentralized delivery of services. In such a situation, there may be a director of career services for the university who then coordinates the provision or availability of career services from several locations within an institution. In some circumstances, these decentralized locations for delivery may be considered satellites of a central career center.

California State University (CSU) at Long Beach is one example of how a career center can be organized to combine centralized and decentralized services. Unlike many other institutions of higher education, CSU-Long Beach is primarily a commuter school with most of its students traveling by car from Los Angeles. When they complete their classes, they tend immediately to leave campus and return to work or to their families. Thus, communication with students about career services is even more difficult than is true on a campus where most students are full-time and live on campus. According to Babbush, Hawley, and Zeran (1986), in order to keep staff and other costs for the career planning and placement center at CSU-Long Beach to a minimum, the organizational structure for the center is nontraditional. For example, rather than each professional staff member's reporting to only one supervisor, in this instance all staff report to all three associate directors, who in turn report to the director. The three associate directors have different responsibilities. One is in charge of placement activities. One is in charge of cooperative education, job development, and student employment and job information functions. The third is in charge of career planning, multimedia, and the Career Resource Center. Because the responsibilities of each of these directors tend to peak at different times in the year, having staff responsible to each tends to enable the creation of staff workloads that are even across the year. It also demonstrates commitment to the assumption that those engaged in career counseling should also be engaged in placement, referral, and related activities so that the various functions of the center complement each other and the career counselors understand and can do these various activities.

The decentralized aspect of the center is manifested by assigning each career counselor to a particular academic school (e.g., Business Administration, Engineering) so that individual career counselors understand the major academic disciplines available in different aspects of the university and maintain close communications with faculty and students in these disciplines. While these counselors remain in the centralized career center, they are charged with getting out to that facility and spending time with administrators, faculty, students, and student associations in the departments and programs of the school to which they are assigned. In this way they are known by and get to know constituents in their assigned areas. They also achieve close contact with those persons in their assigned areas by developing and presenting specialized workshops (e.g., job search, skill identification) to departments for which they are responsible. Because of the transient nature of a commuter student population, workshops and seminars are videotaped and made available in the central Career Resource Center for students to view whose schedule did not permit their attendance at the workshop. The career counselors assigned to the particular schools also do job development with employers seeking students who have majored in the disciplines encompassed by the departments and programs for which each career counselor is accountable.

These job development activities enhance the career counselor's understanding of employer requirements for skills as well as student competencies related to particular majors. Such information is then able to be fed back into the various resource delivery systems available in the career center.

The career counselors, in addition to specialized or discipline-based assignments, are also expected to be generalized in their skills and knowledge of all of the aspects of the career center's operation. To enhance both their specialized and generalized skills, the counselors are assigned objectives (as part of a management by objectives process) that emphasize their particular forms of training and engage them in the completion of certain projects useful to the school to which they are assigned or to the central office.

Shingleton and Fitzpatrick (1985), as well as Babbush, Hawley, and Zeran (1986), have elaborated the advantages and disadvantages of centralized, decentralized, and combined career services. Some of their major points are summarized below.

Centralized Models—Advantages. A centralized approach to the provision of career services in a college or university may be the most economical approach since the deployment of facilities and staff may be maximized. The communication to students and staff about where to go for services is simplified. Employers, faculty, and central administrators communicate with one person or one office, reducing the likelihood of confusion about needs, objectives, or procedures. Student groups needing special career activities or resources may be easier to accommodate because of the director's ability to tap the total resources available to career services as a "critical mass." A central scheduling operation that matches students and employers from interviews or to career-planning services (e.g., workshops, computer-based career guidance programs) may be more efficient and cost-effective than one separated by departments and disciplines. All interviewing of students from all disciplines can take place in one location, reducing employer downtime and overhead costs. For purposes of career counseling and career advisement of students, a centralized location may provide a more comprehensive picture of opportunities and interactions campuswide than is possible when such advising is done at disparate locations by diverse staffs. A central location can provide a more complete career information library than would be possible if several career libraries exist across campus. This is a matter of both budget and cost-effectiveness. The coordination of student employment, volunteer programs, internships, and cooperative education programs can be achieved more readily if centralized. The opportunity for effectiveness of research studies is likely to be greater in a centralized career center. Overall, there may be greater flexibility for change available.

Centralized Models—Disadvantages. A centralized approach may be seen as too impersonal or too large to provide as much attention to employers or to the placement of students from low-demand disciplines as might be true in decentralized organizations. In order to maximize a comprehensive career counseling or advisement system, individual staff may not be specialists in particular disciplines or majors. Direct contacts with, and knowledge of, faculty in particular disciplines may be limited. Indeed, staff in a centralized career center may tend to become isolated from academic departments, faculty, and students.

Decentralized Models—Advantages. Since in decentralized locations, career staff tend to be housed closer to particular departments or faculty, they may know more about the courses, content, and outcomes associated with such programs. Departmental majors may be provided more relevant and substantive career counseling or placement advice. Decentralized models may be able to provide a more personal, informal, and direct approach to students than is possible in large, centralized units.

Decentralized Models—Disadvantages. Because of the lack of economies of scale, decentralized and smaller units may have higher budgetary and overhead costs. Computer programming and scheduling costs may be much higher than in a centralized system. Thus, per student costs may be greater than in a centralized unit. Individual counselors or career staff may be specialists in specific disciplines or technical fields but not have comprehensive understanding of possibilities for transfer or curriculum changes between technical and nontechnical majors or career fields. Some students may be given less effective career counseling than other students. Employers must contact and interview students at several locations on campus if they want to interview students across majors. This may increase their time on campus and recruiting costs. All-institutional activities such as graduate or career fairs, multidiscipline career-planning seminars, and so on may be less likely to occur in deference to more tailored opportunities for smaller groups of discipline-oriented students.

Combined Models—Advantages. When central leadership of career services coordinates decentralized systems of delivery, it is possible to accent the advantages of both centralized and decentralized approaches. A centralized leadership system may increase the campuswide, comprehensive picture and cost-effectiveness of decentralized delivery systems. They may retain economies of scale in computer usage, scheduling, and coordination of career services and placement while retaining the personal or discipline-based sensitivity that is an advantage of decentralized delivery.

Combined Models—Disadvantages. The demands on centralized leadership and coordination when delivery of career services is dispersed across campus are significantly increased compared with either a totally centralized or decentralized system.

While other chapters in the book will identify examples of procedures or emphases of career centers occurring in colleges and universities throughout the nation, it is useful to affirm that, at base, the models of career centers are either centralized, decentralized, or some combination of the two.

SUMMARY

Chapter 1 has described the college or university career center as reflective of an institutional mission that is dynamic. Career-planning and placement centers have evolved from limited placement offices treating the application of career support to students as an event to contemporary forms of comprehensive career services combining career-planning and placement activities as components of a career development process.

The stimuli to the dynamic and comprehensive approaches to career services that are emerging on a growing number of campuses are responsive to changing employer demands for services from college, to the growing needs of students for help with their career plans, and to the sharpening of theoretical approaches to career behavior that emphasize the need to view career placement as a process, not an event.

Chapter 1 has also examined the placement of career services centers in the organizational hierarchy of higher education institutions. In particular, the advantages and disadvantages of centralized, decentralized, and combined approaches to the delivery of career services were described.

In the last analysis, the overarching rationale for the availability of career-planning and placement services lies with the importance of such services to different subpopulations of students. Such is the content of Chapter 2.

REFERENCES

Babbush, H. E., Hawley, W. W., & Zeran, J. (1986). The best of both worlds. How one career center reorganized to combine the advantages of both centralized and decentralized services. *Journal of Career Planning and Employment*, XLVI (3), 48–54.

Bartel, S. M. (1984). Creating a satellite career services program for a college of continuing education. *Journal of College Student Personnel, 25*, 94–95.

Bishop, J. F. (1966). Portents in college placement. In G. F. Klopf (Ed.), *College student personnel work in years ahead.* Student Personnel Monograph Service No. 7, Washington, DC: American Personnel and Guidance Association.

Blaska, P., & Schmidt, M. R. (1977). Placement. In W. T. Packwood (Ed.), *College student personnel services.* Springfield, IL: Charles C. Thomas.

Broch, S. B., & Davis, E. M. (1987). Adapting career services for the adult student. *Journal of College Student Personnel, 28*, 87.

Career Development and Placement Services, Penn State University. (1990). *1989–90 annual report.* University Park, PA: Author.

College Placement Council. (1991, July). 1991 Career Planning & Placement Survey. Special Report. *Spotlight*, the Council, Bethlehem, PA.

Council for the Advancement of Standards. (1986). *CAS standards and guidelines for student services/development programs.* Iowa City, IA: American College Testing Program.

The Department Chair. (1990). 1(1). Bolton, MA: Anke 8–9.

Educational Testing Service. (1985). SIGI Plus [computer software]. Princeton, NJ: Author.

Goodson, W. D. (1982). Status of career programs on college and university campuses. *Vocational Guidance Quarterly, 30* 230–235.

Hale, L. L. (1974). A bold new blueprint for career planning and placement: Part 1. *Journal of College Placement, 35*(2), 34–40.

Healy, C. C., & Reilly, K. C. (1989). Career needs of community college students: Implications for services and theory. *Journal of College Student Development, 30*(6), 541–545.

Heppner, M. J., & Olson, S. K. (1982). Expanding college career centers to meet the needs of adults. *Journal of College Student Personnel, 23*, 123–128.

Herr, E. L. (1989). *Career guidance and counseling for college students and adults*. Taipei, Taiwan: National Taiwan Normal University.

Herr, E. L., & Cramer, S. H. (1988). *Career guidance and counseling through the lifespan. Systematic approaches*. Glenview, IL: Scott, Foresman.

Koehn, S. (1978). Who's doing what? An update survey of career planning programs. *Journal of College Student Personnel, 18*, 523–526.

Kroll, J., & Rentz, A. L. (1988). Career planning and placement. In *Student affairs functions in higher education*. A. L. Rentz & G. L. Saddlemire (Eds.), Springfield, IL: Charles C. Thomas.

Lorick, B. A. (1987). Career planning and placement services. In J. L. Amprey, Jr. (Ed.), *Student development on the small campus* (pp. 92–126). National Association of Personnel Workers.

McDaniel, C. (1968). Youth: Too young to choose. *Vocational Guidance Quarterly, 16*, 242–249.

McLaughlin, W. L. (1973). Placement's emerging role. *Journal of College Placement, 33*, 79–82.

Maze, M., & Mayall, D. (1983). Micro Skills [computer software]. Richmond, CA: Eureka.

Reardon, R. C., Zunker, V., & Dyal, M. A. (1979). The status of career planning programs and career centers in colleges and universities. *Vocational Guidance Quarterly, 28*, 154–159.

Shingleton, J. D., & Fitzpatrick, E. B. (1985). *Dynamics of placement. How to develop a successful planning and placement program*. Bethlehem, PA: CPC Foundation.

Super, D. E. (1957). *The psychology of careers*. New York: Harper & Row.

Teal, E. A., & Herrick, R. F. (Eds.). (1962). *The fundamentals of college placement*. Bethlehem, PA: College Placement Council.

Weber, D. M. (1982). *The status of career planning and placement*. Research Report. Bethlehem, PA: Career Placement Council Foundation.

Weissburg, M., Berentsen, M., Cote, A., Cravey, B., & Heath, K. (1982). An assessment of the personal, career and academic needs of undergraduate students. *Journal of College Student Personnel, 23*, 115–122.

Whiteley, S. M., Mahaffey, P. J., & Geer, C. A. (1987). The campus counseling center: A profile of staffing patterns and services. *Journal of College Student Personnel, 28*, 71–81.

Wrenn, C. G. (1951). *Student personnel work in college*. New York: Ronald.

2

Career Needs of Students

Chapter 1 described the historical evolution of responses by higher education institutions to students' career needs. Personal advocacy by a professor, the rise of the placement office, and the contemporary combination of career planning and development with placement represent points along a continuum of changing employment demands, changing student career needs, and, in turn, changing career services in higher education. This chapter describes some of the research on the magnitude and foci of the career needs of students, as well as selected theory on the development of career behavior in college students. For the purposes of this chapter, the term *college student* refers to any one of at least four populations: the traditional college student, that is, the late adolescent and young adult; the returning adult, who may be anyone beyond approximately 25 years of age; the student who is a minority group member; or the international student.

COLLEGE STUDENT CAREER DEVELOPMENT

To an increasing degree in the United States and, indeed, in many other parts of the world, college student requirements for career guidance, career counseling, assistance in career planning, and other types of attention to their career development needs have become highly visible. There are undoubtedly many reasons for these circumstances.

One major reason is that college students, like other citizens in nation after nation, have been affected by pressures causing underemployment and unemployment. In this decade an army of unemployed youth in many parts of the world has become a critical factor. Many of the unemployed and many of the underemployed in the countries affected are persons who hold a college degree or are college-trained even if they have not finished degree requirements.

A second reason for the growing requirements for career-related activities in higher education has to do with the fact that a significant portion of college students are experiencing difficulties in relating their educational pursuits to the world of work. A number of research studies at American colleges and universities over the last two decades substantiate the fact that approximately one-half of America's college-going population feel a need for some assistance with career planning and/or career choice (Kramer, Berger, & Miller, 1974; Snyder, Hill, & Darksen, 1974; Williams, Lindsay, Burns, Wyckoff, & Wall, 1974). While specific studies are examined in the next section, collectively this body of research makes clear the need for career planning and placement services in postsecondary institutions: technical, two- year, and four-year. They also affirm that such needs pertain to younger and older students, to traditional and reentry women, to minority students, and to virtually every segment of the collegiate population.

A third reason for the rise in comprehensive approaches to career services in higher education has to do with the nature of career development itself. Career development does not start and end with the college experience. College students are in transition, and they are coping with a broad range of developmental tasks. Some carry the residual effects of tasks that should have been completed in high school or earlier. Others are more mature and dealing in depth with their own identity questions, preparing for marriage, developing capability for marriage, becoming productive persons, mastering skills of an occupation. Others may be preoccupied with learning about and using exploratory resources, relating interests and capacities, formulating a vocational preference, becoming aware of contingencies that affect their vocational goals, differentiating their interests and values, accepting themselves as in process, coming to terms with relationships between present behavior and future possibilities, relationships, learning to defer gratification and set priorities, acquiring knowledge of life in organizations, achieving more mature relations with peers of both sexes, or achieving emotional independence of parents and other adults. Returning adult college students are frequently attempting to cope with reentry to academic demands, the disciplines of study and examination taking, possibly reduced income, changing roles and identity from an adult worker to the more ambiguous status of student, and possibly attempting to parent children and manage home simultaneously. Minority students and international students may experience any or all of the developmental tasks described above and, in addition, deal with the cultural shock occasioned by coming to a new country, or, indeed, leaving one area of the country where ethnic or racial groups are a large proportion of the population and moving to a collegiate setting where minority persons or persons of color are cast into an isolated and marginal status.

College Student Career Needs

In Chapter 1, two studies, Weissburg, Berentsen, Cote, Cravey, and Health (1982) and Healy and Reilly (1989), were used as examples of data that support the needs of students for career services. Those studies will be examined in some greater detail, and other studies will be discussed as well. The essence of the Weissburg, et al. (1982) study is that in this research at the University of Georgia from 50 to 80 percent of the students surveyed (total n =1,625) expressed desires for help with a variety of career-related concerns. This percentage was higher than that of students who expressed desire for help with either academic or personal concerns. Specifically, over half of the students said that they wanted help in exploring their career interests, values, and abilities; in obtaining information and learning how occupations can affect their future life; and in having the opportunity to talk with a career counselor about their career plans. Seventy to more than 80 percent indicated that they wanted help, respectively, with learning how to prepare for their careers; developing job-seeking skills; exploring job opportunities related to their majors; and obtaining work experience in a career area.

As a function of research on the career needs of 1,540 women and 1,386 men from ten community colleges in California and analysis of the responses by those who differed in age and sex, Healy and Reilly (1989) found that all of the student population groups had either minor or major needs in each of the following areas:

1. Knowing more about their interests and abilities
2. Understanding/deciding on career goals
3. Becoming more certain of career plans
4. Exploring careers related to interests and abilities
5. Selecting courses relevant to career goals
6. Developing job-finding skills

The findings of these two studies are complemented by the findings from studies undertaken at other colleges and universities. For example, in a study of freshmen at Bowling Green University (Walters & Saddlemire, 1979) it was found that 85 percent of the students indicated needs in six areas of career development:

1. Information on the occupations that my chosen major will prepare me for
2. Knowledge of places and people on campus that can help in my career planning
3. More direct experiences such as part-time work or job visits in occupations that I am considering
4. Better understanding of myself to choose an occupation that closely fits my values, goals, and life-style preferences
5. Knowledge of the job market
6. Help to plan college courses that will give more flexibility in choosing among different occupations

Haviland and Gohn (1983) studied the career needs of a random sample of Montana State University students stratified by sex, class year, and field of enrollment. The freshmen, sophomores, and juniors indicated that their greatest needs were for information about occupations for which their majors prepared them and for more direct experience in occupations under consideration. The seniors indicated as greatest their needs for knowledge of the job market and of people and places for help with career planning. One-fifth of the seniors had not made a career decision.

In a study of undergraduate students at Cornell University, Kramer et al. (1974) reported that the most prevalent problem perceived by students involved vocational choice and career planning, with 48 percent of the males and 61 percent of the females indicating that they were having problems in these realms. Other research during the 1970's (Williams et al., 1973; Snyder, Hill, & Darksen, 1974) supported the view that approximately one-half of America's college population feels a need for some assistance with career planning and/or career choice. In addition to the perceived need for help with career planning and related matters, Healy, Mourton, Anderson, and Robinson (1984) have reported research findings that indicate that for both community college students and disadvantaged university students, relationships exist between students' career maturity, including such factors as knowledge of differentiated interests, world of work information, and decision making, and their academic achievement and, possibly, their academic retention. Thus, career-planning and placement services respond to the expressed needs of different student populations for help with their career planning and development and also have an instrumental function related to improving academic achievement and purpose for students whose career needs are facilitated and stimulated to greater maturity.

Needs of Different Student Populations

While, as discussed in Chapter 1, there is a range of important career interventions that need to be available in comprehensive career-planning and placement offices in college and universities, it is also clear that different student populations, from potential or incoming students to graduate students and alumni, males and females, minority and disadvantaged, international students and others, will have unique needs that require sensitivity and possibly unique approaches.

Walter-Samli and Samli (1979) studied the needs of international students for help with their career development. They found that the majority of these students do not receive sufficient career development information or guidance. The deficiencies in career needs experienced by these students were found to be a function of issues both in their home country and in higher education institutions in the United States. For example, international students were found to have inadequate information concerning employment opportunity in the home country; difficulty in determining the academic adviser's sensitivity to international concerns; lack of congruence between course work and desired work experience; difficulty of self-expression in an unfamiliar culture; and lack of access to professional career counselors. Within such contexts it was suggested that successful career counseling for international students requires, among other emphases, general knowledge of the student's home country, familiarity with the academic curriculum and identification of internationally oriented academic advisees, and provision of reentry transition counseling.

Cooper and Robinson (1987) studied the career values and needs of males and females in engineering and the sciences. For women these are non-traditional careers, although they are not for men. In this study, it was found that there were differences between males and females with respect to career-related values. For example, women gave higher ratings to the importance of task completion, job involvement, meaning from work, and career importance than did men. They also experienced some interference in their view of career importance by their orientation toward home and family. Such findings support the need for broad-based career and life planning for both men and women students in engineering and science curricula and the delivery of such career services from a developmental perspective across the years of college. In addition, however, these researchers accent the importance of taking into account plans to marry and have children when counselors help women choose careers and design their career paths. Of importance are issues of work salience as well as life-style preference, leisure needs, and related matters.

As the research of Aslanian and Brickell (1980) demonstrate, adult students have at least three reasons for returning to college. They include career changes or implementations, transitions in their family lives, and transitions in their leisure patterns. Griff (1987) has suggested that each of these factors is related to unmet needs in career development experienced by returning adult students. They include possible insecurity over the decision to return to school, uncertainty about ability to succeed academically, concerns about coping with marital and family responsibilities, and apprehension about being able to cope with ongoing work responsibilities, as well as with converting the return to higher education into new career options or career changes. Since academic advisers typically do not have the time nor the expertise to help adult students work through these issues, such content needs to be reflected in programs specifically designed to meet the career development needs of returning adult students. According to Griff, to be successful, such programs require a well-trained staff and making such services available during evening and weekends as well as weekdays. The services available for returning adults should include such emphases as the following:

1. Career and self-awareness exercises
2. Exploration of interests, values, goals, and decisions
3. Realities of the current job market and future trends
4. Career resources and materials, including updated practical information about various careers
5. Telephone and advising network
6. Topical workshops (e.g., risk taking, building learning skills, résumé writing, interviewing)

7. Support groups (e.g., returning women, building assertiveness)
8. Academic advising for specific educational requirements
9. Individual counseling in job searching, interviewing, and résumé-writing skills
10. Recruiting and job placement services for returning students

Addressing the importance of a developmental approach to career planning and placement, McCaffrey, Miller, and Winston (1984) studied the career maturity and career needs of undergraduate and graduate students in a large southeastern university. Their results indicated that freshmen were significantly less career mature than were seniors or graduate students. However, the latter also had career needs but they were different ones from those experienced by freshmen. Thus, freshmen, seniors, and graduate students need the services of career-planning and placement services that are tailored to their particular needs and emphases. In simplified form, the primary career needs of freshmen are exploratory in nature, identifying and choosing a career, connecting their academic experiences and course work to the reality testing of their chosen career, projecting future plans, and similar tasks. In some contrast, seniors and graduate students need to be helped to convert the results of their career explorations into specific plans that reflect their assessed values, needs, skills, and interests and that allow them to examine the interaction of possible work roles, life-style considerations, and the role of advanced training in the options chosen. In addition, they need to be able to convert possibilities into actualities as the career development process of exploration becomes the placement process of establishment.

The importance of a developmental approach to career planning and placement is also reinforced by research findings that suggest that on some campuses today, college students are deciding on careers earlier than before. If career-planning interventions (e.g., career orientation and decision-making courses, individual counseling) do not occur in the freshman or sophomore year, it may be too late to offer such courses later in the college experience. For example, Keller, Piotrowski, and Rabold (1990) found that in their sample of 409 undergraduates from a medium-sized university in the Southeast, the majority of the freshmen and sophomores had already decided on specific careers. Many of these students would benefit from career-planning courses or internships that would help them determine whether these initial choices are based on accurate information and wise decision-making procedures while there is time to alter these choices and create new learning plans.

The importance of an early developmental approach to career planning can also be reinforced by a different population of students: those who begin college and find it difficult to declare a major. Existing research (e.g., Holland & Holland, 1977) suggests that undecided and decided college students differ in their sense of vocational identity and in the ability of an individual to possess a clear and stable conception of goals, interests, and skills. Lacking such identity creates a potential dilemma in choosing either a curriculum or specific courses to pursue or maintaining commitment to being in college. Buescher, Johnston, Lucas, and Hughes (1989) reported research based upon 116 entering, undecided freshmen at a large midwestern university that supported the premise that undecided freshmen who received an early intervention were able to develop a stable vocational identity from which to evolve more effective goal direction in college.

The role of career-planning and placement services on campuses is not confined only to what happens once a student is enrolled as a freshman and begins, in a formal or informal sense, career exploration. A developmental approach to career planning and placement can actually begin during the process of recruitment of students. Apparently, in an era of a decreasing pool of talented students seeking admission to college and one in which many, if not most, entering students and their parents view a primary goal of college as career preparation (Astin, Green, Korn, & Schalit, 1985), many colleges are engaging in the tight competition for students by promoting their career development services in their recruitment materials or providing outreach career services to high school students. Two examples follow.

Reardon and Clark (1987) examined in-depth the recruiting information of some 96 colleges from the South, the Midwest, and the Atlantic coastal region. Of the 96 colleges and universities, 58(60 percent) included specific career-related information in their recruitment literature. Some 12 percent of the schools providing career recruitment materials included full-color photographs, 500- to 1,000-word narrative presentations, and descriptions of multiple career programs available to students. Under multiple career headings (e.g., Career Services, Career Opportunities, Career Preparation), the schools described a range of career interventions with information about such categories as: "(a) cooperative education and intern or extern placements in major fields of study; (b) experiential career education, career shadowing, or other on-site employer visits; (c) networks of alumni and college friends as career resources; (d) computer-based career guidance systems; (e) special career and academic advising; (f) a comprehensive career resource and information center; (g) professional career planning and placement staff; and (h) intern and job placements in major metropolitan centers with Fortune 500 corporations" (p. 468).

A second example of efforts by college and university placement centers to reach out to high school students through career services has been described by Lott (1984). In this case, the summer career development workshop offered by Valparaiso University for students becoming seniors is seen as reflecting, both from the university's standpoint and from the viewpoint of students, that the concept of choosing a career is a developmental process. This one-day, 6 1/2-hour workshop brings potential students to campus, an event that is both important for recruitment and important for the students' career development, since many have never physically been on a college campus nor seen career resource centers or other campus facilities in operation. From the perspective of the unique career needs of a subpopulation to be served by the career-planning and placement center of a college and university, this workshop approach addresses a variety of needs experienced by college-bound students in high school: choice of college and possible college majors; the need to view career development as a process that continues throughout one's life span; ways to gather information about one's work values, abilities, interests, and work-related experience; the relationships between college majors and careers; comparisons between different types of colleges, entrance requirements and procedures, and financial aid; and how to gather relevant career information from available resources and use them in decision making.

Another subpopulation of potential concern to career-planning and placement offices is student athletes. Of particular concern are those in revenue-producing sports, typically football and basketball, who may have experienced impaired career development in high school and a continued lack of career exploratory experiences in college because of their overriding dedication to athletic performance at the expense of the development of other skills or career development perspective (e.g., Blann, 1985) Summarizing such data, Wilkes, Davis, and Dever (1989) suggest that student athletes sometimes lack identification of academic and career plans, experience unrealistic goal setting, and lack self-confidence outside athletics. Many observers have suggested that although the probability of a college student athlete's progressing into professional sports is less than 2 percent, the lure of financial and psychological gain for those who do achieve professional status after college is sufficient to deflect many athletes away from educational and career development.

The research of Kennedy and Dimick (1987) on the performance of athletes and nonathletes on the attitude scale of the Career Maturity Inventory (Crites, 1978) indicates that football and basketball scholarship athletes in a large midwestern university were significantly lower in career attitude maturity than were nonathletes. Those tested included 106 male varsity football players and 16 male varsity basketball players. Of these 122 athletes, 69 percent were white, and 31 percent were black. Compared with the national statistic that 2 percent of college athletes are likely to enter professional sports, in this sample 48 percent of the athletes tested reported that they expected to enter professional sports. Of the black athletes, 66 percent indicated that they expected to play professional sports, compared with 39 percent of the white athletes. To the degree that such research is reflective of national trends among student athletes, it suggests that student athletes need special focus on career services in college in order to help them test the reality of their expectations to enter professional sports and to make specific plans to do so if this is clearly their desire. Beyond plans to pursue professional sports, however, given the few openings actually available, student athletes are also likely to profit from contingency career planning by which they can be helped to examine alternative career options related to their college majors and other transferable skills they may have that relate to occupations other than athletic performance.

A further subgroup for whom career-planning and placement assistance require some tailoring are liberal arts students. In a specific, although not in an absolute, sense, liberal arts students are not engaged in technical or "career" curriculum. They are more likely to pursue generalist, multi-disciplinary studies than specific, occupationally oriented skills. Given the confusion sometimes associated with generalist learning in a society that often accents the importance of specialization in learning and skills, the career opportunities for liberal arts are frequently less sharply defined and more amorphous. Thus, these students frequently need to understand the transferable and occupationally related skills associated with liberal studies.

While the data about liberal arts students compared with majors in other curricula are not precise about how their career needs may differ, several observers have suggested particular emphases that seem appropriate as career-planning priorities assisting students to understand the relationship between liberal arts learning and career and life planning; helping students clarify their values, abilities, and interests as well as their life goals; and facilitating the exploration of relationships among various career and life goals (Bjorkquist, 1987; Branyon, 1987). It is quite likely that, possibly more so than for students in other curricula, liberal arts students will need to coordinate their academic programs with internships and cooperative education as ways to maximize their career exploration and planning opportunities.

THEORIES OF CAREER DEVELOPMENT

The previous section suggested that the needs of college students for help with their career-planning and placement concerns are diverse. It also suggested that different subpopulations of students may have needs that vary or for which career services must be tailored in ways that respond to some specific developmental level (freshman, senior) or group characteristic (student athlete, returning adult). These expressed or demonstrated needs of different subgroups of college students are, in many ways, predictable from current theoretical approaches that attempt to explain career behavior in the populations of interest here.

In Chapter 1 it was noted that over the past quarter century, theoretical approaches to the prediction and the description of how career behavior unfolds have taken a decidedly developmental character. So, too, have approaches to career planning and placement services and, indeed, in a larger sense, student personnel programs in higher education. In parallel with the evolution of career services in higher education from placement to career development, student personnel services have evolved from an array of discrete activities or functions (e.g., admissions, housing, campus ministry) to a more articulated and comprehensive set of interventions focused on student development. The general assumption of the latter is that student development is a subset of the broader perspectives included in the term *human development*. When applied to college populations, the term *student development* is directed to facilitating student maturation in areas deemed to be related to behavioral "end points" or goals that could be expected in college-educated persons and to which student personnel programs, including career services, should be directed. King and Fields (1980), in a classic analysis of perspectives on student development, have argued that there are four areas of emphasis: intellectual development, identity development, interpersonal development, and value development. Each of these areas reflects a variety of skills, abilities, and general concepts that focus on specific goals of development as they have been expressed by various college student development theorists. By definition, King and Fields (1980) suggest that they include the following:

Intellectual Development

Emphasizes a person's capacities as a thinker and as a learner, including the process by which a person gathers information, synthesizes it to create new meaning, and evaluates its merit and potential.

Identity Development

Focuses on the development of one's sense of self: discovering who you are and identifying the type of person you would like to become.

Interpersonal Development

Emphasizes one's interactions with other people, how these interactions affect oneself and others, and how a person can learn to interact with others more effectively and beneficially.

Values Development

Focuses on the formation of moral and ethical principles to guide one's life, the way a person defines his or her own role in society in terms of one's social ideals (pp. 544–545).

In essence the theories that underlie the four areas of student development expressed above provide a conceptual framework to which student services and their interaction with the other aspects of the academic community can be related. In addition, the specifics of these theories tend to elaborate the attitudes, knowledge, and skills that are the "targets" of programming in student services. Further, these theories help planners to determine which student services on a particular campus can most effectively influence or facilitate the acquisition by students of the desired outcomes. Thus, student development theories go beyond what we know of students' needs to how these needs fit into various theoretical frames of reference to which programming of student services can be related. An important subset of student development theories is those dealing with career development.

Perspectives on Career Behavior in College Students

Conceptual approaches to career behavior attempt to explain several phenomena: (1) the types of experiences, knowledge, attitudes, and skills from which one forges a personal identity as it is reflected in self-understanding, educational directions, occupational preferences, and career motivation; (2) how one develops and implements a decision-making process through which one expresses personal identity in choices made; and (3) the interactions that occur in career behavior among time, social structures, and personal attributes. As such, career development can be conceived as a special emphasis within human development in the fullest sense or as college student development in a somewhat narrower sense. With respect to the latter, insights from career development theory are not unrelated to the four areas of student development mentioned above: intellectual, identity, interpersonal, and values development. Each of these emphases also interacts in career behavior.

One of the overarching assumptions that ties career, college student, and human development together is the key word *development*. A fundamental assumption is that as students progress through the collegiate experience, they experience change and develop attitudes, knowledge, and skills that are increasingly mature and that prepare them with the attitudes and behaviors essential to being effectively placed in the next process after college graduation, for example, work or graduate school.

There are many models of the development of career behavior in college that relate to career planning and placement. Kroll and Rentz (1988) suggest that one such model includes five stages: (1) self-awareness, (2) exploration, (3) decision making, (4) preparation, and (5) employment. In slightly paraphrased fashion, according to Kroll and Rentz, assumptions associated with these stages conceive of career development as a dynamic and lifelong process (p. 80). The first three stages of career development become known as career planning. The goal of career planning is to help students (1) learn to identify and transfer career interests to a plan of action, (2) relate interests and goals to opportunities, (3) relate career plans to life goals and opportunities; and (4) evaluate progress toward career goals through academic preparation (p. 81). In such a model, the last two stages are primarily devoted to placement: preparation and employment.

Regardless of the specific model of career development used for college students, there are several important assumptions. One is that career development does not start and end with the college experience. College students are in transition, and they are coping with a broad range of developmental tasks.

The decision to attend college and the specification of an occupational preference are developmental tasks faced by students regardless of age or other group characteristics. They are important for the adolescent and for the adult attending college. Election of a college, the selection of a major field of study, and the indication of an occupational preference require significant information, planfulness, and adequate self-assessment.

In the case of college students, career decisions are expressed through educational plans. College is not an end in itself; it is not a cul-de-sac. Its choice and the choice of a major are intermediate occupational or career choices. Recognition of the need to make educational decisions that have career implications and the acceptance of responsibility to implement these decisions are important career development tasks for college students. The ability to think beyond the present, to have some "future orientation," and to commit oneself to the attainment of these future goals is part of such developmental tasks or career development needs (Super & Associates, 1974).

Researchers have varied in their theoretical approach to the process involved in career decision making, but most agree that the process of deciding involves understanding oneself, understanding career alternatives being considered, assessing the desirability of each alternative, determining priorities and impediments, and selecting a course of action.

Some researchers emphasize that decisions among college students are made from a loss-gain or investment perspective. The evaluation of available college, curriculum, or career alternatives is determined by the prediction of success and the cost of failure. Risk-taking capacity affects this evaluation of possible success or failure. Some individuals will consider only those decision options that stress security; others will give high priority to the potential of rewards and little thought to the consequences of failure (Witwer & Stewart, 1972). Some individuals become so anxious about the decision or commitment that they are unable to make a career choice (Maier & Herman, 1974; Mendonca & Seizz, 1976). Lack of decision-making skills may result from inaccurate self-appraisal skills, inadequate information-gathering skills, lack of problem-solving behavior, avoiding the choice task, anxiety about the choice commitment, lack of general maturity, and lack of training in accepting choice responsibility (Holland, Gottfredson, & Naziger, 1975).

A variation on the issue of decision making among college students is the issue of self-efficacy. Essentially, self-efficacy is a process by which persons appraise whether they can adequately perform some action required by a particular job or curriculum. An efficacy expectation is an estimate that one can successfully execute the behavior required to produce the outcomes sought. Whether or not the appraisal is accurate, persons will likely act on the basis of their feelings of self-efficacy in a particular situation. Bandura (1977), the originator of self-efficacy theory, contends that the level and strength of self-efficacy will determine whether a coping behavior will be initiated, how much effort will result, and how long the effort will be sustained in the face of obstacles. Self-efficacy theory has become an important explanatory system to describe why some people choose some things and not others or, put more clearly, why they avoid choosing some areas. For example, women tend to be less evident in mathematics and science majors in college for reasons that many observers attribute to self-efficacy expectations: women are not ''supposed'' to be good at masculine areas such as math and science, men do not find bright women attractive, and so on. Such feedback to women may be incorrect, but it is the type of content or feedback that enters into the processing of alternatives on self-efficacy bases.

In several important studies, level and magnitude of self-efficacy have been found to relate to such areas as mathematics performance, to career entry behaviors such as choice of college major and academic performance, and to gender differences pertinent to a variety of career behaviors (Betz & Hackett, 1981, 1983; Campbell & Hackett, 1986; Lent & Hackett, 1987). Of particular significance have been studies indicating self-efficacy differences between those who choose mathematics courses or majors and those who do not. Mathematics is so critical as a foundational skill or knowledge for scientific and technical occupation that avoidance of courses providing such skills likely eliminates women or men who have low self-efficacy in mathematics from such occupations. As such, career services providing success experiences and other counteractions to low self-efficacy in mathematics and in other areas become major career interventions.

The results of studies done on certainty of career choice on the part of college students have been somewhat mixed. Differences between being decided and undecided about a field of study or future career goal have been studied in relation to a variety of factors: interest development, career maturity, concept of self, sex differences, persistence in school, persistence in field of study, and grade point average while in college. A higher proportion of those who are certain about their academic major and career goals typically persist to graduation (Montgomery, 1975). Thus, career uncertainty is one of the factors typically associated with college attrition (Montgomery, 1975). In a major national study of this criterion, Cope and Hannah (1975) cite commitment to an educational or career goal as the single most important determinant of persistence in college (p. 19). In a related manner, a review of the literature by Groccia and Harrity (1991) indicates that "undecidedness about which major to pursue has been shown to be a major factor in adjustment to college and attrition. Students are clearly 'drop-out' prone unless they get assistance with the decision-making process involved in declaring a major. Many capable students leave college because they possess unclear vocational identities or lack appropriate information, experience, or the skills necessary to work through the major/career-choice process in an orderly, planned way" (p. 178).

Reasons for coming to college are also related to the career development or career maturity of college students. For example, more than two decades ago Baird (1969) reviewed data on 59,618 college-bound students, who were asked to choose among ten reasons for attending college. Baird found that students who were undecided about their career choice emphasized the goal of developing their minds, while those students who were decided about their career choice chose professional training as their most important goal. This result was confirmed later in studies done at the University of Texas and at the University of Washington (Appel & Witzke, 1972; Lunneborg, 1976). Those students who were undecided were less concerned about college as a vehicle for occupational preparation and more concerned about increased self-awareness and personal growth.

A lack of decision-making progress is related theoretically to personal conflict, unclear preprofessional goals, academic problems, and dissonance, which threaten the student's career development in college. Madison (1969) cautioned that developmental crises center around student inability to integrate oneself with institutional expectations about the choice of college major and the after-college career. This is partially a function of unresolved matters of life-style desired, clarity of values, and understanding of expectations. Too frequently, students base their decisions on stereotypes of what majors or jobs might be rather than on exploration or accurate information.

Holland and Holland (1977) concluded from their research that college students who have difficulties in making career choices consistently show dysfunctional attitudes, interpersonal incompetence, lack of involvement, unclear identity, and poor decision-making skills. To confound the problem, however, many undecided students merely delay decisions until situations or necessity forces action, rather than being unable to make choices. Holland and Holland further caution that college student indecisiveness may be a reflection of a multiplicity of unfavorable personal and situational forces, rather than totally the result of anxiety or tensions.

Various researchers have found career maturity in college students to be related to their level of self-esteem. For example, Barrett and Tinsley (1977) found that individuals with high self-esteem also had more highly crystallized vocational self-concepts than low self-esteem individuals. Similarly, Maier and Herman (1974) found vocationally undecided college students attached great importance to the opinion and values of others. Their locus of control was invested in others, not themselves. They were more dogmatic and had lower self-esteem than decided students. These data and others indicate support for the broad hypothesis that adequate career decision-making ability depends on self-understanding, knowledge of vocational roles, and perceptions of future decisions (Holland et al., 1975).

In more developmental terms, Knefelkamp and Slepitza's research (1976) indicates that college students typically move from a simplistic categorical view of career through four stages, culminating in a complex pluralistic view of career. The movement of college students through these stages can be predicted and described through the unfolding of nine variables, each of which represents a substage. By definition, the stages in paraphrased form are as follows:

1. Dualism. This stage is dominated by simplistic, dichotomous thinking about career planning that is largely controlled by information obtained from external sources.
2. Multiplicity. In this stage, student decision making becomes more cognitively complex and more oriented to the possibility of making right and wrong choices. More factors are considered in the process and cause-and-effect relations are worked into the decision making process.
3. Relativism. In this stage, the student's point of reference tends to shift from a predominantly external to a predominantly internal one. Students are more analytical in their decision making, tend to assume responsibility for decisions made, and create a decision-making process that is tailored to their own characteristics and perceptions.
4. Commitment within relativism. In this stage, increased responsibility for the decision-making process is taken, choice of a career is seen as a personal commitment, and career identity and self-identity become more closely intertwined.

According to the research of Knefelkamp and Slepitza, the nine variables that affect the maturity of career planning among college students, as the stages just cited evolve, include:

1. Locus of control—the external-internal sources that students use to define themselves and their environments.
2. Analysis—the individual's ability to break down a decision into its diverse elements and to consider cause-and effect relationships.

3. Synthesis—the individual's ability to integrate the diverse aspects of a problem or decision into a whole, and to look at a problem whole as a series of related elements or components that can be examined.
4. Semantic structure—the continuum of absolute or open verbs and qualifiers students use in their written and spoken expressions; the rigidity or flexibility with which students see themselves.
5. Self-Processing—the ability to examine oneself and take into account one's defining factors: aptitudes, values, goals, interests, risk-taking ability.
6. Openness of alternative perspectives—the degree to which a student knows about and considers alternative points of view about options.
7. Ability to assume responsibility—the students' willingness to accept the consequences of actions or decisions taken and to be independent rather than letting someone else live through them vicariously.
8. Ability to take on new roles—the student's ability to accommodate the characteristics of new roles or activities; one's ability to adopt or compromise with role realities or change to another curriculum.
9. Ability to take risks with self—the student's ability to risk self-esteem when new learnings and experiences so demand.

Any one of these substages can represent a specific hurdle for which some students need help through various career interventions. They are, in general, not fixed effects but can be modified through systematic exposure to career planning and placement services described elsewhere. If such interventions do not occur, however, it is quite possible that a student will become fixated at one of these stages or unable to behave adequately in accordance with one of the variables identified.

It is particularly important to note that a major expectation of higher education is to make persons activists in their own behalf and to help them to be able to identify and effectively act upon the choices available to them. Thus, in order to meet such a goal, most persons, whether youth or adult, must be educated to choose. Simply providing information and expecting them to use it rationally and on their own initiative have been shown in many research studies to be inadequate. In fact, most people do not know what information they need, what information is available, or how to use what they have.

In broad terms, the two requirements of good decision making are "adequate information" and "an effective strategy for analyzing, or organizing, and synthesizing that information to arrive at a choice" (Clarke, Gelatt, & Levine, 1965). It is the latter that is at issue here. College students live in a knowledge-rich but action-poor world. Information is all around them, but they frequently do not know what is relevant to their needs or how to process what they have. Information is the fuel of the decision maker, but it is inadequate in itself; it must be systematically evaluated, weighed as to its personal relevance, and placed into a plan of action.

It is likely that each person enrolled in a community college or four-year higher educational institution or graduate school has certain unique informational and counseling needs that should be addressed. But there are also major categories of information that will be common needs of most persons around which systematic program planning can be developed. In broad terms, this information includes dealing with knowledge and attitudes about the (1) self, (2) occupational and other environmental opportunities, and (3) decision-making or career-planning processes. These three categories represent both the content and the process of choice.

In the first place, then, college students need to be assisted to come to terms with who they are; what kinds of commitments they are willing to make; the nature of their aptitudes, interests, values, and goals; their feelings of competence and confidence or the lack of these. In essence, the provision and consideration of self-information provide a base to which anything else can be related. Knowing one's strengths and weaknesses, preferences, and goals defines an evaluative foundation to which any option or action can be referred to determine its relevance. This base of information also helps one determine what information one has, what one needs, and what should be secured.

In the second place, the college student needs to know about and consider the range of occupational and other environmental options available to him or her and how these might be accessed. This requires having knowledge about and considering the personal relevance of such matters as the characteristics of curricular majors available, their prerequisites and content, the relationship between subject matter and occupations in which that subject matter is required, the outcomes of pursuing various curricula (What's the placement record? Into what kinds of jobs are people placed?), and the matching of personal characteristics with those required in preferred curricula or occupations.

In addition, considerations of environmental alternatives will likely require information about methods of access. Are the preferred occupations available locally? If not, where are they available? How are potential employers identified? What's the best procedure to use to make contact with an employer? What information or procedures are pertinent to the completion of letters of inquiry, résumés, and applications? What types of questions or other conditions are likely to prevail in an interview situation? How does one follow up a contact with an employer?

The third area of needed information is likely to deal with the decision-making process itself. Here the emphasis is not so much on acquiring and incorporating information about personal characteristics or educational, occupational, and other environmental alternatives but applying this information within a decision-making process. The assumption in career planning, counseling, or career guidance is that once such a process is learned, it can be used repeatedly as a logical or systematic approach by which to process information and to weigh alternatives. There are several major models appropriate here.

Pitz and Harren (1980) have indicated that any decision problem can be described in terms of four elements:

1. The set of objectives that the decision maker seeks to achieve
2. The set of choices, or alternative courses of action, among which the decision maker must choose

3. A set of possible outcomes that is associated with each choice

4. The ways each outcome might be assessed with respect to how well it meets the decision maker's objectives, the attributes of each outcome (pp. 321–322)

As Gelatt originally suggested in 1962, the individual needs both a prediction system and a value system to make decisions among preferences and expectancies for action within a climate of uncertainty. In 1989, Gelatt amended his 1962 model to respond to new knowledge about and conditions under which decision making occurs. Gelatt has argued for positive uncertainty as the new decision-making framework. He argues that "what is appropriate now is a decision and counseling framework that helps clients deal with change and ambiguity, accept uncertainty and inconsistency, and utilize the nonrational and intuitive side of thinking and choosing" (1989, p. 252). Thus, in the information society with its ambiguity and paradoxes, Gelatt has suggested a new definition of decision making as "the process of arranging and rearranging information into a choice or actions" (1989, p. 253). Gelatt specifically contends that in his amended model, reflections, flexibility, and both rational and intuitive thinking must occur in a holistic way. Therefore, "helping someone decide how to decide must move from promoting only rational, linear, systematic strategies to recommending, even teaching, intuitive situations and sometimes inconsistent methods for solving personal problems or making decisions" (153). In subsequent chapters, specific approaches to the teaching or facilitating of decision making will be described as it relates to career interventions used with different subgroups.

SUMMARY OF COLLEGE STUDENT CAREER BEHAVIOR

As the needs of college students for career planning and placement and theory and research related to such goals are examined, perspectives emerge that undergird the planning for career services, as well as the range of interventions provided to various college populations. These perspectives include the following:

1. The mix of aspirations, self-knowledge, and ability among college students is so wide that no one model or process of career planning and placement is likely to be adequate to the diversity of needs present. Some students need only reassurance that their choices make sense, others need specific information, and still others need much more comprehensive assistance to deal with their indecision, inaccurate self-efficacy, and lack of connection between the choice of majors and career options.

2. Many college students are not clear about their own characteristics and may be very fragile in motivation and self-esteem. Most decisions are not impulsive but are the outcomes of related decisions. They are public testimonies to how people feel about themselves and about their alternatives. If they view themselves as losers, they choose as losers choose; if they view themselves as winners, they choose accordingly. Whitehead (Tyler, 1978, p. 5) argues that decisions are the ways people create their own reality. To put it another way, careers are unique to each individual; they are created by the

decisions people make. Thus, the facilitation of effective decision-making procedures is a necessary part of programs of career planning and placement.

3. Some persons are in college because they do not know where else to be, and they choose majors because they must, not because they understand or are committed to them. These persons need a developmental process of career planning that begins no later than the freshman year and carries them incrementally through the stages of awareness, exploration, and commitment.

4. Some persons are unaware of the expectations that college or a particular major holds for them. In essence, they lack a socialization in their family or in their previous education to prepare them to engage the college experience knowledgeably and confidently. The point of induction to these expectations is critical and deserves career support systems and orientation appropriate to such importance.

5. Some persons know very little about the relationship of course requirements to subsequent career choices or patterns. Such connections are important aspects of career-planning and placement programs.

6. Some persons know very little about how to access occupational or career opportunities and how to interview employers and implement the mechanics of an application process. These, too, are important aspects of career planning and placement programs.

7. Adult and adolescent college students will differ in their feelings of urgency for, and specificity in, planning.

8. There is a variety of subpopulations of college students for whom career planning and placement programs need to be tailored.

In summary, the primary planning considerations relating to the provision of career guidance and counseling in higher education are institutional commitment, responsiveness to immediate needs, and comprehensive, articulated delivery of services.

GOALS FOR CAREER GUIDANCE AND CAREER COUNSELING

Goals for career guidance and counseling in higher education should be such that all types of career concerns and needs are addressed. It is, therefore, unlikely that very many students will require all of the outcomes listed below; however, almost all students in higher educational institutions could probably benefit from one or more. In a truly comprehensive career guidance and counseling program, provisions will be made to achieve the following goals.

1. Assistance in the selection of a major field of study. A majority of freshmen will change their major field at least once during their collegiate experience. Many will pursue many changes because they have no idea what they really want to do. Each change of academic discipline entails a commensurate alteration in career planning to which career guidance should respond.

2. Assistance in self-assessment and self-analysis. Reasonable career choices cannot be made by individuals who do not have a fairly clear notion of who they are, of their

strengths and weaknesses, of what they value, of their motivations, of their psychological characteristics, and of their interests. Without such an evaluative base, it is difficult to sort out the personal relevance of the multiple options available. In short, students must be aided to discover both a personal and a vocational identity that can subsequently be related to the world of work.

3. Assistance in understanding the world of work. At the collegiate level, it is likely that most students will have a broad and basic understanding of the occupational structure. However, many students may need help in exploring specific segments of that structure in personally-relevant terms (e.g., What work is related to a given major?)

What these interventions are and where they occur must be tailored to the characteristics of the institution in which they are to be implemented. For this reason and others, they must be viewed within the context of an explicit institutional commitment that is planned systematically and that provides multiple approaches to the diversity of career-related needs present in the college student populations to be served in that institution. Such an approach rests on several propositions

1. An individual can choose only from among those alternatives of which he or she is aware. Therefore, college students and others need ways to identify and classify relevant career opportunities and evaluate them.

2. The phenomena that appear most likely to bring career-related alternatives into the awareness of college students and that thus serve as linkages are experiences, both job-related and curricular, and persons who serve as role models or give advice. Reading seems to serve only to a limited extent.

3. Most career-related decisions result in further experiences or interactions with persons, leading them to subsequent decisions. Thus career-related decisions tend to be sequential and cumulative.

4. A wider range of alternative experiences and interactions with persons seems likely to generate a wider range of career alternatives for college students to consider.

5. It is appropriate for career counselors and other specialists to analyze the developmental decision points required of students during the four years of college to determine the extent of supportive services provided by the staff and faculty to assist students with their decisions. Further analysis would then seem to suggest a potential plan of action designed around the lead-up decisions. For example, a well-timed intervention, such as a discussion group following an experience (internship, summer job, and so on), could assist in raising the students' level of awareness about themselves and their career planning.

6. The increasing numbers of college graduates currently entering the job market present a strong argument for introductory courses to include some planned learning experiences focusing on career development, for example, an examination of the intellectual skills appropriate to that discipline that are then transferrable to a variety of job settings.

7. Students with helping skills are a potential resource to each other, facilitating constructive discussions in the residence halls and student centers where doubts, insights, and strategies are most often shared.

8. When teaching decision-making skills, there seems to be value in encouraging students to consider their usual patterns of decision making and then to explore ways of strengthening their preferred style with an alternative mode.

9. That career planning is a process and not an event is important for students to comprehend. Encouraging them to examine the experiences and persons that have attracted them to specific career alternatives might (1) help convey this concept, (2) help identify the basis of their decisions, and (3) help individuals assume responsibility for their lives and perceive some control over them (Padgett, 1978).

SUMMARY

Just as the development of career behavior and its endless reaffirmations and refinements is a lifelong process, career counseling and career planning have come to be seen as lifelong responses important at every life stage and in each career transition in which one engages. Career transition as a term has initiated new language systems and many conceptual models, particularly of career development for college students and adults. These perspectives on career behavior and the obstacles to it have enriched the practice of career counseling and career planning for many groups of persons not traditionally served and, in turn, expanded the repertoire of counselor interventions implemented in an enlarging range of settings, including colleges and universities.

REFERENCES

Appel, V. H., & Witzke, D. B. (1972). *Goal orientation vs. self orientation: Two perspectives affecting indecision about college major and career choice.* Paper presented at the American Educational Research Association Convention, Austin, TX.

Aslanian, C. B., & Brickell, H. M. (1980). *Americans in transition: Life changes and reasons for adult learning.* New York: College Entrance Examination Board.

Astin, A., Green, K., Korn, W., & Schalit, M. (1985) *The American freshman: National norms for fall 1985.* Los Angeles: University of California, Graduate School of Education, Higher Education Research Institute.

Baird, L. L. (1969). The undecided student: How different is he? *Personnel and Guidance Journal, 47*(5), 429–434.

Bandura, A. (1977). Self-efficacy: Toward a unifying theory of behavioral change. *Psychological Review, 84,* 191–215.

Barrett, T. C., & Tinsley, H. E. (1977). Vocational self-concept crystallization and vocational indecision. *Journal of Counseling Psychology, 24*(4), 301–307.

Betz, N. E., & Hackett, G. (1981). The relationship of career-related self-efficacy expectations to perceived career options in college women and men. *Journal of Counseling Psychology, 28,* 399–410.

Betz, N. E., & Hackett, G. (1983). The relationship of mathematics self-efficacy expectations to the selection of science-based college majors. *Journal of Vocational Behavior, 23,* 329–345.

Bjorkquist, P. M. (1987, July). Career development for the liberal arts student. *Journal of College Student Development, 28* 377.

Blann, F. W. (1985). Intercollegiate athletic competition and students' educational and career plans. *Journal of College Student Personnel, 26*, 115–118.

Branyon, S. D. (1987, March). Career and life planning: No magic answers. *Journal of College Student Personnel, 28*, 187–188.

Buescher, K. L., Johnston, J. A., Lucas, E. B., & Hughes, K. F. (1989). Early intervention with undecided college students. *Journal of College Student Development, 30*(4), 375–376.

Campbell, N. K., & Hackett, G. (1986). The effects of mathematics task performances on math self-efficacy and task interest. *Journal of Vocational Behavior, 28*(2), 149–162.

Clarke, R., Gelatt, H. B., & Levine, L. (1965). A decision-making paradigm for local guidance research. *Personnel and Guidance Journal, 44*, 40–51.

Cooper, S. E., & Robinson, D.A.G. (1987, January). A comparison of career, home, and leisure values of male and female students in engineering and the sciences. *Journal of College Student Personnel, 28*, 66–70.

Cope, R., & Hannah, W. (1975). *Revolving open doors*. New York: Wiley.

Crites, J. O. (1978). *Career Maturity Inventory Administration and Use Manual*. Monterey, CA: CTB/McGraw-Hill.

Gelatt, H. B. (1962). Decision-making. A conceptual frame of reference for counseling. *Journal of Counseling Psychology* . 9, 240–245.

———— . (1989). Positive uncertainty: A new decision-making framework for counseling. *Journal of Counseling Psychology*. 36(2), 252–256.

Griff, N. (1987, September). Meeting the career development needs of returning students. *Journal of College Student Personnel, 28*, 469–470.

Groccia, J. E., & Harrity, M. B. (1991). The major selection program: A proactive retention and enrichment program for undecided freshmen. *Journal of College Student Development, 32*(2), 178–179.

Haviland, M. G., & Gohn, L. A. (1983, Spring). Career planning needs of college students. *NASPA Journal, 20* 28–33.

Healy, C. C., Mourton, D. L., Anderson, E. C., & Robinson, E. (1984, July). Career maturity and the achievement of community college students and disadvantaged university students. *Journal of College Student, 25*, 347–352.

Healy, C. C., & Reilly, K. C. (1989). Career needs of community college students: Implications for services and theory. *Journal of College Student Development, 30*(6), 541–545.

Holland, J. L., & Holland, J. E. (1977). Vocational indecision: More evidence and speculation. *Journal of Counseling Psychology, 24*, 404–414.

Holland, J. L., Gottfredson, G. E., & Naziger, D. (1975). Testing the validity of some theoretical signs of vocational decision-making ability. *Journal of Counseling Psychology, 22*, 411–422.

Keller, J. W., Piotrowski, C., & Rabold, F. L. (1990). Determinants of career selection in undergraduates. *Journal of College Student Development, 31*(3), 276–277.

Kennedy, S. R., & Dimick, K. M. (1987, July). Career maturity and professional sports expectations of college football and basketball players. *Journal of College Student Personnel, 28* 293–297.

King, P. M., & Fields, A. L. (1980). A framework for student development: From student development goals to educational opportunity practices. *Journal of College Student Personnel, 21*, 541–548.

Knefelkamp, L. L., & Slepitza, R. (1976). A cognitive developmental model of career development—an adaptation of the Perry scheme. *The Counseling Psychologist*, 6(3), 53–58.

Kramer, H. C., Berger, F., & Miller, G. (1974). Student concerns and sources of assistance. *Journal of College Student Personnel*, 15(5), 389–393.

Kroll, J., & Rentz, A. L. (1988). Career planning and placement. In A. L. Rentz & G. L. Saddlemire (Eds.). *Student affairs functions in higher education*. Springfield, IL: Charles C. Thomas.

Lent, R. W., & Hackett, G. (1987). Career self-efficacy: Empirical status and future directions. *Journal of Vocational Behavior, 30*, 347–382.

Lott, J. K. (1984, January). A career development workshop for high school seniors: Reaching out further. *Journal of College Student Personnel, 25*, 80–81.

Lunneborg, P. (1976). Vocational indecision in college graduates. *Journal of Counseling Psychology, 23*(4), 402–404.

McCaffrey, S. S., Miller, T. K., & Winston, R. B., Jr. (1984, March). Comparison of career maturity among graduate students and undergraduates. *Journal of College Student Personnel, 25* 127–131.

Madison, P. (1969). *Personality development in college*. Reading, MA: Addison-Wesley.

Maier, D., & Herman, A. (1974). The relationship of vocational undecidedness and satisfaction with dogmatism and self-esteem. *Journal of Vocational Behavior, 5*(1), 95–102.

Mendonca, J. P., & Siete, T. F. (1976). Counseling for indecision. *Journal of Counseling Psychology, 23*(4), 339–347.

Montgomery, E. F. (1975). A study of the effects of career and personal group counseling on retention rates and self- actualization. Unpublished doctoral dissertation, University of Southern Mississippi.

Padgett, K. (1978). How do they decide: Factors affecting career decisions of liberal arts students. In Ginny Riser-Schoch (Ed.), *Career planning and placement in the small college. Proceedings*. Alma, MI: Alma College.

Pitz, G. F., & Harren, V. A. (1980). An analysis of career decision-making from the point of view of information processing and decision theory. *Journal of Vocational Behavior, 16*, 320–346.

Reardon, R., & Clark, J. (1987, September). Career development in student recruitment: A case study. *Journal of College Student Personnel, 28*, 467–469.

Snyder, J. F., Hill, C. E., & Darksen, T. P. (1974). Why some students do not use university counseling services. *Journal of Counseling Psychology, 19*(4), 263–268.

Super, D.E., & Associates. (1974). *Measuring vocational maturity for counseling and evaluation*. Washington, DC: National Vocational Guidance Association.

Tyler, L. E. (1978). *Individuality, human possibilities and personal choice in the psychological development of man and woman*. San Francisco: Jossey-Bass.

Walters, L., & Saddlemire, G. (1979). Career planning needs of college freshmen and their perceptions of career planning. *Journal of College Student Personnel, 20*, 224–229.

Walter-Samli, J. H., & Samli, A. C. (1979, September). A model of career counseling for international students. *Vocational Guidance Quarterly, 28*, 48–55.

Weissburg, M., Berentsen, M., Cote, A., Cravey, B., & Heath, K. (1982). An assessment of the personal, career and academic needs of undergraduate students. *Journal of College Student Personnel, 23*, 115–122.

Wilkes, S. B., Davis, L., & Dever, L. (1989). Fostering career development in student athletes. *Journal of College Student Development, 30*(6), 567–578.

Williams, G. D., Lindsay, C. A., Burns, M. A., Wyckoff, J. H., & Wall, H. W. (1973). Urgency and types of adult counseling needs among continuing education students. *Journal of College Student Personnel, 14*(6), 501–506.

Witwer, G., & Stewart, L. H. (1972). Personality correlates of preference for risk among occupation-oriented junior college students. *Vocational Guidance Quarterly, 20*(4), 259–265.

3

Planning for the Career Center

In the first two chapters we have described the historical evolution of the modern university career center and reviewed the literature describing student needs that have led to the establishment of comprehensive career development and placement centers. In this chapter we attempt to show how this evolution, changing student needs, and other factors have affected and continue to affect planning for the career center. The emphasis here is on identifying those factors that determine and shape the goals of the university career center and, perhaps most important, on the process that leads to a practical plan that can realistically be implemented.

In their chapter entitled "Systematic Planning for Career Guidance and Counseling," Herr and Cramer (1988) review the process of systematic planning for career services and advocate a five-stage planning model as follows:

Stage 1 - Developing a Program Rationale and Philosophy

Stage 2 - Stating Program Goals and Behavioral Objectives

Stage 3 - Selecting Alternative Program Processes

Stage 4 - Developing an Evaluation Design

Stage 5 - Milestones (specifying critical times when major events must take place)

While the planning process we advocate in this chapter is based principally on practical experience in the management of university career centers, the similarities between the process we advocate here and the five-stage model described by Herr and Cramer will be obvious.

In nearly any enterprise, planning must take place on at least two levels. First, one must plan strategically for the long run based on factors that are universal and relatively unchanging, yet be responsive to those factors that change from year to year or even month to month. There is a whole series of strategic factors that will impact on the nature of the university career center plan. These are factors such as behavioral expectations of students for which the center will be accountable, beliefs about human nature (career development theory), professionally developed standards (CAS standards), institutional mission and commitment, demographics of the student body, and position of the career center within the university organizational structure. These factors tend to remain fairly constant over time. Many are beyond the control of the planner, but all will have a significant impact on the final plan and its successful implementation.

At the second level there is a set of factors that are constantly changing. These are factors like the economy, current student issues, staff strengths and weaknesses, institutional politics, social issues, and short-term fluctuations in those factors previously identified as strategic factors. Short-term factors are more elusive than strategic factors. Getting a handle on them requires a well-developed system of both formative and summative evaluation techniques. This chapter will provide some examples of proven evaluation techniques and speculate on others that may be helpful but that are far from proven.

STRATEGIC FACTORS

Clearly there is some overlap between strategic factors and short-term changing factors, but for purposes of discussion we deal with them as though they are independent of one another. We begin with strategic factors.

Strategic Factor #1: Behavioral Expectations

One of the key strategic factors that must be taken into account in planning for career services is behavioral expectations or outcomes, sometimes called behavioral objectives. While behavioral objectives could be developed for all constituent groups that interact with the career service office, students are clearly the primary constituent group. To provide the reader with a sense of the nature of what we regard as appropriate behavioral expectations or objectives, we present here a fairly universal set of behavioral objectives for student clients of the career center:

1. Increased exploration of careers and self
2. Increased awareness of the need to plan and to take responsibility for one's own career destiny
3. Greater understanding of one's self, occupations, and the relationship between self and occupations
4. A realistic, appropriate, and congruent occupational choice
5. Knowledge of available options and means of attaining such options
6. Knowledge of appropriate job search strategies and job-seeking skills and experience utilizing those strategies and skills
7. Placement into a job, acceptance into further education or training, or some client-approved acceptable alternative

Clearly, the most important factor in planning for career services is to have identified and articulated behavioral outcomes for the principal clients. Such outcomes need to be no more specific than those seven cited above. As a service agency the ultimate goal of the career service office is to affect student behavior in ways that facilitate career development. How one goes about implementing programs and services to accomplish these outcomes will depend on many factors, but one thing is certain: just as in the case of career planning, "If you don't know where you're going you'll probably end up somewhere else" (Campbell, 1974). Establishing a set of behavioral outcomes is the first and perhaps the most important step in planning for the career center. Career center professionals seeking assistance in the process of developing program goals and behavioral objectives may wish to refer to Herr and Cramer (1988, pp. 207–216). In their chapter on planning for career guidance and counseling, they provide a blueprint for establishing program goals and behavioral objectives for a wide range of career services settings.

Strategic Factor #2: Career Development Theory

It should be apparent from Chapters 1 and 2 that the authors hold a certain conception of the career development and placement process and that this conception provides a basis for planning a comprehensive array of services that are the core of the modern career center. Several key tenets of that conception (or theory) are enumerated and discussed here in terms of their implications for the planning process.

Career Development Is a Lifelong Process (Super, 1957; Herr & Cramer, 1988). If one accepts this basic premise, then a comprehensive career development and placement service must provide services across a considerable span of an individual's life. The bulk of the services offered in a college or university career center will be targeted toward the needs of enrolled students, and at most institutions many of these students will be between the ages of 18 and 22. Of course, one must also consider that among the 18–22 year olds, there are considerable individual differences in terms of career maturity and needs, depending on socioeconomic background, ethnicity, gender, and demographic variables. Additionally, universities, by definition, have a significant enrollment of graduate and professional students, most of whom are in different stages of career development than the average undergraduate.

Beyond services for enrolled students, there is increasing pressure from alumni and alumni associations to provide for the long-term career development needs of alumni. Indeed, a number of universities are providing retirement planning workshops in conjunction with their career development and placement services. At the other end of the continuum, it has become increasingly important for career development offices to provide at least informational services, if not counseling services, to "potential students" (often in collaboration with the admissions office), all the way down to elementary school. In fact, several universities, in the interest of assisting parents with financial planning for college (which is clearly a form of career planning), are providing college cost planning brochures at obstetric and pediatric clinics throughout their service areas.

In a very real sense college and university career centers are being asked to provide comprehensive career services "from cradle to grave" in response to the growing conviction among practitioners that career development truly is a "lifelong process." Even if such comprehensive services are not being provided, career services professionals must be aware of, and attuned to, the "lifelong process nature" of the career development enterprise to assure that the services they do provide are relevant and supportive of the larger process.

Planning Implications: The conviction that career development is a "lifelong process" dictates that career services must be more than a job service–oriented placement office. No matter how career services are configured, they must be comprehensive and flexible, recognizing the developmental and demographic differences that exist within an increasingly diverse university student body. An underlying commitment to meeting student career development needs across the life span must drive the planning process.

Career Development Is an Integral Part of the Educational Process. The assumption that career development is an integral part of the educational process has significant implications for planning in terms of (1) the geographic location of career services on the campus; (2) the position of career services within the organizational structure of the university; and (3) the relationship of those services to the academic programs of the various colleges and the academic departments within them.

Planning Implications: If career development is viewed as an integral part of the educational process, a strong case can be made for ensuring that career services are housed centrally on campus where access is assured for the broad mass of students. Given such an assumption, locations on the periphery of the campus in barnlike quonset huts are not acceptable. Similarly, sharing facilities with mental health or psychological service units is inappropriate because of the stigma that is unfortunately often associated with such units. Incorporating career services as a component of some other unit within the student services organizational structure often obscures the identity of career services and is likely to create confusion in the minds of students, faculty, and staff. Beyond this, the staff of the service must have credibility with, and must integrate and interact positively with, faculty from all the academic units of the institution. In brief, the geographic location and quality of the physical facility in which the university career center is located must communicate to students, employers, and faculty alike that the service is a valued and integral component of the educational mission of the institution and that it is not some type of remedial service or marginal office operating on the fringe of respectability with little or no relationship to the core goals of the institution.

Finally, there must be formal linkages between academic units and the career services office to assure the uninterrupted and direct flow of information in both directions. This critical, interdependent relationship will not exist accidentally. It must be planned.

Career Development Is an Important (Perhaps the Most Important) Component of Human Development. Throughout our discussions we have assumed that career development is a significant component of human development and that, as has been previously described, it takes place over the life span (Herr & Cramer, 1988). As such, it is an important element of normal human development, perhaps one of the key elements that lead to identity formation and a source of purpose and meaning in life. Its significance should not be trivialized by thinking of it as "getting kids jobs." While job placement is important, it is just one element of career development.

Planning Implications: In planning for the university career center, care must be taken to ensure that the focus remains on the broader goal of meeting student career development needs with equal emphasis and allocating resources to the freshman, sophomore, and junior years rather than placing the primary focus on seniors and the achievement of a high placement rate.

The "Four Critical Years" During the Undergraduate Experience May Be the Most Critical Years of the Lifelong Career Development Process. If one accepts Super's (1957) conception of life stage career development, the years from ages 18 to 22 are among the most turbulent and yet the most critical years to satisfactory career development and self-concept implementation. Although career development is a lifelong process, some portions of that process are more critical than others; the stage that Super refers to as "exploration" and that Astin (1977) has labeled "four critical years" offers a "window of opportunity" for young adults to transcend their environment and take control of their career destiny.

Planning Implications: Because of the critical role that the undergraduate years play in the career development process, career services must be "saturation-loaded" on students during this brief four-year period. Students must graduate with competence in the career development curriculum. In a sense, career development is to placement what a liberal arts education is to vocational education. In parable form, "Give a man a fish, and he'll eat for today; teach him how to fish, and he'll eat forever." A worthwhile paraphrase might be, "Give a student a job, and she or he will be satisfied for today; teach her or him the career development process, and she or he will be satisfied for a lifetime."

Career Development Is the Undergraduate Experience. While we believe that the modern career center has an obligation to provide a comprehensive array of services in support of healthy career development, it will take place with or without those services. In fact, we believe career development *is* the undergraduate experience. Everything a student does, every experience a student has during his or her undergraduate years will have an impact on that student's career destiny. It is the responsibility of the career center to enhance the value of that undergraduate experience as a vehicle for personal career development—to show students how decisions they are making, activities in which they are engaged, and courses in which they are enrolled affect their career destiny. Thus, planning for student career development requires an understanding of the academic curriculum available and an array of career center–sponsored services that integrate with the curriculum (and the extra curriculum—those out-of-classroom activities, programs, and events that are such an important part of college life) to ensure that the undergraduate experience is also a unifying career development experience.

Planning Implications: Planning for career services must take into account the undergraduate curriculum and provide an array of services that integrate with it and enhance it. To borrow an often used term, career development theory and services must be "infused" into the curriculum. In our experience that infusion will not happen without its being carefully planned, and the impetus for it must come from the career center.

Strategic Factor #3: Professionally Developed Standards

Planning for the career center must also take into consideration certain professional standards that have evolved within the profession and that have been codified by professional associations external to the college or university. In the case of career services, the appropriate, professionally developed standards are those of the Council for the Advancement of Standards for Student Services/Development Programs (CAS). This consortium of student affairs professional associations includes three associations with particular relevance to college and university career centers: the American Association for Counseling and Development (AACD), the American College Personnel Association (ACPA), and the College Placement Council (CPC).

The CAS Career Planning and Placement Standards represent an external benchmark that was alluded to in Chapter 1 and that we believe should be the cornerstone for all university career services planning. The standards themselves are presented in their entirety in Appendix 3.1 for the convenience of the career services professional because in our experience they are rather difficult to locate on most campuses. Readers interested in reviewing the standards complete with associated guidelines should consult *CAS Standards and Guidelines for Student Services/Development Programs* (1986) and the *CAS Standards and Guidelines for Career Planning and Placement* (1988). Key topics are addressed in the standards as follows:

1. Mission
2. Program
3. Leadership and Management
4. Organization and Administration
5. Human Resources
6. Funding
7. Facilities

8. Legal Responsibilities
9. Equal Opportunity, Access, and Affirmative Action
10. Campus and Community Relations
11. Multicultural Programs and Services
12. Ethics
13. Evaluation

To provide a flavor for the CAS standards, the first standard, entitled "Mission," is quoted here:

The institution and its career planning and placement services must develop, review, and disseminate regularly their own specific goals for student services/development, which must be consistent with the nature and goals of the institution and with the standards in this document.

Career planning is a developmental process and must be fostered during the entire period of a student's involvement with the institution.

The primary purpose of career planning and placement must be to aid students in developing, evaluating, and effectively initiating and implementing career plans.

Planning Implications: While it will be clear to the reader that the CAS standards are necessarily generic, with many of the flaws that committee-developed standards exhibit, they provide a fundamental basis for planning that has evolved in the profession. The danger with any set of minimum standards is that they sometimes foster a sort of "IRS mentality." That is, rather than providing a model of excellence to which career centers might aspire, they may be misconstrued to provide a license to "get by" with the minimum. This mind-set can be particularly destructive of career center quality if it is embraced by the director of career services and/or university central administration. Professionals involved in planning for the career center must be mindful of this possibility and take steps to ensure that the role that CAS standards play in the planning process will be a positive one. Planning must be driven by aspirations for excellence, not by compliance with minimum standards.

Strategic Factor #4: Position of Career Services Within the University Structure

The position that career services occupies within the university structure is a crucial factor in planning. While there are an almost infinite number of ways in which the career services units might "fit" within the university structure, the major issues related to this strategic factor may be summarized as follows:

Issue #1: Reporting Lines. Most university career service offices report either to the vice president for student services or to the provost or chief academic officer of the institution. According to the 1991 Career Planning and Placement Survey

(College Placement Council, 1991), the most common structure is for career services to report to the vice president for student services (74.5 percent). The typical alternative to this approach is for career services to report to the provost or chief academic officer if the service is centralized. In cases where career services are decentralized, the most common reporting line is to individual academic deans.

Advantages of reporting to the vice president for student services

- Career services is often one of the larger and stronger student service units and is thus likely to compete successfully with other student service units for resources.

- The vice president for student services is more likely to be sympathetic to the service nature of career services and embrace a ''student development point of view.''

- Most student services vice presidents view career development as a developmental process and are more supportive of the costly counseling and programming functions that are critical to a comprehensive approach to career services.

- Reporting to the same vice president as other student services enhances the probability that quality communications will exist between career services and other related student services (e.g., financial aid, student counseling service). It also enhances the likelihood of appropriate and expeditious referrals between student service agencies.

Advantages of reporting to the provost or academic dean

- The academic side of the university invariably receives top priority when it comes to resources and facilities. Being allied with an academic department can be very helpful in maintaining the career services resource base and is likely to enhance credibility with the faculty.

- When career services is seen as part of an academic unit, it often enhances the quality of the communication and cooperation with faculty and may lead to stronger faculty support for the service.

- In most universities the provost has more political clout than the vice president for student services. As in any business or enterprise, the closer you are to the central power structure, the more control you are likely to have over your destiny.

Issue #2: Centralized Versus Decentralized Services. The debate over whether career services should be centralized or decentralized has raged for years. In most cases career services have evolved based on the historical development and unique character of the particular institution in which they are located. For example, the University of Illinois has a long history and commitment to decentralization. It seems inconceivable that a centralized approach to career services would be successful there. On the other hand, other universities, for example, Penn State, Michigan State, Texas A & M, Georgia Tech, have histories of strong central management and control. Clearly centralized career services are more likely to be successfully implemented in such institutions. Our experience suggests that high-quality career services of both the centralized and decentralized variety exist; however, each has its advantages.

Advantages of centralized career services

- Centralized career services are less confusing to students, faculty, and employers because everything is located in one place and everyone knows where.

- There are significant efficiencies and economies of scale that occur in terms of interview room utilization, career resources, placement library, copy facilities, clerical support, audiovisual services, and others.

- A centralized service is more likely to achieve a critical mass in terms of professional staff size, which allows individual staff to achieve higher levels of specialization and skill to the benefit of all staff and students.

- The administrative overhead will be lower since fewer people will hold the position of director. Some large universities have as many as 15 directors of placement.

- Long-standing relationships with employers who traditionally seek technical students (engineers, scientists, and business majors) can be exploited to create opportunities for nontechnical students.

- Because a centralized career service draws a very heterogeneous and diverse student population, it creates a more vibrant, challenging, and interesting environment for students and staff alike.

Advantages of decentralized career services

- The service is likely to be perceived by students as being more personal, because the career services staff is likely to interact more frequently with students and in a more focused way.

- The facilities are likely to be located much nearer to the students who actually use them, thus enhancing convenience and utilization and reducing the probability that students in need of services will "fall between the cracks."

- Because the facilities are typically located within the college they are serving, it is much easier to secure faculty involvement with the staff of the service and with employers. Decentralization usually enhances faculty-employer relations as well as faculty-career center staff relations, with resultant higher faculty participation in the career development and placement process.

One common compromise to the issue of whether to offer centralized or decentralized career services is to implement some combination of the two whereby certain functions are centralized, (e.g., on-campus interview center or career information center) while others are decentralized (e.g., career counseling and/or programming) (Babbush, Hawley, & Zeran, 1986).

Issue #3: Comprehensive Career Services Versus Specialized Placement Services Alone. Despite the fact that many placement offices have changed their names to career development and placement services or career services, many career service offices are still functioning as narrowly defined placement offices where little programming beyond résumé preparation and interview skill building is done and where nothing vaguely resembling career counseling occurs. When we use the term *comprehensive career services office*, we are talking about an office that offers services including career counseling and assessment to freshmen as well as upperclassmen and alumni. Such an office must have a well-developed career resource center as well as a placement library and offer a comprehensive array of career counseling, programming, and placement services.

Advantages of a comprehensive career service office

- Career counselors get continuous exposure to employers and the placement function. This contact brings a reality base to their counseling that does not often exist when career counseling is provided through a university counseling center.

- A comprehensive service can offer one-stop shopping for all career needs and minimize the tendency for students to fall through the cracks as they are ping-ponged around the university from one office to another.

- Combining career counseling, programming, and placement functions allows the director to draw on corporate contributions (external resources) that flow principally from the placement function in support of the often underfunded counseling and programming functions.

- When career counseling is combined with the placement function, it is more likely to be perceived by students and faculty as an integral part of the educational mission of the institution rather than a remedial one, as is often the case when career counseling is combined with psychological counseling. Hopefully, this will remove the stigma sometimes associated with seeing a counselor and result in a larger number of students seeking and utilizing career counseling services.

Advantages of single-purpose placement services

- A single-function placement office is less likely to be confused in the minds of students, faculty, and staff.

- A career service that offers placement only is easier to staff and manage because of the clarity of its objectives.

- The placement office can utilize all external corporate contributions for the purpose of enhancing placement facilities and services without sharing those resources with counseling and programming staff. Such an arrangement can lead to placement offices with elegant physical facilities.

Issue #4: Relationship to Other Student Service Units. While there are a number of different models, most universities choose to deliver career counseling and assessment through the counseling center rather than through career services. There are certain advantages to this arrangement, which we have enumerated below, but in general we favor the separation of career counseling and assessment from psychological counseling.

Advantages of career counseling and assessment being delivered through the university counseling center together with psychological counseling

- Students get one-stop counseling service. Because career issues are often intertwined with personal issues, an integrated career and personal counseling service has the potential to assure that students get the counseling support they need without being referred.

- Certain economies are likely to exist with respect to clerical support, copy service, reference materials, waiting area, and so on.

- Career counselors and psychological counselors benefit professionally through day-to-day association. They develop a better understanding of the similarities and differences in their counseling techniques and strategies and more appreciation for each other's profession.

Advantages of career counseling being provided through career services rather than the university counseling service

- Career counselors are "first-class citizens" in a career services office while the career counseling done in counseling center settings is often regarded as being of secondary importance to psychological counseling. The perception of "second-class citizenship" is a frequent source of morale problems for career counselors functioning in counseling center settings.

- When career counseling is done in a career center, it is more likely to have a strong "reality base" because of the day-to-day interactions with employers and placement staff. Career counseling done through a counseling center is often very client-centered and may lack this desired reality base.

- External resources that usually flow from the placement function are available to support the career counseling and programming functions.

- When career counseling is provided through career services, it is more likely to be perceived as an integral part of the educational process. When career counseling is combined with personal counseling, students often perceive it as less of an integral part of the educational process, and the association with personal counseling may stigmatize career counseling and frighten students away.

Other student services units that sometimes have a formal relationship with career services are cooperative education and student employment. Both can be, and often are, legitimately incorporated into a comprehensive career service, where they seem to present few problems. In our experience student employment is increasingly seen as a student aid function and as such is most often housed there. On the other hand, cooperative education and similar experiential education programs seem to be a logical extension of the placement function, involving many of the same processes as on-campus interviewing. Similarly, the occupational exploration and personal career growth aspects of experiential programs are an integral component of the career development process. We, therefore, advocate that cooperative education and internship programs be at least partially administered through career services.

Planning Implications: The position of career services within the university structure, including reporting lines, degree of centralization, degree of comprehensiveness, and relationship to other student service units, has significant implications for the planning process. Throughout the remainder of this chapter we assume a centralized, comprehensive career service reporting to the vice president for student services. Offices with different configurations are likely to find our discussions to be useful but somewhat less relevant.

Strategic Factor #5: Institutional Goals and Mission

While much has been made of changing demographics (see short-term factors in a later section of this chapter), the mission of many large universities has remained remarkably constant. For example, land-grant institutions continue to enroll relatively large numbers of first-generation college students, and a disproportionate number of those students enroll in agriculture, business, science, and engineering. Similarly, a very high percentage of undergraduates from Ivy League universities continue to go on to graduate and professional schools, and a high percentage of undergraduates from the AASCU-type (American Association of State Colleges and Universities) institutions go into teaching or business. The point here is that the career service emphasis in a land-grant university must be quite different from that of an Ivy League university or a regional university of the type that would be a member of the AASCU. To a considerable degree, the nature of services being offered in a university career center will be determined by the goals and mission of the university. A viable career services plan must be based in considerable measure on the goals and mission of the institution.

The strategic factors enumerated here will be pivotal in the development of a long-range career center plan. But short-term factors must not be overlooked, and we turn to a discussion of them now.

SHORT-TERM FACTORS

While the long-term strategic plan for career services is determined principally by the strategic factors discussed above, short-term factors also have a significant impact on planning for the day-to-day operation of the career center. In many ways incorporating short-term factors into the planning process is more difficult than incorporating strategic ones. Strategic factors can almost always be agreed upon by the planners, while there may be disagreement about which short-term factors should be incorporated into the planning process. Indeed, identifying short-term factors may be problematic unless the center has well-established formative and summative evaluation systems to enhance understanding of the short-term factors. Examples of factors that are key to short-range planning are the economy, changing student demographics, current staff strengths, institutional politics, and other political and social issues of the day. These factors must be monitored constantly and reacted to in the context of the broader strategic plan to ensure the relevance of the service package being offered.

The Economy

Few student services are as directly affected by the cyclical swings of the economy as the career service office. When the economy is strong, students feel confident about securing employment. They register for placement services in relatively smaller numbers, seek less career assistance and counseling, and generally have lower expectations of the career center. On the other hand, in recessionary times, students register for placement services in larger numbers, place greater demands on career professionals, and often exhibit a rather unforgiving attitude toward career center policies and procedures. In a very real sense, when the economy goes sour, students expect more from the career center at the very time that fewer and fewer organizations are seeking to hire students through the on-campus recruitment program. Such economic downswings cause career centers to alter their programs in accordance with changing needs. For example, more staff time and energy must be put into programs to assist students to "take the job search to the employer," and less reliance is placed on the on-campus recruitment program. Clearly, the economy is an important short-term factor in planning for the career center. Its effects must be closely monitored and program changes implemented accordingly.

Changing Student Demographics

Long before the publication of "Workforce 2000" (Hudson Institute, 1987), career services professionals were aware of the need to monitor closely changing student demographics. While the major thrust of career services remains the same for all students, the increasing diversity of the student body has demanded a more diverse array of outreach programs directed to the special needs of women, minority populations, disabled students, international students, gay and lesbian students, returning adults, and others. Not only is it necessary to develop special programs to serve the unique needs of these populations, but it is also important to provide human relations and sensitivity training to existing staff to assure that programs and services for the broad mass of students are being sensitively delivered. As the student population becomes more and more diverse, long-standing traditional approaches to the delivery of career services must be revised, modified, and, in some cases, abolished. Planning for diversity in the career center is a challenge that must be met.

Staff Strengths and Weaknesses

Inevitably, every career center experiences staff turnover. When turnover occurs, the new staff members are likely to have different strengths and weaknesses from those of their predecessors. Planning for the career center must take this into account. While strategic factors determine the major thrust of career services planning, short-term fluctuations in staff strengths and weaknesses will have an impact on the quality and number of programs that can be reasonably delivered. For example, it would be unfortunate, if not a waste of staff resources, not to offer career planning time management seminars if there is a member of the staff with expertise in that area and a strong commitment to conduct such seminars. On the other hand, such seminars are probably not an absolutely necessary offering for a career center. In cases where there is a perceived need for special programs and the career center staff does not have the necessary expertise to conduct them, referrals might be made to other service units on campus, or services could be purchased on a short-term basis from a consultant outside the career center. At any given time the university career center is likely to experience short-term staff strengths and weaknesses that must be taken into consideration in the planning process.

Current Social and Political Issues of the Day

Program planning must be responsive to current social and political issues that may fluctuate radically over short time spans. Typical was the issue many placement offices faced in the late eighties regarding whether or not to allow corporations doing business in South Africa to recruit on campus. Poor planning regarding this issue led to protests, disruption and, even violence on some university campuses. Similarly, the issue of preemployment drug testing led to significant controversy for a short period of time in the late eighties. Educational seminars and discussions had to be planned to address this short-term issue, which went away almost as suddenly as it appeared. More recently, employer policies regarding discrimination on the basis of sexual orientation have led some university career centers to ban certain organizations from recruiting on campus. In order to be both timely and responsive, social and political issues must be continuously monitored and incorporated into the career services planning process.

Administrative Directives

Sometimes administrators issue directives that must be complied with. Such directives might have either a positive or a negative impact on planning. For example, recently a U.S. congressman in a northeastern state directed through University Central Administration that the career center at the land-grant university conduct a statewide career day. Less than six months' notice was given to the director of the career center. The career fair simply had to be carried out. In the end the career fair was very successful, despite the fact that it was not a part of the annual strategic plan. However, such short-term directives can just as easily end in disaster.

Miscellaneous

In addition to the major factors cited previously, there are other short-term factors: budget fluctuations, staff vacancies, and the like. The important point here is that short-term factors play a significant role in the planning process, and because of their shifting and changing nature, they must be monitored closely.

MONITORING STRATEGIC AND SHORT-TERM FACTORS THROUGH EVALUATION

Formative Evaluation

As we have suggested, many of the strategic factors that become inputs to the planning process are easily identified and agreed upon by those involved in planning. Short-term factors, on the other hand, are more elusive and difficult to identify. Crucial to planning for the career center is the ability to perceive and capture information and data from the day-to-day operations of the center. The formal term for securing this information is evaluation. Two types of evaluation are utilized: formative evaluation, which consists of results used to improve performance, and summative evaluation, which provides a means of estimating the aggregate or total impact of a program, service, or individual or group activity (Kuh & Andreas, 1991) on some predetermined set of criteria.

Formative evaluation techniques vary in terms of their formality, complexity, and convenience, but a wide range of techniques must be employed in support of the planning process. We have here developed a short list of the more common formative evaluation techniques and provided examples of several survey evaluation forms that might be used to capture information and input crucial to planning.

Advisory Boards. Advisory boards are not often thought of as elements of an evaluation strategy, but if they are effective, they will perform that function. Student advisory boards are the most important of such mechanisms, but many career centers also employ faculty and employer advisory boards. The key characteristic of advisory boards is that they are usually made up of consumers (of one sort or another) of the services of the career center. As such, their members interact with, and relate to, their peer consumers frequently and are thus in a position to represent views beyond their own about the quality and appropriateness of career center services. Individual members, because of their dual role as both consumer and advisory board member, usually take a very positive approach to providing feedback to center staff. Their vested interest in ensuring that the center provides the very highest quality career service makes them a key source of feedback for the planning process.

Program Evaluation Forms. Another useful method of securing formative evaluation data is through the continuous and ongoing use of program and presenter evaluation forms. An example of a fairly universal program evaluation form is presented in Figure 3.1. Such a form can be used for nearly any type of center-sponsored program. Our experience has shown that very high percentages of program participants will respond via such forms if the programmer implores them to do so at the beginning and again near the end of the program. We find that between 90 and 95 percent of program participants complete and submit evaluation forms when the programmer presents them as a means of improving both the quality and relevance of future programs. Forms are collected by the presenter and reviewed immediately. Then they are forwarded to the assistant director for programming, who collates the information and provides feedback and suggestions to all presenters

Figure 3.1
Career Services Outreach Program Evaluation Form

```
Program Title:   _____
Date:            _____
Presenter:       _____
```

1. How did you find out about this event?
   _____Flyer   _____Counselor Referral
   _____University Newspaper   _____RA/Academic Advisor Referral
   _____Class Assignment   _____Word of Mouth
   _____Other (please specify)_____

2. What were your reasons for attending or expectations of the
   program? Please list.

		Strongly Agree 1	Agree 2	Disagree 3	Strongly Disagree 4
3.	My expectations of the program based on my concerns and questions were fulfilled.	1	2	3	4
4.	The presenter(s) delivered information in a clear, organized, and interesting manner.	1	2	3	4
5.	I found the program to be helpful for my career planning/job search.	1	2	3	4
6.	I enjoyed the program.	1	2	3	4

7. What I liked best about the program includes:

8. What needs to be improved upon or strengthened:

9. Other topics about which I am interested in learning more include:

DEMOGRAPHIC INFORMATION:
In an attempt to meet the unique needs of various populations, we ask
that you complete the following:

```
STATUS:   ____Freshman    ____Sophomore   ____Junior     ____Senior
____Graduate Student  ____Alumnus   ____Faculty/Staff  ____Non-Student

RESIDENCE:   ____On campus      ____Off campus      ____Greek House

SEX:        ____Female        ____Male

AGE:        ____16 through 24  ____25 and over

ETHNIC STATUS: ____African-American  ____Asian-American  ____Hispanic
               ____Native-American   ____International   ____Caucasian

SPECIAL POPULATIONS:  ____Veteran  ____Returning Adult  ____Disabled
```

at the end of each semester. The purpose of such forms is not to evaluate individual presenters. Rather, they are to be used developmentally to assist presenters to improve the quality of their programming efforts.

Recruiter Checkout Forms. Recruiters represent a crucial source of feedback about the quality and character of various elements of the on-campus recruitment process. Key among these elements are: (1) number of no-shows for interviews, (2) students who might benefit from assistance with interview skills, (3) suggestions /comments pertinent to placement service and accommodations, (4) suggestions pertinent to the relevance of the curriculum in various academic programs, and (5) general comments and suggestions. Feedback from such forms provides useful support for planning change in training programs, the curriculum, and placement policies and procedures, as well as university parking policy. An example of a typical recruiter checkout form is presented in Figure 3.2.

The Suggestion Box. One should never overlook or undervalue this obvious and perhaps simplistic means of securing user feedback. In our experience, some very innovative and useful ideas result from placing a suggestion box in high traffic areas within the career center and providing users with easy to use, eye-catching forms with which to provide their suggestions (see Figure 3.3). We have found that moving the suggestion box from one service area of the center to another from week to week or month to month has a tendency to stimulate user input.

Spot Evaluations. From time to time it is useful to identify a random sample of service users and send them service evaluation forms via direct mail. Such "spot evaluations" can be extremely useful in evaluating the effectiveness of various existing services and in modifying and improving services in accordance with client perceptions and expectations. These one-shot, random evaluations are easy and inexpensive to administer and, if well designed and carried out within two weeks of the date service was rendered, they usually result in a high response rate.

Written and Verbal Complaints. Often complaints about service are regarded as a nuisance, and some of them are; but nearly every complaint contains a kernel of truth that can provide context and insight that will be of value to the planning process. Clients should be encouraged to express their complaints, comments, and suggestions both verbally and in written form, and every such complaint, comment, or suggestion should be acknowledged and taken seriously. Such a policy is not only good for public relations, but just good business.

Evaluation by Walking About. Peters and Waterman (1982) and others have advocated that a key to excellence is getting close to the customer. We know of few better means of formative evaluation than for the director and other staff members to get out on the front line, mingle with the customers (students and employer representatives), and listen to what they are saying. Often the best front line position for feedback is that of the office receptionist or clerk. Few experiences provide greater insight for planning than a short walk in the shoes of the customer or the frontline service purveyor.

Figure 3.2
Recruiter Checkout Form

Please give this form to the receptionist in the Interview Center prior to your departure at 5:00 p.m. We appreciate your interest in our students and look forward to your next visit to campus.

Company/Organization Name _____

Recruiter's Name _____ Date _____
(Please print the requested information or attach your business card to the form.)

I.   Please list any "no shows" below:

STUDENT NAME   MAJOR   SCHEDULED INTERVIEW DATE

II. Please identify any students on your schedule today who could benefit from counseling on their interview skills. We will follow up in an effort to assist them in improving their skills. This information is confidential--neither your name nor that of your organization will be revealed to the students.

STUDENT NAME   MAJOR   COMMENTS ON INTERVIEWING SKILLS

III. What was most impressive about your best interviewees?

IV. Suggestions/comments pertaining to our placement service and accommodations.

V.   Suggestions/comments pertaining to Penn State's academic programs. (We will share these comments with deans/department heads unless you specify otherwise.)

VI. If you have any material for your permanent literature file, leave it with the receptionist in the Interview Center, or visit the placement library in 413 Boucke. It is open from 8:00 a.m. to 5:00 p.m. Also, if you want copies of the transcripts for students whom you have interviewed, please submit your completed form to the receptionist before your departure.

                    THANKS FOR YOUR ASSISTANCE.

Summative Evaluation

While the emphasis in formative evaluation is on improving performance of the individual elements of career services, summative evaluation focuses on estimating the impact of career services. How many students got jobs as a result of participation in on-campus interviews? Were students who participated in the mock interview program more successful in securing employment offers than students who did not? What behavioral change resulted from (1) the use of DISCOVER or SIGI Plus? and (2) participation in individual career counseling?

Figure 3.3
Suggestion Form

WE'D LIKE TO DO A BETTER JOB!
Please give us your comments and suggestions.

Date _____ Semester _____ College _____

Which of the following CDPS service(s) did you use?

☐ Intake counseling   ☐ Education career services
☐ Individual counseling   ☐ Alumni career services
☐ Group counseling   ☐ Career information center
☐ On-campus recruiting/scheduling☐ DISCOVER
☐ Placement library   ☐ Other (specify)

Please comment on these or any additional career
services/information/materials you believe should
be developed to assist Penn State students:

Which services were most helpful and why?

Which services were least helpful and why?

What has been the impact of our advertising program? Are more minority students utilizing our services as a result of our minority outreach programs?

Answers to these and countless other similar questions are fundamental to planning university career services. Summative evaluation is primarily about accountability. Are career services doing what career service administrators (planners) say they are doing and for whom?

Some elements of a summative evaluation process essential for university career center planning are:

1. Some form of registration system for placement services that captures the information shown on the registration card presented in Figure 3.4

2. A computerized system designed to capture and describe comprehensive on-campus interviewing activity that can be used for report generation, including annual reports. Year-to-year comparisons of such data are particularly useful.

3. An intake form to be completed by counselors on each client that inventories key client demographics, presenting problems, recommended services, services provided, and referrals made. Such a form should be machine-readable so that weekly, monthly, and yearly summaries can be generated quickly.

4. A follow-up postgraduation activities survey of all graduates at all degree levels by direct mail after each graduation. A machine-readable survey form like that shown in Figure 3.5 will greatly enhance the speed and accuracy of the tabulating process.

5. Periodically, in-depth random surveys of client satisfaction with counseling, placement, programming, and other career services. The results of such surveys are a crucial input to the planning process.

Summative evaluation not only provides the essential statistical data to generate annual reports and to justify career services to central administration but is fundaental input information to the planning process.

SHAPING STRATEGIC AND SHORT-TERM FACTORS INTO A PLAN: THE IMPORTANCE OF THE PLANNER(S) AND THE PROCESS

The strategic and short-term factors discussed above provide the "warp and woof" of planning for the career center. These are the essential raw materials that one must have to weave a successful career center plan. But successful planning requires more than raw materials. Central to the success of any plan are two additional ingredients that are in many ways even more crucial than the raw materials: the planner(s) and the planning process.

The Planner(s)

Planning for the career center must be done carefully. It must be done strategically. It must be done with vision and dynamism. But by whom? The short answer is "Everyone." The director certainly must be involved; but so, too, must the associate director(s), the assistant director(s), the career counselors, the office manager, the recruitment scheduler, the clerical staff, various advisory board members, and, perhaps, even the physical plant and custodial personnel. To paraphrase John Kennedy, every success has many parents, and every failure is an orphan. If the career center plan is to avoid being orphaned, it, too, must have

Figure 3.4
On-Campus Recruiting System: Candidate Registration Card

SOCIAL SECURITY NUMBER _____

NAME _____ _____ _____
        (Last)   (First)   (MI)   (Mr. or Ms.)

LOCAL ADDRESS _____ _____ _____ _____
                    (Street)   (City)   (State)   (Zip Code)

LOCAL PHONE _____   GRADUATION DATE _____
              (Area Code & Number)   (Month & Year)

ACADEMIC COLLEGE _____   ACADEMIC MAJOR _____

MAJOR GPA _____   CUMULATIVE GPA _____

CHECK DEGREE TO BE RECEIVED:
ASSOCIATE _____ BACHELOR _____ MASTER'S _____ DOCTORATE _____

TYPE OF PLACEMENT SOUGHT:
PERMANENT _____ SUMMER _____ INTERNSHIP/CO-OP _____

I HEREBY AUTHORIZE CAREER DEVELOPMENT AND PLACEMENT SERVICES TO RELEASE THE INTERVIEW REQUEST FORM, WHICH I HAVE REVIEWED, TO PROSPECTIVE EMPLOYERS.

_____   _____
      (Signature)   (Date)

CONTINUED ON REVERSE SIDE

Figure 3.5
The Pennsylvania State University Graduate Follow-up Survey

Use a #2 pencil only to complete this form. Fill in the appropriate coding areas completely.

SOCIAL SECURITY NUMBER

NAME _____
Last   First   Middle/Former

CURRENT ADDRESS _____
Street   City   State   Zip

TELEPHONE (_____) _____
Area Code

Fill in here if above address is different from
that shown on this survey envelope → ⊃

⊃ MALE   ⊃ FEMALE

I. Education

1. Fill in the highest degree you received at Penn State:
   - Associate
   - Bachelor
   - Master
   - Doctoral
   - Professional (e.g., M.D.)

2. Fill in college from which you received degree:
   - Agriculture
   - Arts & Arch.
   - Bus. Administration
   - Communications
   - Earth & Min. Sc.
   - Education
   - Engineering
   - Health & Human Dev.
   - Liberal Arts
   - Medicine
   - Science

3. Academic Major _____

4. Fill in semester and year you received highest degree.
   - Summer
   - Fall
   - Spring
   - 1986
   - 1987
   - 1988
   - 1989
   - 1990
   - 1991
   - 1992

II. Post Graduation Plans

Fill in the most appropriate response:
- Upon graduation, I sought employment related to my career objective.
- Upon graduation, I sought interim employment with the idea of pursuing additional education to prepare me for employment related to my career objective.
- I did not seek employment upon graduation.

III. Employment Status

Where there is a choice of responses, please fill in the most appropriate one.

If employed: To what degree does your employment match your post-graduation career objective? Fill in one item and go to Part IV.

- A. Very much. My job closely relates to my career objective.
- B. Somewhat. I am employed, by choice, in a position somewhat related to my career objective.
- C. Very little. I took this job because I was unsuccessful in finding a position that was related to my career objective.
- D. None. I am employed but I did not have a career objective.
- E. Career objective delayed. I took an interim job. After completing further education, I will seek a position related to my career objective.

If unemployed: Fill in one item and go to Part VII.

- F. I am unemployed but actively seeking employment.
- G. I am presently unemployed; however, I intend to pursue further education and then seek employment.
- H. I am unemployed and not seeking employment at this time.

If pursuing further education full time: Fill in one item and go to Part VI.

- I. I wish to strengthen the skills/specialty that I was exposed to in my undergraduate program.
- J. I wish to develop new skills or a specialty unrelated to my undergraduate program.

many parents. Involvement in the process of planning is far more crucial than the resulting plan itself. If the career center plan is going to be implemented successfully, it will be implemented by those who were involved and invested in the process of producing it. Fundamental to successful career center planning is the notion that planning is a process and that it is inclusive and participative.

Involvement and participation do not mean getting together once a year at an annual planning retreat. Involvement begins with regular and well-conceived professional and clerical staff meetings held at least biweekly. Involvement presupposes the effective functioning of numerous staff committees and task forces where working relationships are established and communication proceeds not only from the top down, but from the bottom up and laterally. In short, the involvement we advocate is similar to that advocated by many of the "total quality management" gurus (Deming, 1982; Crosby, 1984; Imai, 1986; Juran, 1988). The trust that is forged through the conduct of regular, participative staff and committee meetings will go a long way toward ensuring that the planning process is an inclusive one, because these regular staff interactions are at the core of the planning process.

The Process

In George Keller's (1983) classic book on strategic planning for institutions of higher education, he begins the definition of planning by explaining what strategic planning is not. We have paraphrased liberally from his explanation of what planning is not and shaped our list specifically to the planning process of the university career center:

1. *Planning is not the production of a blueprint.* The idea is not to produce a fat, detailed document that everyone should follow but rather to get all the key people (clerical as well as professional) thinking innovatively and acting strategically, with the future in mind.

2. *Planning is not a set of platitudes.* Often an office's goals are given as "meeting the career development needs of our clients" or "achieving the highest possible placement rate." This is like saying, "We believe in apple pie and the American Way." A useful plan must be formulated succinctly and stated operationally. It is specific, not vague and vapid.

3. *Planning is not the personal vision of the director.* A strategy will be based on an analysis of the strategic and short-term factors outlined above as well as the office's traditions and political realities of the institution. It will of necessity include a measure of the director's own vision, but never to the exclusion of the consideration of other realities.

4. *Planning is not a collection of individual operating unit plans, compiled and edited.* A strategy or plan for a comprehensive career center will always be more than the sum of the strategies of the individual units. One cannot simply take the placement plan, the career counseling plan, the employer development plan, and the career programming plan, draw a line under them, and add them up. Individual unit plans are not additive; rather, they must be integrated and mutually supportive.

5. *Planning is not done by professional planners.* As should be evident from the previous section, the role, if any, of professional planners is as consultant to the planning process. Planning itself is done by everyone on the staff of the career center all of the time.

6. *Planning is not something done on an annual retreat.* It is ongoing, continuous, not an activity done separately, away from students, employers, budgets, interview rooms, and the day-to-day operation of the career center. Special sessions are necessary during the formulation stage and when special threats arise, but planning itself is integral, not occasional.

7. *Planning is not a way of eliminating risks.* If anything, planning increases risk taking. It fosters an entrepreneurial spirit, a readiness to start new ventures. It encourages boldness about opportunities and aggressiveness in the face of threats. In so doing, it often causes disruption.

8. *Planning is not a totally rational process.* Although it would be nice to believe that the process of planning operates on a linear, rational decision-making model, reality suggests that superb plans have been known to evolve from a process that is often not linear and is sometimes downright irrational. Both planning and management are increasingly looked upon as an art rather than a science (Vaill, 1989).

If planning is none of these things, then what is it? There is no neat, single answer to this question, and certainly no one answer that would be correct for every university career center. However, there are several features of successful planning that can be identified:

1. Strategic planning means that a university career center and its staff are active, rather than passive, in the process of planning.

2. Planning looks outward and is focused on keeping the career center in step with the changing environment.

3. Planning concentrates on decisions, not on documented plans, analyses, forecasts, and goals.

4. Planning is a blend of rational and economic analysis, political maneuvering, and psychological interplay. It is therefore participatory and highly tolerant of controversy.

5. Planning cannot be artificially separated or isolated from management (the subject of the next chapter).

6. Successful planning presupposes that the staff members of the career center are committed to constant and perpetual improvement; that they understand there has never been a service, product, or professional that cannot be improved upon; and that, in effect, "you don't have to be sick to get better."

Producing a Plan That Can Be Implemented: A Recipe for Career Center Planning

To this point we hope we have communicated our conviction that planning is a critical and highly complex process; that it involves the identification of strategic as well as short-term factors; and that it is a continuous and ongoing process that requires the active participation of the entire professional and clerical staff of the center. What we have not done is provide a step-by-step recipe for planning. We have some reluctance in doing this because we believe that each center must develop its own unique strategy for planning within the broad guidelines we have suggested. Nevertheless, we realize that a step-by-step example of the annual planning cycle for a university career center might have some heuristic value. It is with this in mind that we offer the following "planning recipe," a 13-step recipe for planning.

In Preparation for Planning

Step 1. Staff must be trained to understand the planning process and be committed to the fact that their involvement is crucial to the success of the process. This training is done on an ongoing basis, although real understanding is best achieved through having experienced one complete planning cycle.

Step 2. A core group of staff (normally the director and associate directors—a group small enough to function efficiently) must produce a broad-based set of center goals based on their understanding of the strategic and short-term factors affecting the career center, and this broad plan must be distributed to the entire staff. An example of such goals is presented in Figure 3.6

Year-Round Planning Processes

Step 3. Formative and summative evaluation techniques must be employed throughout the year to accumulate data, facts, impressions, ideas, and so on that can be integrated into the planning process and the ultimate plan. Specific examples of these techniques have been offered in a previous section of this chapter.

Step 4. Subcommittees of the career services staff will take responsibility for addressing certain issues in depth, reporting on these issues throughout the year, and making specific recommendations for incorporation into the planning process. Examples of typical subcommittees might be:

Professional Development Committee

Office Information Systems Committee

Facilities and Equipment Committee

Publications Committee

Research Committee

Career Information Center Committee

External Funding and Grant-Writing Committee

Alumni Services Committee

In addition, task forces might be formed to address short-term, nonrecurring issues and make recommendations.

Step 5. Staff involvement must be solicited and maintained throughout the year at regular staff meetings, with particular emphasis on how the goals and plans to achieve those goals will change from the previous year.

Tasks for the Month of April

Step 6. A special "issues session" involving the entire staff should be held two weeks prior to the all-day planning retreat to get everyone's juices flowing. The emphasis in the issues session should be on anticipated problems and changes for the coming planning cycle.

Figure 3.6
Goals of University Career Services

---

1. To assist students, alumni, and employees in crystallizing and specifying career goals.
    a. Assist students, alumni, and employees to identify self-characteristics (values, attitudes, interests, and abilities).
    b. Assist students, alumni, and employees to expand their knowledge of career alternatives.
    c. Assist students, alumni, and employees to understand an effective decision-making process and acquire appropriate strategies and skills to carry out the process.

2. To assist students, alumni, and employees in implementing career goals.
    a. Assist students, alumni, and employees to acquire appropriate strategies and skills to implement chosen career goals (employment/education, other).
    b. Assist students, alumni, and employees in contacting potential employment/educational sources to implement career goals.

3. To assist other professionals and paraprofessionals in developing knowledge and skill in the delivery of career services.
    a. Promote a systematic exchange of information with Career Services personnel at the Commonwealth Campuses and other University locations.
    b. Develop a cooperative relationship with those academic departments preparing professionals or paraprofessionals in areas related to career development.
    c. Promote the systematic exchange of information with other professionals in the area of career development.

4. To develop a cooperative relationship with other University staff/faculty to gain their active support in the delivery of career services.
    a. Inform other student service offices, student programs and service offices, and academic units of the functions and services provided by Career Services.
    b. Develop a referral mechanism with other student services offices, student programs and services, and academic units.
    c. Promote the delivery of career services with other student service offices, student programs and services, and academic units.
    d. Establish and develop liaison with all colleges and certain departments.

5. To research career development and placement issues and provide systematic feedback to the University community and the business community concerning career issues.
    a. Provide information on labor market developments from a national and state perspective and the implications for the University community.

Figure 3.6 (continued)

      b.   Provide information on the career development patterns of college students and alumni with recommendations for appropriate institutional programming.

      c.   Conduct evaluations concerning the effectiveness of a wide range of career development and placement services.

6.   To enhance the professional growth of Career Services staff.
      a.   Maintain and upgrade professional competence.
      b.   Assist staff to expand their knowledge of career development.
      c.   Encourage staff members to promote a mutually supportive atmosphere for individual professional development.
      d.   Prepare and submit articles for professional publication.
      e.   Encourage networking within the profession.
      f.   Maintain an on-going commitment to human relations training.

7.   To cultivate positive relationships with potential employers to insure the efficient flow of information and graduates.
      a.   Address issues of ethnic/racial bias, sexual orientation, sex bias, age bias, and handicapped student bias as they impact our student clientele.
      b.   Monitor the issues of Affirmative Action/EEO in our daily activity as it relates to employers and students.
      c.   Make corporate plant information exchange visits.

Tasks for Early May

Step 7. An all-day planning retreat will be held involving the entire staff, at which the following tasks will be accomplished:

1. Broad goals and objectives are reviewed, revised, and approved (those presented in step 2 above). While these goals are not likely to change much from year to year, it is important for the entire staff to have the opportunity to review and modify them annually.
2. Detailed, supportive subgoals and objectives will be reviewed and updated with an emphasis on current issues. In the example provided in Figure 3.7, the subgoals of Goal #1 from the broad goals listed above are enumerated. In a real planning session this same task would be done for all of the broad goals.
3. The detailed subgoals and objectives will be agreed upon, and individual staff names will be assigned to accomplish those goals wherever possible. Fictitious names have been inserted in Figure 3.7.
4. Committee and task force membership will be established.

Tasks for Mid-May

Step 8. All staff will be given the opportunity to review the product of the planning retreat (a document of no more than 15 pages) and provide additional input and feedback.

Tasks for Late May

Step 9. The director will integrate staff feedback and additional input and publish the final plan, which will be distributed to the entire staff.

Tasks for Early June

Step 10. Individual staff members, in conjunction with their supervisors, will produce individual yearly goals and objectives, which must be supportive of the overall center plan. Individual goals and objectives will include the following three sections: routine objectives, innovative

Figure 3.7
Detailed Subgoals and Staff Assignments

> GOAL 1
> To assist students, alumni, and employees in crystallizing and specifying career goals.

Item 1
SUMMER/FALL: Update, maintain, and increase publications, handouts, and other resource materials for use in the Unit. Consider all client users, i.e., nontechnical majors, education majors, and nontraditional students. (Interns, volunteers, work-study will assist staff.)
    [Sue, David, Denise, Eva, Mary, and Paul]

SPRING: same

Item 2
SUMMER/FALL: Update, standardize, and increase publications, handouts, and other materials for use in the Career Information Center. Consider all client users, i.e., nontechnical majors, education majors, and nontraditional majors students. (Interns, work-study will assist staff).
    [Dana, Denise, Gail, Mary, Paul, and Tina]

SPRING: same

Item 3
FALL: Develop a rotating schedule of professional staffing for the library. One staff member will spend approximately 1/2 day per week providing direct assistance to students using the Unit for the first two weeks of the semester.
    [Ronald and John will assign]

SPRING: same

Item 4
FALL: Staff members will serve on a rotating schedule as intake counselor for 1/2 day each week. (Sue, David, Denise, Eva, Gail, Mary, Mona, Paul, and Tina -- Backup: James, John, Ronald, and Graduate Students).
    [John and Ronald will assign]

SPRING: same

Item 5
FALL: Continue to offer the Minority Internship Program to under-graduate members of ethnic groups. Attempt to facilitate 10 intern placements.
    [Sue and Graduate Students]

SPRING: same

SUMMER: Attempt to facilitate 5 placements.

Figure 3.7 (continued)

Item 6
FALL: Offer the EXTERN Program to students in (nontechnical colleges)
the colleges of Liberal Arts, Arts and Architecture, Health and Human
Development, and the School of Communications for Winter break.
     [Sue and Graduate Students]

SPRING: same

Item 7
FALL: Staff to see a minimum of 150 appointments (students,
University employees, and alumni) per week for individual counseling.
     [All]

SPRING: same

Item 8
FALL: Advertise Career Services programs and services through the
university newspaper. Prepare one promotional insert.
     [Bonnie and Denise]

SPRING: same

Item 9
FALL: Offer a minimum of 6 career counseling groups, some geared to
specific populations, i.e., African-Americans, Latino/Hispanic
students, women, international students, returning adult students, gay
and lesbian students and deciding students.
     [John and Counseling Staff]

SPRING: same

Item 10
SUMMER/FALL: Continue outreach efforts to underclass students.
(A) Meet with selected Residential Life staff in their complexes and
train and offer programs to hall assistants when appropriate. Offer
programs for selected residential life housing areas for the purpose
of orienting underclass students to our services. Maintain
audiovisual materials and outreach programming files.
     [Counseling Staff]

(B) Offer Career Exploration Trips to New York City and Washington,
D.C., for students in Liberal Arts, Art and Architecture, Health and
Human Development, and the School of Communications, subject to
funding from the colleges.
     [Sue]

SPRING: same

(C) Invite representatives (including counselors; advisors) from The
Division of Undergraduate Studies, Counseling and Psychological
Services, The Center for Women Students, The Returning Adult Center,
Academic Assistance Programs, The Veterans' Administration, Core
Advising Units, The Office of Disability Services, The Office of
International Education, The Freshman TestingCounseling and Advising
Program, etc., to counseling staff and general staff meetings to
discuss undecided student issues and cooperative programming.

Figure 3.7 (continued)

[Designated Liaisons]

SPRING: Offer in-service training workshops for Student Services agencies for undecided students with The Division of Undergraduate Studies, College Advising Centers, Counseling and Psychological Services, The Center for Women Students, The Returning Adult Student Center, and the Academic Assistance Program.
[Designated Liaisons]

Item 11
SUMMER/FALL: Continue special programs for students in nontechnical colleges and negotiate new programs as time and resources permit.
[Sue]

SPRING: same

Item 12
SUMMER/FALL: Maintain computerized guidance system. Continue with DISCOVER and SIGI PLUS. Continue to evaluate outcome of systems.
[Dana, Denise, and Eva]

SPRING: same

Item 13
SUMMER/FALL: Identify special populations using our services, then promote usage of services.
[All]

SPRING: same

Item 14
FALL: Offer two sections of Liberal Arts 100 (Personal and Career Decision Making).
[John, Counseling Staff, Graduate Assistants]
(A) Select and train new instructors for Liberal Arts 100.
(B) Employ graduate assistants to support Liberal Arts 100 instruction.
(C) Continue research regarding the effects of Liberal Arts 100 on student career planning progress.
(D) Continue to revise Liberal Arts 100 course content. [John]
(E) Pursue making Liberal Ars 100 a 3-credit course with application toward General Education Requirements.

SPRING: If enrollment warrants, add a 3rd section of Liberal Arts 100.

Item 15
FALL: Maintain a career planning assessment file for use in career counseling.
[John]

Item 16
SUMMER: Assist The Division of Undergraduate Studies with the Freshman Testing, Counseling and Advising Program for out-of-state parents.
[John and selected staff]

Figure 3.7 (continued)

```
Item 17-
SUMMER/FALL:    Establish   an   Audio/Visual   equipment   coordinator.
Explore possible initiatives in producing audiovisual programs using
new technologies.
    [Ken]

Item 18
SUMMER/FALL:  Maintain bulletin board outside intake counseling office
and maintain career issues bulletin board.
    [Gail and Lorna]

Item 19
SUMMER/FALL:   Complete manual on counseling procedures.
    [Denise]

Item 20
SUMMER/FALL:  Continue with the experimental model of providing career
services to University employees.  Monitor this activity and modify
our involvement as conditions dictate.
    [John]

Item 21
SUMMER/FALL:   Establish and maintain the Center  for  the Review of
Career Information.
    [Paul and Staff]

SPRING:   same

Item 22
SUMMER/FALL:  Investigate the feasibility of a security system for the
Career Information Center.
    [Paul]

SPRING:  If  resources  are  available,  implement Career  Information
Center security system.
    [Paul]
```

objectives. Figures 3.8 and 3.9 present examples of individual goals for two staff members: an associate director and a counselor, respectively.

Tasks for Mid-June

Step 11. Individual staff plans will be placed on file with supervisors and the director and used throughout the year to monitor staff member performance.

Tasks for October

Step 12. Individual staff performance will be evaluated against the individually approved plan, and "mid-course corrections" will be negotiated between supervisors and staff.

Tasks for February

Step 13. Individual staff performance will be evaluated against the individually approved plan, and formal performance appraisals will be conducted.

The Cycle Repeats Itself

Because of the order in which events have been presented, the formal performance appraisal appears to be the final event in the planning cycle. The reality is that the planning cycle is a continuous process with no real beginning or end. The major events in the process (annual goal-setting session, establishment of individual staff goals and objectives, performance appraisal, and so on) do come in sequential order, but they may be moved forward

Figure 3.8
Associate Director Goals and Objectives

<u>ROUTINE</u>
A. Employer Relations and Placement Services
    1. Direct and manage all Placement Services including On-Campus Recruiting Service, Alumni Career Services, Education Career Services, the Interview Center, and the Placement Library;
    2. Supervise and evaluate assigned professional (2) and clerical staff (6);
    3. Serve as backup intake counselor for each semester (Summer/Fall/Spring);
    4. Coordinate staff assignments for Interview Request Form (IRF) Workshop presentations; conduct IRF workshops during the first weeks of each semester as part of a predetermined schedule (Fall/Spring);
    5. Schedule staff for "recruiter duty" and serve as backup for coverage on an emergency basis (Fall/Spring);
    6. Participate in professional staffing of the placement library during the first weeks of each semester (Fall/Spring);
    7. Serve as Career Center liaison contact with the College of Earth and Mineral Sciences (Summer/Fall/Spring);
    8. Serve as Career Center liaison to the Admissions Office (Summer/Fall/Spring); participate in Spend a Summer Day Program, hosting guidance counselors, etc.;
    9. Present workshops as part of the Career Seminar Series (Fall/Spring);
    10. Participate in outreach programming efforts (Fall/Spring);
    11. Schedule staff, obtain space, revise format of presentation, and coordinate the delivery of the orientation programs to on-campus recruiting (Summer);
    12. Coordinate the revision of the <u>Placement Manual</u> (Spring/Summer);
    13. Assist with the establishment of the annual Career Center goals and objectives (Spring/Summer);
    14. Continue to develop and maintain effective employer/Career Center relations; meet with employers to discuss recruitment procedures and strategies; respond to employer inquiries for assistance; attend employer-sponsored symposiums, visits, workshops (Summer/Fall/Spring);
    15. Manage the on-campus recruiting system (Summer/Fall/Spring);
    16. Prepare advertisements and appropriate articles for inclusion as part of the Career Center newspaper (Summer/Fall);
    17. Participate in Division of Undergraduate Studies-Freshman Testing Counseling Advising Program for parents of out-of-state students (Summer);
    18. Assist with work-study training sessions (Fall/Spring);
    19. Review and revise, as appropriate, forms used as part of on-campus recruiting system (Summer);
    20. Prepare and distribute report to deans and department heads, as appropriate, regarding employer perceptions of academic program offerings (Fall/Spring);
    21. Assist with the recruitment and selection of clerical staff for the recruitment scheduling office and other Career Center units as appropriate (Summer/Fall/Spring);
    22. Coordinate video interviewing activity (Fall/Spring);
    23. Assist with implementation of computerized master scheduling system in support of on-campus recruiting (Summer/Fall/Spring);
    24. Assist with development of rotation schedules for intake and semester start-up activities (Summer/Fall/Spring);
    25. Assist with preparation of Career Center Annual Report.

Figure 3.8 (continued)

B. Western Region Liaison Activities
1. Serve on the committee to develop program content for the system-wide conference of career counseling and placement personnel serving at the satellite campuses; assist with management of the conference (Spring);
2. If funds are available, visit one-half of the campuses in the Western Region each semester to review the delivery of Career Center programs and services;
3. Upon invitation, develop and deliver presentations to members of professional guidance and counseling organizations;
4. Assist campus locations in the Western Region with the evaluation and selection of professional personnel responsible for Career Center programs and services; establish interview schedule(s) and transmit results to appropriate campus location (Summer/Fall/Spring);
5. Continue in-service development programs for new personnel (Summer/Fall/Spring).

C. Other
1. Coordinate project providing access by students to on-campus recruiting system (Fall/Spring);
2. Serve as an appointee to the University Appeals Board (Summer/Fall/Spring);
3. Serve as a member of the Student Organization Appeals Board;
4. Serve as a member of the following Career Center committees/task forces:
   a. Counseling Conference
   b. Career Interview Program (CIP)
   c. Minority Career Awareness Day
   d. Electronic Resumes/Computer Programs
   e. Swipe Card Registration
   f. Research Committee
   g. Career Day
5. Continue liaison relationship with the University newspaper (with Denise);
6. Continue to provide corporate recruitment data to the staff of the Development Office (Summer/Fall/Spring);
7. Serve as liaison to the Office of Corporate Relations.

INNOVATIVE

A. Complete logistical arrangements for staff to conduct an informational visit to the GE Aerospace Center in Valley Forge, PA (Summer);
B. Assist with the development of a meeting of the various Career Day Coordinators to exchange ideas, issues, and concerns (Fall/Spring);
C. Explore the feasibility of expanding the video interviewing service (Summer/Fall);
D. Implement and monitor new procedures for Interview Request Form submission and alternate signup procedures (Fall/Spring).

PROFESSIONAL DEVELOPMENT

A. Attend a regional conference;
B. Attend the national meeting of the College Placement Council;
C. Review a minimum of two professional publications on an ongoing basis.
D. Maintain membership in the following professional organizations:
1. Middle Atlantic Placement Association
2. American Association for Higher Education

Figure 3.9
Counselor Goals and Objectives

Counselor
Goals and Objectives

Routine Objectives
-Meet with students individually to discuss career-related issues
and concerns (between 14-16 appointments per week) (Fall,
Spring)
-Present at least 8 outreach programs per semester (Fall, Spring)
-Serve on rotating schedule for intake counseling (Fall, Spring)
-Assist in the Fall and Spring Seminar Series (Fall, Spring)
-Assist in providing Interview Request Form Preparation Workshops
(Fall, Spring)
-Serve in the rotating schedule for recruiter duty (Fall, Spring)
-Serve in the rotating schedule for library staffing during the
first two weeks of each semester (Fall, Spring)

Innovative Objectives
-Serve as coordinator of computerized guidance systems (DISCOVER,
SIGI PLUS) (Fall, Spring):
-Upon request, conduct programming sessions for selected
administrators, faculty, and staff on computerized guidance
systems
-Work with other staff on conducting research on SIGI PLUS
and DISCOVER
-Continue process of obtaining evaluations, and record and
publish evaluation data for computerized guidance systems
-Serve as coordinator of Mock Interview Programs; train and
supervise up to 14 undergraduate interns each semester (Fall,
Spring)
-Serve as co-chair of the Career Center Spring Counseling
Conference Committee (Fall, Spring)
-Coordinate and edit the insert for the University newspaper
(Summer, Fall)
-Serve as liaison to North and East residence halls (Fall,
Spring)
-Serve as chair of the Professional Library Committee (Fall,
Spring)
-Serve as member of the Career Information Center Committee
(Fall, Spring)
-Serve as member of the Publications Committee (Fall, Spring)
-Review publications for the Center for the Review of Career
Information (Fall, Spring)
-Serve as member of the Office Furniture Task Force (Fall,
Spring)
-Serve as member of the Computer Software/Hardware Task Force
(Fall, Spring)
-Review videotapes on the career implementation process (Fall,
Spring)
-Assist in conducting regional Alumni Career Planning and Job
Search Workshops (Fall, Spring)
-If necessary, serve as discussion group leader in LA100 (Fall,
Spring)
-Assist Director and Associate Directors with editing and writing
miscellaneous reports and articles (Fall, Spring)
-Assist in the installation and implementation of Counseling
Psychologists Press assessment software, i.e., SII, MBTI, CPI
(Fall, Spring)
-Complete Counseling Procedures Manual (Summer, Fall)
-Visit selected commonwealth campuses when feasible to observe
general counseling service and to see how computerized guidance
systems are used with counseling (Fall, Spring)

Professional Development
-If feasible, attend at least one professional conference/
workshop related to counseling/career planning issues
-Maintain memberships in the following professional
organizations:
MAPA
AACD/ACPA
-Remain current on counseling and career issues by reviewing
professional publications

SUMMARY

We believe that a planning cycle like the 13-step one presented here incorporates most of the critical planning features we have tried to stress in this chapter: that planning is a year-round process; that it is participative; that individual staff member plans must support the overall center plan but that the center plan is more than the sum of individual staff member plans; that both formative and summative evaluation techniques must be used to secure and incorporate as much information as possible into the process; and that only through planning can university career services evolve to meet the ever-changing career development and placement needs of the university community.

Finally, we believe that such a planning process will lead to the establishment of an array of services, whose elements are presented in Figure 3.10 in outline form. These are the basic services that have evolved in most modern, comprehensive career centers, and these services are described and commented upon in subsequent chapters of this book.

Figure 3.10
Comprehensive Career Center Services—An Outline

Placement services

      Placement advising

      On-campus recruiting

      Job listing services

      Educational and graduate/professional school credential
            service

      Resume referral services

      Training and skill development seminars and workshops

            Interview skills

            Job search strategies

            Resume preparation

            Summer job search workshops

            Internship search workshops

            Other topics

      Career days and job fairs

      Placement library

      Alumni job search workshops

Career planning and counseling services

      Courses for credit

      Career planning workshops and seminars

      Intake counseling (counseling available on a drop-in basis)

      Individual career counseling

      Group career counseling

      Computer assisted career counseling

      Assessment

      Alumni life-career planning workshops

Figure 3.10 (continued)

<u>Career programming services</u>

    Maintenance of an array of resources in support of

        programming

    Evaluation and support of programs

    Clearing house function for requests and assignment of

        staff

    Outreach programs

    Special topics workshop and seminar series

    Experiential education program coordination

        Cooperative education

        Internship programs

        Externship programs

<u>Information support systems</u>

    Placement library

    Career information center

    Student advisory board

    Suggestion box

    Follow-up surveys

    Office handouts

    Salary survey

    Employer advisory board

<u>Communications</u>

    Career trends, career success

    Topical office handouts

    Placement manual

    Electronic message board

Figure 3.10 (continued)

      Office brochures

      Career planning news (office newspaper)

      Annual report

      Electronic bulletin board (via modem to students)

      College newspaper to students

          Advertisements

          News releases

      Radio spots

      Television spots

Training functions

      Work study

      Volunteers

      Undergraduate interns

      Graduate interns

      Practicum students

      Graduate assistants

      Sponsored research

Research function

      Annual post graduation follow-up studies

      Periodic evaluations of individual services

          Counseling

          Placement

          Programming

          Efficacy studies of career interventions

REFERENCES

Astin, A. W. (1977). *Four critical years*. San Francisco: Jossey-Bass.

Babbush, H. E., Hawley, Wade W., & Zeran, Jack. (1986). The best of both worlds. *Journal of Career Planning and Employment, XLVII*, 48–53.

Campbell, D. P. (1974). *If you don't know where you're going, you'll probably end up somewhere else*. Niles, IL: Argus Communications.

College Placement Council. (1991). *1991 Career Planning and Placement Survey*. Bethlehem, PA: Author.

Council for the Advancement of Standards. (1986). *CAS standards and guidelines for student services/development programs*. Iowa City, IA: American College Testing Program.

Council for the Advancement of Standards. (1988). *CAS standards and guidelines for career planning and placement*. Iowa City, IA: American College Testing Program.

Crosby, P. (1984). *Quality without tears: The art of hassle-free management*. New York: McGraw-Hill.

Deming, W. E. (1982). *Out of the crisis*. Cambridge, MA: Productivity Press.

Herr, E. L., & Cramer, S. H. (1988). *Career guidance and counseling through the life span*. Glenview, IL: Scott, Foresman.

Hudson Institute. (1987). *Workforce 2000—Work and workers for the 21st century*. Indianapolis, IN: Author.

Imai, M. (1986). *The key to Japan's competitive success*. Cambridge, MA: Productivity Press.

Juran, J. M. (1988). *Juran on planning for quality*. Cambridge, MA: Productivity Press.

Keller, G. (1983). *Academic strategy: The management revolution in American higher education*. Baltimore: Johns Hopkins University Press.

Kuh, G. D., & Andreas, R. E. (1991). It's about time: Using qualitative methods in student life studies. *Journal of College Student Development, 32*, 397–405.

Peters, T. J., & Waterman, R. H. (1982). *In search of excellence*. New York: Warner Books.

Shingleton, J. D., & Fitzpatrick, E. B. (1985). *Dynamics of placement*. Bethlehem, PA: College Placement Council.

Super, D. E. (1957). *The psychology of careers*. New York: Harper & Row.

Vaill, P. B. (1989). *Managing as a performing art: New ideas for a world of chaotic change*. San Francisco: Jossey-Bass.

Appendix 3.1
CAS Career Planning and Placement Standards

Part 1: Mission

The institution and its career planning and placement services must develop, review, and disseminate regularly their own specific goals for student services/development, which must be consistent with the nature and goals of the institution and with the standards in this document.

Career planning is a developmental process and must be fostered during the entire period of a student's involvement with the institution.

The primary purpose of career planning and placement must be to aid students in developing, evaluating, and effectively initiating and implementing career plans.

Part 2: Program

The overall career planning and placement services program must be (1) purposeful, (2) coherent, (3) based on or related to theories and knowledge of human development and learning characteristics, and (4) reflective of the demographic and developmental profiles of the student body.

Career planning and placement services must promote student development by encouraging such things as positive and realistic self-appraisal, intellectual development, appropriate personal and occupational choices, clarification of values, physical fitness, the ability to relate meaningfully with others, the capacity to engage in a personally satisfying and effective style of living, the capacity to appreciate cultural and esthetic differences, and the capacity to work independently and interdependently.

Career planning and placement services must assist students in overcoming specific personal, physical, or educational problems or skill deficiencies.

Career planning and placement services must identify environmental conditions that may negatively influence welfare and propose interventions that may neutralize such conditions or improve the environment.

The educational experience of students consists of both academic efforts in the classroom and developmental opportunities through student services and development programs. Institutions must define the relative importance of these processes.

Career planning and placement services must offer the following programs:

1. Career counseling, which assists students at any point in time to:
   - analyze interests, aptitudes, abilities, previous work experience, personal traits, and desired life-style to promote awareness of the interrelationship between self-knowledge and career choice;
   - obtain occupational information including, where possible, exploratory experiences such as cooperative education, internships, externships, and summer and part-time jobs;
   - make reasoned, well-informed career choices that are not based on race/gender stereotypes; and
   - set short-range and long-range goals.
2. Placement counseling and referral, which assists the student to:
   - clarify objectives and establish goals;

- explore the full range of life and work possibilities including graduate and professional preparations;
- prepare for the job search or further study;
- present oneself effectively as a candidate for employment or further study; and
- make the transition from education to the world of work.

3. Student employment, including part-time, vacation, and experiential education programs which assist students in obtaining work experiences, financial resources, and/or the opportunity for academic credit.

Part 3: Leadership and Management

The institution must appoint a leader of career planning and placement or designate an individual to fulfill that role. This leader must be positioned in the organization so that the career development needs of students are represented at the highest administrative level of the institution. This leader must be an experienced and effective manager, must have substantial work experience in the field of career planning and placement, and either be an acknowledged leader on the campus or have obvious background and experience to command such respect. The specific title and reporting relationship of this individual may vary among institutions. The individual must be selected on the basis of personal characteristics and formal training.

The leader must create an effective system to manage the career planning and placement office. The leader must plan, organize, staff, lead, and assess programs on a continuing basis. The result should be an integrated system of career planning and placement activities and services for the institution, funded and otherwise supported at a level that permits the effective delivery of these programs.

The leader must be able to develop, to advocate, and to use a statement of mission, goals, and objectives for career planning and placement on the campus. The leader must attract and select qualified staff members who make effective decisions about policies, procedures, personnel, budgets, facilities, and equipment. The leader must assume responsibilities for program and personnel development, assessment, and improvement of the services and development activities of the organization.

Part 4: Organization and Administration

Career planning and placement services must develop its own set of policies and procedures that include a detailed description of the administrative process and an organizational chart showing the job functions and reporting relationships within and beyond the program.

Part 5: Human Resources

Career planning and placement services must have adequate and qualified professional staff to fulfill the mission and to implement all aspects of the program. To be qualified, professional staff members must have a graduate degree in a field of study relevant to the particular job in question or must have an appropriate combination of education and experience. In any functional area in which there is a full-time director, that director must possess levels of education and/or professional experience beyond that of the staff to be supervised.

Preprofessional or support staff members employed in career planning and placement services must be qualified by relevant education and experience. Degree requirements, including both degree levels and subject matter, must be germane to the particular job responsibilities. Such staff members must be trained appropriately and supervised adequately by professional staff.

Paraprofessionals must be carefully selected, trained with respect to helping skills and institutional services and procedures, closely supervised, and evaluated regularly. Their compensation must be fair and any voluntary services must be recognized adequately. Paraprofessionals must recognize the limitations of their knowledge and skills and must refer students to appropriate professionals when the problems encountered warrant.

To ensure that professional staff members devote adequate time to professional duties, career planning and placement services must have sufficient clerical and technical support staff. Such support must be of sufficient quantity and quality to accomplish the following kinds of activities: typing, filing, telephone and other receptionist duties, bookkeeping, maintaining student records, organizing resource materials, receiving students and making appointments, and handling routine correspondence.

Salary level and fringe benefits for staff must be commensurate with those for similar professional, preprofessional, and clerical positions at the institution and in the geographic area.

To ensure the existence of suitable and readily identifiable role models within the campus teaching and administrative ranks, staff employment profiles must reflect representation of categories of persons who comprise the student population. However, where student bodies are predominantly non-disabled, of one race, gender, or religion, a diverse staffing pattern will enrich the teaching/administrative ranks and will demonstrate institutional commitment to fair employment practices.

All career planning services must have a regular system of staff selection and evaluation, and must provide continuing professional development opportunities for staff including in-service training programs, participation in professional conferences, workshops, and other continuing education activities.

Professional staff members must be skilled in career planning, placement, and counseling, and must have the ability to function effectively with students, faculty, administrators, and employers.

Part 6: Funding

Career planning and placement services must have funding sufficient to carry out its mission and to support the following, where applicable: staff salaries; purchase and maintenance of office furnishings, supplies, materials, and equipment, including current technology; phone and postage costs; printing and media costs; institutional memberships in appropriate professional organizations; relevant subscriptions and necessary library resources; attendance at professional association meetings, conferences, and workshops; and other professional development activities. In addition to institutional funding commitment through general funds, other funding sources may be considered, including: state appropriations, student fees, user fees, donations and contributions, fines, concession and store sales, rentals, and dues.

Part 7: Facilities

The career planning and placement services program must be provided adequate facilities to fulfill its mission. As applicable, the facilities for career planning and placement services must include, or the program must have access to, the following: private offices or private spaces for counseling, interviewing, or other meetings of a confidential nature; office, reception, and storage space sufficient to accommodate assigned staff, supplies, equipment, library resources, and machinery, and conference room or meeting space. All facilities must be accessible to disabled persons and must be in compliance with relevant federal, state, and local health and safety requirements.

Part 8: Legal Responsibilities

Staff members must be knowledgeable about, and responsive to, relevant civil and criminal laws and must be responsible for ensuring that the institution fulfills its legal obligations. Staff members in career planning and placement must be well versed in those obligations and limitations imposed on the operation of the institution, particularly in their program area, by local, state, and federal constitutional, statutory, regulatory, and common law and by institutional policy. They must utilize appropriate policies and practices to limit the liability exposure of the institution, its officers, employees, and agents. The institution must provide access to legal advise to professional staff as needed to carry out assigned responsibilities.

Part 9: Equal Opportunity, Access, and Affirmative Action

Career planning and placement services must maintain good relations with relevant campus offices and external agencies, which necessarily requires regular identification of the offices with which such relationships are critical.

The career planning and placement services must adhere to the spirit and intent of equal opportunity laws in all activities. The program must ensure that its services and facilities are accessible to and provide hours of operation that respond to the needs of special student populations, including traditionally under-represented, evening, part-time and commuter students.

Personnel policies shall not discriminate on the basis of race, gender, color, religion, age, national origin, and/or handicap. In hiring and promotion policies, student services professionals must take affirmative action that strives to remedy significant staffing imbalance, particularly when resulting from past discriminatory practices. Career planning and placement services must seek to identify, prevent and/or remedy other discriminatory practices.

Part 10: Campus and Community Relations

Career planning and placement services must maintain good relations with relevant campus offices and external agencies, which necessarily requires regular identification of the office with which such relationships are critical.

Career planning and placement service must:

- develop job opportunities on a continuing basis from a variety of employers;
- provide all employers the opportunity to consider candidates for employment;
- maximize students' exposure to employers through a variety of programs;
- collect information on occupational trends and employers' needs;
- encourage dialogue among employers, faculty, and administration concerning job needs and trends; and
- encourage employers to recognize career planning and placement services through public acknowledgment and/or avenues of support.

The career planning and placement service must:

- develop a working relationship that encourages the academic administration and faculty to maximize and give active support to an effective program for students and graduates;
- promote better understanding between the institutions and employers of the relationship of curricular and other activities to the career needs of and opportunities for students; and

- promote a systematic flow of information to faculty members and students from alumni concerning their academic preparation and employment experiences.

Part 11: Multicultural Programs and Services

The institution must provide to members of its majority and minority cultures educational efforts that focus on awareness of cultural differences, self-assessment of possible prejudices, and desirable behavioral changes.

The career planning and placement service must provide educational programs that help minority students identify their unique needs, prioritize those needs, and meet them to the degree that numbers of students, facilities, and resources permit. The career planning and placement service must orient minority students to the culture of the institution and promote and deepen their understanding of their own culture and heritage.

Part 12: Ethics

All persons involved in the provision of services to students must maintain the highest standards of ethical behavior. Career planning and placement services staff members must develop and adopt standards of ethical practice addressing the unique problems that face personnel in that area. The standards must be published and reviewed by all concerned. In the formulation of those standards, ethical standards statements previously adopted by the profession at large or relevant professional associations may be of assistance and must be considered.

Certain ethical obligations apply to all individuals employed in career planning and placement programs, for example: All staff members must ensure that confidentiality is maintained with respect to all communications and records considered confidential. Unless written permission is given by the student, information disclosed in individual counseling sessions must remain confidential. In addition, all requirements of the Family Educational Rights and Privacy Act (Buckley Amendment) must be complied with and information contained in students' educational records must not be disclosed to third parties without appropriate consent, unless one of the relevant statutory exceptions applies. A similar dedication to privacy and confidentiality must be applied to research data concerning individuals.

All staff members must be aware of and comply with the provisions contained in the institution's human subjects policy and in any other institutional policy addressing ethical practices.

All staff members must ensure that students are provided access to services on a fair and equitable basis. All staff members must avoid any personal conflict of interest so they can deal objectively and impartially with persons within and outside the institution. In many instances, the appearances of a conflict of interest can be as damaging as an actual conflict. Whenever handling funds, all staff must ensure that such funds are handled in accordance with established and responsible accounting procedures.

Staff members must not participate in any form of sexual harassment. Sexual harassment is defined to include sexual advances, requests for sexual favors, as well as other verbal or physical conduct of a sexual nature if "(1) submission to such conduct is made either explicitly or implicitly a term or condition of an individual's employment, academic progress, or any other outcome of an official nature, (2) . . . is used as a basis for such decisions or outcomes . . . , (3) . . . has the purpose or effect of unreasonably interfering with an individual's work performance or creating an intimidating, hostile, or offensive working environment" (29 Code of Federal Regulations, C.F.R., Section 1604.11 [a]).

All staff members must recognize the limits of their training, expertise, and competence and must refer students in need of further expertise to persons possessing appropriate qualifications.

Referral of an employed graduate to another employer must be preceded by that person's request for referral.

Career planning and placement office personnel must use their best efforts to ensure that the student's selection of a career or a graduate school is protected from improper influence by faculty, administrators, placement staff, and employers.

Conditions of employment and salary offers made to an individual by an employer must not be divulged in a personally identifiable form by career planning and placement office staff members.

Unless permission is given by the student, information disclosed in individual counseling sessions as well as information contained in records must remain confidential.

Part 13: Evaluation

There must be systematic and regular research on and evaluation of the overall institutional student services/development program and career planning and placement services to determine whether the educational goals and the needs of students are being met. Although methods of evaluation may vary, they must utilize both quantitative and qualitative measures. Data collected must include responses from students and other significant constituencies. Results of these regular evaluations must be used in revising and improving the program goals and implementation.

4

Management of the Career Center

Many organizations are well administered, and some are well managed, but few are well led. While the "leadership difference" (Peters & Austin, 1985) that seems to be everyone's aspiration eludes most of us, we believe a well-managed career center is an achievable goal, and we are confident that this chapter will assist the reader to manage a career center better and maybe even to achieve a "leadership advantage." Although the emphasis in this chapter is on management, it should be stressed that the planning functions described in the previous chapter go hand in glove with the management function. Simply put, a career center cannot be well managed without a "vision" in the form of a well-developed plan. Both planning and management are ongoing, year-round activities that are essential to the successful operation of an effective career center. Indeed, the capacity to identify (through the planning process) and take advantage of opportunities (through careful management) is an important characteristic of extraordinary student service agencies (Samson, Graue, Weinstein, & Walberg, 1984; Kuh, 1985).

The management concepts presented here are down-to-earth, practical ones that emphasize rational approaches. Despite our penchant for the practical and the rational, we acknowledge that present-day managers increasingly find themselves in what Vaill (1989) has termed "permanent white water." That is, they confront a world (and office) of chaotic change (Peters, 1987) that does not always respond to rational concepts of management. It is important not to let our focus on rational approaches detract from the fact that, now more than ever, the management of a career center involves as much art as science, and perhaps some luck as well.

The management of a university career center, while similar to the management of any other complex student services organization, also has certain unique characteristics, which are discussed here to provide a context for the remainder of the chapter.

MANAGEMENT CHARACTERISTICS OF THE CAREER CENTER

A Businesslike Function in an Educational Environment

The placement component of a university career center must be run very much like a business enterprise. Placement staff interact on a day-to-day basis with representatives from business, industry, and government. The function performed is basically a brokering function, that is, making all the arrangements necessary to get the right student in the right room at the right time with the right employer. This brokering function must be performed with a high degree of accuracy often under severe time constraints. Because placement personnel interact so directly and so frequently with representatives from business, industry, and government, they must know and understand the "business subculture" and interact accordingly with employers. There is a very real "press" within the university career center to adopt the culture of business and industry to assure success. That is, placement staff must be very goal-oriented because there is a very real "bottom line" in the placement business, and that bottom line is "placement rate." The characteristics necessary to be effective in placement are a strong goal orientation, maximum attention to detail, excellent follow-through, and ability to work under great time pressure. The business of placement consists of making relatively rapid judgments about human character on the basis of limited interactions under the press of time.

In contrast to the subculture of the placement function, the counseling function of the career center is principally "process"-oriented. While there are some time pressures and constraints, the interactions with students are largely facilitative, nonjudgmental, and supportive. Effective counselors tend to be less goal-oriented, more forgiving, and more concerned about the quality of client relationships than about the numbers of clients they see or whether they see them on time. The business of career counseling focuses on creating a facilitative, nonjudgmental environment while providing ample information resources to ensure quality career development and choice.

Managing and leading career counseling and placement staff working in these two quite disparate functions present a unique challenge. Indeed, few universities or colleges have successfully incorporated both career counseling and placement functions into an integrated, full-service career center. Bridging this disparity between placement and counseling staff goals, values, and skills may be one of the most challenging tasks confronting the director of a comprehensive career center, but it is also one of the most important and, if it is done well, one of the most rewarding. The natural tendency is for the placement function (and, in particular, on-campus recruitment) to drive the whole center. Too often the "placement tail wags the career development and counseling dog." It is the director's responsibility to ensure that balance is maintained and that the counseling and programming functions receive adequate staff and resource support. Besides the distinct subcultures of placement and counseling, the career center presents other unique management challenges.

The (Sometimes) Unfortunate Linkage of the Development Function to the Placement Function

Another unique and difficult aspect of managing a career center office is the tendency for faculty and central administration to allow the placement function and the development function to become linked to one another in unfortunate ways. In an era of scarce resources when universities look increasingly to corporations as a major source of funding, faculty and administrators often feel the need to offer their "best and brightest students" in return for corporate contributions. Bluntly put, corporate grants are solicited in return for inside access to top graduates.

Similarly, when the staff of the university development office seeks a large grant or endowment from a corporation, the corporation frequently requests that placement services provide it with special favors. Often a census is done to determine just how many graduates of the university are currently employed by the "target" corporate donor. Presumably the greater the number of alumni the corporation employs, the greater should be its obligation to deliver grant monies and other forms of resource support to the university's development coffers.

This type of relationship has its advantages, but it also makes it increasingly difficult to assure that the universitywide placement function is operating in accord with professional ethical standards, including affirmative action/equal opportunity guidelines. Interesting "networking" arrangements develop between faculty and corporate representatives that deny students equal access to on-campus job interviews. Individual students in high-demand majors are provided with exclusive access to interviews with certain "generous" corporations that conduct their interviews in faculty offices while the majority of students are referred to the placement office or simply turned away.

It becomes the distasteful responsibility of the director of a large university career center to identify these faculty-run, "guerrilla" on-campus recruitment operations and keep them under control. He or she must also endeavor to dissuade faculty and staff from the view that the solicitation of funds from corporations necessitates special favors from the faculty in the form of exclusive access to the best and brightest students.

Attempting to keep faculty interested and involved in the placement function while operating in accordance with ethical standards requires both patience and diligence on behalf of the director.

MANAGEMENT PHILOSOPHY

Defining the Culture: Establishing and Then Communicating Management Philosophy to Current and Potential Employees

Perhaps the most important single thing a director can do to enhance the professionalism and productivity of the career center is to commit to writing a management philosophy, live the philosophy, and then communicate that philosophy to current and potential employees in as direct and open a way as possible. This approach, based on Ouchi's Theory Z (1981), is predicated on the notion that every organization or office has a certain set of values and expected behaviors that create a culture. Persons who share the core values of the culture will be successful, productive, and satisfied staff members. Those who do not will be better off elsewhere and should be "assisted" to migrate there. Potential employees, professional as well as clerical, should be provided with a written copy of the office management philosophy during the interview process and asked to read it carefully and believe it. By making explicit the office culture through this formally prepared management philosophy, the potential employee will be better able to judge whether or not to accept an offer of employment, should one be made. Simply put, the management philosophy defines the office culture and can be used as a standard against which potential employees can be judged and against which current employee behavior can be evaluated. The philosophy is less a rigid set of rules about office behavior than it is an ideal of how one hopes the office will operate. If potential employees can "buy into" this basic philosophy and hold it as a vision of how things should work, it is more likely that they will strive toward this vision no matter how unreachable an ideal it might be. Put another way, "If you never have a dream, you'll never have a dream come true."

For the purpose of illustration we have included in Figure 4.1 the management philosophy of the Career Development and Placement Service at Penn State University. While there is nothing sacred about the Penn State philosophy, it illustrates the types of issues and the degree of specificity that we believe are necessary to ensure the successful use of a "management philosophy" as a management tool.

Note that this philosophy addresses four broad areas of management, including office objective, management style, work ethic, and student services orientation. While it should be clear to the reader that articulating a management philosophy is neither sufficient nor necessary to assure the efficient management of a university career center, we believe that the establishment of such a philosophy sets the tone for the work environment and can be a useful management tool. We advocate that such a philosophy be included as a preface to the office procedures handbook and that it be referred to frequently as a cornerstone of effective management.

PERSONNEL NEEDS

Nothing is more crucial to the success of a service agency than the careful selection, training, and professional development of the staff. A comprehensive university career center requires a staff with a wide range of interests, skills, abilities, academic backgrounds, and training. The staff is likely to be comprised of at least six different types on the basis of function.

Figure 4.1
Office Management Philosophy

OFFICE OBJECTIVE
Our office objective is to perform and be recognized as the best, the leader, number one in student services among all departments and agencies at The Pennsylvania State University and throughout the nation. If as an office we achieve this objective, then it will clearly reflect positively upon us as individuals. It is assumed that it is not possible to be an outstanding success as an individual if the office is mediocre or average. Our ego is strongly tied to this aspect of our philosophy.

Innovativeness, creativity and above all quality are stressed in all our programs and services and in our approach to the delivery of these programs and services. We must continuously strive to improve in every way. "You don't have to be sick to get better." -- No matter how well we do it, we can always do it better.

It should always be our practice in working cooperatively with any individual (student, staff member, faculty member, recruiter or anyone else) or any other office or department to display a willingness to go "more than half way" to insure the success of such cooperative efforts.

We are sensitive to our image with students, the business and university communities. Commitments to students and other clients are considered sacred and we are upset with ourselves when we do not meet our commitments. We strive to demonstrate to the entire university and business community on a continuing basis that we are credible in describing the nature of our programs and services and that we are well organized and in complete control of all things that lead to the successful delivery of those programs and services.

MANAGEMENT STYLE
Career Development and Placement Services is an office of individuals each with their own personalities and characteristics. And while this is true, certain general characteristics of the management style will allow us to achieve our objectives.

1. The staff is self-critical. Everyone must be capable of recognizing and accepting mistakes and learning from them.

2. Open, constructive confrontation is encouraged at all levels, and is viewed as a method of problem solving--conflict resolution. Hiding problems is not acceptable. Covert political activity is strongly discouraged.

3. Decision by consensus is the rule. Decisions once made are supported. Position in the organization is not the basis for quality of ideas. Decisions are encouraged to be made at all levels within the organization, wherever the facts are. What people help create, they support.

Figure 4.1 (continued)

4. A highly communicative/open management approach is part of our style. People want to know as much as possible about their work environment, and not knowing hurts. It hurts their pride, insults their intelligence, arouses their fears, and results in counter-productivity. We must have "enough" meetings. Problems must be discussed in an open forum, decisions must be made in an open forum and so on. Staff members at all levels must be accessible.

5. A high level of organizational skill and discipline is demanded. Consistent with our office objectives, staff are expected to be organized in their approach, and a high degree of planning is required. The relationship between performance and commitments should be closely monitored and viewed as a key indicator of an individual's overall performance.

6. Staff members must be ethical. Decisions and actions must be consistently beyond question from an ethics standpoint. By telling the truth and by treating everyone within and without our organization equitably, we establish our ethical credibility.

7. Trust in relationships is important. Without trust, any human relationship will inevitably degenerate into conflict. With trust, anything is possible.

8. Staff must face up to difficult work-related decisions, whether they are professional, organizational, or personal.

9. The responsibility for individual development rests to a considerable degree with the immediate supervisor. To behave in an ethical manner here means that time and effort must be put into the professional development of subordinates. This means "pushing" subordinates and encouraging continued improvement in both skills and performance while creating an environment conducive to professional development.

WORK ETHIC
It is the general objective of our office to arrange individual work assignments which are consistent with individual career objectives.

Further, we must work to create an environment that allows each employee to enjoy his/her work while achieving his/her career goals.

We should strive to provide an opportunity for personal career development. this implies the necessity for a strong commitment to training but does not imply that the sole responsibility for this training lies with the supervisor.

Our office is results oriented. The focus is on substance vs. form, quality vs. quantity.

We believe in the principle that hard work and high productivity are things to be proud of. A high degree of discipline is to be expected and admired. Timeliness is a key element of our work ethic. It is not good enough to deliver a quality product - the quality product must be delivered on time.

Figure 4.1 (continued)

```
The concept of assumed responsibility is accepted.  If a task needs to
be done, assume that you have the responsibility to get it done and do
it.

We desire to have all staff involved and participating in their
relationship with this office.  We want the staff to care about their
office.  To aid in achieving this end, we stress good communications
in the hope of establishing a sense of identify and closeness.

STUDENT SERVICE ORIENTATION
Students are:

...the most important people on the campus, without students there
would be no need for our office or this institution.

...not cold enrollment statistics, but flesh and blood human beings
with feelings and emotions like our own.

...not people to be tolerated so that we can do our thing.  They are
our thing.

...not dependent on us.  Rather, we are dependent on them.

...not an interruption of our work, but the purpose of it.  We are not
doing them a favor by serving them.  They are doing us a favor by
giving us the opportunity to do so.
```

Staff Types

Administrative Staff. This staff consists of the director and perhaps one associate director or an administrative assistant/office manager, with primary responsibility for maintaining the resource base, fighting the political battles within the university, handling all budgetary and personnel matters, representing the office to the greater university and the outside world, and generally managing the office. Also included is an office information specialist/systems person with responsibility for evaluating, recommending, installing, implementing, and integrating computer information systems within career services.

Placement Staff. This staff consists of an associate director and additional professional staff whose primary responsibilities are to supervise and conduct the placement-related services, including employer relations, on-campus recruitment, credential service, placement library, career information center, placement advising, and programming related to the placement function.

Counseling Staff. This staff consists of an associate or assistant director and counselors with specialized training in career counseling whose primary responsibilities are to supervise, evaluate, and conduct individual and group counseling sessions, to teach career decision-making courses for credit, and prescribe and interpret assessment devices and other standardized treatment modules, including computer-assisted career guidance.

Programming Staff. This staff has excellent presentation skills and an interest in, and flair for, delivering a wide range of career programs, including seminars, workshops, lectures, and so on to diverse groups of students and prospective students.

Some of the programming staff are likely to be counselors, placement staff, and administrators, as few career centers will have the luxury of single-purpose programming specialists.

Graduate Assistants. These are likely to be of two principal types: master's-level student personnel administration students interested in programming, placement, and management tasks and master's- and doctoral-level counseling students with an interest in individual and group career counseling, assessment, and teaching.

Support Staff (Clerical Staff). Each of the five types of professional staff described above will require quality clerical support. This will include receptionists, scheduling clerks, word processing/data entry clerks, and administrative assistants.

In addition to these six types of staff, many comprehensive career centers supplement their staff with volunteers, interns, and work-study support. Such supplementary staff are likely to be assigned to various functional roles identified here on the basis of need and/or individual skill.

Dimensions of Diversity

While university career center professional staff generally work in the functional areas described above, it is necessary to assure diversity along several key dimensions that cut across these functional areas if success is to be achieved. The dimensions of diversity that we regard as most important at this point in the historical development of university career centers are enumerated here.

Gender. Wherever possible, it is desirable to maintain as close to a 50/50 balance on the basis of gender as possible. This gender balance should cut vertically through the hierarchy of the professional staff. That is, it is important to have both women and men at all levels of the organization. Too often women are concentrated in the entry-level positions while men are concentrated at the upper management levels. With the undergraduate student gender ratio in most universities being nearly 50/50, it is important to maintain a similar gender ratio among staff. In recent years it has been increasingly difficult to recruit men into entry-level positions within career centers. According to the 1991 CPC *Career Planning and Placement Survey*, "Of . . . professional staff, other than the director more than three-fourths were female (76.1%)." This feminization of the profession should be of concern, just as the concentration of males at the upper management levels is a concern. An appropriate gender balance must be maintained.

Ethnicity. As the ethnic diversity of university enrollments grows, so too does the need to assure appropriate ethnic diversity among the staff of the career center. At most modern university career centers it is reasonable to expect that at least some of the professional staff will be African American and Hispanic. The degree and nature of the ethnic diversity within the student body should dictate the degree and nature of the ethnic diversity of the career services staff, and a good-faith effort must be made to achieve that degree of ethnic diversity.

Academic Background. While it is natural for career center staffs to be dominated by individuals with degrees in education and counseling, it is highly desirable to assure some diversity in terms of academic background. Where possible, the disciplines of engineering, science, liberal arts, education, and business administration should be represented on the university career center staff. Such diversity of academic background not only allows for specialization but enhances the richness of staff and staff-student interactions and ensures the probability that a variety of viewpoints will be represented in the delivery of career services. Few diversity issues are as critical to the successful delivery of career services to the multiple colleges of a comprehensive university as academic background of the staff, and yet this is one area of diversity that receives little attention.

Experience Background. Just as it is desirable for staff to exhibit considerable diversity in terms of academic background, diversity of work experience is also important. All too frequently, career services staff have little work experience outside the educational setting. Where possible, the background experience of staff should complement their academic backgrounds to assure that career counseling and advising have a strong reality base. In brief, it is not desirable to employ career counselors who have never held employment outside an educational institution.

Age. Diversity along the age dimension may be more important in the career center than in other student service offices. On one hand, undergraduates may find it easier to relate to young staff, who have recently graduated from master's programs. On the other hand, young staff with limited life experiences often lack the credibility to provide effective career counseling to returning adult students, graduate students, and postdoctoral students, and faculty. To some degree the nature of the student body and the relative mix of graduate to undergraduate students should dictate the age range of the staff, but clearly an attempt should be made to maintain some balance.

There are other dimensions of diversity that we have not addressed here but that may be of greater or lesser importance depending on the nature of the student body and the mission of the institution. The important issue here is that a high level of awareness be maintained regarding staff diversity and that this awareness be translated into action every time a hiring decision is made.

SAMPLE POSITION DESCRIPTIONS

The role of director of university career services has become increasingly complicated in recent years as students, faculty, and administrators have demanded much more in the area of career counseling and programming. Now, in addition to having excellent management and organizational skills, it is necessary for a director to have a strong background in career and counseling psychology in order to provide the necessary leadership and supervision to assure that the core of the career center is solidly based in counseling theory and technique. In addition, continued fiscal constraints have increasingly forced directors to supplement their budgets with external grant monies. Many university career centers depend on external sources for up to 50 percent of their operating budget. This funding condition has forced the role of development officer upon many career center directors—a role that often conflicts with other duties that many have only reluctantly accepted. Yet another demand confronting directors is the increasing complexity of management information systems, computerization, and technology generally. While directors do not have to be systems analysts or technocrats themselves, they are confronted daily with decisions about hardware, software, database management systems, local area networks, and the like; and most directors at large universities find themselves increasingly involved, for better or worse, with technology.

Finally, to assure the credibility necessary to function effectively within the increasingly credential-oriented university community, a doctorate and at least affiliate faculty rank in an appropriate academic department are almost a necessity. The days of the "Mr. Chips" placement director are definitely over. Figure 4.2 presents a typical position description for the directorship of a large university career center. It is followed (Figure 4.3) by a position description for the other most common career services position, that of career counselor. We have also included in Appendix 4.1, eight additional position descriptions of the most common professional positions in existence at university career centers: associate director for placement; associate director for counseling and programming; assistant director for career counseling; assistant director for career programming; assistant director for career information systems; assistant director for alumni career services/educational career services; coordinator, experiential education programs; and office information specialist. While position descriptions will necessarily vary depending upon the organizational structure of the institution and the mission and goals of the Center, these basic position descriptions provide models which can be easily modified to meet the needs of nearly any career center.

ORGANIZATIONAL STRUCTURE, REPORTING LINES, AND SUPERVISION

In Chapter 3 we discussed in some detail the importance of the position of the career center within the organizational structure of the college or university. The way career services itself is structured is of equal importance. In general, university career center organizational structures are of three types: (1) centralized and hierarchical, (2) centralized and flat, or (3) decentralized and flat. Because career center staffs are usually not large, the structure is normally fairly flat. We believe that a flat structure is generally superior to a more hierarchical one becasue it encourages direct communications between and among all staff and it shortens turnaround time (Townsend, 1970). However, the structure of career services at most universities will be dictated to a considerable degree by the structure of student services and the greater university itself. Clearly, the structure of career services must be compatible with the institution in which it operates. Our experience has been that excellent career services often exist despite, rather than because of,

Figure 4.2
Career Services Position Description: Director

Title of Position: Director

Classification: Professional

Department: Career Services

Function of Position:

Responsible to the Vice President for Student Services for the direction and management of University Career Services. Has overall responsibility for and authority over planning, organizing, developing, administering, and budgeting career-related programs and delivery systems for the University.

Principal Duties and Responsibilities:

1. Responsible for overall administration of Career Services including:
    a. Overseeing operation of established services and programs, including evaluation, improvement, policy enforcement, change and approval;
    b. Establishing long-range plans for office;
    c. Developing and administering the budget;
    d. Developing and assessing the effectiveness of day to day management and communication procedures, policies and forms;
    e. Assessing, maintaining and improving office physical environment including equipment, furnishings and facilities;

2. Responsible for staff supervision including:
    a. Developing and maintaining staff patterns as office needs dictate;
    b. Developing and overseeing the hiring process for all staff including selection and/or approving selection of all staff;
    c. Developing and conducting and/or overseeing training and development of all staff (professional and clerical);
    d. Conducting ongoing supervision and evaluation of staff.

3. Responsible for representing the Career Center to the University and public including:
    a. Publicizing office programs and services to faculty, staff, and students;
    b. Serving on University committees;
    c. Representing the Center on consortium institution committees and programs;
    d. Representing the Center to employers locally, regionally, and nationally.

Figure 4.2 (continued)

4. Responsible for representing the Career Center and the University to the profession including:
   a. Attending, participating, and presenting at professional conferences and communicating relevant information to Center staff and University faculty and staff;
   b. Staying abreast of the professional literature as well as contributing to it on a regular basis;
   c. Integrating information and knowledge gained through (a) and (b) into office planning and practices.

5. Participate as a Management Team Member in Student Services including:
   a. Attending all appropriate meetings and communicating information about Career Services to other departments and from other departments to Career Services;
   b. Participating in Student Services decision-making, planning and problem solving as appropriate;
   c. Working with other Student Services Unit Directors and Units to plan and implement programs, training, and collaboration as appropriate;
   d. Maintaining of high quality two-way communication with the Vice President for Student Services.

6. Interpret University policy and government (state and federal) rules and regulations to students, faculty, executive staff, governmental officials, and representatives from business and industry in all matters pertaining to career development and professional employment. Ensure that the University adheres to current national and state guidelines on equal opportunity and affirmative action insofar as career placement activities are concerned.

7. Serve as spokesman for the University to media for articles, forecasts, quotes, and appearances (radio, TV, and business/civic groups) as expert on the job market for graduates, employment data and trends, and related research.

Supervision:

Duties and responsibilities are performed under general direction and through the interpretation of University policy based on general objectives. Thorough knowledge of University policies and procedures is required in their application to cases not previously covered. Work is performed independently toward general results and requires the ability to devise new methods or modify existing procedures to meet new conditions. Problems are rarely referred.

Figure 4.2 (continued)

<u>Minimum Qualifications</u>:

An earned Doctorate in Counseling Psychology, Higher Education, Industrial Psychology or related area plus a minimum of 8 years effective administrative experience in Higher Education, Career Services or related areas. Excellent interpersonal and communications skills, strong theoretical and practical knowledge of the career development field and proven ability to translate ideas/concepts into successful career programs/services. Must be qualified for immediate affiliate faculty rank in counseling psychology, counselor education, industrial psychology, or other academic department.

a particular organizational structure and that while the choice of a structure is not trivial, it is seldom critical. Nevertheless, we include here a brief discussion of the advantages and disadvantages of each structure, together with a graphic depiction of each.

Centralized/Hierarchical Structure

In this type of organizational structure (Figure 4.4), the director has full responsibility and authority for career services universitywide. Under this model, most large university career centers will have a professional staff of from 10 to 20 persons and a clerical staff of from 5 to 10. Such a structure will probably have at least four levels or grades of professional staff and perhaps four clerical grade levels as well. Depending on the size of a college and its student affairs staff, it may be necessary to collapse these levels to three or even two.

Advantages of the Centralized/Hierarchical Structure

1. A hierarchical structure provides a "career ladder" for staff. Entry-level professionals can aspire to a progression up the ladder with concomitant increases in responsibility, authority, and salary. (This is the corporate model.)
2. Centralization allows for more specialization of function and provides the flexibility to draw better on the special skills and talents of staff.
3. It recognizes that certain functions are more crucial to the operation of the center than others and rewards persons performing those functions with appropriate authority, responsibility, titles, and salary.
4. Reporting lines are clear, and if the organization functions in accord with the reporting lines, responsibility should follow authority.

Disadvantages of the Centralized/Hierarchical Structure

1. If the structure is rigidly adhered to in terms of communication within the organization, turnaround time on decisions can be time-consuming and decision making can become inefficient.
2. Specialization can lead to boredom and a perceived lack of variety in work assignments.
3. Staff at the lower levels of the hierarchy can feel as though they are isolated from the decision-making process and thus feel uninvolved and uninvested in the goals and mission of the center.

Figure 4.3
Career Services Position Description: Counselor

Title of Position: Counselor

Classification: Professional

Department: Career Services

Function of Position:

Responsible to the Assistant Director for Counseling for providing career development and placement services.

Principal Duties and Responsibilities:

1. Provide professional assistance and/or consultation to any student who requests help in planning or implementing his/her life/career direction.

2. Provide professional referral services for any student requiring extended treatment for social, personal adjustment or psychiatric problems.

3. Assist in the development and delivery of life/career education and outreach programs.

4. Assist with the liaison and consultative relationships with faculty, staff, and appropriate student organizations.

5. When qualified, occasionally teach formal courses in career development.

6. Maintain such records as appropriate for performance of the counseling functions.

7. Assist as required, with any evaluative procedures to be used to measure the effectiveness of Career Services.

8. Occasionally represent Career Services at campus/community functions such as career day programs and various educational, religious, and social meetings.

9. Perform other duties as assigned.

Supervision:

Duties are performed under general direction and the employee plans and arranges own work which is directed toward an established objective. Employee determines action to be taken handling all but unusual cases. Knowledge of established policy, procedures, and practices is required.

Minimum Qualifications:

Masters degree (or equivalent) in clinical or counseling psychology, counselor education, student personnel administration, or related area, plus one to two years of effective career counseling experience is required.

Figure 4.4
Centralized Hierarchical Structure

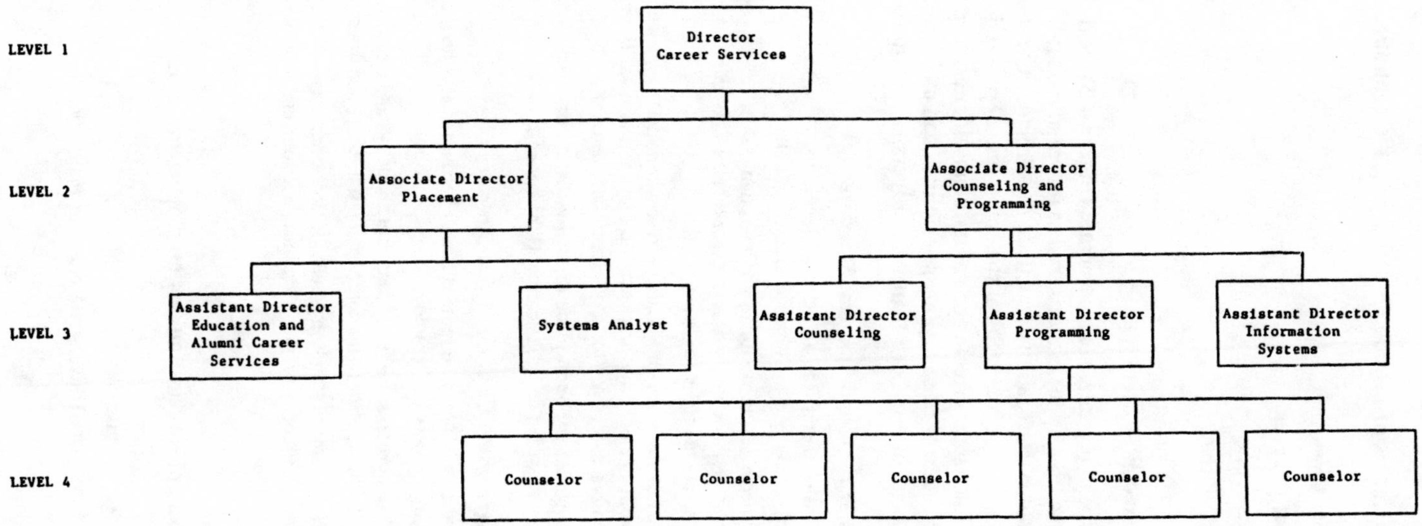

LEVEL 1

LEVEL 2

LEVEL 3

LEVEL 4

```
                          ┌─────────────────┐
                          │    Director     │
                          │ Career Services │
                          └────────┬────────┘
               ┌───────────────────┴──────────────────────┐
      ┌────────┴────────┐                        ┌─────────┴──────────┐
      │Associate Director│                       │ Associate Director │
      │   Placement     │                        │  Counseling and    │
      └────────┬────────┘                        │   Programming      │
               │                                 └─────────┬──────────┘
       ┌───────┴────────┐                   ┌──────────────┼──────────────┐
┌──────┴──────┐  ┌──────┴──────┐    ┌───────┴──────┐ ┌─────┴──────┐ ┌─────┴──────┐
│  Assistant  │  │   Systems   │    │  Assistant   │ │ Assistant  │ │ Assistant  │
│  Director   │  │   Analyst   │    │  Director    │ │ Director   │ │ Director   │
│ Education and│  │             │    │  Counseling  │ │Programming │ │Information │
│Alumni Career │  │             │    │              │ │            │ │  Systems   │
│   Services  │  │             │    │              │ │            │ │            │
└─────────────┘  └─────────────┘    └──────────────┘ └─────┬──────┘ └────────────┘
                                          ┌────────┬────────┼────────┬────────┐
                                    ┌─────┴──┐ ┌───┴────┐ ┌─┴──────┐ ┌┴───────┐ ┌────────┐
                                    │Counselor│ │Counselor│ │Counselor│ │Counselor│ │Counselor│
                                    └────────┘ └────────┘ └────────┘ └────────┘ └────────┘
```

Some examples of institutions employing the centralized/hierarchical model:

Arizona State University
University of Maryland
Michigan State University
Penn State University

Centralized Flat Structure

In this type of organizational structure (Figure 4.5) the director has full responsibility and authority for career services universitywide; however, nearly the entire professional staff reports directly to the director. The staff may be just as large as in the centralized hierarchical structure, but all professional staff have similar titles (e.g., assistant director or career counselor) and are at approximately the same level in terms of salary, responsibility, and authority. This model is more likely to occur in a college than in a university structure.

Advantages of the Centralized Flat Structure

1. All professional staff are at the same level, and thus, ideally a collegial atmosphere will exist. (This is clearly the academic model.)
2. Since in theory all professionals are interchangeable, work assignments can be rotated and shared, enhancing variety of work tasks and minimizing the burnout that is sometimes associated with specialization.
3. There are less compartmentalization and specialization of work tasks; thus, staff coverage in the event of sick leave and vacation leave is more easily arranged. In theory, any staff member can cover for any other staff member.
4. Such a system may be in place to assure that all professional staff within the career center are regarded as "management" as a means of dealing with staff unionization.

Disadvantages of the Centralized Flat Structure

1. The director's job may be more difficult because she or he must direct and supervise such a large number of employees.
2. Rarely do all professional staff contribute equally, and this structure limits the options available to the director to reinforce high productivity and discourage poor performance.
3. The lines of authority and responsibility are often vague, leading to confusion about who has the authority to direct certain functions and who has the responsibility for those functions.

Some examples of institutions employing the centralized flat structure:

Carnegie Mellon University
Members of the State University System in Pennsylvania

Figure 4.5
Centralized Flat Structure

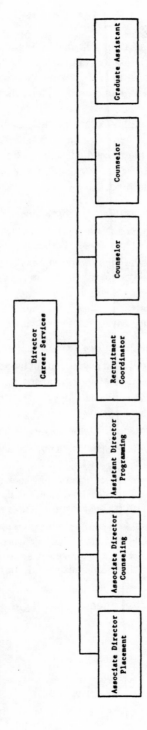

Decentralized Flat Structure

In this type of organizational structure (Figure 4.6) there are several (and may be as many as 10 to 15) directors of placement and/or career development. Generally such directors run one- to three-person operations affiliated with individual colleges or schools within the university. There may also be a director of the career development center, which may serve all colleges (the University of Illinois and Cornell University model). Another variation on this theme is the centralized career development and placement service with individual assistant directors affiliated with, and housed in, the individual colleges but with joint reporting lines to the central director of career services and the dean of their particular college (the University of Virginia model).

Advantages of the Decentralized Flat Structure

1. Placement staff are located close to the faculty of their respective college and presumably can give more specialized service and attention to both students and faculty of the college.
2. Day-to-day involvement with the faculty and staff of a particular college or school enhances the probability of faculty involvement in both career development and placement functions.
3. Individual college staff size is small, and thus, there is more variety in the work load and staff feel that they have more individual autonomy.

Disadvantages of the Decentralized Flat Structure

1. Communication between and among staff of the separate colleges often becomes difficult, and geographic separation exacerbates it.
2. Destructive competition often develops between individual college offices for access to employers at student expense.
3. Duplication of services and facilities is almost inevitable.
4. Students and employers may become confused about which office to use and where they are welcome.
5. Engineering and business administration generate much interest, interviews, and resources, while liberal arts, health and human development, and other nontechnical colleges with fewer natural linkages to business and industry struggle.
6. Such systems often result in conflicted loyalties on the part of staff. If a student's interests, values, and abilities suggest a transfer to another college, will the staff members who counsel be in sympathy with the student's needs or with those of the college, which are maintaining enrollments/minimizing attrition?

Some examples of institutions employing the decentralized flat structure:

Cornell University
University of Illinois
Iowa State University
University of Virginia

Figure 4.6
Decentralized Flat Structure

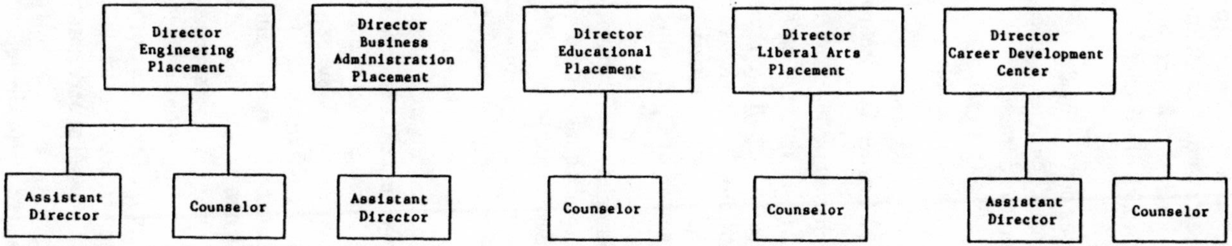

The Best (Worst?) of Both Worlds

Finally, some institutions have endeavored to combine various aspects of both centralized and decentralized approaches, claiming to achieve the efficiencies of a centralized career planning and placement operation with the ease of communication and more personal approach of a decentralized operation (Babbush, Hawley, & Zeran, 1986).

Beyond the reporting lines defined by the three basic organizational types and the advantages and disadvantages cited here, there are several important supervisory issues that we have chosen to address.

SUPERVISORY ISSUES

Licensed Supervision of Career Counselors

As career centers have evolved, so too have the quality and nature of the career counseling done in them. From the very early years (late 1920's through the seventies), the focus was principally on placement and placement-related "counseling issues." Until the late seventies career counseling was thought to consist mostly of assisting seniors with such issues as résumé preparation, developing job search strategies, and providing advice to engineers and business majors regarding starting salaries, interviewing skills, plant trips, and other placement-related tasks (Shingleton & Fitzpatrick, 1985). Most career counselors during that era had no formal counselor training. They were typically faculty members who had taken a particular interest in placement and who enjoyed working with students. While there were always some career services professionals who had a broader view of career counseling, most were employed in counseling centers rather than career centers.

Throughout the seventies and eighties there was a significant change in the profession. Nearly all placement offices expanded their role to include at least some career counseling. Many are now involved in assessment, the use of computer-assisted career counseling systems, the teaching of career decision-making courses for credit, the provision of life/career planning workshops, and the delivery of sophisticated interview training programs. In short, career counseling has become much more sophisticated, and with that sophistication have come certification and licensure. These new career counselor skill requirements are reflected in the position descriptions offered earlier in this chapter, and they carry with them the need for quality counselor supervision. We advocate that all career counselors be supervised by an individual with a strong academic and experience background and that all supervisors be certified. Indeed, large career centers should, in our judgment, have a licensed psychologist with a specialization in career counseling on staff to provide appropriate supervision and training.

Clerical-Staff Relationships and Supervision

The effective management of clerical (support) staff is essential to the success of the career center. Client perceptions of career center services are often based as much on the quality of clerical staff interactions with clients as on those with professional staff. Several keys to clerical staff productivity and morale in the career center are:

- Every clerical staff member should be directly supervised by a professional staff member. This is in keeping with our belief in flat supervisory structures. Such an arrangement typically increases the two-way communication between professional and clerical staff and keeps both groups knowledgeable of the other's issues and problems.

- If at all possible, clerical and professional staff meetings should be held jointly. Such an arrangement builds trust, enhances information flow, and includes vital clerical viewpoints in the decision-making process. If joint meetings are not possible, then regular clerical staff meetings should be held during which professional staff "cover" key clerical workstations to allow all clerical staff to participate.

- As was pointed out in Chapter 3, clerical staff should be involved in annual planning sessions and serve actively on career center committees and task forces. If continuous quality improvement is a desired goal, the ongoing involvement of cross-functional teams, including clerical and professional staff, is a must (Deming, 1982; Crosby, 1984; Imai, 1986; Juran, 1988).

- A well-conceived and adequately funded clerical staff training and professional development program must be a part of the clerical staff management strategy.

Supervisory Patterns

Perhaps the most important thing to be said about supervision is that it is a sacred function that must be performed on a regular basis and that it must be regarded as a vital component of every employee's and supervisor's job. Too often in our experience, career center supervision is "put off" in the interest of providing direct service or solving more pressing problems. There is no more pressing problem than quality supervision for either employee or supervisor. Some supervisory issues of special concern for career center staff follow.

General Nature: Supervision should be viewed as a continuous and ongoing process occurring every minute of the working day. The emphasis in supervision should be on growth and development within a supportive professional environment. Quality supervision is the process that culminates once each year in a performance appraisal.

Frequency. While supervision is an ongoing process, regular supervision sessions should be held at least once every two weeks. It is important to set aside quality time for supervision sessions. Assuming that adequate supervision will occur on an unscheduled basis invites problems, particularly in high-energy offices like career centers. Some staff may require or request supervision sessions once a week or even more often. High-frequency supervision should be negotiated between supervisor and supervisee to their mutual satisfaction.

Group Versus Individual Supervision. We believe that some combination of group and individual supervision is desirable. On the one hand, individual sessions provide a forum for role modeling, trust building, confidentiality, and growth. On the other hand, group sessions encourage a camaraderie and cohesion, while providing peer pressure for improvement and growth.

If supervision is provided consistently and conscientiously, the performance appraisal process becomes its natural extension.

THE PERFORMANCE APPRAISAL PROCESS

Our belief is that a quality system of performance appraisal is one of the most critical tools for effective staff management and development. While an in-depth discussion of performance appraisal techniques and strategies is beyond the scope of this handbook, we here provide (1) a brief outline of the performance appraisal process, (2) examples of two forms for use in the performance appraisal process, and (3) a list of 12 tips for the conduct of quality performance appraisals that we believe will assist the reader to implement better the performance appraisal process.

Outline of the Performance Appraisal Process

1. Every staff member's performance should be evaluated "against" his or her position description (general goals) and against his or her personal goal statement for the year (employee-specific goals prepared as a part of the planning process outlined in the previous chapter). The key point here is that performance appraisals are not done in a vacuum. The appraisal process seeks to compare the actual performance of the employee with ideal performance as described in both the position description and the personal goal statement which is negotiated each year as a part of the planning process.

2. Each staff member should be asked to complete a preappraisal summary (discussion guide) of the year's accomplishments and disappointments and submit it to his or her supervisor at least a week prior to the performance evaluation. The purpose of this summary is to provide focus for both the employee and supervisor prior to the actual evaluation. Such a summary may also be done verbally during a regular supervision session. (See Figure 4.7.)

3. The performance appraisal form (see Figure 4.8) is completed by the supervisor and presented to the employee in a personal supervision session lasting at least one hour. It is hoped that such sessions will be comprised of direct, honest dialogue, with attention being given both to praise for positive contributions and to specific suggestions for improved performance.

4. In all cases, after the employee and supervisor have met and discussed the appraisal, a copy is placed in the employee's personnel file and the employee is given a copy for his or her records. Signing the appraisal does not indicate an employee's agreement with the content; rather, it simply indicates that the employee has read and understands the appraisal and has discussed it with his or her supervisor. If an employee disagrees with the appraisal, he or she may always attach a letter explaining his or her position.

Figure 4.7
Performance Appraisal Discussion Guide

THE PENNSYLVANIA STATE UNIVERSITY
Career Development and Placement Services

Annual Performance Appraisal
<u>DISCUSSION GUIDE</u>

Name: _____

===

1. With reference to the personal goal statement you prepared
    last summer, list and <u>briefly</u> comment on your CDPS
    accomplishments during the past year.

2. List those areas where your accomplishments were greater and/
    or less than anticipated, and briefly describe your
    perceptions of why.

3. List CDPS-related activities which you regard as most
    significant for the utilization of your time and effort
    during the months ahead. (Include only activities that you
    regard as <u>priority</u> items.)

Figure 4.8
Staff Performance Appraisal

Objectives

The staff performance appraisal system is designed to enhance:

1. COUNSELING AND COMMUNICATION. An employee should be evaluated on his/her performance on a regular basis; work-related issues of mutual concern to the employee and the supervisor should be discussed, and efforts to establish performance goals should be initiated.

2. PROFESSIONAL DEVELOPMENT. The evaluation process should be used to identify individual professional development needs and opportunities, consistent with the professional goals of the employee and the advanced training skills appropriate for the job and office.

3. PERSONNEL DECISIONS. Performance appraisals can contribute to a variety of personnel actions, including among others, considerations for promotions and salary increases.

NOTE: Some employees have been called upon or have volunteered to participate in University affirmative action activities. These activities are frequently in addition to an employee's regular job. Any involvement in such activities should be considered along with the employee's regular work performance when completing an appraisal. While it is important for each employee to perform all of his or her regular duties well, performance appraisals should take into account the employee's entire contribution to the University.

Instructions

The first eight PERFORMANCE CRITERIA may be utilized for all Staff Exempt and Staff Nonexempt employees. The ninth criterion (Supervisory Ability) should be utilized only for employees with supervisory responsibilities.

For each PERFORMANCE CRITERION (sections A through I), the appraiser must:

(1) Provide a performance rating by circling the appropriate number (1 to 12), or
(2) Write a narrative appraisal in the "Supporting Comments" section, or
(3) Provide both a rating and a narrative in the "Supporting Comments."

For the OVERALL EVALUATION (section J), the appraiser MUST provide a numerical performance rating (1 to 12).

Appraisers are reminded of the added value of the narrative sections and are encouraged to supplement the rating with supporting comments and, where appropriate, suggestions. For each PERFORMANCE CRITERION on which the employee is given an inadequate rating (i.e., 1 to 3), the appraiser MUST provide supporting comments.

In any case where performance under a specific criterion or the OVERALL EVALUATION of an employee is considered to be inadequate, the "Suggestion" portion of the form should also be used. It may be helpful if suggestions, such as recommendations for training or the development of performance objectives, are discussed and jointly agreed upon between the supervisor and the employee.

Some of the PERFORMANCE CRITERIA may not be appropriate to a particular position. In such circumstances, simply indicate "Not Applicable" under the narrative for the criterion. You may attach a separate piece of paper listing any other criteria which are more applicable to the employee's position, utilizing the same evaluation procedures outlined above.

The descriptive phrases under each PERFORMANCE CRITERION are intended only as suggestions of attributes to be considered. If a particular phrase or behavioral example appears to be inappropriate in appraising an employee, the supervisor may simply cross that phrase out. Further clarification of any evaluation may, of course, be added in the "Supporting Comments" section.

Blank copies of the appraisal form may be made available to employees at any time. Furthermore, a mutual review of the employee's position description either during or prior to the interview is encouraged to insure the currency and accuracy of the position description, as well as establish a basis for understanding the duties being appraised.

Figure 4.8 (continued)

STAFF EXEMPT AND STAFF NONEXEMPT EMPLOYEE PERFORMANCE APPRAISAL

EMPLOYEE NAME: _____ POSITION TITLE: _____

COLLEGE/DEPT.: _____ PERIOD COVERED: FROM _____ TO _____

DATE STARTED AT UNIVERSITY: _____ DATE STARTED THIS POSITION: _____

PERFORMANCE CRITERIA

A. JOB KNOWLEDGE: The demonstration of technical, administrative, managerial, supervisory or other specialized knowledge required to perform the job. Consider degree of job knowledge relative to length of time in the current position. If applicable, consider the individual's endeavors to increase job knowledge through additional formal or informal study, seminars, readings, and other professional activities both on and off the job.

1 2 3 Displays deficiencies in job knowledge; further training required.

4 5 6 Shows strength sometimes but is not consistent.

7 8 9 Demonstrates average to high level of job knowledge.

10 11 12 Demonstrates consistently high level of job knowledge.

Supporting Comments: _____

_____

Suggestions: _____

_____

B. PLANNING AND ORGANIZATIONAL EFFECTIVENESS: The extent to which the employee effectively plans, organizes, and implements tasks or programs. Consider the extent to which the employee's performance displays the basic fundamentals of good organization and work planning and the employee's effectiveness in time management. Consider the degree to which the employee meets deadlines, handles emergencies, and appropriately establishes goals and priorities. Assess the individual's productivity compared to the standards of the position.

1 2 3 Displays poor planning; lack of organization apparent even in routine assignments; frequently misses deadlines.

4 5 6 Does routine tasks adequately; difficulty in managing multiple or complex assignments; occasionally misses deadlines.

7 8 9 Average or better; most tasks are planned, organized, and implemented effectively and on time.

10 11 12 Displays outstanding ability to plan, organize, and implement tasks and programs and to meet deadlines.

Supporting Comments: _____

_____

Suggestions: _____

_____

C. INTERPERSONAL RELATIONS: How well the employee gets along with other individuals in the performance of job duties. Consider effectiveness of relations with co-workers, subordinates, supervisor and, if applicable, the general University community and the public in the handling of position responsibilities. Consider the employee's cooperativeness, tact and courtesy.

1 2 3 Has difficulty in relating to others; not readily cooperative.

4 5 6 Relates to others fairly well; works better with some persons than others.

7 8 9 Works well with others; facilitates cooperation.

10 11 12 Is very effective interpersonally; works extremely well with subordinates, peers, and superiors.

Supporting Comments: _____

_____

Suggestions: _____

_____

Figure 4.8 (continued)

D. ATTITUDE: Enthusiasm, dedication and interest displayed regarding position responsibilities and duties. Consider whether the employee expresses willingness to undertake projects, supports organizational goals and endeavors, and demonstrates flexibility in response to changing circumstances.

1	2	3	Generally displays negative attitude toward job; criticizes without offering constructive suggestions; inflexible.
4	5	6	Accepts job duties, occasionally with reluctance.
7	8	9	Displays interest in duties and responsibilities; flexible in response to changing circumstances.
10	11	12	Highly dedicated and enthusiastic; strongly supportive of organizational goals.

Supporting Comments: _____

_____

Suggestions: _____

_____

E. INITIATIVE: The degree to which the employee is self-starting and assumes responsibilities when specific directions are lacking. Consider how well the employee follows through on assignments, taking appropriate independent action when necessary, and the relative amount of supervision required.

1	2	3	Needs detailed instructions; requires constant supervision to keep assignments going.
4	5	6	Follows through on some assignments without continuous direction; requires some follow-up to keep assignments progressing.
7	8	9	A self-starter; follows through on assignments independently.
10	11	12	Exceptionally self-reliant; completely follows through on assignments.

Supporting Comments: _____

_____

Suggestions: _____

_____

F. RESOURCEFULNESS: Extent to which employee devises ways and means to deal with challenges in the performance of job duties. Consider the modification of, or recommendations for the modification of, existing methods or procedures to meet new or changing circumstances and the development of new ideas or methods.

1	2	3	Rarely develops more effective ways of handling assignments.
4	5	6	Occasionally offers worthwhile ideas and suggestions when encouraged to do so.
7	8	9	Has necessary resourcefulness to devise or suggest new methods, or to modify existing ones, to meet changing circumstances.
10	11	12	Frequently makes worthwhile suggestions; readily develops ideas and solutions to problems.

Supporting Comments: _____

_____

Suggestions: _____

_____

G. JUDGMENT: Evidence of ability to analyze available data or circumstances concerning a situation, develop alternative solutions, and recommend or select a proper course of action.

1	2	3	Makes frequent errors in judgment; often overlooks consequences of decisions.
4	5	6	Judgment usually sound under normal circumstances; occasionally exercises questionable judgment.
7	8	9	Exercises good judgment; aware of impact of decisions on related areas.
10	11	12	Exceptionally sound and sensible judgment; foresees and evaluates impact of decisions on related areas.

Supporting Comments: _____

_____

Suggestions: _____

_____

Figure 4.8 (continued)

H. COMMUNICATION SKILLS: Effectiveness in conveying ideas, information and directions to others. Consider clarity of oral and written communications as related to the employee's responsibilities.

1	2	3	Displays an inability to communicate clearly.
4	5	6	Sometimes lacks clarity or conciseness; generally can communicate desired information.
7	8	9	Communicates in an organized, clear and concise manner.
10	11	12	An outstanding communicator; can communicate complex information extremely well.

Supporting Comments: _____

Suggestions: _____

I. SUPERVISORY ABILITY: COMPLETE ONLY FOR INDIVIDUALS WITH SUPERVISORY RESPONSIBILITY. Extent to which the employee applies sound, acceptable supervisory practices in the execution of his/her supervisory responsibilities. Consider evidence of demonstrated skill in arousing interest and enthusiasm in subordinates rather than solely relying on authority to get the job done. Consider the employee's effectiveness in selecting and developing personnel.

1	2	3	Causes morale problems: does not adequately handle employee relations.
4	5	6	Somewhat competent as supervisor but is not consistent.
7	8	9	Encourages subordinates in self-development; creates and maintains a comfortable, cooperative work environment.
10-	11	12	Dynamically leads subordinates to discover their own potential within their positions; provides inspiration and outstanding leadership to subordinates.

Supporting Comments: _____

Suggestions: _____

J. OVERALL EVALUATION: The overall evaluation should reflect the assessment of the employee's total performance, based upon the foregoing criteria. In making the assessment, consider the criteria according to the employee's duties and responsibilities, taking care not to overemphasize one particular criterion.

1	2	3	Improvement is required in order to perform at an acceptable level.
4	5	6	Generally performs adequately; need for improvement in specific areas is evident.
7	8	9	Performs duties and responsibilities well; occasionally excels.
10	11	12	A noteworthy employee; this employee is a top performer.

Supporting Comments: _____

Suggestions: _____

Signature of the Appraiser   Date

Concurrence of Administrative Officer   Date

---

*Signature of Individual Appraised   Date

*Signature indicates only that the evaluation has been reviewed, and does not necessarily signify concurrence. A response to this appraisal may be made on a separate sheet and attached.

5. The performance appraisal should become the major basis for the merit component of individual employee salary increments.

6. Performance appraisals should be done at least once each year but may be done more often at the request of either the employee or employer.

7. This basic process should be utilized for both clerical and professional staff performance appraisals, though the basic appraisal form will probably differ for the two different employee classifications.

Twelve Tips for the Conduct of Quality Performance Appraisals

1. Don't wait until review time to let your supervisee(s) know what you expect from them. Let them know early what specific goals, standards, and deadlines you expect them to meet and how you plan to evaluate and reward their performance. This should be done in conjunction with the negotiation of their annual goals and objectives as a part of the planning process.

2. Keep a written record of each supervisee's performance throughout the year so that you can cite specific examples to back up criticism and praise during the performance appraisal review session. We suggest that you maintain a file for each employee and keep nearly every document you receive through the course of the year that reflects either positively or negatively upon that employee's performance. Even notes jotted on scratch paper will be helpful.

3. Never give a numerical evaluation of an employee (see Figure 4.8) without supporting it with some narrative. The numbers alone have limited usefulness.

4. Go over your written evaluations with your supervisees to let them know how you rate their strengths and weaknesses. Find out if they feel your ratings are fair. If they do not, they are less likely to try to improve their performance.

5. Keep the performance appraisal review focused on the particular supervisee's performance. Show that you care about your supervisee's career by providing quality time during the review.

6. When critiquing a supervisee's performance, make sure you reinforce quality performance and good work habits with praise. Be careful not to focus only on areas where improvement is necessary.

7. Whenever possible, try to base your judgments on observable behavior, not on opinions or general impressions. Even when rating personality or character traits, try to recall specific examples of such traits in actual practice on the job.

8. Be specific and constructive in your criticism. Don't just tell someone she or he is not doing well in some area. Explain how improvement can be made. Provide examples.

9. Critique the behavior, not the employee. Keep the discussion on a professional level, not personal. Try to avoid confrontation but not at the expense of honest evaluation.

10. Be fair but do not be afraid to give honest criticism. Most employees want to know where they stand and how they can improve.

11. Follow up each performance review with periodic, informal progress reports or "minireviews." Keep up a continuing exchange so that you will both spot problems before they become serious. Nothing in the performance appraisal should come as a surprise to your supervisee. Rather, it should be an affirmation of the many interactions you have had throughout the course of the year. If either you or the supervisee so

desires, it may be desirable to have several performance evaluations throughout the course of the year.

12. Make an honest effort to achieve some range in your distribution of evaluation scores and comments. Sometimes it helps mentally to rank order all supervisees from strongest performer to weakest. It is important to review all supervisees before assigning final numerical evaluation scores to individuals to assure equity.

In summary, the performance appraisal process is one of the most sacred of management tasks. If done well, it has the potential to be a very powerful management and leadership tool. If done poorly, it will severely limit the effectiveness of the career center. Supervisors desiring to improve their performance appraisal process are encouraged to consult the following sources:

Baird, L. S., Beatty, R. W., & Schneier, C. E. (Eds.). (1982). *The Performance Appraisal Sourcebook*. Amherst, MA: Human Resources Development Press.

Brown, R. D. (1988). *Performance Appraisal as a Tool for Staff Development*. San Francisco: Jossey-Bass.

DeVries, D. L., Morrison, A. M., Shullman, S. L., & Gerlach, M. L. (1981). *Performance Appraisal on the Line*. New York: Wiley.

BUDGETING AND FUND-RAISING

The budgets of most university career centers are characterized by three things: (1) they are dominated by personnel salaries, (2) operating budgets are meager, and (3) increasingly, career centers are expected to secure a greater and greater portion of their total operating budget through shifting costs to employers or to other departments within the institution, fees for service, or external fund-raising.

Personnel Salaries

Like most student services, personnel salaries in career services comprise about 75 and 90 percent of total budget (*1991 CPC Career Planning and Placement Survey*). Typically, individual personnel salaries are governed by some form of human resources classification system that specifies salary ranges by grade and leaves little flexibility. Within the constraints of such a classification system, we strongly urge the adoption of some form of merit system with a direct and positive linkage to performance. Without such an incentive system, the largest portion of the career center budget (personnel salaries) is likely to be appropriated on a flat, across-the-board increase basis, which ultimately leads to inefficiency and marginal performance.

Operating Budget

The operating budget of most university career centers is approximately 10 to 15 percent of the total budget. In actual dollars most university centers that serve

10,000 undergraduates or more had operating budgets that ranged from $30,000 to $100,000 in 1991. In the entire nation only 17 institutions (presumably universities) with enrollments in excess of 10,000 had operating budgets of greater than $100,000 in 1991, according to the 1991 *CPC Career Planning and Placement Survey*. The trend in career center operating budgets in recent years has been disappointing:

- Increases have been minimal.
- Actual operating budgets have increased by 50 to 75 percent in the last ten years—barely keeping pace with inflation.
- There has been an expectation that operating budgets will be supplemented by the implementation of fees for service or by external fund-raising.

There is probably no "typical" operating budget, but the sample career center operating budget provided here is reflective of the major operating expenses incurred by most university career centers. For the sake of simplicity, this sample (Figure 4.9) is based on an annual total operating budget of $100,000. Column 3 indicates the amounts budgeted for each class of expense, and column 4 indicates the percentage of the total operating budget devoted to each particular class of expense. It should be noted that nearly 50 percent of the typical career center operating budget is devoted to four areas: office supplies, telephone and fax services, postage and mailing services, and printing and copying services.

Supplementing the Career Service Budget

Ask any entrepreneur what the key to success is, and you are likely to hear, "Using OPM" (other people's money). In recent years it has become necessary to supplement career center operating budgets in creative ways. Many university career centers spend twice what is officially budgeted on operating expenses. While such means of creative financing have enhanced the ability of career centers to provide service, they also demand that a significant portion of staff time be spent seeking alternative sources of support, and they carry with them certain obligations that can limit flexibility. Nevertheless, creative financing has become a necessary aspect of career center survival. Here are the most common ways that career centers supplement their budgets.

Advertising. One obvious way to supplement the career center operating budget is to solicit employers to advertise in office publications and manuals. Most university career center placement manuals are supported totally through advertising. Similarly, electronic message boards, career center bulletin boards, and career center newsletters are increasingly supported through advertising. At large universities, advertising support often accounts for up to $25,000 in additional operating funds, and the trend is likely to continue.

Shifting Operating Costs to Employers. Many career centers have made arrangements to shift the cost of telephone and fax services to employers through

Figure 4.9
Sample Career Services Operating Budget

1	2	3	4
OBJECT CLASS	DESCRIPTION	AMOUNT	PERCENT
201	Work Study and Wage Pay roll	3,000	3
301	Office Supplies	8,000	8
304	Catering and Food Supplies	1,500	1.5
309	Miscellaneous Supplies	2,000	2
310	Supplies and Materials for Resale	500	0.5
321	Telephone and Fax	8,000	8
322	Postage and Mailings	15,000	15
331	Conference Registrations	600	0.6
332	Group Meals	700	0.7
336	In State Travel	2,000	2
337	Out of State Travel	6,000	6
341	Publications	6,000	6
342	Subscriptions	2,000	2
360	Building Rentals	300	0.3
361	Equipment Rentals	400	0.4
371	Equipment Maintenance	7,000	7
372	Repair or Maintenance of Building	1,000	1
391	Honoraria or Consulting Fees	1,000	1
393	Professional Services	400	0.4
401	Unemployment Compensation	1,000	1
403	Tuition and Fees	1,500	1.5
407	Auxilliary Enterprise Charges	400	0.4
410	Freight Charges	300	0.3
411	Purchased Services	1,000	1
412	Photographic Services	200	0.2
414	Printing and copying	18,000	18
447	Advertising	1 500	1.5
452	Software	1,500	1.5
454	Memberships	500	0.5
455	Non Capital Equipment (under $1,000)	1,000	1
458	Promotional Printing	500	0.5
499	Other miscellaneous	200	0.2
710	Capital Equipment	5,000	5
715	Lease/Purchase Agreements	1,000	1
730	Video tapes/Films	1,000	1
		100,000	100%

the use of collect calls. Similarly, some career centers have made arrangements to utilize employer account numbers with Federal Express and other overnight delivery services so that mailing and shipping costs are billed directly to the employer. The cost of résumé books and copy service is also often borne by employers. Such cost-shifting measures may save the career center thousands of dollars in just a year's time.

Equipment Grants from Corporations. In an era of rapid technological change, many corporations find it easy to make substantial equipment grants to career centers. Among the most common types of equipment grants are fax machines, personal computers and related hardware and software, copy machines, phone equipment, audiovisual equipment, and so on. In some cases these grants are for new equipment, and in others they may be grants of used or obsolete equipment that is still serviceable. In either case equipment grants can significantly supplement career center operating budgets.

Shifting Operating Costs to Other Academic Departments. Another trend in most large universities is for individual operating units to be treated as individual profit centers. Thus, interdepartmental billing for services is becoming increasingly prevalent. Some career centers now routinely bill individual colleges and academic departments for such things as employer mailing lists, materials in support of career courses taught by career center staff for various academic units, postgraduation follow-up study placement reports, career counseling and assessment conducted for faculty and staff, and other services that go beyond the scope of the career center's mission.

Contracted Services. Various external vendors are prepared to install equipment (e.g., copy machines for student use) or provide services (e.g., computerized job-listing services or résumé distribution services and an array of other services) through the career center and then collect fees from employers or other third parties to cover costs and perhaps even pay the career center a royalty. While such arrangements carry with them considerable risk, they do represent a way to supplement meager operating budgets.

Corporate Sponsorships. An increasing number of college and university career centers have established corporate sponsorship or corporate associate programs. The essence of such programs is that corporations contribute an annual sum of several thousand dollars to the career center in return for public recognition in the form of having their corporation's name and logo appear prominently in the foyer of the career center on a bronze plaque. Corporate sponsorships can provide thousands of additional discretionary funds in support of the career center. Corporate sponsorships appear to work fairly well for large, prestigious engineering and business colleges but have enjoyed less success elsewhere. One disadvantage of the corporate sponsorship arrangement is a predictable expectation on the part of corporate sponsors that they receive certain scheduling, parking, and other favors as a quid pro quo.

While most career centers engage in these and other means of supplementing their operating budgets, such techniques are not without their disadvantages. Relying on external funds shifts a certain amount of control to those who provide the funds. Ethical dilemmas sometimes develop as contributors (usually employers) seek favors in return for contributions. Of perhaps more concern is the tendency to develop a dependence on "soft money" that may dry up in hard times, leaving the career center without the necessary operating budget to deliver expected services. Despite these disadvantages, career centers are likely to become increasingly dependent on creative financing in the future.

Fees for Service. Another way that career centers supplement their meager operating budgets is through user fees charged to student, alumni, employers, or the general public. Such fees usually take two forms: general fees or specific fees for specific services. Figure 4.10 provides a snapshot of current career center fee practices.

Figure 4.10
Office Fees

| | Percent of Respondents | | |
	1981	1987	1991
Student fees:			
General fee	10.1	6.3	6.4
Specific fee	31.3	34.9	33.0
Alumni fees:			
General fee	9.3	6.7	9.8
Specific fee	32.5	35.7	36.0
Employer fees:			
General fee	0.4	0.7	0.1
Specific fee	4.8	9.1	22.0
General public			
General fee	—	1.7	3.0
Specific fees	—	13.0	13.7

Source: 1991 Career Planning and Placement Survey (CPC, 1991b).

Two interesting fee trends are apparent from this figure. First, general fees are uncommon for any of the four user types, and there doesn't seem to be a trend toward increasing them. Second, about one-third of career centers charge students and alumni specific fees for specific services, and there is a clear trend to increase specific fees for services to employers. In their summary of fee data from the 1991 Survey, the College Placement Council (CPC, 1991) concluded: "The service for which both students and alumni were most often charged was for credentials. The next most common charges were for testing/assessment and vacancy bulletins. Employers were most often charged for participation in career days and fairs. The most common charge for the general public was for testing/assessment" (p. 29).

In general we are opposed to user fees for two reasons. First, we believe that quality career services are an integral part of an undergraduate education and as such should be available to all students free of charge. Second, fee collection is a costly, time-consuming activity that drains staff time away from the business of delivering career service. However, if financial exigencies dictate that some form of fee be charged, we regard fees for specific services to alumni and the general public as being far preferable to general fees or fees for undergraduates.

Fund-Raising. Beyond the budget supplementing techniques already suggested, some career centers have mounted capital fund-raising drives to support specific projects. We know of one career center that raised $400,000 to convert the basement of a classroom building into a state-of-the-art interview center. Others have written grant proposals to corporate foundations or governmental agencies for the establishment of career resource centers, interview training centers, and computerized guidance centers, as well as for the purchase of more mundane things like new typewriters, personal computers (PCs), or copy machines. Fund-raising of this type has never been easy for student service units because of an often held perception by central administration that such efforts siphon off funds that would otherwise go to academic units. While we don't wish to discourage the pursuit of external funding, the competition for such funds has intensified in recent years to the point that many college and university development offices will not allow student service units to engage in such efforts. Career center staff should develop a strong working relationship with the development office to enhance the possibilities for external funding.

A Separate Development Budget

Another budgeting strategy that some career centers have turned to is the establishment of a development budget. A development budget is simply a budget totally separate from the operating budget of the career center. Essentially all income is generated through grants and contributions from external sources (principally, corporate contributions). The development budget has several features that greatly enhance financial flexibility:

1. Resources can be transferred to the operating budget to supplement ongoing operations. Thus, the development budget provides a kind of safety net against unanticipated cost overruns.
2. Resources can be used to purchase certain enhancements like professional development and travel that may be restricted by university policy but that are important to the professional development of staff and greatly enhance the quality of career services.
3. The balance of the development budget carries over to successive years rather than reverting to the general fund of the university. Thus, one need not spend every dollar each fiscal year or lose it. This minimizes the kind of ''frenzied'' buying that sometimes occurs near the end of the fiscal year when it becomes apparent that there will be some balance left in the operating budget and encourages a more careful and considered approach to year-end spending.

While not all institutions will allow the establishment of a development budget or fund, the advantages of such a fund far outweigh the potential for abuse. In an era of severe fiscal constraint, the flexibility provided by a development budget can have an enormous positive impact on the quality of career services.

Budgeting Summary

One of the most important management prerogatives a career center director must have is the authority and flexibility to move funds from the personnel budget to the operating budget and from the development budget to the personnel budget or operating budget. Vice presidents typically like to control this resource flow.

If at all possible, an effort should be made to retain this prerogative. Budgetary authority and control are fundamental necessities to the successful management of the career center or any other enterprise.

ADVERTISING AND PUBLIC RELATIONS

The advertising and public relations needs of a career center vary greatly depending on the size and type of center and on the size and type of institution. In general the small, private, liberal arts institution has few advertising and public relations needs. Small residential colleges often enjoy both high-quality and high-frequency communication among faculty, staff, and students. Thus, knowledge of career center services and events is typically high, and student participation is encouraged and expected, with little need for special advertising and public relations initiatives. Similarly, technically oriented small colleges like Worcester Polytechnic Institute often achieve 100 percent career services registration rates. In short, small institutions may need little beyond an office brochure and a placement manual to advertise their services sufficiently.

Large universities served by one centralized career center, on the other hand, may have to invest considerable time, energy, and money in the establishment of an effective advertising and public relations program. We recommend that career center advertising begin with a core of basic items including the following:

1. A basic office brochure (see Figure 4.11 for an example)
2. A placement manual
3. A quality annual report
4. The use of campus mail, bulletin boards, and inexpensive posters and fliers to advertise and promote services
5. A strong liaison and two-way referral system between career center staff and all academic departments and other student services units
6. Faculty announcement of events and services

Beyond these core methods of advertising, there is no limit to the resources and creativity that may be applied to the task of promoting career services. Here are examples of techniques used on various campuses around the nation.

College or University Newspaper. Most colleges and nearly all universities have daily newspapers, which are generally regarded as one of the most effective ways to communicate with students. There are a number of ways that student newspapers can be used effectively to promote career services. First, the topic of career development and placement is always newsworthy. A good relationship with the editor and student reporters can lead to lots of free news coverage of career center events. Some career centers have even worked out deals with their daily newspaper to write regular columns on career-related topics—a sort of Dear Abby of careers. Second, advertising in the campus newspaper is an effective way to communicate

Figure 4.11
Career-Planning Steps

Career-Planning Steps

Freshman Year

Increase Self-Awareness

—meet with a CDPS counselor to help identify your interests,
  values, and abilities
—test your interests through courses, volunteer jobs, student
  activities, and summer work
—interview friends and family about the nature of their jobs
—identify majors that relate to your abilities and interests

Sophomore Year

Explore Career Alternatives

—obtain information about occupations
—begin to identify what is important to you in a job
—attend meetings of student professional organizations
—target electives that will make you more employable
—explore relevant work experiences such as internships,
  externships, co-op education, and summer jobs

Junior Year

Link Self-Knowledge With Occupational Information

—relate your values, interests, and abilities to career fields
—interview people in areas that interest you about the nature
  of their jobs
—develop relationships with faculty and professionals
—continue increasing your skills through meaningful
  activities and work
—begin learning about job-search strategies

Senior Year

Career Implementation

—if feasible, do an internship in your field to gain relevant
  experience
—come to CDPS early fall semester to sharpen job-search
  skills and take advantage of on-campus recruiting
—join a career or job-search skills group
—talk with professionals in your field about job-search
  techniques and opportunities

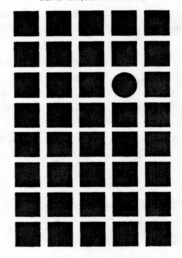

**CAREER DEVELOPMENT
AND PLACEMENT SERVICES**

CAREER-PLANNING ASSISTANCE
FOR ALL STUDENTS AND ALUMNI
INCLUDING COUNSELING,
WRITTEN INFORMATION,
OUTREACH PROGRAMS,
SEMINARS, AND COURSES

THE PENNSYLVANIA STATE UNIVERSITY
413 BOUCKE BUILDING
UNIVERSITY PARK, PA 16802
(814) 865-2377

PENNSTATE

with the university community. While this can be expensive, it does allow the career center totally to control the content of the communication, which is sometimes desirable. Third, some college newspapers regard the printing of career center press releases as a public service. Though not always possible, this is a very inexpensive and effective way to reach students. Fourth, running announcements of key workshops, seminars, and other programs in the want ad section of the student newspaper can be effective. Finally, we are aware of several career centers at large universities that publish a monthly tabloid-style insert to their daily student newspapers supported totally by employer advertisements. These 8- to 12-page inserts can convey a tremendous amount of useful career center information and are often saved by students for reference throughout the semester.

Electronic Message Boards. Many colleges and universities now have rather elaborate electronic mail systems or other computer networking capabilities that allow the career center to communicate to students electronically either via their own PCs plugged into the campus network or via terminals located in labs around the campus.

Campus Radio and TV Stations. Most colleges and universities own and operate radio stations. Often such stations are willing to make public service announcements that can be quite effective in promoting services. Radio and TV spots typically take two forms: general services announcements—promoting the services of the office generally and providing information about location, hours of operation, and the like—and advertisements of specific events—promoting specific events like a career day or seminar or workshop.

Commercial Radio and TV Stations. The placing of TV and radio spot advertisements on key stations to which students listen a great deal can be effective, but such ads are also quite expensive.

Direct Mail. Some career centers promote their services by direct mail. One particularly effective way of promoting placement services is to target all students classified as seniors and time the promotional mailing to arrive at their summer address about one week before the start of fall semester. This approach not only reaches students but often also reaches the parents, who sometimes have more interest in placement services than the students.

Another direct mail technique involves identifying special populations by doing a computer sort of all those registered on the particular variables of interest. For example, a mailing could be made to all disabled seniors, offering a workshop on job search strategies for the disabled. Targeted, direct mail promotional efforts of this sort can be both effective and efficient.

Dial-Access Telephone. More and more campuses have dial-access information systems. While we've had direct experience with such systems, we have found that the most often accessed program is usually the weather report!

Information Booths. Staffing a career center information booth at various career fairs, health fairs, housing fairs, activities fairs, and other such campus events is an inexpensive and interactive way of promoting career services to students. Such booths provide a particularly useful means of distributing office brochures and other printed promotional materials.

Public Address Announcements at Athletic Events. At many institutions public service announcements can be made over the public address system at basketball, football, and other major athletic events. One such announcement at a key game may reach thousands of students.

Giveaways. Some career centers have engaged in giving away novelty items with the name, address, and phone number of the career center prominently displayed. One interesting novelty item we've seen recently was a combination beer bottle opener/key chain with the career center name and phone number on it, together with the following slogan: "Your Future Starts Here." In general we're skeptical about the cost/benefit ratio of such promotional techniques.

MANAGEMENT INFORMATION SYSTEMS

The term *management information system* is simply a hi-tech term for those data storage and retrieval systems that any administrator uses to support the decision-making process. Many such systems are very low-tech. For example, some administrators keep a file on each of their staff members, and they put any note, report, letter of congratulations, project, or anything else related to that particular employee in that file throughout the course of the year. Such an employee file is a management information system. It provides documentation upon which personnel decisions are based. Similarly, all colleges and universities have a computerized accounting system that provides the information on which budgetary decisions are made. Indeed, all the formative and summative evaluation techniques described in Chapter 3 are components of a management information system. Advisory board input, outreach program evaluation forms, recruiter checkout forms, suggestions received through the suggestion box, spot evaluations, and written or verbal complaints or compliments are all formative evaluation techniques that are part of the management information system. Similarly, summative evaluation techniques, like placement and counselor registration systems, postgraduation follow-up surveys, and random, in-depth surveys of client satisfaction, are also part of the management information system. The real key to the effectiveness of such a system is how quickly and accurately necessary information can be brought together in a meaningful way to support the decision-making process. Some software packages on the market are specifically designed to support the career center, for example, UNICORE (Marcus, 1986) and Placement Data Manager (Roka, 1987), but most are piecemeal systems designed more to facilitate the delivery of service than to provide an integrated decision support system. It seems likely that the decade of the nineties will see the development of true computerized management information systems designed specifically for career centers. At present most career centers are hobbling along with some combination of piecemeal, computerized database systems, traditional information storage systems like filing cabinet and shoe boxes, and whatever knowledge and information key staff members can dredge from memory. With few exceptions, the era of computerized management information systems for the career center still lies ahead.

LAWS AND POLICIES AFFECTING CAREER CENTERS

While there are several legal issues that merit attention, the fact is that a very small number of legal actions are taken related to college and university career centers each year throughout the nation. Perhaps the best measure of how seldom legal actions are taken within the profession is the low premiums charged to those career center staff who carry professional liability insurance. Therefore, while it is prudent to be knowledgeable about legal issues, one should recognize that the legal risks in the career services profession are minimal.

Those legal issues that arise most frequently fall into the following five categories:

Affirmative action issues
Issues surrounding EEO and the employment process
Issues related to reference letters and checks
Responsibilities under the Americans with Disability Act
Issues related to the Buckley Amendment

As a service to their members, the College Placement Council publishes a series of legal monographs on these five topics as follows:

CPC. (1990a). *Affirmative Action Today*. Bethlehem, PA; Author.

CPC. (1990b). *EEO and the Employment Process*. Bethlehem, PA: Author.

CPC. (1988a). *A New Dilemma: Reference Letters and Checks*. Bethlehem, PA. Author.

CPC. (1991a). *New Responsibilities Under the ADA*. Bethlehem, PA: Author.

CPC. (1988b). *Understanding the Buckley Amendment*. Bethlehem, PA: Author.

In addition, the College Placement Council publishes timely and frequent legal briefs in its twice-monthly newsletter, *Spotlight*, and also conducts occasional teleconferences and telebriefings on legal issues. Member institutions of the College Placement Council may also call upon CPC's legal counsel staff for assistance and advice on legal issues as they arise. Membership in CPC is worth this service alone! Finally, staff should never be hesitant to obtain the opinions and advice of their own college or university's legal counsel, though our experience has shown that CPC is generally a far better source of legal advice regarding employment- and placement-related legal issues.

ETHICAL ISSUES

There are three chief reference documents that guide the ethical behavior of career center professionals. The first two present guidelines for those engaged principally in the counseling and assessment aspects of the profession. *Ethical Standards of the American Association for Counseling and Development (1988)* provides standards for career counseling practice while *Standards for Educational and Psychological Testing (1985)* provides standards for the use of tests and other assessment devices. Both these documents are too large to include here, but copies should be on file in the professional library of every career center. Most professional counselors receive exposure to these standards as a part of their formal counselor training, and many will have copies of the standards in their personal professional files.

The other important ethical reference document, which was recently revised by the College Placement Council, is entitled *Principles for Professional Conduct for Career Services and Employment Professionals (1990c).* Developed by the 1990-1991 Board of Governors of the College Placement Council as a "framework within which the career planning, placement, and recruitment processes should function," this booklet offers ethical guidelines for the interactions among colleges and universities, employers, and students. A copy of the text of this booklet, which applies specifically to career services professionals, appears in Appendix 4.2. In addition to having copies of the document on hand for ready reference, CPC members may request an advisory opinion regarding an interpretation of the principles at any time. This is yet another valuable service available to members of CPC for the price of membership.

SUMMARY

As we pointed out in the introduction to this chapter, the management of a career center is similar to that of managing any other complex service agency. Perhaps the most intriguing and challenging aspect of career center management is bridging the differences that exist between the business and educational/counseling cultures that the career center straddles. Within this context we have tried to provide practical tools that practitioners can employ to increase the organizational effectiveness of the career center. We have advocated the importance and utility of establishing and effectively communicating a management philosophy, described the personnel needs of the career center, and provided sample position descriptions. We have examined probable organizational structures and outlined the strengths and weaknesses of each. We have addressed some supervisory issues unique to the career center and provided practical suggestions to enhance the performance appraisal process. We have dealt, in turn, with the issues of budgeting and fundraising, advertising and public relations, and management information systems. Finally, we have addressed some of the laws and policies that affect the career center and provided references that address the major ethical issues confronting the profession. Throughout we have attempted to present management techniques and strategies that are proven and practical yet tempered with a thoughtful basis in career development and management theory. For the career center practitioner who seeks "quick and dirty" solutions we close with ten trite but true secrets to better career services management:

1. If you haven't already done so, establish an intake counseling function staffed on a rotational basis by professional staff to perform the triage function. This will eliminate student lines and waiting and enhance the probability that students will receive the appropriate career service in the shortest possible time.

2. Use technology to improve the quality of career services. Don't let technology dictate office policies and procedures. Too often career centers change what were sensible, meaningful procedures because those procedures can't be done conveniently on existing software or hardware. Don't be seduced by technology, which is often a cheap and inferior solution to human service problems.

3. If at all possible, include and involve clerical staff in weekly or biweekly staff meetings together with professional staff. Clerical staff are on the front line. They know what works and what doesn't, and they have a strong, vested interest in solving office problems. Their involvement in the decision-making process will go a long way toward assuring the successful delivery of high-quality career services.

4. Train academic advisers (working in academic departments) to make appropriate direct referrals to career counselors in the career center. Having trained surrogates will multiply your effectiveness, and it will save ping-ponging students all over campus, reduce the number of students you must see through intake, and increase the total number of students you will be able to serve.

5. If at all possible, secure faculty endorsement of a career decision-making course that carries credit and have that course cross-listed in all colleges. The academy has socialized students to believe that anything worth doing must carry credit. Credit is the academy's way of saying, "It's important."

6. Cultivate a "can do" bias for action among your staff. Many counseling agencies seem to cultivate a "we're overworked and ain't it awful" attitude. Virtually all of the best-run organizations have a bias for action (Peters & Waterman, 1984).

7. Don't let poorly performing staff dominate your management agenda. Surgically remove clerical or professional staff who do not perform, and do it as quickly, courteously, and graciously as possible within the constraints of university policy.

8. As a manager, devote most of your time to eliminating the obstacles that stand in the way of your staff's productivity and professional development. Use your relationship with those administrators above you to liberate your staff from bureaucratic obstacles and the frustrations that accompany them.

9. Produce a detailed office procedures guide so that all staff will know how routine business is conducted within the office. Don't be afraid to let your people know "how the office works." Of course, your office management philosophy will be included in this guide.

10. Cultivate an attitude among your staff that "you don't have to be sick to get better." Constant and continuous improvement must become a way of life in the career center. There has never been a perfect employee, product, or service. There is no status quo. As an organization, you're either improving or you're falling behind.

REFERENCES

American Association for Counseling and Development. (1988). *Ethical standards of the American Association for Counseling and Development*. Alexandria, VA: Author.

American Educational Research Association. American Psychological Association and National Council on Measurement in Education. (1985). *Standards for educational and psychological testing*. Washington, DC: American Psychological Association.

Babbush, H. E., Hawley, Wade W., & Zeran, Jack. (1986). The best of both worlds. *Journal of Career Planning and Employment, XLVII*, 48–53.

Baird, L. S., Beatty, R. W., & Schneier, C. E. (Eds.). (1982). *The performance appraisal sourcebook*. Amherst, MA: Human Resources Development Press.

Brown, R. D. (1988). *Performance appraisal as a tool for staff development*. San Francisco: Jossey-Bass.

College Placement Council. (1988a) *A new dilemma: Reference letters and checks.* Bethlehem, PA: Author.

College Placement Council. (1988b). *Understanding the Buckley amendment.* Bethlehem, PA: Author.

College Placement Council. (1990a). *Affirmative action today.* Bethlehem, PA: Author.

College Placement Council. (1990b). *EEO and the employment process.* Bethlehem, PA: Author.

College Placement Council. (1990c). *Principles for professional conduct for career services and employment professionals.* Bethlehem, PA: Author.

College Placement Council. (1991a). *New responsibilities under the ADA.* Bethlehem, PA: Author.

College Placement Council. (1991b). *1991 career planning and placement survey.* Bethlehem, PA: Author.

Crosby, P. (1984). *Quality without tears: The art of hassle-free management.* New York: McGraw-Hill.

Deming, W. E. (1982). *Out of the crisis.* Cambridge, MA: Productivity Press.

DeVries, D. L., Morrison, A. M., Shullman, S. L., & Gerlach, M. L. (1981). *Performance appraisal on the line.* New York: Wiley.

Hersey, P., & Blanchard, K. H. (1977). *Management of organizational behavior: Utilizing human resources.* Englewood Cliffs, NJ: Prentice-Hall.

Imai, M. (1986). *The key to Japan's competitive success.* Cambridge, MA: Productivity Press.

Juran, J. M. (1988). *Juran on planning for quality.* Cambridge, MA: Productivity Press.

Kuh, G. D. (1985). What is extraordinary about ordinary student affairs organizations. *NASPA Journal, 23*(2), 31–43.

Marcus, J. (1986). *UNICORE (Universal College Recruiting System)* [Software package]. Lakewood, CO: UNICORE.

Ouchi, W. (1981). *Theory Z.* Reading, MA: Addison-Wesley.

Peters, T. J. (1987). *Thriving on chaos: Handbook for a managerial revolution.* New York: Knopf.

Peters, T. J., & Austin, N. (1985). *A passion for excellence: The leadership difference.* New York: Random House.

Peters, T. J., & Waterman, R. H. (1984). *In search of excellence.* New York: Warner Books.

Roka, E. (1987). *Placement Data Manager*[Software package]. Needham, MA: Roka Data Systems.

Samson, G. E., Graue, M. E., Weisntein, T., & Walberg, H. J. (1984). Academic and occupational performance: A quantitative synthesis. *American Educational Research Journal, 21*, 311–321.

Shingleton, J. D., & Fitzpatrick E. B. (1985). *Dynamics of placement.* Bethlehem, PA: College Placement Council Foundation.

Townsend, R. (1970). *Up the organization.* New York: Knopf.

Vaill, P. B. (1989). *Managing as a performing art: New ideas for a world of chaotic change.* San Francisco: Jossey-Bass.

Appendix 4.1
Career Services Position Descriptions

Title of Position: Associate Director for Placement

Classification: Professional

Department: Career Services

Function of Position:

Responsible to the director, Career Services for the direction and management of Employer Relations and Placement Services, for the development and implementation of Management Information Systems, and for the development, coordination and evaluation of these functions.

Principal Duties and Responsibilities:

1. Responsible for directly supervising and evaluating assigned professional and clerical staff in Placement Services and Information Systems.

2. Responsible for the direction and management of all Career Services including the On-Campus Recruiting Program, Educational Career Services Office, Alumni Career Services Office, and the Interview Center.

3. Responsible for the development and maintenance of a program of effective employer-Career Services relations.

4. Responsible for ensuring adherence to appropriate government regulations and to the professional practices and standards as prescribed by the College Placement Council.

5. Responsible for the development and implementation of Management and Placement Information Systems for Career Services.

6. Assist with the establishment of the annual goals and objectives of Career Services.

7. Research and provide recommendations on new Career Services programs and services and act as project leader in the implementation of programs.

8. Responsible for ensuring that progress is made toward meeting annual goals and objectives for assigned areas of responsibility. Prepare and disseminate periodic activity reports.

9. Responsible for administering allocated budget. Make effective recommendations for program expenditures and ensure that budgetary goals and targets are maintained.

10. Develop and deliver invited presentations to members of professional guidance and counseling organizations.

11. When qualified, teach formal courses in career development.

12. Assist other university offices with the collection and interpretation of data for research purposes on associate degree students and job market outlook.

13. Provide direct assistance or referral for students seeking help with career decision/career implementation issues.

14. Serve as a liaison to at least one college or other major administrative unit within the university.

15. Serve on university committees as assigned.

16. In the absence of the director, assume assigned responsibilities.

17. Perform other duties as assigned.

Supervision:

Duties and responsibilities are performed under general direction and by interpreting university policy with regard to general objectives. Thorough knowledge of university policies and procedures is required in their application to cases not previously covered. Work is performed independently toward general results and requires devising new methods of modifying or developing standard procedure to meet new conditions. Problems are rarely referred.

Minimum Qualifications:

A master's degree in counselor education, higher education, industrial psychology, business administration, or related area plus a minimum of five years effective administrative experience in higher education, career services, and related areas.

Title of Position: Associate Director for Counseling and Programming

Classification: Professional

Department: Career Services

Function of Position:

Responsible to the director, Career Services for the direction and management of Career Counseling and Programming Services.

Principal Duties and Responsibilities:

1. Supervise and evaluate assigned professional and clerical staff in counseling and programming services.

2. Direct and manage all Career Services counseling and programming services including intake counseling, individual and group counseling, computerized counseling, assessment, the Career Information Center, seminars, workshops, outreach programs, experiential educational programs, nontechnical programming, and career courses for credit.

3. Assist with the establishment of the annual goals and objectives for Career Services.

4. Research and provide recommendations on new Career Services counseling and programming services. Act as project leader in the implementation of these programs, when appropriate.

5. Ensure that progress is made toward meeting annual goals and objectives for assigned areas of responsibility. Prepare and disseminate periodic activity reports.

6. Develop and deliver invited presentations to members of professional guidance and counseling organizations.

7. Supervise doctoral dissertations and clinical experiences for doctoral interns.

8. Provide assistance or referral for students seeking help with career decision/career implementation issues.

9. Serve on university committees as assigned.

10. Assume assigned responsibilities, in the absence of the director.

11. Prepare and disseminate semester and annual reports on Career Services activities.

12. Serve as the key liaison between Career Services and at least one academic college within the university.

13. Participate in all Career Services rotating staff schedules, for example, recruiter duty, intake, seminar series, and so on.

14. Perform other duties as assigned.

Supervision:

Duties and responsibilities are performed under general direction and by interpreting university policy with regard to general objectives. Thorough knowledge of university policies and procedures is required in their application to cases not previously covered. Work is performed independently toward achieving general results and requires devising new methods of modifying or developing standard procedures to meet new conditions. Problems are rarely referred.

Minimum Qualifications:

Doctorate (or equivalent) in counseling or clinical psychology with license or licensable in the state of Pennsylvania plus five to seven years effective administrative/supervisory experience in career counseling and programming.

Title of Position: Assistant Director for Career Counseling

Classification: Professional

Department: Career Services

Function of Position:

Responsible to the associate director for Counseling and Programming for the operations related to the delivery of career counseling and planning services to students.

Principal Duties and Responsibilities:

1. Responsible with the associate director for Counseling and Programming for the planning and management of all career counseling and career planning services (includes individual and group counseling programs).

2. Responsible for the in-service training of full-time staff, graduate assistants, and part-time staff participating in the counseling functions of Career Services.

3. Conduct career counseling research for the purpose of publishing said research.

4. Responsible for the supervision and evaluation of all junior professional staff, as well as graduate assistants, assigned to counseling roles.

5. Responsible, together with the associate director for Counseling and Programming, for developing and implementing a system of record keeping and evaluative procedures to be used with the counseling services offered by Career Services.

6. Responsible for the selection and procurement of psychometric instruments used in connection with the counseling services.

7. Provide professional assistance and/or consultation to any student who requests help with planning or implementing his or her life/career direction.

8. Provide professional referral services for any student requiring extended treatment for social, personal adjustment, or psychiatric problems.

9. Assist in the delivery of career education and outreach programs.

10. Serve as consultant to faculty, staff, and appropriate student organizations, providing information about available career development and placement services and the related needs of students.

11. Responsible for ensuring adherence to the professional practices and standards for counselors as prescribed by the Code of Ethics.

12. Assist with the establishment of the annual goals and objectives of Career Services.

13. Assist in the selection of professionals hired as counselors.

14. Responsible for hiring graduate assistants assigned to counseling roles.

15. Perform other duties as assigned.

Supervision:

Duties and responsibilities are performed under general direction and by interpreting university policy with regard to general objectives. Thorough knowledge of university policies and procedures is required in their application to cases not previously covered. Work is performed independently toward general results and requires devising new methods of modifying or developing standard procedures to meet new conditions. Problems are rarely referred.

Minimum Qualifications:

Doctrate in counseling psychology or equivalent required (with license or licensable in the state of Pennsylvania) plus a minimum of three years of effective experience in career counseling of college students and three years of effective counselor supervision (or equivalent). Administrative experience in higher education highly desirable.

Title of Position: Assistant Director for Career Programming

Classification: Professional

Department: Career Services

Function of Position:

Responsible to the associate director, Career Services for developing, organizing, and implementing career development courses, programs, and services, for initiating and coordinating job placement services for nontechnical majors, and for providing staff liaison to assigned colleges and various offices of the university.

Principal Duties and Responsibilities:

1. Develop, coordinate, and instruct academic courses related to career development for various colleges. Work with associate deans and faculty in the approval process.

2. Develop, organize, and provide innovative career education programs such as seminars and career days for various student and nonstudent groups throughout the commonwealth.

3. Evaluate career development programs and services, including the instruction. Responsible for periodic reports, publications, and presentations regarding programming efforts.

4. Coordinate career development services to nontechnical students. Supervise graduate assistants providing direct services to students.

5. Develop, coordinate, and implement experiential career education programs such as internships.

6. Supervise graduate interns, faculty aides, and so on involved in career development services.

7. Represent Career Services at various meetings. Serve as liaison with various colleges and administrative units.

8. Assist in the development of annual goals and objectives for Career Services.

9. Assist in the development of professional and clerical staff as it relates to career programming.

10. Provide professional assistance and/or consultation to any student who requests help in planning or implementing life/career direction.

11. Provide professional referral services to any student requiring extended treatment for social, personal adjustment, or psychiatric problems.

12. Perform other duties as assigned.

Supervision:

Duties and responsibilities are performed under general direction and through the interpretation of university policy based on general objectives. Thorough knowledge of university policies and procedures is required in their application to cases not previously covered. Work is performed independently toward general results and requires the ability to devise new methods or modify existing procedures to meet new conditions. Problems are rarely referred.

Minimum Qualifications:

Master's degree (or equivalent) in a counseling-related discipline with a minimum of three years of effective experience.

Title of Position: Assistant Director for Career Information Systems

Classification: Professional

Department: Career Services

Function of Position:

Responsible to the associate director for providing career and manpower information systems.

Principal Duties and Responsibilities:

1. Responsible for conducting universitywide follow-up studies of the graduates each term. Prepare written and statistical findings.

2. Responsible for the management and ongoing development of the Career Information Center.

3. Responsible for the development and implementation of the universitywide career information delivery systems. Periodically review and validate existing career information resources; develop additional printed audio and visual resources when void exists in current resources.

4. Coordinate Career Services career information efforts with those personnel, offices, and services that have an interest in career and manpower planning and can benefit from having accurate, up-to-date, and pertinent career information available.

5. Establish and maintain contact with national, regional, state, and local agencies responsible for the development and dissemination of manpower information. Review and report appropriate data to university community on a periodic basis.

6. When qualified, occasionally teach formal courses in career development.

7. Conduct studies to determine student reaction and evaluation of career information materials and related delivery systems.

8. Manage that portion of the Career Services budget allocated to career information delivery.

9. Serve as consultant to academic departments, campus agencies, and other interested professionals in the area of career information dissemination.

10. Identify potential outside funding sources to support career development services. When appropriate, develop and submit proposals for funding.

11. Supervise and evaluate support staff necessary to carry out the above described activities.

12. Perform other duties as assigned.

Supervision:

Duties and responsibilities are performed under general direction and by interpreting university policy with regard to general objectives. Thorough knowledge of university policies and procedures is required in their application to cases not previously covered. Work is performed independently toward general results and requires devising new methods of modifying or developing standard procedures to meet new conditions. Problems are rarely referred.

Minimum Qualifications:

A master's degree (or equivalent) in economics, counselor education, industrial psychology, higher education administration, vocational education, or related area, plus minimum of three years of effective experience in manpower planning, information delivery systems, or career information.

Title of Position: Assistant Director, Education Career Services and Alumni Career Services

Classification: Professional

Department: Career Services

Function of Position:

Responsible to the associate director, Placement Services for the management and supervision of Education Career Services and Alumni Career Services and for liaison to the College of Education and the Alumni Association.

Principal Duties and Responsibilities:

Responsible for the Management and Operation of the Education Career Services Office.

1. Maintain liaison with academic departments and administrative offices of the College of Education in matters pertaining to the mission of Career Development and Placement Services.

2. Establish and periodically review procedures used to carry out the functions of this office.

3. Ensure confidentiality of records and adherence to federal laws governing rights of privacy.

4. Provide advice and assistance to students and alumni seeking employment in the field of education, particularly those interested in the teaching profession.

5. Responsible with the associate director for the selection, training, supervision, and evaluation of clerical and wage payroll employees assigned to the Education Placement Credentials Office.

6. When qualified and as the need arises, teach formal courses in career development for College of Education students.

7. Responsible for developing a broad employer-recruiter base for the College of Education graduates.

8. Coordinate and supervise on-campus educational recruitment activities, including coordination of the annual Education Career Day Program.

9. Plan, develop, and implement career development and outreach programming for students interested in the education field or related career areas.

10. Inform students, alumni, and employers of services available through the Education Career Services Office.

11. Supervise the collection of fees for educational credentials; ensure the proper accounting procedures for all transactions.

12. Prepare and submit reports annually to the Pennsylvania Department of Education on teacher supply and demand.

13. Responsible for providing the associate director with periodic reports on the operation of the Education Career Services Office.

14. Supervise the publication of the weekly education vacancy listing.

15. Perform other duties as assigned.

Responsible for the Management and Operation of the Alumni Career Service Office:

1. Coordinate career services to alumni with the Alumni Association and Career Services staff.

2. Represent ACS to employers and alumni through correspondence and personal conferences.

3. Responsible with the associate director for the selection, training, supervision, and evaluation of clerical and wage payroll employees assigned to the Alumni Career Services Office.

4. Solicit employer and alumni participation in ACS through correspondence and brochures and by telephone.

5. Advise alumni on résumé and cover letter writing, job search strategies, and the interview process.

6. Collect and submit data regularly in reports on ACS operations.

7. Supervise the collection, accounting, and deposit of ACS funds through fee structure.

8. Establish and oversee practices for handling ACS confidential records in accordance with federal guidelines.

9. Monitor procedures and respond to requests for reciprocal services requested by university alumni and alums of other institutions.

10. Perform other duties as assigned.

Supervision:

Duties and responsibilities are performed under general direction and by interpreting university policy with regard to general objectives. Thorough knowledge of university policies and procedures is required in their application to cases not previously covered. Work is performed independently toward general results and requires devising new methods of modifying or developing standard procedures to meet new conditions. Problems are rarely referred.

Minimum Qualifications:

Requires master's degree, or equivalent in education with teaching certification and three years of effective teaching experience plus three to five years of administrative experience in higher education. Eligibility for affiliate rank in the College of Education is highly desirable.

Title of Position: Coordinator, Experiential Education

Classification: Professional

Department: Career Services

Function of Position:

Responsible to the assistant director for Programming, Career Services, for developing, organizing, and implementing experiential education opportunities, programs, and services and for providing information and resources about such experiential education opportunities to Career Services staff, academic colleges, and various offices of the university.

Principal Duties and Responsibilities:

1. Develop, organize, and provide internship, externship, cooperative education, volunteer, and summer job opportunities; seek out new opportunities for students and maintain resources in the Career Information Center.

2. Develop, coordinate, and provide educational programs such as seminars, workshops, and handouts on the process by which students obtain experiential education opportunities.

3. Maintain contact with colleges, departments, and offices on internship offerings, policies, and procedures. Act as a liaison and resource person to such groups as needed.

4. Provide professional assistance and/or consultation to any student who requests help with planning or implementing experiential education opportunities.

5. Serve on university committees as assigned.

6. Develop, coordinate, and provide externship opportunities for students in nontechnical colleges. Work in consultation with the Alumni Association, the college assistant deans, and the college Advising Centers.

7. Assist the assistant director with general programming functions and responsibilities.

8. Assist in the development of annual goals and objectives for Career Services.

9. Provide professional referral services for any student requiring extended treatment for social, personal adjustment, or psychiatric problems.

10. Perform other duties as assigned.

Supervision:

Duties are performed under general direction, and the employee plans and arranges own work, which is directed toward an established objective. Employee determines action to be taken, handling all but unusual cases. Knowledge of established policy, procedures, and practices is required.

Minimum Qualifications:

Bachelor's degree with one to two years of effective programming and administrative experience in a college or university setting.

Title of Description: Office Information Specialist

Classification: Professional

Department: Career Services

Function of Position:

Responsible to the associate director for conducting analyses of data-processing problems, determining detailed requirements to solve problems, formulating logical statements of systems problems and implementing and maintaining appropriate computer systems to satisfy desired end results within Career Services. Serve as an applications consultant to the entire (Career Development and Placement Services) staff in developing, modifying, and testing computer programs and in training of staff in the use of those programs.

Principal Duties and Responsibilities:

1. Maintain a comprehensive understanding of the workings of career development and placement services units and an overall understanding of other units of Student Services including Career Services activities within the Commonwealth Educational System through active but limited participation in the following:

- Provide educational and occupational information to students when appropriate.
- Counsel students in a career intake facility on a rotational basis.
- Conduct workshops on résumé and cover letter preparation and interview skills on a rotational basis.
- Participate in recruiter orientation on a rotational basis.
- Serve as a liaison to students, faculty, and administrators in the College of Science.
- Support computerized assessment tools.

2. Conduct studies of application problems, analyze the problems, and develop solutions utilizing systems analysis techniques.

3. Develop problem definitions, prepare flowcharts, design input and output forms, define input and output data elements.

4. Perform feasibility studies and investigations of systems equipment and system techniques to gather data necessary to support system design recommendations.

5. Develop, modify, test, and document computer programs.

6. Test, evaluate, install, and maintain commercially available software packages.

7. Train clerical, professional, and administrative staff in the use of microcomputer and mainframe software and systems. Design presentations for applicability to targeted audiences. Conduct training sessions for other Student Services units as time permits.

8. Maintain currency in new developments in data-processing hardware as appropriate and relevant.

9. Make purchase recommendations for microcomputer hardware and software.

10. Maintain thorough familiarity with databases, systems, and procedures of Management Services and the Center for Academic Computing, as well as microcomputer hardware and software applicable to local processing.

11. Perform operational audits of installed systems and make systems adjustments to increase system effectiveness.

12. Coordinate service/maintenance agreements with appropriate vendors of computer hardware and software utilized by Career Services.

13. Keep abreast of new developments in the university's information resources and services through the use of all available educational sources.

14. Maintain a working knowledge of computer systems, languages and application software such as VM/CMS, SAS, ISIS, PL/1, ROSCOE, and NATURAL.

15. Serve as a statistical consultant to staff on research projects.

16. Serve as Area Security Representative for Career Services; authorize access requests to Administrative Computer System; attend meetings convened by Management Services Security Office.

17. Serve as consultant to other Student Services units as time permits.

18. Attend professional conferences.

19. Perform other duties as assigned.

Supervision:

Duties are performed under general direction, and the employee plans and arranges own work, which is directed toward established objectives. Employee determines action to be taken, handling all but unusual cases. Knowledge of established policy, procedure, and practice is required.

Minimum Qualifications:

A bachelor's degree (or equivalent) with an emphasis on basic computer systems and one to two years of effective experience in computer programming and analysis is required. A knowledge of PL/1, VM/CMS, Interact, AIS, basic statistical packages, microcomputer systems, and database packages is required. Knowledge and experience of the operation of a large multicampus university career development and placement service are highly desirable.

Appendix 4.2
Principles for Professional Conduct for Career Services and Employment Professionals

1. Career services professionals, without imposing personal values or biases, shall assist individuals in developing a career plan or making a career decision.

2. Career services professionals shall know the career services field and the educational institution and students they represent and shall have appropriate counseling skills.

3. Career services professionals shall provide students with information on a range of career opportunities and types of employing organizations. They shall inform students of the means and resources to gain access to information that may influence their decisions about an employing organization. Career services professionals shall also provide employing organizations with accurate information about the educational institution and its students and about the recruitment policies of the career services office.

4. Career services professionals shall provide generally comparable services to all employers, regardless of whether the employers contribute services, gifts, or financial support to the educational institution or office and regardless of the level of such support.

5. Career services professionals shall establish reasonable and fair guidelines for access to services by employers. When guidelines permit access to organizations recruiting on behalf of the employer and to international employers, the following principles shall apply:

   a. Organizations providing recruiting services for a fee shall be required to inform career services of the specific employer they represent and the specific jobs for which they are recruiting and shall permit verification of the information. Students shall be informed of any fees for service.

   b. Employers recruiting for work outside the United States are expected to adhere to the EEO policy of the career services office. They shall advise the career services office and the students of the realities of working in any country and of any cultural and foreign law differences.

6. Career services professionals shall maintain EEO compliance and follow affirmative action principles in career services activities in a manner that includes the following:

   a. Notifying employing organizations of any selection procedures that appear to have an adverse impact upon a protected classification;

   b. Assisting recruiters in accessing protected groups on campus;

   c. Informing protected groups about employment opportunities, including those occupational areas where they are under-represented;

   d. Developing awareness of, and sensitivity to, cultural differences and the diversity of students and providing responsive services;

   e. Providing referral services that do not exclude students based upon their protected class status; and

   f. Responding to complaints of EEO noncompliance, working to resolve such complaints with the recruiter or employing organization, and, if necessary, referring such complaints to the appropriate campus department or agency.

7. Any disclosure of student information outside the educational institution shall be with prior consent of the student unless health and safety considerations necessitate the

dissemination of such information. Career services professionals shall exercise sound judgment and fairness in maintaining the confidentiality of student information, regardless of the source, including written records, reports, and computer databases.

8. Only qualified personnel shall evaluate or interpret tests of a career planning and placement nature. Students shall be informed of the availability of testing, the purpose of such tests, and the disclosure policies regarding test results.

9. If the charging of fees for career services becomes necessary, such fees shall be appropriate to the budgetary needs of the office and shall not hinder student or employer access to services. Career services professionals are encouraged to counsel student and university organizations engaged in recruitment activities to follow this principle.

10. Career services professionals shall advise students about their obligations in the recruitment process and establish mechanisms to encourage their compliance. Students' obligations include providing accurate information; adhering to schedules; accepting an offer of employment in good faith; notifying employers on a timely basis of an acceptance or nonacceptance and withdrawing from the recruiting process after accepting an offer of employment; interviewing only with employers for whom students are interested in working and whose eligibility requirements they meet; and requesting reimbursement of only reasonable and legitimate expenses incurred in the recruitment process.

11. Career services professionals shall provide services to international students consistent with U.S. immigration laws; inform those students about these laws; represent the reality of the available job market in the United States; encourage pursuit of only those employment opportunities in the United States that meet the individual's work authorization; and encourage pursuit of eligible international employment opportunities.

12. Career services professionals shall promote and encourage acceptance of these principles throughout their educational institution and shall respond to reports of noncompliance.

Principles for Employment Professionals

1. Employment professionals shall refrain from any practice that improperly influences and affects job acceptances. Such practices may include undue time pressure for acceptance of employment offers and encouragement of revocation of another employment offer. Employment professionals shall strive to communicate decisions to candidates within the agreed-upon time frame.

2. Employment professionals shall know the recruitment and career development field as well as the industry and the employing organization that they represent and work within a framework of professionally accepted recruiting, interviewing, and selection techniques.

3. Employment professionals shall supply accurate information on their organization and employment opportunities. Employing organizations are responsible for information supplied and commitments made by their representatives. If conditions change and require the employing organization to revoke its commitment, the employing organization shall pursue a course of action for the affected candidate that is fair and equitable.

4. Neither employment professionals nor their organizations shall expect, or seek to extract, special favors or treatment that would influence the recruitment process as a result of support or the level of support, to the educational institution or career services office in the form of contributed services, gifts, or other financial support.

5. Employment professionals are strongly discouraged from serving alcohol as part of the recruitment process. However, if alcohol is served, it shall be limited and handled in a responsible manner in accordance with the law and the institution's and employer's policies.

6. Employment professionals shall maintain EEO compliance and follow affirmative action principles in recruiting activities in a manner that includes the following:

a. Reviewing selection criteria for adverse impact;

b. Avoiding use of inquiries that are considered unacceptable by EEO standards during the recruiting process;

c. Developing a sensitivity to, and awareness of, cultural differences and the diversity of the work force;

d. Informing campus constituencies of special activities that have been developed to achieve the employer's affirmative action goals; and

e. Investigating complaints forwarded by the career services office regarding EEO noncompliance and seeking resolution of such complaints.

7. Employment professionals shall maintain the confidentiality of student information, regardless of the source, including personal knowledge, written records/reports, and computer databases. There shall be no disclosure of student information to another organization without the prior written consent of the student, unless necessitated by health and/or safety considerations.

8. Those engaged in administering, evaluating, and interpreting assessment tools, tests, and technology used in selection shall be trained and qualified to do so. Employment professionals must advise the career services office of any test conducted on campus and eliminate such test if it violates campus policies. Employment professionals must advise students in a timely fashion of the type and purpose of any test that students will be required to take as part of the recruitment process and to whom the test results will be disclosed. All tests shall be reviewed by the employing organization for disparate impact and job-relatedness.

9. When using organizations that provide recruiting services for a fee, employment professionals shall respond to inquiries by the career services office regarding this relationship and the positions that the organization was contracted to fill. This principle applies equally to any other form of recruiting that is used as a substitute for the traditional employer-student interaction.

10. When employment professionals conduct recruitment activities through student associations or academic departments, such activities shall be conducted in accordance with the policies of the career services office.

11. Employment professionals shall cooperate with the policies and procedures of the career services office, including certification of EEO compliance or exempt status under IRCA (Immigration Reform and Control Act), and shall honor scheduling arrangements and recruitment commitments.

12. Employment professionals recruiting for international operations shall do so according to EEO standards. Employment professionals shall advise the career services office and students of the realities of working in that country and of any cultural or foreign law differences.

13. Employment professionals shall educate and encourage acceptance of these principles throughout their employing institutions and by third parties representing their employing organization on campus and shall respond to reports of noncompliance.

Source: Excerpted from CPC's *Principles for Professional Conduct for Career Services and Employment Professionals*, with the permission of the College Placement Council, Inc., copyright holder.

5

Career Center Services

This chapter reviews services that are fundamental to most college and university career centers. As discussed in previous chapters, career centers will vary widely in mission and scope. The extent to which career centers are charged with the role of providing counseling for career choice, are centralized or decentralized, or offer on-campus recruitment services will influence the services delivered. However, regardless of mission, staff size, or nature of the college or university, most career centers will provide some measure of direct counseling or advising services, outreach programming, and placement assistance. Therefore, career services that are reviewed include:

Counseling services
   Intake counseling
   Counseling by appointment
   Assessment
   Group counseling
Placement and on-campus recruiting services
Career information
Programming and outreach

COUNSELING SERVICES

The foundation of career center services is counseling. Historically, offices providing career counseling or placement services have been viewed as student services and, most often, have been administratively anchored in student affairs.

It is important, however, that career centers maintain a student services perspective and be responsive to client career issues through providing a range of counseling services. Without counseling services, career centers can easily be seen as only a job or placement center, thereby fostering an image of an administrative office that is limited in scope, providing clients only with career information or facilitating only client use of job search services such as on-campus recruiting. Counseling services, however, enable the career center to embrace a developmental-process approach to career choice and empower clients with the knowledge and skill to clarify and implement career plans.

If counseling services are seen as the heart of the career center, then individual counseling continues to be seen as a primary counseling service. A great deal has been written about the importance of providing group-based programmatic career services (Pyle, 1986), and many of these approaches are reviewed later in the chapter. However, in providing a range of services, the career center must maintain its ability to respond to client issues on an individual basis. Without individual counseling services, the career center loses its image as a student service unit and may be viewed by clients as unresponsive and can easily become out of touch with current career issues presented by clients. Indeed, the image of the career center should also be that of a counseling center. This is not to suggest that the career center apply all of its time and resources to respond to client issues through individual counseling. Rather, individual counseling should represent a portion of a full range of career services, including group counseling, assessment, outreach programming, career education courses, and career information and placement services.

Intake Counseling

Because client issues are so varied, some form of intake counseling is necessary to enable the career center to address client questions quickly and to screen and refer clients to appropriate career center services and programs. Intake should be viewed as an individual career counseling service and must be brief. Most commonly, intake career counseling is made available on a walk-in basis. Large career centers may be able to offer walk-in services during all business hours through a staff rotation utilizing full-time professionals, graduate assistants, interns, and/or trained paraprofessionals. In this case, each staff serving in the rotation may serve as an intake counselor one-half day each week. Career centers with limited staff may offer a number of one-half day blocks of intake counseling on a weekly basis.

Career centers providing individual counseling by appointment without intake will quickly become deluged with clients presenting a wide range of career issues and will develop a substantial waiting list. While responding to a large career counseling appointment caseload with long waiting lists may make the career center and its staff feel needed, overworked, and in need of additional resources, counseling by appointment without intake is an inefficient and unrealistic service in most environments. Problems associated with career counseling by appointment without intake include: (1) students waiting two to three weeks for an appointment may have the issue resolved by the time the appointment occurs, (2) longer waiting times for appointments contribute to cancellations and no-shows, thereby fostering inefficient use of professional time, (3) after waiting for the appointment, students may present a concern that is not within the scope of career center services, (4) after waiting for the appointment, clients may present a concern, such as a review of an application form, that could have been dealt with immediately and taken only a few moments of professional time.

Intake counseling, therefore, allows a career center to respond to many presenting client issues or questions immediately. Many career issues are information-based and can be addressed in 10 to 20 minutes. For example, résumés and cover letters can be reviewed, graduate and professional school applications read, job search questions addressed, career information provided, and questions regarding career center services answered. Student clients with information-based issues can be culled from the individual counseling appointment schedule through intake, leaving counseling by appointment for more in-depth issues such as career choice or goal clarification. Intake services provided on a walk-in basis offer further advantages, including: (1) intake may serve as a conduit for referrals to a variety of career center programs and services and (2) intake enables a career center, at least, to respond and provide immediate assistance to students who have not made appointments.

All career centers experience the unfortunate situation in which a client walks in expecting immediate service. For example, a graduate visiting campus may stop in with career questions or inquiries regarding services. Culturally diverse clients may have different perceptions and expectations concerning time, structure, and schedules (Cheatham, 1990) and, as a result, are not as prone to schedule appointments. In either case, staff members serving on intake can also respond immediately to phone inquiries and thereby reduce other counseling appointments.

All staff serving as intake counselors must be familiar with all career center services. As a result, even staff with specialized responsibilities must understand and be able to respond to varied career issues, thereby enhancing their investment in the career center as a whole. Staff with primarily administrative responsibilities may enjoy and benefit from contact with clients through rotation through the intake counseling function. A further advantage of intake counseling is that clients presenting more involved career issues can be oriented to the career counseling process and given assignments prior to their appointment, thereby contributing to the efficiency and effectiveness of career counseling by appointment. In addition, well-organized and publicized intake services can facilitate the referral process between the career center and other student services and academic units, and since the staff member serving on intake is representing the office as the primary contact, questions and client screening are placed in the hands of the intake professional rather than clerical staff members.

Intake counseling should not be seen as a substitute for individual counseling by appointment. Rather, career center counseling services should be balanced through providing both brief intake and more in-depth counseling services by appointment. Furthermore, the option of providing counseling appointments as a follow-up to intake removes pressure for intake staff to answer all questions or resolve all presenting issues immediately. When intake staff are in doubt, referrals can be made to counseling by appointment.

Intake services require minimal space, but a small room in a career center should be made available to ensure confidentiality and clearly labeled as the intake office. A waiting area is necessary for students, and, ideally, the intake office should be close to a career information library, a counseling receptionist, and/or a scheduling clerk. Since intake is immediate and brief service without follow-up, counseling records such as client name, background, and case notes are not necessary. However, for accountability purposes, data should be collected regarding number of contacts, client demographic information, presenting career issues, and referrals. A scannable form such as the example shown in Figure 5.1 can be developed for efficiently collecting and recording intake counseling data.

Counseling by Appointment

As noted at the beginning of this chapter, individual career counseling by appointment should be viewed as the heart of career planning and placement services. Counseling by appointment should be balanced by intake services and group-based career programs. The availability of, at least, limited career counseling appointments offers a number of advantages for the career center. For example, despite the availability of a full range of group-based programmatic career services, many clients will continue to demand individual services and wish to focus on career concerns with a professional on an individual basis. Individual career counseling by appointment provides a "safety net" that allows the career center to be responsive to clients presenting more complex career concerns or experiencing personal concerns that are influencing career choice. Effective career outreach programs most often stimulate client interest in further involvement with career center services. Following participation in outreach programs, many clients will visit the career center seeking individual services. Individual counseling appointments with professionals contribute to the development of a strong referral network; that is, frequently faculty and staff as well as past clients will refer others to particular career center staff. The use of a variety of assessment measures currently available in career centers requires individual counseling to provide adequate interpretation and integration of the information into the career-planning process.

Clearly, the range and sophistication of career counseling services will vary across institutions depending on the career center staff size and its counseling-oriented mission. For example, at many universities, counseling for career indecision and assessment is provided within a centralized counseling unit that also provides psychotherapy. In such a model, the career center primarily provides career information, programming, and counseling for internships and employment.

Figure 5.1
Intake Scan Form

CAREER DEVELOPMENT AND PLACEMENT SERVICES

GENDER	COLLEGE						REFERRAL TO
O Female	O AG	O A&A	O BA	O Comm	O EMS	O Ed	O Division of Undergrad
O Male	O Engr	O HHD	O LA	O SC	O DUS	O Non-Degree	Studies

O Continuing Education

YEAR IN SCHOOL

O Freshman O Sophomore O Junior O Senior O Community
O Master's O Doctoral O Alumni O Employee

O Counseling and
Psych Services
O International Student
Programs
O Academic Advisor -
Department

QUALITY

O African-American O American Indian O Asian American O Latino/Hispanic
O International O Returning Adult O Veteran O Disabled

O Returning Adult Student
Center
O Academic Assistance
Programs
O Veterans Affairs
O Center for Women
Students
O OTHER
_____

1st	2nd	CONCERN	1st	2nd	ACTIVITY
O	O	Career planning/major choice	O	O	On site intake assistance
O	O	Occupational information	O	O	Individual Counseling
O	O	Internship/Summer Jobs	O	O	Group Counseling
O	O	Resume preparation	O	O	DISCOVER or SIGI
O	O	Cover Letter	O	O	Career Information Center
O	O	Interview Skills	O	O	Credit Courses
O	O	Job Search	O	O	Seminar Series/Outreach
O	O	Recruiting Information	O	O	On Campus Recruiting
O	O	IRF Preparation	O	O	Education Career Services
O	O	Graduate/Professional School	O	O	Alumni Career Services

GENDER	COLLEGE						REFERRAL TO
O Female	O AG	O A&A	O BA	O Comm	O EMS	O Ed	O Division of Undergrad
O Male	O Engr	O HHD	O LA	O SC	O DUS	O Non-Degree	Studies

O Continuing Education

YEAR IN SCHOOL

O Freshman O Sophomore O Junior O Senior O Community
O Master's O Doctoral O Alumni O Employee

O Counseling and
Psych Services
O International Student
Programs
O Academic Advisor -
Department

QUALITY

O African-American O American Indian O Asian American O Latino/Hispanic
O International O Returning Adult O Veteran O Disabled

O Returning Adult Student
Center
O Academic Assistance
Programs
O Veterans Affairs
O Center for Women
Students
O OTHER
_____

1st	2nd	CONCERN	1st	2nd	ACTIVITY
O	O	Career planning/major choice	O	O	On site intake assistance
O	O	Occupational information	O	O	Individual Counseling
O	O	Internship/Summer Jobs	O	O	Group Counseling
O	O	Resume preparation	O	O	DISCOVER or SIGI
O	O	Cover Letter	O	O	Career Information Center
O	O	Interview Skills	O	O	Credit Courses
O	O	Job Search	O	O	Seminar Series/Outreach
O	O	Recruiting Information	O	O	On Campus Recruiting
O	O	IRF Preparation	O	O	Education Career Services
O	O	Graduate/Professional School	O	O	Alumni Career Services

O O O O   O O O O   O O O O   O O O O   O O O O O O O O

Other institutions, however, charge the career center with the mission of providing a full range of career counseling services, including academic/career choice, assessment, and placement. Still other institutions may have a less defined mission for providing career counseling services; counseling and assessment for career choice may be provided both within a centralized counseling center and through the career center. Broad career issues that should be addressed through individual counseling include (1) career indecision, (2) choice of major (it should be noted that while the selection of an academic major may be seen as part of the academic advising process, it frequently involves career choice; i.e., the choice of marketing or psychology as a major may be seen as an academic decision, but it clearly has implications for career paths and plans), (3) exploring linkages between academic majors and careers, (4) assistance with experiential education planning, (5) assistance with the job search process, and (6) assistance in the application process to graduate/professional school.

The primary clients for a college career center are obviously students. As a result, the primary structure, goals, and programs of the career center should be based on student services. As individual counseling is seen as the heart of the career center, students must be viewed as the principal client population. As noted earlier, the mission of the career center is rooted in student services. Because career choice is so tied to college attendance and the process of selecting academic majors, we suggest that the career center adopt a liberal classification of students qualifying for career counseling services. For example, persons with applications on file at the university and part-time or continuing education students, as well as students on leave from the university, would be viewed as prospective clients. Students utilizing career counseling services would include returning adults, culturally diverse clients, international students, the disabled, veterans, graduate students, and traditional undergraduate students, as well as students of varied semester standings and majors.

While career centers must focus primarily on matriculated students, other "nonstudent clients" who have a relationship with the university, such as alumni or university employees, may be provided with individual counseling services. The staff size and budget and the geographic location of the career center will influence the extent to which services can be provided to alumni and employees. A career center with a comparatively small counseling staff located in an urban area may find it challenging to offer career counseling services to all alumni. However, counseling staff may enjoy and develop professionally from providing services to alumni or university employees who are considering a career change, require assistance in conducting a job search, or are experiencing professional plateauing. By expanding the scope of counseling by appointment to include alumni or employees, the career center may be able to generate funding and add to its staff size. For example, students would be provided with free career counseling while the career center would collect fees from alumni or employees who wish to utilize career counseling services. Such fees may be collected directly from the client, or, in certain cases, other university departments such as an alumni association or office of human resources may subsidize costs for counseling. Additional career services to alumni and university employees and funding considerations associated with these clients are discussed later in this chapter. While students should be the principal client population for career counseling services, the career center should, to some extent, extend its mission to enable alumni and employees of the college or university to gain access to individual counseling services. This is not to suggest that the career center offer unlimited career counseling to all prospective clients requesting services. Most career centers would limit services to those clients who have a formal relationship with the college or university. As a result, clients from the community would be referred to appropriate private or public career counseling services.

The scope and practice of career counseling can be varied and quite complex in nature and often are not understood by professionals or clients. The career center should clarify its philosophy and the practices that are associated with the following questions:

- To what extent does the counselor serve as educator or provide information in career counseling?
- How much follow-up and how many career counseling sessions are available to clients?
- To what extent is assessment used in the career counseling process?
- To what extent are personal issues addressed and dealt with in career counseling?

While these issues must be addressed by the career center, client expectations of the career counseling process are often varied and must be clarified during intake or in the initial phases of the counseling appointment. Indeed, client expectations of the career counseling process as well as the role of counselor and client are often more misunderstood in career counseling than in psychotherapy. Many clients demonstrate a fundamental understanding of psychotherapy (Garfield & Wolpin, 1963); that is, they expect multiple sessions and expect the therapist to listen to their concerns, develop a positive relationship, and suggest a structure for dealing with emotional concerns. Career counseling, however, can be quite misunderstood by clients, and their expectations may include only one counseling session, an information only approach, attention (or inattention) to personal issues, expert advise provided by the counselor, advice based on testing, or a placement or job matching approach in counseling for employment issues. Some clients will present multiple and complicated issues associated with career indecision. They may demand attention to personal process issues and require multiple counseling sessions. Other clients, however, may experience positive outcomes with rather simplistic career counseling interventions such as receiving feedback through an assessment measure or receiving accurate, realistic information concerning an academic program or career. In providing individual counseling services, the career center needs to plan to maintain its versatility, adaptability, and responsiveness in addressing a wide range of client career issues.

The student population using individual career counseling services should be balanced by level and type of demand. For example, freshman and sophomore undergraduates should be encouraged to become involved in the career counseling process early while upper-division graduates are more likely routinely to seek career counseling and placement services. Students in vocationally oriented majors such as business or engineering will often become involved in career center services. However, it is particularly important that students in the humanities and sciences utilize career counseling since the linkages between the academic programs and career alternatives are less defined.

Therefore, it is suggested that a counseling service be embedded within a career center. In a small college or university career center with decentralized placement, the counseling component may include one or two professionals. In a large centralized career center, the counseling staff may include a blend of professionals, graduate assistants, interns, or peer counselors. Regardless of the size and staffing pattern, the counseling component of the career center should be well defined and flexible in providing services ranging from addressing career indecision to providing job search or placement counseling. Also, counseling within the career center would adhere to *Ethical Standards* and guidelines as provided by the American Association for Counseling and Development (AACD, 1988).

The length of appointment time provided to clients may vary by career center size, staffing patterns, and client needs. Counseling by appointment should not be less than 30 minutes while most counseling appointments are from 45 to 60 minutes. Occasionally, appointments of longer duration may be appropriate. For example, alumni clients who are traveling some distance for services may be scheduled with a two-hour appointment. The number of follow-up counseling sessions available to clients will also vary among career centers. Many clients will require only one appointment to address a career question or issue while others may require long-term counseling. Many college and university counseling centers have embraced the short-term counseling model since clients requiring long-term counseling reduce the counseling center's responsiveness to client demands for services (Pinkerton & Rockwell, 1982). This should also be the practice of the career center. Even career centers providing extensive and sophisticated individual counseling should develop a session-limit policy. Often, college or university counseling or career centers will limit counseling services to ten appointments per client each academic year.

Confidential individual counseling records should be maintained and adhere to AACD *Ethical Standards*. It is suggested that client career counseling records be maintained at two levels. One record would include client demographics, appointment activity, assessments completed, and referrals. These records would be used principally for the career center's scheduling and accountability requirements. Often, as discussed in Chapter 7, such data can be maintained or converted to computer-based records. A second record or client file would be maintained for career counseling case notes and additional client records such as copies of assessments, academic records, or résumés. Professionalism and ethical standards demand adequate counseling case notes. However, moderation in the length and in the diagnostic sophistication of career counseling case notes maintained by the career center is appropriate. For example, case notes for individual career counseling need not rival psychotherapy case notes maintained by a counseling center in length or use of diagnostic terminology. However, informal, sketchy counseling case notes maintained in the counselor's desk would be considered unprofessional. Career counseling case notes should be clear and thorough and include sufficient information regarding client background and presenting issues, as well as present and planned counseling interventions. Such notes should be maintained in a centralized, secured, and confidential file. Also included with records should be a form addressing the policy and limits of confidentiality to be signed by the client, and, when sessions are taped, a form should be included indicating client awareness and agreement. Figure 5.2 includes examples of records and forms used in support of individual career counseling services.

Assessment, Vocational Testing, and Computer-Based Career Guidance Systems

Career centers should offer formal vocational assessments in support of individual counseling by appointment. Tests and assessments for use with career counseling not only serve as tools in facilitating positive client outcomes but also contribute to the identity of the career center as a counseling-oriented student service with responsibility for assisting clients in the self-exploration of personal attributes such as interests, values, and skills. As noted earlier, primary responsibility for career counseling and self-exploration is divided between a career center and a counseling center at some universities. For example, at some universities career-related tests and assessments are primarily provided at a counseling center that also has responsibility for providing psychotherapy. This situation would be considered erosive to the counseling identity and mission of the career center. Therefore, career centers embracing a counseling identity and mission would also embrace testing and assessment in support of counseling. Career assessment and testing bring focus to the counseling and career exploration mission of the career center.

Much has been written concerning the effectiveness of vocational testing and assessment within the career counseling process (Crites, 1974; Prediger, 1974). The presence of vocational assessment and testing in the career center is not to suggest that career counseling interventions rely on or foster routine counselor use of assessment. Such routine structured reliance on assessment is associated with a "test 'em and tell 'em" approach to career guidance rooted in a diagnostic medical model that contributes to client passivity in the career counseling process. Rather, vocational assessment and testing, when used appropriately with clients, provide an additional source of information as part of the career exploration process. More than process-oriented career counseling interventions, the results of assessment are tangible and can be taken from the career counseling process

Figure 5.2
Counseling Record Forms

<u>CONFIDENTIALITY</u>

Career Development and Placement Services
THE PENNSYLVANIA STATE UNIVERSITY

We realize that you might be concerned about what happens to any records or notes
kept by our office in providing you with Career Counseling Services. Please note
that all records kept by CDPS are STRICTLY CONFIDENTIAL.

Information provided by you, interview session notes, career planning assessment
measures, and other information such as academic records, will be kept confidential
except under the following conditions:

-- Only if you request in writing, may any part of your record be
released to appropriate individuals or agencies;

— We reserve the right to seek supervision and consultation as well as
to review your record with other professional colleagues within CDPS
which will aid us in providing career counseling services to you;

— Since career counselors do not have privileged communication in court
cases, it is possible that your records would have to be released
to courts if subpoenaed; and

— If we become aware of a life threatening situation, we may need to
notify family or other responsible personnel.

I have read and understand these conditions of CONFIDENTIALITY.

_____
Signature

<u>CODES</u>

Appointment:

R	-	Rescheduled (Counselor changed appointment)
CC	-	Career Counseling
CF	-	Career Follow - Up
PC	-	Placement Counseling
PF	-	Placement Follow - Up
C	-	Cancelled
N	-	No Show

External Referral

DU	-	DUS
CP	-	CAPS
CL	-	College
AP	-	Academic Assistance Program
DS	-	Disabled Student Services
RA	-	Returning Adult Student Center
IN	-	International Student Programs
SA	-	Student Aid
VA	-	Veterans Affairs
OT	-	Other

Assessment Measure:

DC	-	DISCOVER
SC	-	Strong Campbell
SD	-	Self Directed Search
MB	-	Myers Briggs
CP	-	California Personality Inventory
OT	-	Other
SP	-	Sigi Plus

sSCs

160

Figure 5.2 (continued)

CAREER DEVELOPMENT AND PLACEMENT SERVICES COUNSELING

PENN STATE

Name _____ Phone _____
    (Last)   (First)   Please Print

ADDRESS _____ Social Security No. _____

Semester Standing _____ College/Major _____

Sex _____ Age _____ GPA _____ U. S. Citizenship Yes _____ No _____

Ethnic Background _____ African/American _____ Latino _____ American Indian _____ Asian _____ White
    _____ Other

Permanent Resident _____ (Nationality) Student Visa _____ Do you have any disabilities? _____
Are you involved in any activities, on or off campus, that are important to you? Examples could be student government, volunteer human service agency, greek life, religous organization or student athlete If so, please note briefly

How can our office be of assistance to you? _____

COUNSELOR	DATE	TIME	APPT	EXTERNAL REFERRAL

EXTENDED COUNSELING RECOMMENDED: After ten (10) completed sessions

Measure						
Date						
Time						
Activity						

CODES
(on back)

CONSENT FOR AUDIO/VIDEO RECORDING
Career Development and Placement Services
THE PENNSYLVANIA STATE UNIVERSITY

Ocasionally, for supervisory purposes, career counseling session(s) will be taped. The confidentiality of all such tapes will be strictly safeguarded and they would be reviewed only by CDPS professional staff. I also understand that I will be notified prior to such taping.

If taping is requested by a counselor, I give the above permission with full knowledge that access to career counseling services is not contingent on the granting of such permission.

_____
Signature

_____
Date

Figure 5.2 (continued)

THE PENNSYLVANIA STATE UNIVERSITY

Career Development & Placement Services
Counseling Interview Summary

Student_____Time_____Date_____

Appointment number_____Counselor_____

<u>Session Summary</u>:

<u>Planned Activities and Referrals</u>:

(See reverse side for first session student background
or continued summary)

Counseling Interview Summary -- page 2

<u>Check one of the following</u>:

_____Student Background

_____Continued Session Summary

_____Continued Planned Activities and Referrals

to foster additional client reflection or to share with parents, spouses, or additional significant others. Not only does assessment become a "tool" in career exploration, but it can also be viewed as a "carrot" used by career centers to stimulate the referral process as well as client interest and involvement in career development. Often, clients will be referred to the career center or seek career counseling services to become involved in testing or computer-based guidance systems. It is important for career centers to accept this reality and to publicize and offer assessments but to ensure that clients be assisted in the timing and use of relevant testing and understanding of its meaning and relationship to other interventions. As a result, clients will become more sophisticated regarding the relative importance of the information received from assessment.

Tests and assessments utilized by career centers can be classified as follows: (1) traditional assessment of client internal attributes such personality type, interests, values, and abilities, (2) computer-assisted career guidance systems (CACG), and (3) diagnostic measures of client career maturity, progress, or satisfaction in the career planning process.

Traditional Assessment. The heart of the career center assessment program rests in the measurement of client internal, career-related attributes such as interests, values, and skills. In most instances, these assessments, unlike computer-assisted career guidance systems, are noninteractive and single administration measures focused on particular client attributes. Typically, these assessments are in paper-and-pencil form, but, increasingly, many traditional measures are becoming available in computer-based administration and scoring systems. These software programs will be reviewed in Chapter 7. Furthermore, unlike interactive CACG systems, these measures most often are used in support of individual counseling by appointment and require professional interpretation by the career counselor. As discussed earlier, career counseling by appointment enables the career center to be flexible and responsive to individual client needs. As a result, the timing, selection, and interpretation and use of particular assessments tailored to the client career concern should be part of the individual career counseling process. Traditional assessment can often be incorporated into group-based career interventions such as small group counseling, career planning workshops, or career development courses for credit. A thorough review of all assessments pertinent to the goals and client diversity of the typical career center is beyond the scope of this chapter. However, some measures commonly used by college and university career centers for the assessment of client internal attributes include:

Personality Type:

Myers-Briggs Type Indicator (MBTI). I. B. Myers and K. C. Briggs. Consulting Psychologists Press, Inc.

Sixteen Personality Factor Questionnaire (16 PF). R. B. Cattell. Institute for Personality and Ability Testing, Inc.

Interest:

Strong Interest Inventory (SII). E. K. Strong, Jr., J. C. Hansen, and D. P. Campbell. Consulting. Psychologists Press, Inc.

The Jackson Vocational Interest Survey (JVIS). D. N. Jackson. Research Psychologists Press, Inc.

Career Assessment Inventory (CAI). C. B. Johansson. National Computer Systems.

Vocational Preference Inventory (VPI). J. L. Holland. Psychological Assessment Resources, Inc.

The Self-Directed Search (SDS). J. L. Holland. Psychological Assessment Resources, Inc.

Values:

The Value Scale (VS). D. E. Super and D. D. Nevill.

Consulting Psychologists Press, Inc.

Aptitude:

The Differential Aptitude Test (DAT). G. K. Bennett, H. G. Seashore, and A. G. Wesman. Psychological Corporation.

If the measurement of career-related client attributes is the foundation of a career center assessment program, then interest assessment through measures such as the Strong Interest Inventory should be seen as the heart of traditional vocational testing. More than any other form of assessment, interest measurement contributes to facilitating client career exploration. Unlike interactive CACG systems, interest assessment can be controlled by the counselor; that is, the counselor refers the client to complete a particular measure, provides an interpretation, and assists the client in integrating the assessment information into the career planning process. Furthermore, more data have been collected regarding the psychometric qualities of traditional interest assessments than for relatively newer CACG systems (Johnston, Buescher, & Heppner, 1988). While interest testing may be viewed as the focal point of traditional assessment, additional assessment of client attributes is often appropriate. For example, a measure of personality type such as the Myers-Briggs may help bring focus to client self-concept. The Jungian-based scales of the MBTI may be considered in relationship to the Holland-based scales in the SII and the client's career-related belief systems as measured by Krumboltz's Career Beliefs Inventory (CBI) published by Consulting Psychologists Press, Inc. Caution must be exercised, however, in the use of information acquired through the MBTI in career counseling. For example, the College Placement Council (1991b) has reported the need for further evaluation of the MBTI as a career counseling assessment tool.

Values, by nature, can be amorphous and difficult for clients to understand and clarify. Instruments such as the Value Scale can facilitate client clarification and understanding of the relationship of values to the career-planning process. Students can be helped to focus on the intrinsic and extrinsic values of most importance to them in curriculum and in work. Because of the availability of a variety of ability indexes such as grades, scholastic aptitude test results, and freshman placement test results, aptitude tests may not be commonly used by the career center. This is particularly the case with traditional-age college students. However, as career centers respond to more diverse clients, limited aptitude testing may be appropriate. For example, returning adult students or university employees engaged in part-time college study may require feedback concerning their academic-vocational aptitudes through the use of the Differential Aptitude Tests, which have been recently revised for use with adults. Frequently, adult college students are unsure about their abilities or have not had such abilities challenged since leaving high school. Therefore, aptitude results may be more important to them in choosing majors or careers than to young students.

Computer-Assisted Career Guidance Systems. It is suggested that CACG systems be included in the mix of assessment and testing that is available to clients through the career center. CACG systems provide interventions and information not available through traditional career assessment. For example, CACG systems may be used effectively without active counselor involvement or interpretation (Sampson & Stripling, 1979; Garis & Bowlsbey, 1984). They are interactive, and, by including a variety of information such as exploration of interest, values, and skills, education and career information, and assistance in the decision-making process, they educate the user in the ingredients and process of career exploration. In addition to the self-exploration exercises, CACG systems are excellent sources of updated career information. A more in-depth review of CACG use and evaluation is provided in Chapter 7.

Because CACG systems are interactive and can stand alone from other career center services, their use by clients may be more difficult to control by the career center. Therefore, it is suggested that clients wishing to use CACG systems at least be screened through intake counseling. When clients are referred to CACG through individual counseling by appointment, care must be taken in considering the most appropriate CACG modules that meet client needs as well as the relationship of CACG use with other traditional assessments used in career counseling. Because CACG includes such comprehensive self-assessment and career information, it can be used as a stimulus to facilitate client involvement in the career center and the career-planning process. As clients become involved with CACG systems, the career center may wish to encourage client involvement in additional programs or counseling services.

Diagnostic, Career Development, and Career Maturity Measures. A variety of instruments have been developed that may be used by career centers to measure client level of functioning, knowledge, confidence, or maturity in career development. These assessments frequently focus on client skills in the "process of choice" rather than in dealing with the "content of choice." Such measures serve two purposes: (1) they assist career center counselors in understanding current client attitudes, knowledge, or progress concerning career planning. This information can help professionals in planning interventions with clients, and this feedback may be provided to clients to foster further understanding of career issues and behavior; and (2) since these measures are often diagnostic in nature, they may be used, as discussed in Chapter 4, as dependent measures in research and empirically based evaluations of career center services to measure client progress concerning career-related behavior (Crites, 1974). In addition to measuring career maturity, instruments have been developed to measure client work-related attitudes or behavior such as occupational stress and client belief systems associated with the career-planning process. Measures available to the career center in assessing career maturity, beliefs, or progress in career planning include such examples as:

Career Maturity.

Career Development Inventory (CDI). D. E. Super, A. S. Thompson, R. H. Lindeman, J. P. Jordaan, and R. A. Myers. Consulting Psychologists Press.

Career Maturity Inventory (CMI). J. O. Crites.

Career Planning Knowledge and Progress:

Career Decision Scale (CDS). S. H. Osipow. Psychological Assessment Resources, Inc.

My Vocational Situation (MVS). J. L. Holland, D. C. Daiger, and P. G. Power. Consulting Psychologists Press.

Adult Career Concerns Inventory (ACCI). D. E. Super, A. S. Thompson, and R. H. Lindeman. Consulting Psychologists Press, Inc.

Assessment of Career Decision Making (ACDM). J. N. Buck and M. H. Daniels. Western Psychological Services.

Work-Related Behavior or Beliefs:

Career Beliefs Inventory (CBI). J. D. Krumboltz. Consulting Psychologists Press.

Occupational Stress Inventory (OSI). S. H. Osipow and A. Spokane. Psychological Assessment Resources, Inc.

Work Salience Inventory. D. E. Super and D. D. Nevill. Consulting Psychologists Press.

While the above measures hold utility for the career center as diagnostic or research evaluation instruments, they are not as central as traditional assessment or CACG intervention tools in facilitating client progress in the career exploration process. Because career maturity measures address a comprehensive set of career development attitudes and behavior, they can be employed effectively in evaluating career center services such as individual counseling or credit career-planning courses (Garis & Bowlsbey, 1984). Career-planning attitude or progress measures such as the My Vocational Situation or Career Decision Scale have been used to evaluate the effectiveness of CACG (Garis & Niles, 1990). Instruments such as the Career Beliefs Inventory provide rich information regarding client assumptions or irrational beliefs associated with the career choice process. Information gathered through the Career Beliefs Inventory, such as client beliefs concerning the amount of control that they have in the choice process, can be incorporated into the individual career counseling process. As career centers extend services to alumni or university employees, instruments such as the Occupational

Stress Inventory or Adult Career Concerns Inventory can be used in support of individual counseling services or group-based workshops for clients with work experience who are attempting to cope better in their present career or are considering a career change.

Summary. The career center can embrace assessment as an intervention, diagnostic, and research-evaluation technique. To the degree that these purposes are sought, career centers should develop a systematic approach to the content of the assessment file. Staff should be carefully trained in the use of each measure. Rather than falling into routine use of selected measures, career center staff must carefully plan for the use of measures that are appropriate to client needs and center goals. As career centers use traditional assessment, CACG systems, and diagnostic measure, it is critical that staff understand the relationship and linkages between measures, carefully communicate with clients concerning the rationale for selected assessments, provide ethical interpretation of assessment results, and help clients to understand the meaning of the assessment information in relationship to other career center interventions and the client career choice process. Hood and Johnson (1991) provide a thorough review of assessment in counseling, and this resource would be quite appropriate for inclusion in the career center professional library.

Groups

Regardless of staff size, budget, or breadth of goals, it is suggested that career center interventions be packaged and delivered through a range of treatment modalities. In addition to individual interventions, assessment, and computer-assisted guidance, group-based career counseling should be offered by the career center. For the purposes of this discussion, group career counseling is defined as (1) including a relatively small number of members ranging from 5 to 15, with an optimal size of 5 to 8 members, (2) focusing on a particular topic common to all members, (3) being interactive in nature, and (4) meeting for more than one session, most often ranging from three to seven sessions (Hansen & Cramer, 1971). Advantages of group career counseling include efficiency in delivering interventions to several members simultaneously rather than to only one individual, as well as the sharing and modeling common to interactive counseling groups. A great deal has been written about the advantages of group interventions in counseling and psychotherapy (Yalom, 1975). Despite the advantages associated with group counseling, it can often present challenges to the career center as a career intervention delivery system. For example, groups may quickly lose their efficiency as delivery systems if they require substantial amounts of staff preparation time and publicity only to be fraught with spotty attendance and attrition by members. Furthermore, groups can lose quality as an intervention if members feel that their career concerns have not been addressed adequately in the group, become frustrated, and seek individual services. The authors have observed that given a choice between group-based approaches and individual counseling, many clients will request individual services; group career counseling can be very difficult to organize (i.e., in providing adequate publicity, and finding a meeting time that enables members to attend even the initial group session); and, even after building a group, maintaining attendance and avoiding attrition of significant numbers of members can be quite challenging.

In essence, career centers must strike a balance in the emphasis placed on group-based career counseling interventions. Career centers should not view group counseling as group psychotherapy. Rather, career centers should take advantage of groups as an efficient and effective mode of delivering career interventions in carefully planning groups designed to consider (1) particular career issues, (2) specific client populations, (3) desirable group size, (4) appropriate number of group sessions, and (5) group focus and purpose ranging from an information-based orientation to process counseling orientations (Herr & Cramer, 1988). A brief discussion of each of these factors to be considered by the career center in developing a group counseling program follows.

Client Career Issues. Career issues commonly addressed by career center group counseling include:

1. Career exploration and choice of major
2. Computer-assisted guidance users' group
3. Internship-summer job search
4. Interview skills enhancement
5. Job search strategies and support
6. Graduate and professional school decisions and search

Client Population. In addition to addressing information and goals common to all members, the real power of a group-based approach is in the support, interaction, and understanding that can be achieved when small group career counseling is offered to particular populations sharing common experiences. For example, many of the above career issues ranging from career exploration to the elements of the employment search can be tailored to specific populations, including:

1. Traditional-age college students, including undecided freshmen and graduating seniors
2. Returning adult students
3. African American students
4. Asian American students
5. Academically at-risk students
6. Hispanic students
7. Women
8. Academically gifted-scholar students
9. International students
10. Disabled students
11. Veterans
12. Graduate students

When planned carefully, group career counseling focused on particular populations can be an efficient intervention with low client attrition and with the capability to foster client progress in career-related issues. Some of the above populations can be combined, facilitating even further commonality among client needs and characteristics. For example, an interview skills group can be offered for African American women, a career exploration group can be offered to returning adults who are academically at risk, or a job search group can be provided to disabled veterans. Such commonality of client experience may contribute to group efficiency, cohesion, and sharing. Group focus and commonality can be achieved by considering additional client attributes. For example, job search groups can be developed for students in almost any major. However, job search groups for specialized fields such as the arts or communications may hold particular promise. Furthermore, skill development and support groups for students considering application to medical schools could be offered by the career center. Due to the increase in social awareness and collectivity aspects of culturally diverse populations (Cheatham, 1990), group approaches to selected career or postgraduate education issues may be especially appropriate for African American or Hispanic clients.

Group Size, Session Number, and Focus. The size of the career counseling group, its total number of meetings, and focus are addressed collectively since they should be interrelated. It is suggested that the focus of career groups may vary more than therapy groups in their orientation to information, content, or process. It is assumed that, due to their attention to personal concerns, most therapy groups will attend to client process issues, for example, through the use of group dynamics. Such groups will frequently span several sessions. Some career groups, however, may be informationally oriented with an instructional focus while others may be highly interactive and process-oriented. Group size and number of sessions should be linked directly to group focus; that is, a content-information–oriented job search group might be offered to a relatively large number of students (12–15) and meet for only three sessions. A process-oriented group such as career exploration for undecided and academically gifted students may include only 5 to 7 members and meet for several sessions. A job search support group for disabled students may include a relatively small number of members and meet over a long period of time. Regardless of focus on content or process, it is important that all career counseling groups, to a differing extent, take advantage of group dynamics and be interactive in nature through involving all members in discussions.

Career Groups: Examples and Summary. A thorough review of the types of career counseling groups that can be offered by the career center cannot be covered fully in this chapter. However, outlines of three career counseling groups are provided to illustrate the variability of group counseling in content and focus on particular populations. The first example, shown in Figure 5.3, represents a career counseling model for traditionally aged, academically gifted freshmen who are undecided in the choice of major and career plans. This group meets for five sessions and includes a blend of group exercises and discussion, assessment, and

Figure 5.3
Career Planning Group for Scholars

Career Development and Placement Services, 403-A Boucke.
Thursday, October 19 through Thursday November 16; 1:00 - 2:15
Don Timmons, leader.

Session 1, October 19
      Introduction of members, discussion of members' current plans
and relationship to goals of this group. Overview of the process and
issues involved in choosing majors/careers, and how the group will
address them.
      Complete Survey of Career Development, Career Planning
Confidence scale. Assign life-line, Strong-Campbell Interest
Inventory, Myers-Briggs Type Indicator, DISCOVER or SIGI, Values
checklists.

Session 2, October 26
      Review life-lines and discuss their relevance. Discuss
developmental issues, general and specific. The importance of
knowing oneself--e.g., interests, values, skills. Review Holland's
typology, assign functional skills and Self Directed Search.

Session 3, November 2
      Interpretation and discussion of Strong-Campbell Interest
Inventory, Myers-Briggs, and SDS. Review SIGI and DISCOVER. Relate
to individual. Discuss additional ways of learning individual
trends/patterns, such as experiences, activities, coursework.

Session 4, Novewmber 9
      Issues in academic planning at Penn State. Resources for
academic advising and information. Relationship of majors to
careers. Resources for career information; visit to Career
Information Center. Strategies for learning about careers. Assign
career research.

Session 5, November 16
      Discussion of strategies for trying out tentative career
choices, such as internships, externships, summer jobs, foreign
study, leadership and various development experiences. Summary of
current status and possible directions. Review of problem-solving
and decision-making strategies. Interacting with the world of work
and adult changes and development. Wrap-up and termination.

presentations. Because of the discussions and group exercises, interpretation of
assessments, and focus on a specific population, this group would likely include
a relatively small number of members, that is, five to seven students.

A second example is provided for an information-based job search group for
seniors. Unlike the intervention outlined above, this group could be provided to
12 to 15 members and would meet for only three sessions.

Session 1: Introduction of group members and discussion of career goals; review of a job
    search outline; discussion of resources for identifying and contacting employers; review
    of career center job search services and the career library

Session 2: Discussion of networking; review of correspondence associated with the job search process—cover letter, résumé, and follow-up letters

Session 3: Review and practice of interview skills; discussion of members' future job search strategies

The final example represents a workshop provided to a specialized population, in this case returning adult women. Unlike the above examples, this group would be highly process-oriented and interactive in nature. As a result, it would include five to seven members, with each session being relatively unstructured.

Session 1: Introduction of group members, discussion of career goals; review of job search techniques, time management and dealing with role conflict

Session 2: Résumé writing and cover letter design

Session 3: Interview skills; dealing with illegal interview questions

Session 4: Dealing with transition to the workplace; sexual harassment issues, coping with stress

As noted earlier, groups can be time-consuming and difficult services to organize for career center staff. Care must be taken in planning group services. In developing each group, consideration must be given to group focus, target population, and direction to ensure its efficiency and effectiveness. Unlike individual services, groups associated with specific topics and populations can be planned and publicized, thereby contributing to the career center's identity as a service that is responsive to student needs. For example, in difficult, economically recessionary times, the career center may offer and promote increased numbers of job search groups. Furthermore, a group program enables the career center to be responsive to the career-related needs of particular client populations such as women and ethnically diverse clients. In some cases, the career center may choose to cosponsor groups with other student service agencies, such as a center for women students, academic advising services, or a returning adult student center. The career center's group program for each academic year should reflect diverse career topics and be addressed to varied client populations. An example of a group program offered by a comprehensive career center for an academic year is shown in Figure 5.4.

PLACEMENT

As discussed in Chapter 1, the scope of placement services provided by the career center will obviously vary in relationship to the extent to which a centralized or decentralized placement model is utilized in the respective college or university. For example, no placement services may be present in a centralized career center of a university in which a placement function exists in each college. In contrast, large, sophisticated placement services will often be available through a career center with a mission of providing placement assistance to students enrolled in

Figure 5.4
Career Groups

- Groups start throughout the semester.

- An intake counselor is available in 412 Boucke to answer your
  questions.

- The purpose of each group is to provide **support and encouragement** as
  well as to help you develop needed skills and obtain relevant
  information.

CHOOSING A MAJOR/CAREER
Are you confused about how to choose a major and how to plan career
direction? This group focuses on:
- exploring your interests and values
- ways of obtaining information about occupations
- developing criteria for career planning and choosing your major
ASSERTIVE JOB SEARCH:
ASSERTIVE JOB SEARCH FOR MINORITIES
Is it hard for you to put your career goals into words? Are you unsure
about the kind of job you're looking for? This group focuses on helping
you:
- describe what you would like to do
- identify where those jobs are
- develop strategies for assertively contacting employers
SUMMER JOB SEARCH
- designed for sophomores and juniors wanting a worthwhile job related
  to the major
- similar in content to the assertive job search group in helping you
  define goals and develop strategies
INTERVIEW SKILLS:
INTERVIEW SKILLS FOR INTERNATIONAL STUDENTS
Several sessions, identifying and discussing:
- the factors that influence the interview process
- ways to answer difficult questions positively and honestly
- myths versus the reality of the employer's perspective
TIME MANAGEMENT
Valuable now, essential on the job:
- only 4 sessions
- ways to break down tasks into manageable parts
- methods of setting and completing your priorities
- how to make use of unexpected free time or waiting time
PLANNING FOR GRADUATE OR PROFESSIONAL SCHOOL
- three sessions
- for students considering medical, dental, law, vet, or graduate
  school
- discussions about all your concerns, from admissions criteria to
  career concerns
CAREER ISSUES FOR WOMEN
Designed for women in all fields. Issues which affect the work world
are discussed, such as:
- power and influence
- developing support networks
- the dual career family
- personal and professional goal setting

mr2.3 (WP)
9/1/92

all colleges of the university. Additional factors that may influence the characteristics of placement services offered by the career center include college/university size and enrollment, breadth and nature of academic programs, and geographic location. The placement services of a small, rural liberal arts college may be limited in job placement and place more emphasis on graduate/professional school admissions than would placement services in an urban university with large business and technical colleges. The extent to which placement services are provided by the career center may influence the title of the office. A title of "Placement Office" suggests more focus on job search services than the title of "Career Center." Many other offices offer a balanced set of developmental career services as well as commitment to providing employment assistance by using a title of "Career Planning and Placement." The definition of "placement" may vary, as some career centers may view it as solely an on-campus recruiting service. However, we prefer that placement be viewed as a set of career center services to assist clients in the implementation of career plans. This view of placement sees it as a process, not an event. Such a view of placement transcends on-campus recruiting to include career exploration and placement counseling, assistance in graduate/professional school admissions, computer-based job search systems, networking services, employment listing services, and employment-oriented career days.

Due to the varied models for delivering placement services in colleges, it is not realistic to recommend a package of placement services that are applicable to all career centers. Rather, a range of placement services will be reviewed briefly, leaving career centers with the task of selecting and implementing placement services that are most consistent with their mission and applicable to their client needs.

On-Campus Recruiting

While placement includes many other implementation services, on-campus recruiting remains the foundation of placement. Through an on-campus recruiting system, the career center bridges the gap between academe and the external career environment. By developing a system and offering a service that brings students and employers together in order to discuss employment opportunities, the career center amplifies its mission to assist students not only in career development but in the implementation of career plans. The on-campus recruiting service creates a mission for the career center that is often unique to the college or university; that is, few other college services systematically bring representatives of business, industry, and government on campus to meet with students. This is not to suggest that career centers focus primarily on placement and on-campus recruiting. Such focus would cause career centers to be viewed as traditional placement offices, which, at one time, were evaluated solely on the basis of the number of organizations recruiting on campus. Often, the mix of organizations participating in on-campus recruiting cannot be controlled by the career center. Characteristics associated with the college or university such as those noted earlier, coupled with the economic climate, will influence recruiting activity. In addition, many types of employers such as communications organizations, the human services, or small businesses do not participate in on-campus recruiting activities. Even when corporations or government agencies are conducting on-campus interviews, their hiring needs and interests in interviewing students from only certain desired academic programs are often narrow in scope. Therefore, it is suggested that career centers maintain an on-campus interview system that is appropriate to their mission and campus environment. Such recruiting services create a high profile on campus for the career center, obviously help certain students in obtaining employment, and keeps the career center in contact with employers. An ongoing recruiting system, however, should be augmented with a variety of other placement services.

Career centers charged with a placement mission should develop a well-organized system for notifying and providing students access to opportunities for on-campus interviews. Methods used in the selection of students for on-campus interviews are quite varied, including first-come, first-served selection, an interview bidding system based on allocation of a limited number of points for each registrant, lottery systems, and employer prescreening and selection, as well as a combination of these interview selection systems. Due to the information-based and systemic nature of on-campus recruiting systems, computer-driven applications to maintaining employer information, as well as candidate notification and selection processes, are increasingly common, and a number of these systems are reviewed in Chapter 7. Regardless of paper-driven or computer-based applications, the on-campus interview process should be well organized, routinized, and well publicized to foster early registration and use by students. Typically, upperclass as well as graduate students are sent letters describing the on-campus interview system just prior to their final year of study. As a result, students can be registered and oriented to the use of the recruiting system shortly after their return to campus. In most instances, students will register and request interviews through the use of a form, including information comparable to that provided in résumés, that is, career interests, education, experience, and college/community activities. Such information can be paper- or computer-based. An example of an interview request form is shown in Figure 5.5. Obviously, the format and content of request forms will vary according to the interview selection system employed by the career center. However, a standardized format for providing employers with information regarding professional attributes of student registrants will be necessary.

As noted earlier, a variety of systems may be used for the selection of students for on-campus interviews. Regardless of the recruiting system used, the career center should consider several questions associated with the implementation of an on-campus interviewing system, including:

1. What are the roles and responsibilities of the career center, students, and employers involved in the recruiting system?
2. How are students informed of employer recruiting visits?

Figure 5.5
Interview Request Form

(PSU Student Use Only)   (Type or Print)

Request interview with _____

Division (if given) _____

Job Title: 1st choice _____ 2nd choice (Optional) _____

Date of Visit _____ Job Location _____

Applying for: (Check one)   Perm _____   Summer _____   Intern _____

I UNDERSTAND THAT I MAY EXCLUDE ANY OF THE INFORMATION REQUESTED ON THIS FORM.

NAME _____ Social Security No. _____
      (Last)   (First)   (M.I.)

PRESENT   Telephone No.
ADDRESS _____   (   )
         (Street)   (City)   (State)   (Zip Code)

PERMANENT   Telephone No.
ADDRESS _____   (   )
         (Street)   (City)   (State)   (Zip Code)

Check One: U.S. Citizen (   )   Permanent Resident (   )   Student Visa (   )

CAREER INTEREST OR DESCRIPTION OF WORK DESIRED

_____
_____
_____

DATE AVAILABLE _____ GEOGRAPHIC PREFERENCE _____

EDUCATION

Names of Colleges Attended	Dates (MO/YR) From	To	Degree (BA, BS, MBA)	ACADEMIC MAJOR (Include minor or emphasis if relevant)	Grade Basis	GPA (1) Major (2) Cum
The Pennsylvania State University					A = 4.0	(1) (2)
					A =	
					A =	

ACADEMIC PROFILE: List courses most relevant to your career objectives. Show the number of credits earned and planned.

COURSE TITLE	CREDITS Earned Upon Graduation	COURSE TITLE	CREDITS Earned Upon Graduation

NOTE: This form is not an official transcript. It includes courses completed, in progress, and anticipated.

Figure 5.5 (continued)

NAME _____

(Last)   (First)   (M.I.)

WORK EXPERIENCE: Include Part-Time, Summer, Coop. Education, Intern, Military, Etc.

Employer's Name	Dates (MO/YR) From	To	Hours Per Week	Job Titles

JOB DUTIES/RESPONSIBILITIES/ACCOMPLISHMENTS

CAMPUS/CIVIC ACTIVITIES (Honors, Academic or Special Projects, Internships, Etc.)

DISCUSS YOUR BACKGROUND, INTERESTS, ABILITIES, AND ACHIEVEMENTS AS THEY RELATE TO THE POSITION DESIRED

BY PREVIOUSLY SIGNING THE UNIVERSITY PLACEMENT CENTER'S REGISTRATION CARD, I HAVE AUTHORIZED THEM TO USE THIS INFORMATION WHICH I HAVE CHOSEN TO PROVIDE ON MY BEHALF AND TO RELEASE IT TO PROSPECTIVE EMPLOYERS.

3. How are interviews requested by students?

4. How are students selected for interviews?

5. How are students notified when selected for interviews?

6. How are employers provided with student interview requests?

7. When selected, how do students schedule the interview time?

8. How do employers or the career center inform registrants concerning qualifications necessary to interview on a particular schedule?

9. How are employers provided with information concerning their completed interview schedule?

10. To what extent are computers used in each step of the on-campus interview system, ranging from maintaining a database of employers and student registrants to developing the interview schedule?

Although career center budgetary and facility resources are often limited, every effort should be made to ensure that the environment associated with the on-campus interview system is as professional as possible. All too often, corporate recruiters and students engage in professional interviews in basements, large public rooms with temporary dividers, or offices used for other purposes such as a health center. The physical setting for on-campus interviews should be quiet, private, and comfortable and include a waiting area for students. Frequently, one of the first priorities for career center funding requests from employers is to improve interview facilities. Such facility needs are addressed further in Chapter 8. In addition to addressing the physical environment for on-campus interviews, the career center should ensure the professionalism of the recruiting system through orienting recruiters and providing students with adequate interview preparation. Printed and video-based information describing organizations recruiting on campus should be collected, updated regularly, and made available to students. Information regarding employer group meetings should be obtained and provided to students well in advance of the recruiting visit.

Most career centers with a placement mission offer an ongoing, systematized, on-campus interview system. These systems are often rather traditional in nature, static, and passive; that is, the career center responds with an on-campus interview system to employers who traditionally recruit at a particular college or university. While such systems should be maintained, it is critical that career centers assume a proactive and dynamic role in developing on-campus interview systems. For example, the career center may be able to add to or change its recruiting mix through publicizing particular academic programs, employer site visits, and further efforts in employer development. In addition to maintaining a continuing on-campus interview system, career centers may wish to augment their existing systems in developing specialized on-campus recruiting programs. For example, a particular group of students, such as liberal arts or communications majors, who do not routinely benefit from an on-campus recruiting system may be targeted, and a specialized career interview program could be planned to create on-campus interview opportunities (Garis & Hess, 1985). Such a program, unlike the ongoing recruiting system, may be brief, that is, one to three days, and focused on a particular academic program or student population. These programs are proactive in that the career center sets a date, identifies a target student population, and develops an employer-based interest in recruiting at the college or university. In some cases, these focused recruiting visits can be tied to career days for an academic program such as a college of education or a particular student population such as a minority career day. Because these on-campus interview programs are specialized, the career center may vary the interview selection system from its routine process associated with the ongoing recruiting system. For example, a university offering a continuing recruiting system based on employer prescreening and selection may wish to create interview opportunities for all students participating in a specialized recruiting program such as a liberal arts or minority student career interview program through developing an interview schedule representing a blend of students selected by the employer as well as some students selected by the career center.

Additional Placement Services

In addition to on-campus interview services, career centers may provide a variety of programs and services to assist clients in the implementation of career plans, including:

1. Participation in regional consortia, job fairs, or career programs
2. Maintaining job notices and vacancy listings filed by academic programs and developing vacancy lists or employment opportunity newsletters sent to students or alumni in particular career fields
3. Planning or participating in specialized employment-oriented career programs such as a state career day
4. Developing a job bank or networking program utilizing computer-based and electronic bulletin board applications
5. Offering a credential service for education majors and for students seeking admission to graduate/professional school
6. Developing résumé books for students in specialized academic programs
7. Developing a computer-based résumé matching and referral system for alumni
8. Purchasing computer-based job search systems such as Career Navigator (1987)
9. Maintaining employment and organizational directories as well as job search self-help books in the career information center
10. Subscribing to employment listings in specialized fields such as government, human services, or law enforcement
11. Providing career education outreach programs and credit courses to assist clients in the development of job search skills
12. Providing individual and group counseling services to assist clients in the employment search or graduate/professional school application process

Obviously, the range of placement-related programs will vary according to career center mission, staffing, fiscal and spatial resources, and characteristics of the college or university. Some of the above services may be provided solely by the career center while others may be cosponsored by other university offices such as an academic department or an alumni association. Certain services may be free while others, such as a credential service, may be provided on a fee basis. Any career center charged with a placement mission should offer an ongoing on-campus recruiting system, specialized programs that provide further on-campus interview opportunities, and an additional mix of placement programs and services to assist clients in the implementation of career plans. Finally, career centers will need to decide whether placement will be treated as a process of developing skills in career planning and choice, job search, and related elements through the four years of college or as an event of relevance only at the end of the senior year.

INFORMATION USE

A thorough review of career information services is provided in Chapter 6. However, for the purposes of this chapter, the importance of providing information and support of career center counseling and placement services must be acknowledged. The career center must gather and maintain academic and career information for use with clients engaged in counseling services for career exploration. As discussed earlier, while the career counseling process can be varied and complicated, often just a bit of new information, such as gaining a better understanding of the linkages between an academic major and career opportunities, can contribute to a positive counseling outcome. Furthermore, the effectiveness of placement services rests on information availability. For example, employer information such as annual reports or descriptions of career opportunities must be available in support of the on-campus recruiting process. Directories of employers and descriptions of career opportunities are vital in assisting clients in the placement process. A variety of handouts developed by the career center should be maintained in the career library and used in support of outreach programming.

Information made available by the career center will include printed materials such as handouts, brochures, and books, as well as computer-based information and videotapes. Career information offered in support of counseling, placement, and programming would include:

1. Academic information files
2. Career/occupational information files
3. Occupational information directories
4. Occupational information books
5. Internship and summer job information
6. Graduate/professional school information
7. Career information for specialized populations
8. Self-help career planning and job search books
9. Organizational directories
10. Geographic/location files
11. Computer-based occupational information
12. Employment opportunity directories
13. Videotaped academic and occupational information
14. Videotaped job search programs
15. Videotaped company/organizational information
16. Company annual reports
17. Company/organizational career opportunities and recruiting information
18. Career-related periodicals

A review of the types of career information noted above, as well as the organization of a career library, is provided in the following chapter.

PROGRAMMING AND OUTREACH

A great deal has been written in this chapter concerning variability of the career center mission with respect to responsibility for providing career counseling or placement services. However, career education programming is common to all career centers. Career education outreach programs, unlike counseling groups or credit courses, meet once, are relatively brief, are informational or discussion-oriented, and carry no credit. Outreach programs achieve the following goals: (1) they provide a vehicle for the career center to publicize and promote its services, (2) they can be used to orient clients to the career-planning or employment search process, (3) they enable the career center to develop further understanding of career issues and cooperative services with other college and university offices, and (4) they provide a forum for group-based information delivery or skill enhancement in a wide range of career planning and placement issues.

Outreach programs can be provided in a variety of settings and can be offered jointly with other organizations. Program settings would include:

1. Academic classes
2. Colleges and academic departments
3. Student professional organizations
4. Student social organizations
5. Residence halls
6. Student service offices
7. Community organizations
8. Career center–sponsored

Outreach programs in cooperation with a variety of campus organizations enable the career center to gain access to students representing a range of semester standings, majors, and personal qualities such as age, gender, and ethnicity. Career education outreach offered in the classroom at the invitation of faculty can be particularly beneficial in that a captive audience is present, and frequently the instructor becomes more informed of career issues and can serve as an advocate for the career center. Most colleges hold career days, which may be co-sponsored by the career center. In some instances, the career center may be requested to provide specialized outreach programs as part of the college career day activities. All colleges and universities sponsor a variety of student professional organizations. Examples are wide-ranging and include societies for women engineers, professional honor societies, marketing clubs, or societies of student social workers. Since they are professional in nature, almost all student organizations are interested in career-planning and employment issues and frequently request career center outreach programs. Outreach programs to student professional organizations can be advantageous in that the program can often be focused on a particular profession or career area, attendance and student interest in professional development are high, and student organizations can co-sponsor the program, resulting in funding for program publicity.

Career centers can gain access to a variety of students through social organizations such as Greek organizations, veterans groups, or black caucuses. At many colleges residence halls have adopted a living-learning approach, resulting in requests for evening outreach programs. However, unlike student professional organizations or academic classes, student background and interest in career planning can be more diverse, and, as a result, attendance in residence hall–sponsored programs can be unpredictable. Therefore, career centers may request several residence halls to cosponsor and carefully publicize the program to enhance its efficiency. It is important for the career center to cooperate with other student service offices in cosponsoring outreach programs. This is a particularly effective tool for reaching out to diverse student populations. Examples of cooperating student service offices on many campuses include:

1. Returning adult student services
2. Student orientation office
3. Office for women students
4. International student services
5. Student union
6. Admissions
7. University scholars
8. Disabled student services
9. Religious affairs
10. Support centers for student athletes

Through cooperative programs with other student services, the career center can have a systematic and powerful impact on the student body. For example, the office responsible for orienting new students to the college or university could include career planning programs with required attendance for all new freshmen and transfer students. The career center could support its college or university recruitment efforts through offering career-planning or placement orientations to prospective students and families visiting the campus. Furthermore, many student unions offer series of evening workshops and provide space and funding for program publicity. As a community service, the career center may wish to provide limited programs to people in the public area who are not affiliated with a college or university. Examples of relevant community organizations for career outreach include correction facilities, youth organizations, public schools, and business groups. While such programs are not central to the mission of the career center, they can be beneficial in promoting the public image of the college or university, serve as a recruiting tool, and facilitate staff development through exposure to varied environments and populations.

In addition to providing a variety of joint programs, it is necessary for the career center to sponsor and offer a range of programs. These programs should be offered each semester and may include orientations to on-campus recruiting and career center tours, as well as programs for fundamental skills such as résumé preparation and résumé writing.

The career center should offer outreach program topics that address issues associated with all aspects of the college student career development process and are provided to a cross section of its client population. The career center may wish to offer on a weekly basis a series of programs that address routine issues such as résumé preparation or interview skills. Such "career seminar series" are well publicized and available to any client, and no prior sign-up is required. An example of a seminar series is shown in Figure 5.6.

Additional programs held during evening hours can be developed and sponsored by the career center that address a variety of career issues and are targeted to particular client populations. The career center could explore the option of cosponsoring such programs with other organizations to facilitate publicity and attendance. An example of an evening career series that could be offered jointly by a career center and the student union throughout the academic year is provided in Figure 5.7.

Outreach program topics provided in a variety of program settings and cosponsored by other organizations obviously would be quite varied. Examples of relevant topics would include:

Figure 5.6
Seminar Series

Sessions are repeated weekly. *All students are welcome.*
No prior sign-up is required and attendance at only one session per topic is necessary.

INTERVIEW REQUEST FORM PREPARATION	**THE SELF-DIRECTED JOB SEARCH**
September 10 through September 25 Only	*October 1 through October 23 Only*
Tuesdays: 5th period (12:20 - 1:10 p.m.)	Tuesdays, 5th period (12:20 - 1:10 p.m.)
Wednesdays: 3rd period (10:10 - 11:00 a.m.)	Wednesdays: 3rd period (10:10 - 11:00 a.m.)
RESUME PREPARATION	**INTERVIEWING SKILLS**
September 10 through October 23	*September 10 through October 23*
Tuesdays: 6th period (1:25 - 2:15 p.m.)	Tuesdays: 7th period (2:30 - 3:20 p.m.)
Wednesdays: 4th period (11:15 a.m. - 12:05 p.m.)	Wednesdays: 5th period (12:20 - 1:10 p.m.)

ALL WORKSHOPS WILL BE HELD IN **424 BOUCKE BUILDING.**

Figure 5.7
Student Union Career Series

CAREER DEVELOPMENT AND PLACEMENT SERVICES
OFFICES OF THE VICE PRESIDENT FOR STUDENT SERVICES

FALL HUB SERIES
SEPTEMBER 25, 1990 THROUGH NOVEMBER 20, 1990

Five programs are being offered Fall Semester as part of the HUB SERIES. *All students are welcome.*

APPLYING TO GRADUATE AND PROFESSIONAL SCHOOLS. . . . . . .TUESDAY, SEPT. 25, 1990
    Jeff Garis, Associate Director   7:00pm

CAREERS WITH THE FEDERAL GOVENRMENT. . . . . .TUESDAY, OCT. 9, 1990
    Joe McMasters, Philadelphia Office of Personnel Management   7:00pm

WHAT TO EXPECT AT AN ON-SITE INTERVIEW . . . . .TUESDAY, OCT. 23, 1990
    Representatives from GENERAL ELECTRIC and AT&T   7:00pm

INTERNSHIP AND SUMMER JOB SEARCH. . . . . .TUESDAY, NOV. 13, 1990
    Jeff Garis, Associate Director   7:00pm

JOB SEARCH FOR INTERNATIONAL STUDENTS . . . . .TUESDAY, NOV. 20, 1990
    Jack Rayman, Director   7:00pm

ALL PROGRAMS WILL BE HELD IN THE HUB FISHBOWL
Please check with CDPS in 413 Boucke (5-2377) for information on additional programs.

1. Career center orientation

2. Career planning issues

3. Exploring linkages between majors and careers

4. Internship/summer job search

5. Job search skills

6. Résumé preparation

7. Interview skills

8. Orientation to on-campus recruiting

9. Transition from school to work

10. Graduate/professional school admission

11. Time management

12. Stress management

Obviously, the above topics would be tailored to the program setting and student population, as addressed earlier. For example, a job search skills workshop for the accounting club may be quite different in format and content from a job search workshop for students with disabilities. In larger career centers, it is important that all staff become involved in programming to ensure its responsiveness to a variety of settings and populations. It is not uncommon for a large, centralized career center to develop 400 to 500 programs provided to over 20,000 students during an academic year. It may be useful, therefore, to designate one staff member as coordinator of outreach programming to contribute to a systematic, organized approach to the delivery of workshops. The outreach coordinator would also assume responsibility for maintaining records of workshop activity and for program evaluation. It is particularly important for smaller career centers with limited staff to seek cosponsorship of programming activity and, when possible, involve a number of student organizations and staff in joint programming. Also, career centers with limited staff must prioritize program requests and set specific program goals for each year.

Counseling, by nature, can be delivered only to a limited number of clients, and on-campus interviewing often serves students only in certain academic programs. In crossing a variety of career topics with a variety of settings and client populations, programming enables a career center to reach out to larger populations representative of more potential clients than is possible in counseling services or in on-campus recruiting.

Additional Programming

Courses for Credit. Since academic and career planning are often linked, career centers should have close ties with academic departments and colleges. A vehicle for developing such ties with academic units is to offer career-planning and implementation courses for credit sponsored jointly by the career center and an academic department. Credit career-planning courses offer a number of advantages, including: (1) they contribute to the professional credibility of the career center and its staff, (2) credit courses provide a captive audience who are motivated to work on career development issues, and (3) career-planning courses include a comprehensive package of interventions and have been shown to be effective in enhancing decision-making skills and facilitating student career-planning progress (Bartsch & Hackett, 1979; Garis & Niles, 1990).

The development of career courses for credit is increasingly common and will vary in focus and structure. For example, in a career course survey of Pennsylvania colleges and universities, Bolsinger (1991) found that 50 percent of the schools that responded offer a credit course and 9 percent were in the process of proposing a career course. Many career courses are developed for low-division college students and are intended to facilitate the career-planning/exploration process. Often students who are undecided in the choice of major or who are unclear concerning the linkages between a major and career plans enroll in such courses. Self-exploration exercises, assessment, supporting career counseling, educational and career information, review of career development theory, instruction in the decision-making process, and career choice issues for special populations are topics that are frequently included in career-planning courses. Other career courses may be developed for upper-division students and focus on the career implementation process. Unlike career-planning courses offered to students in varied academic disciplines or to students who are academically undecided, career implementation courses are often focused on particular majors or departments. Therefore, career implementation or job search courses may be offered in colleges such as liberal arts, education, business, or engineering. Content of these courses most often includes clarification of career goals, review of job search processes, résumé and cover letter development, interview skills, career management skills, and facilitating the transition from school to work.

Texts frequently used in support of career courses include:

Career Planning Courses

Locke, R. D. (1992). *Taking Charge of Your Career Direction, Career Planning Guide Book I.* Pacific Grove, CA: Brooks/Cole.

Shertzer, B. (1985). *Career Planning: Freedom to Choose.* Boston: Houghton Mifflin.

Mencke, R., & Hummel, R. L. (1984). *Career Planning for the '80s.* Monterey, CA: Brooks/Cole.

Michelozzi, B. N. (1992). *Coming Alive from Nine to Five.* Mountain View, CA: Mayfield.

Career Implementation Courses

Locke, R. D. (1992). *Taking Charge of Your Career Direction, Job Search Career Planning Guide Book II.* Pacific Grove, CA: Brooks/Cole.

Figler, H. (1979). *The Complete Job Search Handbook.* New York: Holt, Rinehart, & Winston.

Greenhaus, J. H. (1987). *Career Management.* Chicago: Dryden Press.

Bolles, R. N. (1987). *What Color Is Your Parachute?* Berkeley, CA: Ten Speed Press.

Experiential Learning. The acquisition of professionally relevant experience through experiential learning can be a powerful career-planning tool. Formal involvement in experiential education is quite varied, ranging from colleges and universities with cooperative education embedded in all academic disciplines to liberal arts schools lacking any formalized experiential education programs. Regardless of the extent to which a college or university is invested in experiential education, it is suggested that the career center provide some measure of support to clients interested in obtaining professionally relevant experience. Students enrolled in academic departments with formalized internship programs may be assisted by the career center in skills such as résumé preparation. In other cases, the career center may augment the academic department through assisting students in identifying internship sites. The career center may play a leading role in helping students acquire an internship or summer job when academic departments lack formal experiential education programs. Experiential education can be classified as follows:

1. Cooperative education—an alternating work-study program that is embedded in the academic curriculum. Students rotate semesters in the classroom and in the work environment. In most cases cooperative education includes both credit and pay.

2. Internships—may be for credit and/or pay. Can be a formal academic requirement of the department or may be a less formal option that can be exercised by students. Unlike cooperative education, internships are most often isolated experiences spanning a semester and/or summer.

3. Externships—provide a comparatively brief period of exposure to a career environment (often one to two weeks). Generally are volunteer in nature and carry no credit or pay. Usually externships are provided to lower-division students as a career exploration tool to test interests and gather information in a particular career environment.

4. Summer jobs—may provide relevant professional experience, such as a management traineeship or involvement in an organization related to student career goals; for example, a finance major may work as a summer bank teller. Summer jobs are paid but carry no credit. Additional summer jobs may be obtained for profit or enjoyment but may not provide professionally relevant experience but help to establish a student's general credibility as a worker.

As noted earlier, career centers should assist clients in the exploration of career plans, in understanding the linkages between majors and careers, and in the implementation of career plans. In this context, experiential education can be an important intervention in enhancing client understanding of the linkages between academic programs and careers. Furthermore, experiential education may contribute to both client exploration and the implementation of career plans. Almost all career center services discussed in this chapter are applicable to assisting clients in their involvement with experiential education. For example, clients may be assisted in career exploration through experiential education as part of counseling. If so, the career information library should include experiential education materials. In addition, outreach programs should be provided that address experiential education and assist clients in skill development required to participate in such programs. Many placement-related services, such as job search programs, résumé preparation, and interviewing skills, are also applicable to the experiential education search. On-campus recruiting systems often include interview schedules for internship opportunities or other experiential education options.

Some career centers may view experiential education planning and implementation as central to their mission and, as a result, may have staff specializing in internship coordination. Internship coordination may include the development of cooperative efforts with academic units and other administrative departments such as an alumni association, internship site development, student counseling for acquiring and adjusting to internship site, and administrative tasks associated with matching students with experiential education opportunities, as well as the development of specialized experiential education programs.

Descriptions are provided in Figure 5.8 and 5.9 of two examples of specialized experiential education programs that can be offered through the career center—externships and a minority intern program.

Figure 5.8
Extern Program

HOW SPONSORS CAN GET INVOLVED: If you believe that you would be able to be or to provide an EXTERN sponsor, complete and return the Sponsor Data Sheet now. Upon receipt of the data sheet, we will send a packet of information on the program. If you have any questions, please contact Career Development and Placement Services, 413 Boucke Building, the Pennsylvania State University, University Park, PA 16802. Phone (814) 865-2377 and ask for the EXTERN Program coordinator.

HOW STUDENTS CAN APPLY: If you are interested in participating in the EXTERN Program, you can pick up the necessary forms and schedule an appointment with the EXTERN coordinator at Career Development and Placement Services, 413 Boucke Building, 865-2377.

Sponsored by Career Development and Placement Services, the Penn State Alumni Association, the Colleges of the Liberal Arts, Arts and Architecture, Health and Human Development, and the School of Communications.

PENN STATE

EXTERN
PROGRAM

Employers
Helping
Students
Explore
Career Fields

Figure 5.8 (continued)

WHAT IS THE EXTERN PROGRAM?

A brief (two- to five-day) experience through which Penn State sophomores and juniors in the sponsoring colleges have the opportunity to work with a professional in an employment setting related to the student's educational and career goals. The student may observe and/or participate in daily responsibilities of the sponsor. Students work without pay or credit during the winter, spring, or summer vacations.

GOALS

— to offer students a chance to test career plans before making a career decision

— to provide a means by which alumni, friends, or organizations can make a meaningful, non-monetary contribution to the University and to the lives of Penn State students

— to enable organizations and sponsors to get an early look at potential future employees

HOW DOES IT WORK?

Participating sponsors develop planned career exposures to offer to students. These, in turn, are advertised to sophomores and juniors in the sponsoring colleges. Prospective EXTERNs complete an application for the experience they prefer, outlining their goals, background, and knowledge of the field. They are then interviewed and matched with the appropriate sponsor by the EXTERN Program coordinator.

IS THIS PROGRAM SUCCESSFUL?

The bottom line of the EXTERN Program is that it works to the benefit of students, sponsors, and organizations. As EXTERNs discover more about themselves and the world of work, they take steps toward effective career decision making. Sponsors have the satisfying experience of helping students at important crossroads in their lives.

ROLES AND RESPONSIBILITIES:

SPONSORS:

EXTERN sponsors are professionals in a variety of work settings including business, government, and the nonprofit sector and represent such professions as law, advertising, management, sales, banking, communications, and more. As a resource person and role model, the sponsor provides a vital part of a Penn State student's education.

Responsibilities of a sponsor involve planning and supervising the visit. An EXTERN experience should be educational and provide the EXTERN with a realistic picture of a career field. Activities should focus on what the sponsor does, how it is done, and why it is important. As a result, participation in the EXTERN Program involves an investment of staff and planning time.

EXTERNS:

Student participants come from various disciplines - from anthropology to nutrition, from art history to journalism. They seek the opportunity to learn firsthand what it is like to work in a specific field and to make judgments about their own preparation for, and commitment to, a career. As EXTERNs, students attend staff meetings, speak with colleagues, get involved in ongoing work projects, and experience typical day-to-day activities of the sponsor's organization and department.

Responsibilities of EXTERNs include participation in an orientation meeting and commitment to the program through a written contract. Students apply to a particular EXTERN experience and provide the program coordinator and the sponsors a background data sheet describing career goals and knowledge of the field. Upon placement, EXTERNs contact the sponsor to make specific arrangements. EXTERNs also are responsible for their own transportation and housing.

Figure 5.9
Minority Intern Programs

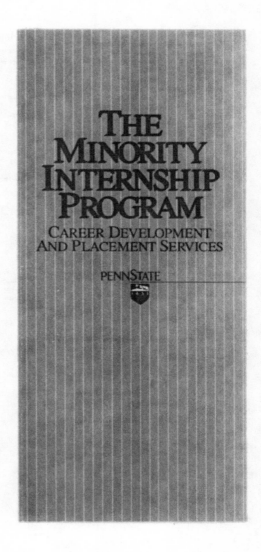

MARILYN LAMORE,
INTERN
*"My internship in health
promotions helped me to decide
to combine my interests in
telemarketing and medicine,
and working in public
health with adolescents and
children. . . . The internship helped
me become more assertive and
strengthened my interpersonal and
workplace skills."*

ARNOLD ADDISON, MAYOR,
STATE COLLEGE
*"Our minority internships have
opened new avenues of knowledge
and understanding for both
students and our municipal
staff. Our efforts have been
greatly rewarded."*

WILLIAM ASBURY, VICE
PRESIDENT FOR
STUDENT SERVICES,
PENN STATE
*"An excellent program
that provides students with
much needed experience
and enhances
'town/gown' relations."*

THE
MINORITY
INTERNSHIP
PROGRAM
CAREER DEVELOPMENT
AND PLACEMENT SERVICES

PENNSTATE

Figure 5.9 (continued)

The Minority Internship Program (MIP) provides undergraduate students at Penn State University Park Campus with work experiences in a setting related to their educational and career goals. Internship opportunities are offered by businesses and industries in and around the State College area.

Opportunities are available in virtually all fields, including accounting, administration of justice, business logistics, community education, computer science, insurance, local government, marketing, and public relations.

Student interns represent all colleges at Penn State and are from majors such as Engineering, Finance, General Arts and Sciences, Marketing, and Speech Communications.

GOALS

■ to provide preprofessional work experiences to minority students at Penn State
■ to assist students in testing career goals
■ to help students gain valuable experience as well as establish a professional network
■ to provide local business and industry with qualified, motivated individuals eager to learn and apply their skills
■ to enhance cultural diversity and community relations at Penn State and in the State College area.

THINGS YOU SHOULD KNOW

■ To participate in the program, you must be at least a fourth-semester undergraduate minority student with a 2.00 or better cumulative grade-point average.
■ Internships may be voluntary or for credit and/or pay. The minimum commitment is generally for one semester; longer internships can be arranged based on the employer's needs and your schedule.
■ Typical work assignments vary from ten to fifteen hours per week, depending on the nature of your responsibilities.
■ Assignments should relate to your career interests and general academic field. They should be designed to expose you to managerial concepts and professional activities within a given area.

HOW THE PROCESS WORKS

Phase 1: Application
In conjunction with the MIP coordinator, you develop the following application materials:
■ an internship/career objective
■ a résumé
■ a brief statement of intent

Phase 2: Placement
Your application materials are distributed to local businesses identified by you and the MIP coordinator as relevant to your internship/career objective. You then prepare for and participate in interviews with personnel at potential internship sites.

Placement results when you are offered and accept an internship.

HOW TO GET INVOLVED

Students: If you are interested in participating in the Minority Internship Program, you can pick up the application packet and schedule an appointment with the Minority Internship Program Coordinator in 413 Boucke Building.

Businesses: If you believe that you can offer an internship or have questions about participating in the program, contact the Minority Internship Coordinator at 865-2377.

FOR MORE INFORMATION, CONTACT:

Minority Internship Coordinator
Career Development
and Placement Services
413 Boucke Building
The Pennsylvania State University
University Park, PA 16802
(814) 865-2377

Career and Job Fairs

Career and job fairs are regularly offered on college and university campuses and will vary in two principal qualities. First, job fairs or career days may be sponsored by one or a combination of different organizations and targeted to a range of populations. For example, a career day may be developed for a population such as African American, Hispanic, disabled, and/or women students. Such programs could be sponsored by the career center or in concert with appropriate student groups or university services. Some specialized academic departments such as nursing or graduate programs in business or public administration could be a prime sponsor of a career day with the collaboration of the career center. Many colleges such as liberal arts, business, or engineering will hold career days. Some may be sponsored solely by the college, while others may be offered in cooperation with the alumni association of the respective college and/or the career center. At larger universities with large numbers of colleges, many career days may be held throughout the academic year, which occasionally may contribute to confusion and competition for employers and student participation. Therefore, even when they are not directly involved, it is suggested that career centers play a role in the planning and coordination of career days that are offered on large campuses to facilitate communication and publicity to students, as well as reduce the confusion of organizations participating in the events. Some career days or job fairs may transcend the student population of a college or a university to include other institutions participating in a regional consortium. Still other career days may be offered statewide to all students attending college in the state as well as residents attending college out of state who wish to return to their state for employment following graduation. For example, Rutgers University sponsors an event entitled "The New Jersey Collegiate Career Day." This event is sponsored jointly by the Rutgers Career Center and the New Jersey Chamber of Commerce, and employers pay a fee for participation. The program primarily involves large corporations and is employment-oriented. Penn State University has developed a Pennsylvania Career Day modeled on the New Jersey program offered by Rutgers. However, no employer fees are involved in the Pennsylvania Career Day, and, as a result, a large variety of nonprofit and for-profit employers participate, including health care agencies and small businesses, as well as Pennsylvania-based large corporations.

Job fairs and career days vary in a second way in that they may provide a forum for employers and/or alumni to offer career information and programs to students in facilitating career exploration, provide an opportunity for participants to make formal contact with employers in seeking internships or full-time employment opportunities, and include both career information to lower-division students and employment opportunities to seniors or graduate students. In cases where career days include contact with organizations regarding employment, the settings may range from those where students wait in line in order to present a résumé to an employer representative to career days that provide a one-day fair of employers interacting with students at booths followed by a second day of formal interviewing with students. The two ways in which career days vary may be crossed. For example, a career day may be sponsored jointly by a college of education and a career center and provide both teaching-oriented career information to participants and interviews to selected students. Furthermore, corporations such as Mobil Oil and IBM have sponsored career days that include both company information and formal interviews. Such events may be sponsored by the career center and selected academic programs. Such focused programs augment an ongoing recruiting system and provide an additional forum for students to interact with employers.

Alumni and Employee Services

While students should always be regarded as the principal client population, some career centers may expand their mission to include nonstudents such as alumni and college or university employees who have a relationship with the university. Increasingly, alumni are turning to the college or university for assistance in issues such as career management, career change, or employment assistance. Many career centers may not have the resources or staff to offer such services, but they must have well-defined responses to alumni inquiries. Career centers may be able to develop services to alumni through cooperative efforts with the alumni association and/or continuing education office. For example, alumni offices can subsidize a career center for developing programs and materials and providing services focused on the career-related needs of alumni. Continuing education offices could organize career planning or job search workshops including career center materials and staff. Furthermore, career centers may be able to provide alumni services through charging fees for materials, workshops, or services. For example, a College Placement Council (1991a) survey shows that 67 percent of career centers at large universities charge alumni users. Alumni career services could include:

1. Individual counseling
2. On-site or regional career-planning and job search workshops
3. Career management programs presented at alumni club meetings
4. Educational credential services
5. Career-planning and job search manuals
6. Employment opportunity listings, newsletters, or job hotlines
7. Computer-based networking and résumé matching services
8. Regionally based satellite alumni career centers
9. Regional alumni job fairs

Obviously, the breadth of alumni services such as those listed above will vary widely. At some colleges or universities, career services may be provided through the alumni office with little or no involvement of the career center. Other institutions may offer services that are jointly sponsored, funded, and staffed by an alumni office and the career center. Some career centers offer services to alumni with no involvement or support from other offices.

A thorough review of alumni career services is well beyond the scope of this chapter. However, a sampling of programs at selected institutions demonstrates the range and variability of alumni career services. For example, the University of Illinois staffs an alumni career center in Chicago that provides the following services:

1. Career resource center
2. Job listings
3. Alumni networking file
4. Résumé referral
5. Résumé books
6. Interviewing facilities
7. Counseling
8. Job vacancy bulletins
9. Seminars, workshops, and job fairs
10. Job hotline

The University of Wisconsin-Madison developed a program entitled Career Connection. This program assists alumni, as well as students, in networking with Wisconsin graduates. The University of Maryland offers several one-day professional development seminars that assist alumni in planning and implementing career changes. These workshops are provided on the Maryland campus and are offered by the Alumni Association and the Career Center. Penn State University also has developed alumni career-planning and job search workshops but offers its programs at various locations, and they are cosponsored by the Alumni Association and Office of Continuing Education. Both the University of Maryland and Penn State provide graduates who are Alumni Association members with discount workshop fees. The University of California at Los Angeles (UCLA) participates in an Alumni Career Fair, which provides a forum for UCLA alumni to interact with employers in a job fair environment at various locations.

Therefore, given the demand for career services by alumni and the range of programs that can be provided, it is important for the career center to establish a policy regarding its response to alumni inquiries and to develop a formal relationship with its institution's alumni association. If the career center chooses to provide alumni career services, they should be well defined, with service content and fees clearly communicated to alumni, and should not be erosive to the career center's ability to provide services to students.

Although not as common as alumni programs, career centers may extend services to their institutions' employees. Increasingly, career-planning, career management, or outplacement services are provided to employees as part of the organization's office of human resources mission. Rather than contracting with private consultants, the career center may be in a position to offer counseling and career-planning or job search workshops to employees. In such instances, the career center would be reimbursed for services by the university office of human resources. As is the case with alumni services, care must be exercised by the career center in developing clear policies and not overextending itself in providing services to employees.

Cooperative Services and Referrals from Other Offices

As a student service unit, it is critical that the career center establish cooperative relationships with a range of other university offices. For career centers charged with the mission of providing counseling for career exploration, it is particularly important to establish a strong referral network with academic advising offices. Unlike academic advising, career counseling is not a requirement. Therefore, as students who are undecided in their choice of major receive advice for course selection, they should be referred routinely to the career center. The referral process between academic advising offices and the career center can be systematized by carefully orienting academic advisers to career center programs and services. If well-informed academic advisers become allies of the career center, they can serve as advocates for the importance of early career planning and refer students to specific services such as individual counseling or a career-planning course. Furthermore, the career center could provide academic advisers with a referral card similar to the example shown in Figure 5.10 that contributes to a systematic referral process between academic advising offices and career centers.

As noted earlier in this chapter, it is important for the career center to provide cooperative services with a range of other student services offices, student organizations, and academic departments in providing career education outreach programs. For example, through cooperative efforts with an office of residence

Figure 5.10
College Advising Center Referral Card

_____
student's name

This student has been referred by an academic adviser
to make an appointment for DISCOVER or SIGI PLUS or
to meet with a counselor as a part of his/her counseling and advising process, and need not go through
Intake Counseling.

_____   _____
Signature of Adviser   Date

life, all resident assistants could be oriented to career development and placement issues as part of their training program and, as a result, serve as a conduit for the referral of students to career center services.

When providing placement services, the career center should develop strong liaisons with colleges and academic departments. Many departments have strongly vested interests in employment opportunities for graduates of their programs. As a result, academic units should be well informed of the career center placement services and understand recruiting activity associated with their disciplines. Therefore, department heads and faculty should be advocates and referral agents for career center placement and on-campus recruiting services. As noted earlier, certain placement programs such as a job fair or career interview program could be sponsored jointly by the career center and an academic department.

PURPOSE AND SUMMARY

This chapter has reviewed a variety of services that can be developed and offered by the career center. Clearly, the package of services offered by the career center will vary in relationship to career center budget and staff size; the extent of its counseling mission; the scope of its placement mission, ranging from offering no recruiting services to decentralized or centralized placement services; and the qualities of the career center's college or university. However, regardless of career center mission and size (ranging from a staff of 1 to 31), ordinarily some measure of assistance is provided to clients through three core services: (1) career counseling, including intake, appointments, groups, and assessment, (2) outreach programming, including a variety of other student service offices, academic departments, and student organizations, and (3) placement, including assistance in the acquisition of experiential education and postgraduate employment. A fourth service—career information—supports career center counseling, programming, and placement. The importance of providing a variety of current, sophisticated information through building and maintaining a career library is discussed in the following chapter.

REFERENCES

American Association for Counseling and Development. (1988). Ethical standards. *Journal of Counseling and Development, 67*, 4–8.

Bartsch, K., & Hackett, G. (1979). Effects of a decision making course on locus of control, conceptualization and career planning. *Journal of College Student Personnel, 20*, 230–235.

Bolles, R. N. (1987). *What color is your parachute?* Berkeley, CA: Ten Speed Press.

Bolsinger, J. A. (1991). *Results of a career course survey of four-year PA institutions.* Unpublished manuscript, Point Park College, Pittsburgh, PA.

Cheatham, H. (1990). Africentricity and career development of African Americans. *Career Development Quarterly, 38*(4), 334–346.

College Placement Council. (1991a). *College Placement Council 1991 membership survey.* Unpublished manuscript.

College Placement Council. (1991b). Testings. *Spotlight, 14*(9), 4.

Crites, J. O. (1974). A reappraisal of vocational appraisal. *Vocational Guidance Quarterly, 22*(4). 272–279.

Drake, Beam, & Marin, Inc. (1987). *Career Navigator Manual: The computer-powered job search system.* New York: Author.

Figler, H. (1979). *The complete job search handbook.* New York: Holt, Rinehart, & Winston.

Garfield, S. L., & Wolpin, M. (1963). Expectations regarding psychotherapy. *Journal of Nervous and Mental Disease, 137,* 353–362.

Garis, J. W., & Bowlsbey, J. H. (1984, December). DISCOVER and the counselor: Their effect upon college student career planning progress. *ACT Research Report.* (85).

Garis, J. W., & Hess, H. R. (1985). A career interview program for liberal arts students seeking business careers. *Journal of College Placement XLV,* (2), 39–44.

Garis, J. W., & Niles, S. G. (1990). The separate and combined effects of SIGI or DISCOVER and a career planning course on undecided university students. *Career Development Quarterly, 38*(3), 261–274.

Greenhaus, J. H. (1987). *Career management.* Chicago: Dryden Press.

Hansen, J. C., & Cramer, S. H. (Eds.). (1971). *Group guidance and counseling in the schools.* New York: Appleton-Century-Crofts.

Herr, E. L., & Cramer, S. H. (1988). *Career guidance and counseling through the life span: Systematic approaches* (3rd ed.). Glenview, IL: Scott, Foresman.

Hood, A. B., & Johnson, R. W. (1991). *Assessment in counseling: A guide to the use of psychological assessment procedures.* Alexandria, VA: American Association for Counseling and Development.

Johnston, J. A., Buescher, K. L., & Heppner, M. J. (1988). Computerized career information and guidance systems: Caveat emptor. *Journal of Counseling and Development, 67,* 39–41.

Lock, R. D. (1992a). *Job search: Career planning guide, Book II* (2nd ed.). Pacific Grove, CA: Brooks/Cole.

Lock, R. D. (1992b). *Taking charge of your career direction: Career planning guide, Book I* (2nd ed.). Pacific Grove, CA: Brooks/Cole.

Mencke, R., & Hummel, R. L. (1984). *Career planning for the 80s.* Monterey, CA: Brooks/Cole.

Michelozzi, B. N. (1992). *Coming alive from nine to five: The career search handbook* (4th ed.). Mountain View, CA: Mayfield.

Pinkerton, R. S., & Rockwell, W. J. (1982). One-or-two session psychotherapy with university students. *Journal of the American College Health Association, 30,* 159–161.

Prediger, D. J. (1974). The role of assessment in career guidance. In E. L. Herr (Ed.), *Vocational guidance and human development* (pp. 325–349). Boston: Houghton Mifflin.

Pyle, K. R. (1986). *Group career counseling: Principles and practices.* Ann Arbor: University of Michigan, ERIC Counseling and Personnel Services Clearinghouse.

Sampson, J. P., & Stripling, R. O. (1979). Strategies for counselor intervention with a computer-assisted career guidance system. *Vocational Guidance Quarterly, 27,* 230–238.

Shertzer, B. (1985). *Career planning: Freedom to choose* (3rd ed.). Boston: Houghton Mifflin.

Yalom, I. (1975). *The theory and practice of group psychotherapy.* New York: Basic Books.

6

Building and Maintaining a Career Library

Regardless of mission (i.e., career counseling or placement), structure and size, centralized or decentralized, small college or large university, all career centers provide some measure of career information through a resource center or library. While career information is used in support of counseling, programming, and placement services, it may also be viewed as an additional and separate service offered by the career center. This chapter reviews types of resources that should be included in the career library, their use, and physical and location considerations, as well as staffing requirements.

CAREER LIBRARY RESOURCES

Obviously, the information provided by a career center library should be related to its mission and range of services. For example, a career center providing counseling for academic/career indecision may require large amounts of self-assessment or academic information, while a decentralized career center emphasizing on-campus recruiting services would place emphasis on company and employment information related to its respective college or academic department. This section of the chapter reviews a variety of resources for inclusion in a comprehensive career center library. Clearly, the range of resources and emphasis placed on each will vary by career center mission, services, and budget.

In reviewing possible library resources, specific publications are cited as examples of different categories of information needed. However, a comprehensive review of all resources to be contained in the career library is beyond the scope of this chapter.

Academic Information—Major Files

One of the initial elements of any career library would be the development of files for each academic program within the college or university. In many instances, academic programs develop fliers, brochures, and booklets describing their majors. Often, a portion of this information addresses career opportunities associated with the major. These resources are commonly made available to admissions departments for recruiting purposes, but such information should be acquired by the career center in order to assist clients in the choice of major/career and in understanding the linkages between academic programs and careers. Major and academic information is almost always free to the career center and, when compared with general career information, is more specific to program characteristics of the university. Therefore, an informational file for each major should be maintained in the career library, and, by surveying department heads, the information should be updated at least biannually. The importance of this information to the career library cannot be overstated. Frequently, academic programs spend considerable time and money in developing materials in order to promote their majors and describe careers associated with the majors. The information is often focused and specific, concise as well as current.

In addition to files describing academic programs, several university degree bulletins or catalogs should be included in the academic program section of the career library. Further, the career center may wish to develop a simple listing of all majors and minors within the university. Such lists of academic programs will span from only one to, perhaps, four pages but can be very functional. For example, students who are undecided in academic/career choice can scan all available majors by reviewing the handout rather than be overwhelmed with the breadth of information contained in the bulletin or major files. Frequently, lower-division college students consider a choice of major before clarifying specific career plans. This is understandable since the student's present environment is in an academic, rather than career-related, setting and their present setting demands a choice of major within two years of beginning to attend college. Furthermore, reviewing, understanding, and choosing among a range of academic alternatives may be more manageable for clients who are undecided in career choice. For example, even in large universities, academic programs rarely include more than 150 majors. The career alternatives are much larger and more complicated. As a major directory of work types, the *Dictionary of Occupational Titles* (U.S. Department of Labor, 1991) includes descriptions of over 20,000 occupations. A common counseling strategy with undecided students in focusing upon alternatives, prior to referring to all career center information resources, is to request that the client carefully eliminate majors that are of no interest, using a handout giving the names of academic programs. Following this procedure, clients can develop a list of majors under consideration and begin to learn about the programs and related careers using the catalogs and files of academic programs. Such an exercise may help the undecided client to gain a structure to begin to explore and acquire career information without overwhelming the client with a full range of resources. This informational exercise rests on the assumption that the undecided student is committed to remaining in the present college or university. To such ends, files of academic programs can be classified alphabetically by college within the university.

Career Information—Files

In addition to academic program files, all career libraries will contain career information files. Information contained in such files includes booklets, brochures, fliers, and articles describing particular careers. Larger career information resources such as books, directories, handbooks, and notebooks would be maintained on separate shelves adjacent to the career files. The most fundamental, and perhaps most important, sources of career information for inclusion in the files are through professional associations. Free or inexpensive information regarding many careers is available through professional associations, for example, the American Anthropological Association, the Geological Society of America, and the American Association for Music Therapy. A complete listing of professional associations is contained in the *National Trade and Professional Association Directory* (Colgate, 1989). This directory contains a subject index, which is particularly helpful in gathering information for careers. Career information provided by professional associations is current, of high quality, and specifically focused on a professional area. Obviously, career information prepared by professional associations often suffers from a favorable bias toward occupations in that field. But the importance of the acquisition of career information through professional associations as a central component of the career library cannot be overstated. A brochure published by the American Association of Advertising Agencies (David Deutsch Associates, 1975) illustrates how powerfully specialized career information can be presented in a relatively brief resource. This association's 16-page publication, entitled, *Advertising: A Guide to Careers in Advertising*, includes the following sections:

1. What is advertising?
2. How advertising works
3. The many facets of advertising
4. What is an advertising agency?
5. What is an account executive?
   a. The marketing plan
   b. Developing the advertising program
   c. Educational preparation
   d. Occupational training
6. What is marketing research?

    a.   Securing information

    b.   The most desirable qualifications

    c.   Educational preparation

    d.   Occupational training

7. What are media?

    a.   The importance of making sound judgments as a media buyer

    b.   Educational preparation

    c.   Occupational training

8. What is the function of an agency's TV-radio department?

    a.   Educational preparation

    b.   Occupational training

9. What is the responsibility of the creative department?

10. Sales promotions departments

11. What is expected of a copywriter?

    a.   Educational preparation

    b.   Occupational training

12. What is expected of an art director?

    a.   Educational preparation

    b.   Occupational training

13. The broadcast area of advertising

    a.   TV commercials

    b.   TV producers

    c.   Educational preparation

    d.   Occupational training

14. What does broadcast operations do?

    a.   Educational training

    b.   Occupational training

15. What are the jobs within an agency's print production department?

    a.   The type director

    b.   The proofreader

    c.   Traffic control

    d.   Educational preparation

    e.   Occupational training

16. What are other opportunities in the agency?

17. Job opportunities in advertising outside of the agency

    a.   Outside suppliers

    b.   Media representatives

    c.   Direct mail advertising

18. Preparing for an advertising career
19. The importance of college
20. Practical experience while you are still in school
21. How do you go about finding a full-time job?
22. Once you are working, what are the chances of advancement?
23. Summary
24. The American Association of Advertising Agencies

Undoubtedly, lower-division clients exploring the choice of advertising as a college major or upper-division students attempting to understand the linkages between a major and advertising careers would become more sophisticated in their knowledge of advertising as a result of reviewing the brochure outlined above.

Other important resources for career libraries that provide career information include reprints of newspaper or trade journal articles, career information booklets produced by private publishing companies, and printouts of occupational descriptions included in computer-assisted guidance systems such as DISCOVER (1988) and SIGI (1988). Newspapers frequently publish articles regarding particular careers or career trends. Copies of recent articles are helpful additions to career information files. For example, as illustrative of such content, the *National Business Employment Weekly* (Capell, 1990) included an article entitled, "Ad Executives Face Tough Jobs." The article addressed current trends such as how mergers and the recession have cut corporate and agency positions. Further, the article reviewed expected advertising career trends over a six-month period and included agency advertisers' salaries for the current year. For persons considering such a career field, both the contextual and the content information obtained from such an article are extremely helpful as choices are evaluated.

A number of companies produce career information booklets that are appropriate for career files. For example, the Institute for Research publishes a series of Career Research Monographs. Their research reports include a variety of information such as a brief history of the career, employment and work descriptions, testimonials from professionals, perspectives on client qualifications, appropriate training and education, earnings, job opportunities, getting started in a career, relevant professional associations, and periodicals related to the career. Other sections that are particularly helpful in the format used by the Institute for Research Career Research Series are descriptions of interesting as well as negative aspects of the career. It is important to note that computer-assisted guidance systems provide career information in addition to interactive self-assessment and career decision-making exercises. For example, DISCOVER for Colleges and Adults includes brief and long descriptions for over 450 occupations. The career center may find it most efficient to print out descriptions of careers and include the hard copy in appropriate career information files. DISCOVER occupational descriptions include:

1. Work tasks
2. Work settings
3. Tools and materials
4. Related civilian occupations
5. Related military occupaticns
6. Education and training possibilities
7. Special requirements
8. Personal qualities
9. Career ladders
10. Salary potential
11. Projected demand for new workers
12. The good and bad side
13. Where to get more information

Therefore, an information file for a career file such as banking could include the following materials:

1. Professional association information
   a. *Your Career in Banking*, American Bankers Association (1987)
   b. *What About Banking?* American Bankers Association (1987)
   c. *Careers in Banking*, National Association of Bank Women (1983)
   d. Reading list of job opportunities in banking (26 entries), the Library American Bankers Association (1987)
2. Periodicals
   a. *NBA Today*, National Bankers Association (1990)
   b. "What I Do on the Job: Bank Manager," *Business Week Careers* (1988)
   c. "New Business Opportunities in Commercial Banking," *Bankers Magazine* (1990)
   d. "Hiring Picks Up for Specialized Bankers," *National Business Employment Weekly* (1991)
   e. "Banking Futures," *New Accountant* (1990)
3. Career information publications, booklets, and brochures
   a. *Jobs and Careers with Banks*, Institute for Research (1987)
   b. *Careers in Banking and Finance*, American Institute of Banking— California (1990)
4. Computer-assisted guidance information
   a. "Long Description for Bank Officer/Manager," DISCOVER for Colleges and Adults (American College Testing, 1988).

Career Information—Books, Directories, and Other Shelved Resources

A wide range of books and directories providing career information is available through publishers and government agencies. Unlike brochures and pamphlets produced by professional associations, such information may require additional shelf space and can be expensive. Career center libraries will vary in their ability to include books for a range of career areas. Certain directories, however, are fundamental in building a career library. For example, *The Dictionary of Occupational Titles* (DOT) (U.S. Department of Labor, 1991), published by the U.S. Department of Labor, includes classifications and descriptions of approximately 20,000 jobs. The DOT is a necessary component for any career library since it provides an occupational classification system using a nine-digit coding system and is referred to as a major resource in other information systems such as the Self-Directed Search (Holland, 1985) and DISCOVER (American College Testing, 1988). A further strength of the DOT is that it provides counselors and clients with a framework by which to understand the diversity and characteristics of the larger career world, as well as in-depth descriptions of specific jobs. However, the complex and thorough nature of the DOT can limit its utility. The *Occupational Outlook Handbook* (OOH) (U.S. Department of Labor, 1991), compiled by the U.S. Department of Labor and published by VGM Career Horizons, offers a more user-friendly approach to providing information for a range of major occupations. The OOH clusters over 200 occupations within 13 categories, and each occupational description follows a standard format:

1. Nature of the work
2. Working conditions
3. Employment
4. Training, other qualifications, and advancement
5. Job outlook
6. Earnings
7. Related occupations
8. Sources of additional information

Because it is current and includes readable summaries of a variety of occupations, the OOH is often the initial resource used with clients as they begin to gather information about particular careers of interest.

Other general directories of occupations and careers are available. For example, *America's 50 Fastest Growing Jobs*, published by JIST Works, Inc. (Farr, 1991), includes occupational information compiled by the U.S. Department of Labor and used in the OOH but focuses on occupations with projected growth opportunities. *The Jobs Rated Almanac* (Krantz, 1988) provides descriptions of over 250 jobs ranked by a variety of criteria, including salary, stress, benefits, and travel. *Jobs! What They Are, Where They Are and What They Pay* (Snelling and Snelling, 1989) includes information that describes responsibilities, earnings, training, and further details for occupations in the following 29 categories:

1. Advertising and sales promotion
2. Agribusiness
3. Architecture and design
4. Clergy
5. Carpenters
6. Counseling
7. Ecology and conservation
8. Education
9. Engineering
10. Federal and municipal government
11. Finance
12. Health services
13. Health technology
14. Hospitality and travel
15. Industry
16. Law
17. Law enforcement
18. Management and office administration
19. Marketing
20. Media and communications
21. Medicine
22. Military
23. Performing arts
24. Physical sciences
25. Retailing
26. Sales
27. Self-employment and temporary
28. Service occupations
29. Social sciences

The categories outlined above make the Snelling and Snelling resource helpful in that the occupations included are well organized to reflect the range of possibilities in each career area. Some resources provide occupational descriptions within certain career areas. An example of this is the *Handbook of Scientific and Technical Careers* (Norback, 1990), published by VGM.

In addition to general directories of occupational information, career libraries include books and directories focused on particular career areas. Therefore, it is often helpful to organize occupational information holdings by the academic program structure of the respective college or university. Care must be taken to acquire specific sources of occupation information that reflects the range of majors or academic programs within the college or university. Often, more information and resources are available for vocationally oriented fields such as business or engineering than for liberal arts fields. However, an increasing range of resources is marketed that provides career information associated with less vocationally oriented majors such as the arts and humanities. Indeed, career libraries in smaller colleges or those with limited majors may place more emphasis on gathering resources in less vocational academic or nontechnical programs since the linkages between academic major and vocational opportunities are less clearly defined and understood and thereby contribute to greater client need for career information. As noted earlier, a comprehensive listing of publications and resources that are available for all career areas is well beyond the scope of this chapter. However, the following sample of 12 resources reflects the diversity of career information:

1. *The Outdoors Career Guide* (1986)
2. *Careers in Engineering* (1989)
3. *Career Choices for the 90's: History* (1990)
4. *Exploring Careers in Foreign Languages* (1990)
5. *Flying High in Travel: A Complete Guide to Careers in the Travel Industry* (1986)
6. *Is Psychology the Major for You?* (1987)
7. *Opportunities in Accounting* (1990)
8. *Magazine Career Directory* (1988)
9. *Careers in Teaching* (1990)
10. *Careers in International Affairs* (1991)
11. *120 Careers in the Health Field* (1989)
12. *Exploring Careers in Science* (1989)

Examples of information resources applicable to just one career area, the arts, follow:

1. *Career Opportunities in the Music Industry* (1986)
2. *Careers in Graphic Arts* (1988)
3. *Opportunities in the Performing Arts* (1991)
4. *How to Survive and Prosper as an Artist* (1988)
5. *Opportunities in Craft Careers* (1988)
6. *Career Opportunities in Art* (1988)
7. *Opportunities in Photography Careers* (1991)
8. *Opportunities in Interior Design Careers* (1988)

Each career field has at least as many diverse and relevant information resources as do the arts, and requires that managers or career libraries think carefully about space and other priority issues pertinent to choosing the number and type of such resources by career field.

Employment Directories

In addition to providing career information that is helpful to students engaged in the career choice process, as well as to students attempting to learn more about career options, most career libraries provide directories of potential employers. As in the case of career information, a wide range of organizational-employer directories are available, and career centers must prioritize their needs with respect to client requirements for employer information. Employer directories are also best classified according to the academic structure of the college or university. The career library may wish to acquire a number of general employment directories that could not be categorized under a particular program. Some excellent general employment directories that illustrate the range of career areas follow. *The Career Guide: Dunn's Employment Opportunities Directory* (Dunn & Bradstreet Corporation, 1991) includes descriptions of thousands of employers and lists: (1) the educational specialties possessed by the employees the company usually hires; (2) a brief history of the company and its line of business; (3) most promising areas of employment prospects and information on recruiting and hiring; (4) an overview of career development opportunities in the company; (5) company locations; (6) a statement of the company's benefits; and (7) the company address and name, title, and telephone number of the person to contact for employment information. Employers are indexed alphabetically and geographically, as well as by Standard Industrial Classification (SIC) codes. Other employer directories helpful to business and technical graduates include *Standard & Poor's Stock Market Encyclopedia* (Standard & Poor's Corporation, 1991), *The National Directory for Corporate Training Programs* (1988), and *Peterson's Job Opportunities for Engineering, Science and Computer Graduates* (Peterson's Guides, Inc., 1991b). *The Job Hunter's Source Book* (1990) includes listings of professional associations, periodicals, and other employment directories helpful to clients seeking employment in a variety of fields. One of the strengths of this resource is that it includes information that spans the continuum of career areas ranging from an accountant to legislative aides to sports officials. Directories helpful to clients interested in non-profit employment opportunities include *Finding a Job in the Non-Profit Sector* (1991) and *Good Works: A Guide to Social Change Careers* (1991). *Finding a Job in the Non-Profit Sector* includes lists of associations, local government, museums, libraries, social services, and schools. *Good Works* includes listings of social interest opportunities and provides the following information for each occupation: (1) purpose, (2) methods of operation, (3) constituency, (4) recent issues and projects, (5) publications, (6) budget, (7) funding, (8) staff, (9) benefits, (10) part-time employees, (11) summer employees, (12) volunteers, (13) interns, and (14) application contacts.

Employer directories that are classified in ways relevant to the academic programs of the college or university will be quite varied. As noted with respect to career information, career centers may wish to create a balance of resources reflecting the needs of clients in all majors. However, particular attention should be placed on obtaining employment directories for nonbusiness and nontechnical career areas that typically are not served through on-campus recruiting or other traditional placement services. A sample of 12 employer directories that reflect a variety of such resources follows:

1. *Artist's Market* (1988)
2. *National Directory of Environmental Organizations* (1988)
3. *National Wildlife Federation Conservation Directory* (1992)
4. *The Fashion Resource Directory* (1990)
5. *Directory of Museums and Historical Organizations in PA* (1991)
6. *Harvard Business School Career Guide for Management Consulting* (1987)
7. *Laboratories Directory* (1989)
8. *Information Technology Services Directory* (1991)
9. *Membership Directory* (Employee Assistance Professionals Association, Inc., 1990)
10. *Directory of Pennsylvania Nursing Homes* (1991)
11. *Patterson's American Education* (1992)
12. *Sports Market Place* (1991)

An example of employer information for one career area—communications—follows:

1. *The Broadcasting Yearbook* (1991)
2. *O'Dweyer's Guide to Public Relations Films* (1988)
3. *O'Dweyer's Guide to Corporate Communications* (1988)
4. *Standard Directory of Advertisers* (1992)
5. *Literary Marketplace* (1989)

Career-Planning and Job Search Directories

Career centers often place emphasis on empowering clients with the knowledge and skills to clarify goals and assertively conduct a self-directed job search. Because traditional placement services such as on-campus recruiting meet career-related needs of only a limited number of college students, large numbers of self-help publications have been developed over the past several years to make information and skills related to career planning and job search accessible to persons not able to use the services of career centers or to augment such services. As with career information and employment directories, career-planning and job search directories will vary in their applicability to particular career fields. Some, such as Bolles's *What Color Is Your Parachute?* (1987) and Powell's *Career Planning Today* (1990), represent excellent general resources for enhancing client knowledge in the employment search process. Bolles's publication is very effective in educating clients to assume personal control of goal clarification and their job search process and in developing tactics assertively to research and contact employers. Powell's book also provides information concerning career exploration and job search skills but is particularly strong in helping the reader to become more sophisticated regarding knowledge of career and employment environments by including major sections addressing a variety of work environments and management career exploration. Other general publications that are often used in support of career-planning and placement credit courses were noted in Chapter 5 and should be included in this section of the career library. These include:

1. *Career Planning: Freedom to Choose* (1985)
2. *Coming Alive from Nine to Five* (1992)
3. *Taking Charge of Your Career Direction, Career Planning Guidebook I* (1992)
4. *Job Search Career Planning Guide, Book II* (1992)
5. *Career Management* (1987)
6. *The Complete Job Search Handbook* (1979)

Employment search directors will vary in their emphases on career planning and goal clarification, general job search strategies, specific content on concrete job search techniques such as résumé writing or interview skills or application to particular career fields. The career library should include employment self-help publications that reflect each of these topics. In addition to the general resources noted above, a sample of 12 self-help career-planning and job search publications include:

1. *High Impact Resumes and Letters* (1990)
2. *Developing a Professional Resume or Vita* (1990)
3. *200 Letters of Job Hunters* (1990)
4. *Interview for Success* (1990)
5. *Resumes for Communications Careers* (1991)
6. *The Advertising Portfolio* (1990)
7. *So You Want to Be in Advertising* (1988)
8. *The Perfect Job Reference* (1990)
9. *Liberal Arts Jobs: Where They Are and How to Get Them* (1986)
10. *Careers for Dreamers and Doers: A Guide to Management Careers in the Non-Profit Sector* (1989)
11. *John T. Molloy's Dress for Success* (1988)
12. *Work in the New Economy: Careers and Job Seeking into the 21st Century* (1987)

Special Sections

Career center libraries may wish to include special categories of information that are of particular importance to clients. For example, library sections could be developed that represent a blend of career information, employment directories, and self-help materials for special populations, international careers, and government.

The career library should represent not only the range of academic/career fields but also the needs of culturally diverse clients of the career center. As a result, the career library should provide information for such special populations, including African Americans, Hispanics, women, international students, returning adults, and students with disabilities. A sample of 12 career information publications for special populations includes:

1. *Minority Organizations: A National Directory* (1987)
2. *The Directory of Special Opportunities for Women* (1981)
3. *Directory of Special Programs for Minority Group Members* (1986)
4. *The Black Woman's Career Guide* (1982)
5. *Resumes Que Consiquen Emplees* (Spanish language version of *Resumes That Get Jobs*) (1989)
6. *Operation Job Match: Guide to Clients with Disabilities* (1987)
7. *Yes You Can: A Handbook for the Physically Disabled (1990)*
8. *The Women's Job Search Handbook* (1991)
9. *Women's Networks* (1980)
10. *Finding a Job in the U.S.* (International students) (1986)
11. *New Horizons: The Educational and Career Planning Guide for Adults* (1985)
12. *Over 40 and Looking for Work* (1991)

Due to the extent of opportunities, complexity, and potential applicability to a wide range of clients, most libraries would develop a special career information section for government opportunities. Through the development of a liaison with federal and state government employment representatives, career libraries can include materials such as SF 171 Forms, the standard application form for the Federal Government Office of Personnel Management, and state application forms, as well as federal and state career information publications, announcements, and bulletins. Similar materials may be obtained from local governments in major cities. Specifically, career libraries would include (1) government application forms, (2) governmental organization information and career opportunity publications, (3) government agency information, and (4) vacancy announcements. Twelve major examples of government career information follow:

1. *Washington Information Directory* (1991)
2. *The 171 Reference Book* (1987)

3. *How to Get a Federal Job* (1986)
4. *The United States Government Manual* (1990)
5. *Information USA* (1986)
6. *The Complete Guide to Finding Jobs in Government* (1990)
7. *Civil Service Handbook* (1988)
8. *The Harvard Guide to Careers in Government and Public Sector* (1987)
9. *Law Enforcement Employment Guide* (1990)
10. *Find a Federal Job Fast!* (1990)
11. *U.S. Geological Survey: Volunteer/Intern/Teaching Opportunities* (1992)
12. *Career America: Federal Career Directory* (1990)

Due to the increase in international careers in many job families and corporations, many career libraries may find it helpful to develop a special international careers section. Again, this section could include a blend of career information, employer directories, self-help books, and specific job announcements. A sample of 12 useful international career resources includes:

1. *International Careers* (1987)
2. *The International Corporate 1000* (1989)
3. *101 Ways to Find an Overseas Job* (1987)
4. *Overseas Employment Opportunities for Educators* (1991)
5. *Almanac of International Jobs and Careers* (1991)
6. *International Businesswoman of the 1990's* (1990)
7. *How to Get a Job in Europe* (1991)
8. *Making It Abroad* (1988)
9. *How To Teach Abroad* (1989)
10. *Directory of Overseas Summer Jobs* (1991)
11. *International Jobs: Where They Are and How to Get Them* (1989)
12. *The Complete Guide to International Jobs and Careers* (1990)

Experiential Education

The importance of the career center's services to clients interested in obtaining experiential education opportunities such as internships, summer jobs, cooperative education, externships, and volunteer experiences was noted in Chapter 5. Therefore, it is important that the career library contain information that describes its services to assist clients in obtaining professionally relevant experience. Since clients may be unclear as to the definition for experiential education, this library section could be labeled as internship, summer job, and volunteer information. Contents of this section could include (1) internships and summer job directories,

(2) current vacancy announcements for summer jobs or internships, (3) files of past internships and summer job opportunities, (4) notices of internships or part-time employment opportunities available through the college or university, (5) listing of campus organizations that provide opportunities for involvement, volunteerism, or leadership development, and (6) referrals to other university services or academic departments that assist students in obtaining internships, volunteer experiences, or part-time employment. Most career centers will be routinely informed of available internships or summer jobs. As a result, the career library should include files of these announcements, classified by internships, that provide professionally relevant experience or part-time/summer jobs. Current opportunity announcements could also be displayed on bulletin boards. Because internships and summer jobs may be applicable to a variety of academic majors, they may be filed in simple alphabetical order. However, the career library may wish to develop an index of opportunities located at the beginning of the file.

Because college and university academic departments vary in the assistance they provide to students to obtain internships, it is recommended that students be referred to their academic department for further information. In addition to current internship or summer job opportunities, career centers may wish to gather information concerning past experiences held by their students. For example, career centers providing on-campus recruiting services could survey registrants on a volunteer basis regarding past internships or summer jobs that they held and would recommend to other students. The logic is obvious: a graduating senior hopefully would no longer be interested in the internship or part-time employment experience, and the sponsor or employer may be interested in another student from the respective college or university. A sample survey form for gathering information about past internships or temporary jobs is shown in Figure 6.1

Because student involvement or leadership experience acquired through student organizations can be such a powerful career-planning and job search tool, it is recommended that the career library maintain information regarding the range of activities and student organizations available to clients. This information may be most appropriate for inclusion in the experiential education portion of the career library. In addition to specific past and present announcements of summer jobs, internships, and volunteer experiences, a sample of 12 resources applicable to experiential education that would be maintained by the career library follows:

1. *New Careers: A Directory of Jobs and Internships in Technology and Society* (1990)

2. *1992 Internships* (1992)

3. *Peterson's Summer Opportunities* (1989)

4. *The National Directory of Internships* (1989)

5. *Connection 1992: A Directory of Lay Volunteer Opportunities* (1992)

6. *Volunteer USA* (1991)

7. *Internships in Foreign and Defense Policy* (1990)

8. *The Complete Guide to Washington Internships* (1990)

9. *The National Directory of Arts Internships* (1989)

10. *Directory of International Internships* (1987)

11. *Summer Employment Directory* (1988)

12. *Internships, Volume I: Advertising, Marketing, Public Relations and Sales* (1990)

Figure 6.1
Best Temporary Job Form

Check One: Please Print:

_____ Internship (for _____ credits)   Your college _____

_____ Summer Job   Your major_____

Job Title _____ Hours per week _____ wage (optional) $ _____

Name of Organization _____

    Street _____

    City _____   State _____

Supervisor _____   Job Title _____

Organization's product/service _____

Check your main responsibilities:

    _____ serving customers   _____ manual labor

    _____ outside sales   _____ operating machines

    _____ helping/counseling others   _____ laboratory or technical work

    _____ teaching/supervising others   _____ working with numbers/data

    _____ other:_____

Additional comments concerning the job:

Undergraduate, Graduate, and Professional School Directories

Some career center clients will be considering a transfer to another college or university while others may be interested in pursuing an additional undergraduate degree. As a result, the career library should include information concerning baccalaureate degree-granting institutions. Furthermore, many career center clients will be in the process of deciding about graduate or professional schools as well as postgraduate training programs in such areas as the allied medical fields, law, or business. A sample of 12 resources that may be of assistance to clients considering additional education and training include:

1. *Peterson's Four-Year Colleges* (Peterson's Guides, 1990a)

2. *The Insiders Guide to the Colleges* (1989)

3. *Peterson's Two-Year Colleges* (Peterson's Guides, 1990b)

4. *Peterson's Graduate Programs Books 1-5* (Peterson's Guides, 1991a)

5. *The Official Guide to MBA Programs* (1990)

6. *The Official Guide to US Law Schools* (1991)

7. *Medical School Admissions Requirements (AAMC)* (1987)

8. *Allied Health Education Directory* (1988)
9. *Graduate Study in Psychology and Associated Fields* (1989)
10. *The Pre-Med Handbook* (1987)
11. *Graduate Admissions Essays* (1991)
12. *Gourman's Report: Graduate and Professional Programs* (1987)

Vacancy Listings

All career centers routinely receive announcements of job opportunities that should be filed by academic program or career field. It may be beneficial for the career center to develop a referral system with academic departments for the exchange of job announcement information. Many announcements of internships, summer jobs, or full-time professional vacancies may be received that are applicable to a variety of majors, and these should be filed and cross-indexed by career field and location. In certain specific career fields such as education, it may be desirable to compile and distribute vacancy listings summarizing opportunities in particular career fields. These vacancy listings can be distributed on-site but may also be sent to alumni or students involved in off-campus internships. Computer-based applications of position announcements are reviewed in Chapter 7.

Salary Information

The College Placement Council (CPC) publishes its Salary Survey (1992) on a quarterly basis and compiles reports from 450 career centers across the United States. Reports are issued in January, March, July, and September. The number of offers included in each report is cumulative from the previous September. The survey is available to CPC members and represents an excellent source of salary information that should be included in the career library. Salary information is provided by functional area for a wide range of employer types. A further strength of the survey is that it provides very specific salary data by including tables cross-indexing beginning salary offers to all candidates by curriculum and employer type as well as curriculum and career functional area. Number of offers, average salaries, and salaries in the 90th and 10th percentiles are included in the tables for bachelor's degree recipients. Less detailed salary offers for graduate degrees are listed by type of graduate program. While the survey is an excellent resource about current salary offers, care must be taken in considering the sample and number of respondents. For example, the number of business and engineering majors is large, enabling more generalization of information compared with certain specific non-technical fields such as the humanities and social sciences.

As noted earlier, the *Occupational Outlook Handbook* includes national salary data compiled by the U.S. Department of Labor for each occupation listed. While this information is helpful and discusses salary for beginning and more experienced employees, the data are more general than information provided by CPC. Some college and university career centers conduct salary surveys for their graduates. When follow-up surveys include a representative sample of graduates, they can be a rich source of employment and salary information since they are focused on the respective academic programs of the university. Therefore, a complete career library should include salary information acquired from CPC, the Department of Labor, and, if possible, localized follow-up surveys conducted by the career center or academic departments.

Employer Information

The breadth of employer information included in the library will be related to the extent of the placement and on-campus interview mission of the career center. However, all career centers will include some measure of employer information, and in career centers with large, centralized placement responsibilities, information may be maintained for hundreds of organizations The types of employer information necessary include (1) annual reports, (2) organizational brochures and descriptions of career opportunities, (3) videotapes describing organizations and reviewing career opportunities, and (4) company history and biographies. Obviously, such information is useful for clients in preparing for on-campus interviews, and it also will be helpful to clients conducting self-directed job searches. In addition to supporting the job search, the above information can be very helpful to clients in exploring career opportunities and in becoming sophisticated in the knowledge of a career area or employer type. Beyond reviewing general information in the career files, a client considering a banking major or career could be referred to employer information in order to learn more about the organization of a large bank, review career opportunities in a bank by reading portions of an annual report, or investigate organizational career opportunities by viewing a videotape of a selected bank. For example, a typical career opportunities packet developed by a large bank and secured for use by the career center might include information such as a financial statement, organizational chart, list of executive management, and a brief history. In addition to these materials, descriptions of various banking careers would be included, addressing topics such as retail banking, wholesale banking (capital markets, global corporate banking, international banking, leasing and market banking), and service products (private clients, institutional service products, wholesale services, cash management, financial data processing, and network services), as well as real estate finance and mortgage banking. A review of such information would assist clients seeking employment in such an organization but would also be extremely helpful to a client considering a banking career. In most instances, annual reports, career opportunity brochures, videotapes, and, occasionally, books reviewing organizational histories are provided free to career centers. The information may be indexed alphabetically by type of employer and/or type of information received. A common limitation to career center employer information is that it often represents only larger business or government organizations that are able to produce and distribute such material, not small organizations with under 100 employees where new jobs are being created.

Video Information

Increasingly, media-based career information is being developed and should be included in a section of the career library. As noted earlier, major companies and government agencies have developed videotapes describing their organizations and career opportunities. Furthermore, many professional organizations are beginning to develop tapes describing their careers. For example, the American Psychological Association has developed a tape entitled, *Careers in Psychology. Your Options are Open* (1991), and the Council of Logistics Management has produced a tape, *Logistics: Careers with a Challenge* (1990). In addition to providing employer and career information, large numbers of videotapes are produced by professional associations and private enterprise. Indeed, a review of catalogs of companies marketing career information reveals the availability of videos addressing almost every facet of the career-planning and job search process, including reviews of career-planning assessments, job search techniques, résumé and cover letter preparation, interview skills, and job survival-career management skills. Occasionally, career centers may wish to develop their own video materials addressing topics such as résumé preparation or interview skills. Tapes may be produced to orient students to the career center in general or to specific career center services such as registration and use of on-campus recruiting or what to expect from the career counseling process. Frequently, academic departments produce videotapes describing majors. These are used in the academic advising or admissions process, and such resources should be included in the career library. With the advent of relatively inexpensive and mobile video-recording equipment, many career centers may film career-related workshops and panel presentations. Many colleges and universities invite alumni and employer representatives to campus for guest lectures and classes or to participate in career-related seminars. Career centers may find it helpful systematically to schedule all returning professionals who are presenting programs with a brief videotaped interview regarding career information or job search techniques in their respective career.

Many career centers, such as the University of Virginia's Office of Career Planning and Placement, have organized a video resource center that is adjacent to the career library. Media-based resource centers could include (1) videos providing company and organization information, (2) career information, (3) privately produced tapes addressing the career-planning or job search process, (4) locally produced orientations to career center services, (5) video-based information about majors, or (6) interviews or programs presented by visiting alumni or employer representatives.

Geographic or Location Information

The career library may include information about cities or locations that commonly attract the school's interns or graduates. Most cities will send free information produced by its chamber of commerce and/or convention and visitors council. Location resources could include (1) visitors guide, (2) community profile (listing information such as population, climate, cultural and recreational resources, educational institutions, work force information, market demographics, major industries, transportation, and tourism information), (3) chamber of commerce directories, (4) hotel/motel guides, and (5) magazines including community information and events. Such materials may be of help to clients in planning interview trips, considering graduate and professional school locations, deciding among internship sites, or considering postgraduation employment offers.

Free Information, Periodicals, and Handouts

The library should place a major focus on the career center's mission of bridging the college or university and the work world. As a result, the career library may wish to subscribe to a local city newspaper, the *New York Times*, the *Wall Street Journal*, and/or the *Chronicle of Higher Education*. These resources should be displayed prominently and be accessible to career center clients. Career centers routinely receive career-related fliers, job announcements, and graduate/professional school information that should be displayed on bulletin boards. Further, a variety of career-related magazines are sent free in bulk to career centers. Examples of current free periodicals should be displayed and copies made available to clients. A sample of 12 periodicals routinely sent to career centers includes:

1. *Graduating Engineer* (1992)
2. *The Wall Street Journal: Managing Your Career* (1992)
3. *Working Woman* (1992)
4. *Careers and the Disabled* (1992)
5. *The Black Collegian* (1991)
6. *Business Today* (1990)
7. *Career Futures* (1992)
8. *Graduate School Guide* (1990)
9. *Looking Ahead: An Overview of Career Paths and Opportunies* (1992)
10. *Equal Opportunity* (1992)
11. *Woman Engineer* (1992)
12. *Hispanic Engineer* (1982)

Almost all career centers will produce handouts in support of their services. These should be displayed and made available through the career library. Handouts developed by a large, comprehensive career center would address topics such as:

Job search strategies

Résumé writing

Letters for the job search process

Interview skills

Planning successful interview trips

Legal/illegal interview questions

How to complete employment application forms

Occupational information interviewing

Seeing a career counselor—what to expect

Using the career library

Computer-assisted guidance orientation and use

Internship and summer job search

Applying to graduate and professional school

The federal government hiring process

Typing, typesetting, and photocopying services

Computer-Based Career Information

Computer-based guidance systems that contain career information, as well as job search network and vacancy information systems, are commonly housed in the career library. Other computer applications that may be contained in the career center include library catalog, indexing, and search systems, as well as computer-based assessment measures used in support of career counseling. Computer-based applications are becoming part of almost all libraries, and the career-related systems will be reviewed in Chapter 7.

CAREER LIBRARY LOCATION AND STAFFING

The career library is one of the most visible components of the career center. Certain career centers are configured such that clients enter the career library first, and the reception area is part of the resource center. This model has an obvious advantage in that career center clients are provided with immediate exposure to the library and may observe others using the resources. A potential disadvantage exists, however, if the environment becomes congested with a variety of clients, not all of whom are actively using career resources. Furthermore, if support staff are serving in dual roles such as receptionist and library assistant, quality of service to clients using the career library may suffer. Another common model for location of the career library is to provide a separate reception and waiting area for career center clients with an adjacent career library and support staff. In this model, the library is separated from the entrance yet represents the center of career services with staff offices located around its perimeter. This configuration keeps focus on the career library yet controls initial client traffic into the career center. A disadvantage of this model, however, is that as staff enter or exit their offices, they may be met with frequent questions and requests for assistance by clients using the library. While this may be beneficial, such configurations could contribute to lack of control and confusion in providing support to clients who are using the career library. Career libraries that are completely separate from reception, waiting areas, and staff offices may enjoy a more secure and controlled environment but may suffer from lack of visibility and utilization.

Allocation of space within college or university departments is always competitive and difficult. Obviously, career center space allocations will influence and place limitations on the size and location of the career library. However, if physical resources permit, an ideal location for the career library would represent a combination of the models noted above. For example, the career library would be located near the career center reception area and would be visible to clients. The library would include separate rooms or sections for computer-based systems and video resources. A copy machine should also be available for career library users. The reception area and waiting areas for counseling or recruiting services would be separate from the career library. Staff offices would be nearby but would not enter directly into the library. A small office shared by staff could be provided within the library for intake purposes.

The central staffing component of the career resource center is the librarian. It is critical that an individual always be present to assist clients, maintain vigilance and organization, and have familiarity with all of the resources. The librarian should be a full time career center employee to provide consistency in the management of career information resources. If the librarian is a clerical staff member, a career center professional should be assigned general responsibility for career information and supervision of library support staff. The librarian should serve a dual role of ordering, indexing, and organizing the resources and also providing staff and clients with assistance in locating and using materials. As noted in Chapter 5, many career centers may find it desirable to develop an intake rotation of staff who are able to respond to immediate client questions. The intake office could be in close proximity to the career library in order to provide walk-in clients with immediate assistance and also could serve as a referral source for the career librarian. Often, career centers may wish to train and use interns, career counselors, or student work-study assistants in staffing the career library. Use of such paraprofessionals will be reviewed in Chapter 9. Staffing of a career information center, therefore, should begin with the librarian and include a blend of professional staff and student assistants. Peterson, Sampson, and Reardon (1991) noted the importance for the librarian to collaborate with counselors and other career center professional staff. For example, the librarian may receive requests from staff regarding acquisition of resources, or the librarian may routinely make recommendations to staff concerning materials or services. As noted earlier, the librarian will focus on technical procedures such as acquiring, categorizing, displaying, or evaluating information but will also assist patrons. Obviously, counselors will also provide clients with assistance in using the library. Therefore, Peterson et al. (1991) best describe the role of counselor and librarian as "complementary."

MANAGEMENT

As pointed out above, a professional staff member should assume responsibility for career information and work with a librarian, support staff, and other career center professional staff in the acquisition, classification, maintenance, application, and evaluation of resources. In large, comprehensive career centers, library resources may be quite varied and complex in supporting all counseling, programming, and placement services. Materials will include printed resources, video information, and computer-based services. In such a center, it may be desirable to develop a career information coordinating committee including staff representing a variety of career center services. Furthermore, the career center librarian may wish to establish a liaison with the college or university library to exchange information, consider cross-indexing of career resources, and develop a client referral system.

Since the resource needs of a career library are dynamic and complex, the librarian may develop a form that can be utilized by staff in requesting additional materials. Furthermore, forms should be made available to clients soliciting requests for information.

A variety of resources are available to assist in the acquisition of information. Professional associations such as the National Career Development Association (NCDA) and the College Placement Council (CPC) produce bibliographies of publications dealing with career information. The U.S. Department of Labor (1980) publishes *A Counselor's Guide to Occupational Information*, which lists government publications relating to careers. National and state networking efforts have been developed that also support the production and distribution of career information. These are the National Occupational Information Coordinating Committee (NOICC) and State Occupational Information Coordinating Committees (SOICC). These organizations publish resources such as the *Occupational Information Systems (OIS) Handbook* (1981), which identifies sources of occupational data. Furthermore, directories of career information resources are produced by publishing companies. For example, the *Professional Careers Sourcebook* (Savang & Dorgan, 1990) is published by Gale Research, Inc., and provides a comprehensive review of informational resources available for an extensive list of careers.

In selecting resources for the career library, consideration should be given to the following NCDA basic guidelines (National Career Development Association, 1980):

1. The material should contain a clear statement of its intended purpose and the group to be served.

2. The presentation of the information should be appropriate to the developmental, educational, and maturity levels of the intended audience.

3. The material should address the cultural diversity of North America society.

4. The occupational descriptions should offer balanced, accurate appraisal of opportunities and working conditions and not be influenced by recruiting or special interests.

5. Career information should include the social and psychological implications of each type of work, including its effects on health and life-style.

Classification of materials included in the career library represents a challenge in information management. In the descriptions of career resources provided earlier in this chapter, an index was suggested that reflects the academic structure of the respective college or university. However, a variety of methods for classifying career information have been developed. For example, the Florida State University Career Center chose the Standard Occupation Code (SOC) (U.S. Department of Commerce, 1980) for classifying its occupational information. Its resources are cross-referenced using a surrogate master card filed under any occupational areas in which the resource may apply. Other classifications systems include the DOT code (U.S Department of Labor 1991a), Holland Codes (Gottredson & Holland, 1989) or Standard Industrial Classification Code (SIC) (U.S. Department of Commerce, 1977). Computer-based systems for classifying library information are available. For example, the Career Key system (Smith, 1983) is available to help users locate library information and is reviewed further in Chapter 7. In any case, the career center staff and librarian should collaborate in developing a classification and coding system that allows for the identification and indexing of each resource within the career library.

STUDENT ACCESS

Career center services and the career library should be organized to encourage accessibility and heavy use of career resources by a wide range of clients. Client use of the career library may be considered in the following ways: (1) walk-in clients browsing through resources and, if necessary, receiving assistance from the librarian or student assistant, (2) clients assisted by an intake counselor in finding and reviewing information, (3) clients assisted by staff during or following a counseling appointment or referred by counselors to return to the library, (4) clients scheduled by appointment to use particular library services such as video or computer-based resources, (5) clients referred to the library from outreach programs or credit courses, (6) clients using the library in support of on-campus recruiting services, and (7) outreach programs and courses holding on-site orientations to the career library. At minimum, the career library should be open and available to clients during all career center hours. In some instances, it may be desirable to offer additional career library hours during evenings or weekends to enhance client accessibility.

PURPOSE AND SUMMARY

The career library should be viewed as central to the career center with respect to both its services and its location. The library should support all career center core services, including counseling, programming, and placement. Beyond supporting services, the career library should be viewed as an additional career center intervention that assists clients in making and implementing career decisions. The complexity and breadth of library resources will be influenced by career center mission, as well as by fiscal, space, and staffing limitations. However, in supporting and providing career services, the library should include a comprehensive blend of files, books, directories, periodicals, handouts, videos, and computer-based information that address the needs of career center clients. The library would be a service that is heavily used and that serves as a focal point for helping the career center bridge its college or university and the career world.

REFERENCES

Allen, J. G. (1990). *The perfect job reference.* New York: Wiley.

Alperin, S. (1989). *120 careers in the health care field.* Miami: U.S. Directory Service.

American Bankers Association. (1987a). *Reading list on job opportunities in banking.* (Available from the library American Bankers Association, 1120 Connecticut Ave. N.W., Washington, DC 20036.)

American Bankers Association. (1987b). *What about banking?* (Available from American Bankers Association, 1120 Connecticut Ave. N.W., Washington, DC 20036.)

American Bankers Association. (1987c). *Your career in banking.* (Available from American Bankers Association, 1120 Connecticut Ave. N.W., Washington, DC 20036.)

American College Testing. (1988). *Discover for colleges and adults.* Iowa City, IA: Publisher.

American Council of Independent Laboratories, Inc. (1989). *Directory* (20th ed.), Washington, DC: Author.

American Psychological Association. (1989). *Graduate study in psychology and associated fields.* Hyattsville, MD: Author.

American Psychological Association. (1991). *Careers in psychology: Your options are open* (videotape). Washington, DC: Author.

Anthony, R. J., & Roe, G. (1991). *Over 40 and looking for work?* Holbrock, MA: Bob Adams.

Asher, D. (1991). *Graduate admissions essays.* Berkeley, CA: Ten Speed Press.

Association of American Medical Colleges. (1987). *Medical school admission requirements, 1988–89.* Washington, DC: Author.

Ball, V (1988). *Opportunities in interior design careers.* Chicago: VGM Career Horizons.

Bard, R. & Elliot, S. (1988). *The national directory of corporate training programs.* New York: Stonesong Press.

Barry, A. M. (1990). *The advertising portfolio.* Lincolnwood, IL: NTC.

Bekken, B. (1991). *Opportunities in performing arts careers.* Chicago: VGM Career Horizons.

Beusterien, P. (1988). *Summer employment directory.* Cincinnati, OH: Writer's Digest Books.

Bloomberg, G., & Holden, M. (1991). *The woman's job search handbook.* Charlotte, VT: Williamson.

Bolles, R. N. (1987). *What color is your parachute?* Berkeley, CA: Ten Speed Press.

Bowker, R. A. (1989). *Literary marketplace, 1989.* New York: Science Press.

Brainard, J. C., & McGrath, R. N. (Eds.). (1988). *The directory of national environmental organizations.* St. Paul, MN: Environmental Directories.

Butterworth, A. S., & Migliore, S. A. (1989). *The national directory of internship.* Raleigh, NC: National Society for Internships and Experiential Education.

Caffrey, E. (1988). *So you want to be in advertising.* New York: Simon & Schuster.

Cantrell, W., & Marshall, T. (1987). *101 ways to find overseas jobs.* Merrifield, VA: Cantrell.

Capell, P. (1990, July 8). Ad executives face tough selling jobs. *National Business Employment Weekly*, pp. 17–18.

Capell, P. (1991, March 10). Hiring picks up for specialized bankers. *National Business Employment Weekly*, pp. 16–17.

Carland, M. P., & Spatz, D. H. (Eds.). (1991). *Careers in international affairs*. Washington, DC: School of Foreign Service, Georgetown University.

Carrol, A. (1991). *Volunteer USA*. New York: Ballantine Books.

Castrovilla, M. (1990). *Graduate school guide*. New Rochelle, NY: Victor Ridder.

Cavin, P., Gorham, J., & Petersen, L. (1990). *Career choices for the 90's: History*. New York: Walker.

Christensen, W. (1989). *National directory of arts internships*. Los Angeles: National Network for Artist Placement.

Cohen, L., & Young, D. (1989). *Careers for dreamers and doers: A guide to management careers in the nonprofit sector*. New York: Foundation Center.

Colgate, C. (1989). *National trade and professional associations of the United States*. Washington, DC: Columbia Books.

College Placement Council. (1992). *Salary survey*. Bethlehem, PA: Author.

Committee on Allied Health Education and Accreditation. (1988). *Allied health education directory*. Chicago: American Medical Association.

Connor, S. (1988). *Artist's market*. Cincinnati: Writer's Digest Books.

Council of Logistics Management. (1990). *Logistics: Careers with a challenge* (videotape). Oak Brook, IL: Author.

Cowan, J. (1991). *Good works: A guide to careers in social change*. New York: Barricade Books.

David Deutsch Associates. (1975). *Advertising: A guide to careers in advertising*. New York: American Association of Advertising Agencies.

Davies, A. (1991). *Washington information directory*. Washington, DC: 1991 Congressional Quarterly.

Doss, M. (1981). *The directory of special opportunities for women*. Garrett Park, MD: Garrett Park Press.

Dunn & Bradstreet Corp. (1991). *Dunn's employment opportunities directory*. Parsippany, NJ: Author.

Edelman, A. (1990). *The fashion resource directory*. New York: Fairchild.

Educational Directories, Inc. (1992). *Patterson's American education*. Mount Prospect, IL: Author.

Educational Testing Service. (1988). *SIGI Plus*. Princeton, NJ: Author.

Edwards, E. W. (1990). *Exploring careers in foreign languages*. New York: Rosen.

Employee Assistance Professionals Association, Inc. (1990). *Membership directory, 1991*. Arlington, VA: Author.

Farr, M. (1991). *America's 50 fastest growing jobs*. Indianapolis: JIST Works.

Field, S. (1986). *Career opportunities in the music industry*. New York: Facts on File.

Figler, H. (1979). *The complete job search handbook*. New York: Holt, Rinehart, & Winston.

Frank, W. (1990). *200 letters for job hunters*. Berkeley, CA: Ten Speed Press.

Friedenberg, J., & Bradley, C. (1986). *Finding a job in the U.S.*. Lincolnwood, IL: Passport Books.

Fry, R. (1988). *Magazines career directory*. Hawthorne, NJ: Career Press.

Fry, R. (1990). *Internships Volume 1: Advertising, marketing, public relations and sales*. Hawthorne, NJ: Career Press.

Garfinkle, D. (1988). What I do on the job: Bank Manager. *Business Week Careers*, pp. 50–51.

Garrett Park Press. (1987). *Minority organizations: A national directory* (3rd ed.). Garrett Park, MD: Author.

Gottfredson, G. D., & Holland, J. C. (1989). *Dictionary of Holland occupational codes* (2nd ed.). Odessa, FL: Psychological Assessment Resources.

Gourman, J. (1987). *Gourman's report: Graduate and professional programs*. Los Angeles: National Education Standards.

Graduate Management Admission Council. (1990). *The official guide to MBA programs*. Princeton, NJ: Author.

Greenhaus, J. H. (1987). *Career management*. Chicago: Dryden Press.

Hammer, H. (1988). *Civil service handbook*. New York: Arco.

Haponski, W. C., & McCabe, C. E. (1985). *New horizons: The education and career planning guide for adults*. Princeton, NJ: Peterson's Guides.

Haubenstock, J. (1988). *Career opportunities in art*. New York: Facts on File.

Hawes, Brownstone. (1986). *The outdoors career guide*. New York: Facts on File.

Helfand R. (1990). *New careers: A directory of jobs and internships in technology and society*. Washington, DC.: Student Pugwash, USA.

Hoffa, H., & Morgan, G. (1990). *Yes you can: A helpbook for the physically disabled*. New York: Pharos Books.

Holland, J. L. (1985). The Self-Directed Search: Professional manual. Odessa, FL: Psychological Assessment Resources.

Howard, R. E., & Mortensen, C. L. (1987). *The Harvard guide to careers in government and the public sector*. Cambridge, MA: Office of Career Services, Harvard University.

Information Technology Association of America. (1991). *Information technology services directory*. Arlington, VA: Author.

Institute of Research. (1987). *Jobs and careers with banks*. (Available from the Institute for Research, P.O. Box 8039, Northfield, IL 60093.)

Johnson, B., Mayer, R. E., & Schmidt, F. (1991). *Opportunities in photography careers*. Chicago: VGM Career Horizons.

Johnson, K. M. (Ed.). (1987). *Harvard business school career guide, management consulting 1988*. Cambridge, MA: Harvard Business School Press.

Johnson, W. (1986). *Directory of special programs for minority group members*. Garrett Park, MD: Garrett Park Press.

Jones, R. (1989). *How to teach abroad*. Plymouth, United Kingdom: Northcote House.

Kazi-Ferrouillet, K. (Ed.). (1991, December). *The black collegian*. New Orleans: Black Collegiate Services.

Kelly, A. (Ed.). (1992, May). *Woman engineer*. Greenlawn, NY: Equal Opportunity.

Kleiman, C. (1990). *Women's networks*. New York: Lippincott & Crowell.

Kocher, E. (1989). *International jobs, where they are, how to get them*. Reading, MA: Addison-Wesley.

Krannich, B. (1990). *High impact resumes and letters*. Woodbridge, VA: Impact.

Krannich, C. R., & Krannich, R. L. (1990a). *Find a federal job fast!* Woodbridge, VA: Impact.

Krannich, C. R., & Krannich, R. L. (1990b). *Interview for success*. Woodbridge, VA: Impact.

Krannich, R. L., & Krannich, C. R. (1990). *The complete guide to international jobs and careers*. Woodbridge, VA: Impact.

Krannich, R. L., & Krannich, C. R. (1991). *The almanac of international jobs and careers*. Woodbridge, VA: Impact.

Krantz, L. (1988). *The jobs rated almanac*. New York: Ballantine Books/Random House.

Kraus, K. (1986). *How to get a federal job*. New York: Facts on File.

Lauber, D. (1990). *The complete guide to finding jobs in government*. River Forest, IL: Planning/Communications.

Law School Admissions Council. (1991). *The official guide to US law schools*. Newton, PA: Law Services.

LeCompt, M. (1990). *Job hunter's sourcebook*. Detroit: Gale Research.

Lee, T. (Ed.). (1992, Spring). *The Wall Street Journal: Managing your career*. New York: Dow Jones.

Lesko, M. (1986). *Information USA*. New York: Viking Penguin Books.

Levitin, H. (1987). *Pre-med handbook*. New York: Warner Books.

Lipsey, R. (1991). *Sports market place 1991*. Princeton, NJ: Sportsguide.

Lock, R. D. (1992a). *Job search: Career planning guide, Book II* (2nd ed.). Pacific Grove, CA: Brooks/Cole.

Lock, R. D. (1992b). *Taking charge of your career direction: Career planning guide, Book I* (2nd ed.). Pacific Grove, CA: Brooks/Cole.

McDaniels, C. (1990). *Developing a professional vita or resume*. Garrett Park, MD: Garrett Park Press.

Madison Newspapers. (1992). *Looking ahead*. Madison, WI: Author.

Markland, J. (1992). *Career futures*. Westport, CT: Career Information.

Mayall, D. (1990). *Careers in banking and finance*. (Available from American Institute of Banking - California, Department A, 550 Kearny St., Suite 310, San Francisco, CA 94108.)

Mellado, C. (Ed.). (1992). *Hispanic engineer*. Baltimore: Career Communications Group.

Michelozzi, B. N. (1992). *Coming alive from nine to five: The career search handbook* (4th ed.). Mountain View, CA: Mayfield.

Michels, C. (1988). *How to survive & prosper as an artist*. New York: Henry Holt.

Molloy, J. (1988). *John T. Molloy's New dress for success*. New York: Warner Books.

Muirhead, G. (1989). *Peterson's summer opportunities*. Princeton, NJ: Peterson's Guides.

Munday, M. (1988). *Opportunities in crafts careers*. Chicago: VGM Career Horizons.

Nadler, B. (1986). *Liberal arts jobs: What they are and how to get them*. Princeton, NJ: Peterson's Guides.

National Association of Bank Women. (1983). *Careers in banking*. (Available from National Association of Bank Women, 500 N. Michigan Ave., Chicago, IL 60611.)

National Bankers Association. (1990, Spring). *NBA Today*.

National Register Publishing Company. (1992). *Standard directory of advertisers*. Wilmette, IL: Author.

National Vocational Guidance Association. (1980). Guidelines for the preparation and evaluation of career information literature. *Vocational Guidance Quarterly, 28*, 291–296.

National Wildlife Federation. (1992). *National Wildlife Federation conservation directory*. Washington, DC: Author.

Nivens, B. (1982). *The black woman's career guide*. Garden City: Anchor Press/Doubleday.

NOICC. (1981). *Occupational information system handbook: Vol. 2. Occupational information analysis, presentation and delivery.* Washington, DC: U.S. Government Printing Office.

Norback, C. (1990). *Handbook of scientific and technical careers.* Chicago: VGM Career Horizons.

O'Dwyer, J. (1988a). *O'Dwyer's directory of corporate communications.* New York: J. R. O'Dwyer.

O'Dwyer, J. (1988b). *O'Dwyer's directory of public relation firms.* New York: J. R. O'Dwyer.

Office of the Federal Registrar. (1990). *The U.S. government manual, 1990/91.* Washington, DC: U.S. Government Printing Office.

PA Federation of Museums & Historical Organizations. (1991). *Directory of museums and historical organizations in PA.* Harrisburg: Author.

Parness, J. (1990). *The complete guide to Washington internships.* Washington, DC: JMP Enterprises.

Peterson's Guides. (1990a) *Peterson's four-year colleges.* Princeton, NJ: Author.

Peterson's Guides. (1990b). *Peterson's two-year colleges.* Princeton, NJ: Author.

Peterson's Guides. (1991a). *Peterson's graduate programs, books 1-5.* Princeton, NJ; Author.

Peterson's Guides. (1991b). *Peterson's job opportunities for engineering, science & computer graduates, 1992.* Princeton, NJ: Author.

Peterson's Guides. (1992). *1992 internships.* Princeton, NJ: Author.

Peterson, G. W., Sampson, J. P., & Reardon, R. C. (1991). *Career development and services: A cognitive approach.* Pacific Grove, CA: Brooks/Cole.

Povich, L. (Ed.). (1992, May). *Working woman.* Harlan, IA: Carol Anderson Taber.

Powell, C. R. (1990). *Career planning today* (2nd ed.). Dubuque, IO: Kendall/Hunt.

Reed, J. (Ed.). (1989). *Resumes que consiquen emplees.* New York: Arco.

Roberson, V. (1988). *Careers in the graphic arts.* New York: Rosen.

Roberts, J., Glizzo, C. A., & Shingleton, J. D. (1987). *Directory of international internships.* East Lansing: Michigan State University.

Rose, M. (1987). *Operation job match: Guide for clients with physical disabilities.* Washington, DC: Operation Job Match.

Rosenburg, M. (1990). *Opportunities in accounting.* Chicago: VGM Career Horizons.

Rossman, M. (1990). *The international businesswoman of the 1990's.* New York: Greenwood.

Rubin, K. (1986). *Flying high in travel: A complete guide to careers in the travel industry.* New York: Wiley.

St. Vincent of Pallotti Center. (1992). *Connections 1992: A directory of lay volunteer opportunities.* Washington, DC: Author.

Sanborn, R. (1991). *How to get a job in Europe.* Chicago: Surrey Books.

Savage, K., & Dorgan C. (1990). *Professional careers sourcebook.* Detroit: Gale Research.

Schenck, A. W. (1990). New business opportunities in commercial banking. *Bankers Magazine, 173* (2), 45–49.

Schnabel, T. (Ed.). (1989). *The international corporate 1000.* New York: Monitor.

Schneider, J. (Ed.). (1992a). *Careers and the disabled.* Greenlawn, NY: Equal Opportunity.

Schneider, J. (Ed.). (1992b). *Equal opportunity.* Greenlawn, NY: Equal Opportunity.

Schuman, H. (1988). *Making it abroad.* New York: Wiley.

Shapiro, S. J. (1989). *Exploring careers in sciences*. New York: Rosen.

Shertzer, B. (1985). *Career planning: Freedom to choose* (3rd ed.). Boston: Houghton Mifflin.

Shockley, Cutlip. (1990). *Careers in teaching*. New York: Rosen.

Smith, E. (1983). Career Key: A career library management system. *Vocational Guidance Quarterly, 32* (1), 52–56.

Snelling, R. D., & Snelling, A. M. (1989). *Jobs! What they are, where they are, what they pay*. (rev. ed.). New York: Simon & Schuster.

Solomon, M. (Ed.). (1990). *Business today*. Princeton, NJ: Foundation for Student Communication.

Standard & Poor's Corporation. (1991). *Standard & Poor's corporate stock market encyclopedia*. New York: Author.

State Health Data Center, Pennsylvania Department of Health. (1991). *Directory of PA nursing homes*. Harrisburg, PA: Author.

Stern, R. (1990). *Law enforcement employment guide*. Mt. Shasta, CA: Lawman Press.

Taft Group. (1991). *Finding a job in the nonprofit sector, 1991*. Rockwell, MD: Author.

U.S. Department of Commerce. (1977). *Standard industrial classification manual*. Washington, DC: Office of Management and Budget.

U.S. Department of Commerce. (1980). *Standard occupational classification manual*. Washington, DC: Office of Federal Statistical Policy and Standards.

U.S. Department of Defense. (1991). *Overseas employment opportunities for educators*. Alexandria, VA: Author.

U.S. Department of the Interior. (1992). *U.S. geological survey Volunteer/intern/teaching opportunities*. Reston, VA: Author.

U.S. Department of Labor. (1980). *A counselors guide to occupational information*. Washington, DC: Bureau of Labor Statistics.

U.S. Department of Labor (1991a). *Dictionary of occupational titles*. Washington, DC: U.S. Government Printing Office.

U.S. Department of Labor (1991b). *Occupational outlook handbook*. Lincolnwood, IL: VGM Career Horizons.

U.S. Office of Personnel Management. (1990). *Career America*. Washington, DC: U.S. Government Printing Office.

VGM Career Horizons. (1989). *Careers in engineering*. Chicago: Author.

VGM Career Horizons. (1991). *Resumes for communication careers*. Chicago: Author.

Wegmann, R., Chapman, R., & Johnson, M. (1989). *Work in the new economy: Careers and job seeking into the 21st century*. Indianapolis: JIST Works.

West, D. (1991). *The broadcasting yearbook*. Washington, DC: Broadcasting.

Williams, C. (Ed.). (1992). *Graduating engineer*. Encinco, CA: Peterson's/COG.

Win, D. (1987). *International careers*. Charlotte, VT. Williamson.

Women in International Security. (1990). *Internships in foreign and defense policy*. Cabin John, MD: Seven Locks Press.

Wood, P. (1987). *The 171 reference book*. Washington, DC: Workbooks.

Woods, Wilkinson. (1987). *Is psychology the major for you?* Washington, DC: American Psychological Association.

Woodworth, D. (1991). *1991 directory of overseas summer jobs*. Oxford United Kingdom: Vacation-Work.

Yale Daily News. (1989). *The insider's guide to the colleges*. New York: St. Martin's Press.

Yingst, R. A. (1990, March). *Banking futures. New accountant*, pp. 38–40.

7

The Use of Computers and Technology in the Career Center

The use of computers is now evident in almost all professions, and, certainly, computer-based applications to information management, record keeping, and service delivery of college and university career centers are increasingly common and continue to evolve rapidly. Computer applications are ubiquitous, and it is difficult to imagine almost any career center function that, to some extent, does not involve computerization. For example, a College Placement Council survey (1991) found that 95 percent of the responding career centers indicated the use of one or more computers in support of their services. Computerized functions identified by college career centers included:

1. Word processing
2. Employer database
3. Career guidance/counseling
4. Statistical reports
5. Position-vacancy listings
6. Student records
7. Alumni files/résumés
8. Student résumés
9. Desktop publishing
10. Budgeting/accounting
11. Career-information indexing
12. Vacancy matching referral systems
13. Scheduling employer visits

14. Interview sign-ups
15. Employer literature

The degree to which computerization is used in support of the center's activities will vary by career center mission, services, size, staffing, and budget. The sophistication of career centers in integrating computer-based applications in support of their services will also vary. The status and quality of computerization within college career centers are very dynamic, with some computer applications offering great utility while other software packages have quickly become obsolete and others were ill-conceived from their inception. A review of all computer-based applications that are available to the career center is an unrealistic goal of this chapter, particularly in light of the rapid evolution of computerization. However, major computer-based applications are reviewed, focusing on their use in a range of career center activities, including information management, record keeping, and placement and recruiting systems, as well as counseling and assessment services. When possible, specific examples of computer-based applications used in support of career center functions are identified and reviewed. Appendix 7.1 includes an alphabetical listing of the developer and address for software noted in this chapter.

For a more detailed review of computer software applications to career centers, the reader is referred to the *Computerization Sourcebook* published by the College Placement Council (CPC) (1991). This publication reviews findings of a national survey regarding career center applications and offers a compendium of currently available software. CPC surveyed more than 100 developers and provided application information, pricing, and acquisition information for software packages applicable to career center services. The software is classified both alphabetically and by the following primary application headings:

1. Alumni records
2. Applicant testing
3. Applicant tracking
4. Candidate information systems
5. Career guidance
6. Career information
7. College selection
8. Desktop publishing
9. Employee records
10. Employer information
11. Information management
12. Job listing
13. Job-search skills

14. Job-search tracking
15. Résumé development
16. Résumé handling
17. Scheduling
18. Sign-up
19. Spreadsheet
20. Word processing

Yet another helpful section of the CPC publication is a listing of 580 college career centers that are indexed under the technological function in which each office expressed experience and a willingness to share its computer applications with others.

It should be noted that the career center functions appropriate for computerization, as described in a number of sections within this chapter, may be served through the same database management or software system. For example, a computer-based recruitment system may create a database of employers, maintain activity records, assist candidates in résumé writing, and facilitate the matching and scheduling of candidates with employers. Within this context, this chapter is structured to reflect many of the fundamental functions of the career center that are most appropriate for computerization. These include (1) basic information and files that should be maintained by the career center, (2) activity records kept by the career center, (3) placement and recruiting services, (4) computer-assisted career guidance systems (CACGS), and (5) computer-based interest and personality assessment.

INFORMATION MANAGEMENT AND THE USE OF DATABASES

Career centers should maintain files and records in support of fundamental services, including employer information, employment listings, client information, and career information. Each of these files can be computerized to facilitate categorization, updating, record keeping, and planning.

Employer Information

Contact persons, address, phone, academic programs of interest, and recruitment activity should be maintained by the career center for employers using the on-campus interview system. The College Placement Council computer/technology survey (1991) found that, aside from word processing, employer databases were the functional area most frequently reported as computerized by career centers. Such files are essential for future communication with employers in planning recruitment visits. An employer database is useful for the referral of candidates outside the on-campus recruitment process, and information could be developed to facilitate employer identification for involvement in specialized events such as career days, participation in outreach programs. conferences, and courses. Furthermore, employers could be tracked according to those solicited for monetary contributions to the university, academic department, or the career center. Career centers can easily develop employer files through general database management packages such as PC File, marketed by Jim Button, or by using more comprehensive software developed specifically for career center placement activity such as the Universal College Recruiting System (UNICORE). UNICORE has a variety of other more sophisticated features applicable to recruiting systems, which are reviewed later in this chapter. However, one facet of UNICORE enables career centers to develop a database of employers involved in the on-campus recruiting system.

Almost all career centers maintain files of employer literature and information in support of the on-campus recruiting process. Employer files include organizational information, annual reports, and descriptions of career opportunities, as well as video-based employer information. A computerized database is helpful for maintaining, categorizing, and updating employer literature and could be developed through software such as PC File.

Employment Listings

Most career centers routinely receive vacancy announcements. Often when poor economic conditions restrict on-campus recruiting by employers, vacancy announcements increase as an efficient method used by employers to increase the candidate pool. A computerized database of employment listings contributes to the career center's classification and updating of vacancy announcements. At minimum, an index and record of vacancies could be generated through the database. More sophisticated localized programs could be developed by the career center to allow candidates to sort through an on-line menu of opportunities. One example is the Texas Job Bank, which is a computer-based listing of statewide employment opportunities developed by the career center at the University of Texas at Austin. Many other computer-based packages for listing employment opportunities and providing a matching service for candidates have been developed at the national level and are reviewed later in this chapter. Other computerized systems have been developed to allow students or alumni to check current job announcements through 24-hour phone access. In any case, career centers should maintain a relatively simple database of position announcements received by mail, fax, or phone and maintain this information in a computer file readily accessible to students and staff.

Alumni Information

A variety of career services that may be provided to alumni were reviewed in Chapter 5, and many of these services can be supported through computerization.

Career centers choosing to offer services to alumni should initially create a database of alumni receiving services. It is common for alumni to become involved in a variety of career center services, including counseling, workshops, credentials, and/or job matching services. Often these services are provided to alumni on a fee basis. As a result, career centers should maintain a file of all alumni receiving services to maintain records of types of services provided, fee schedules and payments, registration, and service period dates, as well as alumni information and demographics.

Many career centers also routinely receive vacancy announcements that are for experienced professionals and that are applicable to their alumni. A database of such listings can be developed, and vacancy announcements may be produced and distributed to alumni. The career center may wish to develop a service through which employment opportunities and candidate career interests and qualifications are coded to enable the computer-based matching of alumni with employers. In addition to databases developed by career centers, a variety of computer-based candidate information and job listing systems have been developed at the national level that are applicable to alumni, as well as to students. A sample of these systems is reviewed in the discussion of placement applications later in this chapter.

The importance of networking as a mentoring and job search strategy has been well documented, and increasingly, career centers in cooperation with alumni associations are becoming interested in developing an alumni database that may be used by students as well as alumni for networking purposes. Computer applications such as database management or electronic bulletin boards are applicable to developing and maintaining such files. For example, an Alumni Information System package marketed by TSM Associates is available to enable students to access information concerning alumni mentors by career fields. The program can print alumni lists, labels, and reports of alumni employment. PC Automated Alumni Career Mentor Records, developed at the Career Services Office at Brooklyn College, stores information on alumni mentors. Home and business address, position, and alumni job descriptions are included in this system. Reports and labels can be produced by the career center. This package offers an optional module that provides students with direct access to the database. Whether the career center uses a localized system or a database management package marketed nationally, care must be taken to define clearly the use and limits of such services for alumni agreeing to be included in the file as well as for students or alumni making contacts from the database.

Student/Client Information

For record-keeping and program accountability purposes, almost all career centers will wish to develop a database for clients receiving services. By actively maintaining computer-based records for ongoing client activity, career centers can easily identify factors such as type and frequency of service used by clients, client semester standing, academic major, demographic information, gender, and ethnicity. Client records for career center service activity can be entered daily through a software package such as PC File. More elaborate client scheduling and record-keeping systems are reviewed later in this chapter.

Career Information

The importance of indexing and maintaining information included in the career library was noted in Chapter 6. The career center may wish to develop a database information management system for library resources or use systems developed and marketed nationally. For example, Career Key (Smith, 1983) is a computer-based system that enables location of information in the library and also classifies records of career information resources. PC Automated Career Library Records, developed at the Career Services Office at Brooklyn College, may be used to maintain databases for career library materials, publishing companies, and clients borrowing materials. The system has the capablity to identify which materials should be reordered from a particular publisher at certain times. Most college and university libraries also maintain career-related materials and have developed computer-based catalog systems. The career center may wish to develop a computer link with the main library and provide a terminal in the career library to review additional career resources available through the university library.

RECORD KEEPING AND EVALUATION OF CAREER CENTER SERVICE ACTIVITY

Program accountability is a critical issue for all career centers, and computer-based applications to data management clearly facilitate record keeping. Records of service activity are of fundamental importance for primary career center programs, that is, counseling, outreach, and on-campus recruiting.

Computer-Based Record Keeping for Counseling Services

The importance of providing intake services was reviewed in Chapter 5, and because walk-in and intake services are brief and used heavily, it is important that a record-keeping system be developed to gather basic client information and record service activity efficiently. For example, a scannable form such as shown in Figure 5.1 can be developed to enable intake staff to acquire client information and record intake activity easily. Scan forms can be scored at any time to acquire, maintain, and report intake activity, including:

1. Number of intake clients
2. Gender
3. Client academic program
4. Semester standing

5. Client characteristics such as ethnicity, citizenship, or other special categories such as disability, returning adult, or veteran

6. Type of career concern presented

7. Intake services provided

8. Referrals

Activity records for counseling by appointment may also be maintained through computer-based systems. Information from counseling records and forms such as those shown in Chapter 5 may be entered daily into a software package such as PC File, resulting in the development of a database for counseling activity. Computer-based information maintained for individual counseling appointments would include:

1. Client information, that is, address, phone, gender, ethnicity, citizenship, and other characteristics such as disabled, returning adults, veterans, or student athletes

2. Counselor

3. Counseling activity, that is, number of appointments, cancellations, or no-shows

4. Other services used, that is, assessment activity

5. Referrals

In addition to maintaining counseling activity records, software has been developed to facilitate counseling appointment scheduling and record keeping. Such systems enable a receptionist easily to identify available counseling appointment times, develop and print professional staff schedules, schedule group meetings, reschedule postponed appointments, enter schedule results, and produce activity reports. An example of a calendar management program is Front Desk, marketed by Peachtree Software. A software package that has been developed specifically for scheduling appointments and workshops for groups of career counselors is PC Automated Appointment Scheduling, developed at the Career Services Office at Brooklyn College. Other group scheduling software packages include (1) the Coordinator II by Action Technologies, Inc., (2) Schedule +1.00a by Microsoft Corp., (3) CaLANder 1.29 by Microsystems Software, Inc., (4) Meeting Maker 1.0 by On-Technology, Inc., and (5) Network Schedule II by PowerCore, Inc. In addition to facilitating counseling scheduling and record keeping, such systems can be used for the calendar management of all career center professional activity and meetings.

Computer-based calendar management can be rather complex. For example, some software packages were developed for business or medical practices and may not be of sufficient flexibility to be used effectively by career centers. Furthermore, larger career centers may experience difficulty in identifying systems to manage comparatively large numbers of professional staff and appointments. When adequate systems are identified, it is important that the career center acquire adequate hardware to develop a scheduling network that can be accessed by all staff involved in the system. However, when appropriate systems are identified and integrated into the career center, they may enable efficient scheduling of client appointments, provide a calendar system for all staff, and include a record-keeping system for counseling activity within the program.

Record Keeping for Outreach Programming

Although career centers often provide outreach programs to large numbers of clients, records of the characteristics of individual participants are not practical or necessary. Therefore, relatively simple records of program activity may be maintained through software such as PC File. Information maintained in this database would include:

1. Program topic
2. Program setting, that is, nature of the sponsoring organization, such as student group, academic class, residence hall, or career center
3. Contact person and organizational information, such as address and phone
4. Number of students attending
5. Participating career center staff

Record Keeping for On-Campus Recruiting Activity

Career centers providing on-campus recruiting services will maintain activity records. More sophisticated computer-based applications to placement services are reviewed in the following section. However, regardless of type of computer application (simple database management systems, nationally marketed interview selection and interviewing systems, or locally developed software packages), most career centers will use technology to maintain records of recruitment activity. For example, PC File or a nationally based placement service software package such as UNICORE enables the career center to gather and report recruiting service activity. Computer-based recruiting activity records should be maintained to enable the career center to report the following information:

1. Number of organizations recruiting
2. Number of interview schedules
3. Number of students registering for on-campus interviews
4. Number of interviews conducted
5. Number of interview requests submitted
6. Interview activity by college and major
7. Interview activity by employer, that is, requests received and interviews conducted

8. Registration and interview activity by candidates, that is, gender, degree type, college/ major, age, type of placement (internship, permanent), ethnic status or specific category (disabled, international, returning adult, veteran)

PLACEMENT AND RECRUITING COMPUTER-BASED APPLICATIONS

All career centers provide placement-related services to clients. Some may offer sophisticated, centralized, on-campus interview systems while others assist clients in résumé writing and/or in developing and conducting a self-directed job search. Regardless of placement service, computer applications can be used by career centers to assist clients in the implementation of career plans. For example, software systems are available to assist clients in producing a résumé while interactive programs are available to help clients in the development and implementation of a job search campaign. Furthermore, systems are rapidly being developed at the national level to create a database of candidates and employers necessary for electronic matching services. This portion of the chapter reviews computer-based résumé, job search, and national job listing/matching services. Once again, it should be noted that the purposes or functions of many computerized placement systems are not mutually exclusive. For example, some national database job search or candidate matching systems help users to develop résumés. In addition to reviewing placement-related software packages, this section also reviews computer applications to career center on-campus recruiting services.

Software for Résumé Development

The Perfect Resume Kit, marketed by Permax Systems, Inc., provides users with instruction regarding résumé construction and offers a variety of examples. The system enables users to alter résumés for particular positions and saves résumés in ASCII files to be produced and printed from a word processing package. Resume Express is a Career Leap program developed by Future Business Leaders of America and Phi Beta Lambda in partnership with Permax Systems, Inc. Resume Express includes the following sections, leading to the development of a computer-based chronological, functional, or targeted résumé:

1. Résumé writing tips
2. Define magnificence (identifies user's top ten capabilities, accomplishments, and leadership qualities)
3. Selection of the best format
4. Completion of résumé sections
5. Arranging résumé sections

6. Designing the résumé

7. Assembling the résumé

In addition to assisting the user in the general construction of a résumé, the Resume Express software package provides over 200 skill- or accomplishment-related words for inclusion in the résumé.

Other résumé development packages include ResumeMaker, marketed by Kane and Associates, which also assists the user in other job search and interview skills. ResumeMaker includes a user appointment calendar to monitor and track the job search campaign. Resume Writer by Bootware Software Company, Inc., and Resumes by Ralph by Resume-Link are yet additional software packages currently available to assist clients in résumé construction. It is important to note that many résumé computer-based packages are marketed either to individuals or to career centers for use with clients. For example, the Perfect Resume Kit, Resumes by Ralph, and Resume Writer are available in career center versions. As noted earlier, many other computer-based job search and candidate matching systems have résumé writing packages embedded in their systems.

Interactive Job Search Software

Career Navigator (Drake, Beams & Morin, 1987) is a comprehensive and interactive computer-based job search system and includes the following sections:

1. Know yourself (identify your interests, define your values, discover your communication style, identify your accomplishments, identify your skills, target your job objective, identify your ideal job preferences)

2. How to communicate (how to use the telephone effectively, how to write effective letters, how to interview effectively, managing communication style, the networking interview, the job interview)

3. Develop your job search tools (understand the job market, develop your contacts, conduct research on organizations, create résumés to market yourself, how to write effective résumés, maintain your personal database, write your résumés, obtain your references)

4. Conduct your job search campaign (manage your campaign, understand campaign plan, identify your campaign plan, develop a weekly action plan, assess your weekly progress, maintain contacts and target organizations, create letters to market yourself)

5. Land that job (negotiate your offers, evaluate your offers, and survive the first three months)

As noted in the above list, Career Navigator includes a section to assist the user in developing a résumé. Computer-based interactive job search systems are relatively new interventions, and research regarding their effectiveness is limited. However, Garis and Hess (1989) conducted research regarding the effectiveness of Career Navigator with a sample of college students majoring in business. They found that, when compared with a job search credit course and a wait-listed control group, clients using the Career Navigator computer-based package demonstrated significantly higher ratings of self-reported confidence and progress in the job search process. Additional job search–oriented, computer-based packages include Job Quest, developed at the Career Planning Office at Hartwick College, the Micro Job Search Tool Kit by Career Development Software, Inc., and the Winning Approach to Interviewing by Professional Resource Center.

Computer-Based Packages for Matching Candidates with Employers

A variety of systems have been developed at the national level to exchange candidate and/or employer information electronically. Because these systems are developing so rapidly, their effectiveness for students, alumni, and employers remains questionable. Clearly, the application of technology to facilitate information management and exchange of client information with employment opportunities is a reasonable concept. However, most systems are so new that their actual use by employers as a recruitment, selection, and hiring tool remains unknown. As a result, their effectiveness in assisting students and alumni in receiving consideration or actually acquiring employment is questionable. An additional concern related to computer-based résumé books or matching services is that they represent a passive approach to the job search process. Increasingly, it is important for career centers to develop client awareness and skill in conducting a comprehensive self-directed job search. However, if kept in proper perspective by candidates and used as only one strategy within the job search process, electronic résumé books and employment listings may hold promise as an additional service offered by career centers.

An example of a national employment network service is JOBLINK by JOBLINK, Inc., which enables students, alumni, and career center staff to access current job opportunities and employer profiles. By specifying criteria such as occupation of interest, location, employer size, and industry, users are able to retrieve job listings related to their backgrounds and interests. From the employers' perspectives, JOBLINK provides a recruiting system and network of over 60 universities, enabling access to over 100,000 undergraduates and 80,000 alumni. JOBLINK was initially developed for western colleges and universities but is expanding to the eastern section of the United States. Presently the program is updated biweekly.

Resume Link, a division of Lundy Associates, Inc., is a computerized résumé placement service and has two databases. Student Resume Link offers employers the following search criteria for graduating seniors at over 100 colleges and universities:

1. Work experience

2. Education
   School
   Grade point average (GPA) overall
   GPA in major
   Majors
   Minors
   Date available
3. Activities
   Leadership positions
4. Skills
   Computer skills
   Special skills
5. Interests
   Geographic preference
   Career interests
6. Personal information
   Name
   Current and permanent address
   Minority recruiting

Professional Resume Link is a database applicable to alumni and provides employers with the following search criteria:

1. Experience
   Specific work experience
   Specific industry experience
   Management experience
2. Preferences
   Occupational preferences
   Willingness to relocate
   Willingness to travel
3. Skills
   Computer skills
   Special skills (e.g., licenses, foreign languages)
4. Personal information
   Educational level
   Address and phone
   Employment status
   Minority recruiting

The service is relatively simple in that Resume Link works directly with colleges and universities in obtaining current résumés for seniors and alumni. Specifically, electronic-based résumés are acquired through candidates' participating in career days. Resume Link, in turn, markets the computerized database to employers or will provide a single search service to employers interested in candidates with specific qualifications.

Resume Expert by Professional Resource Center is a package of four programs that enables the entry, selection, and distribution of information and résumés among students, colleges, and employers. Resume Expert and Resume Expert Personal Print Module provide résumé writing instructions and enable students to construct and print résumés on any remote personal computer. Database Expert and the Electronic Resume Book enable the career center to match employer requests with students and alumni. Career centers may electronically send groups of résumés to employers, and employers, in turn, may perform searches based on 34 categories and print selected résumés on-site.

SkillSearch by SkillSearch Corporation is a computerized database that has been developed for alumni candidates. SkillSearch's concept is to provide one central database by which alumni of colleges and universities can be accessed directly by employers. SkillSearch is publicized and offered to candidates through college and university alumni associations. SkillSearch is provided with a list of alumni from the alumni association. A portion of the fees collected from alumni candidates and from employers utilizing this service is rebated to the college or university. Alumni registrants are sent résumé forms by SkillSearch. After candidates return the form directly to SkillSearch, a copy of the database résumé, formatted by an automated process, is returned to the candidate for review. Alumni database résumés are made available to employers, and individual alumni résumés may be printed by the employer.

kiNexus by kiNexus, Inc., is a job candidate information service in which stuents enter their data directly into a personal computer and provide the career center with the diskette, which is then copied into a candidate database. Career centers send their candidate information to a data clearinghouse maintained by kiNexus, which is then accessed by employers subscribing to the system. Candidates may be students or alumni, and files may be sorted on approximately 30 criteria.

Another computerized networking service, Connexion, attempts to link candidates not only with corporate employers but also with government agencies, nonprofit organizations, and education (teaching positions), as well as graduate schools. The system is marketed by Peterson's and students simply obtain Connexion résumé forms from the career center, and return their completed forms to the career centers, which, in turn, return résumés to Connexion on a weekly or biweekly basis for downloading into a database. It should be noted that Connexion has informed participating career centers that records will be maintained concerning how many times each individual student's name is contacted either by an employer or graduate school and career centers will be informed periodically of the number of times each student's name is sent out.

As noted earlier, national candidate and employer computerized databases are developing rapidly. However, while the concept is reasonable and simple, their utility to career centers and their clients remains questionable. Given the dynamic nature and number of national employer databases, caution should be exercised by career centers in their consideration and selection of a program. Important questions to be asked by career centers are: (1) to what extent does the organization developing and sponsoring the database offer feedback to candidates regarding information provided to employers? (2) to what extent have employers acted on the information, that is, selection and consideration of résumés, interview activity, and employment offers? and (3) to what extent do candidates receive feedback regarding activity associated with their résumés?

On-Campus Recruiting Systems

As noted in Chapters 5 and 8, on-campus recruiting systems vary widely among career centers. Some career centers with decentralized college or university placement services may offer no recruiting systems while centralized career-planning and placement offices may conduct a large, comprehensive on-campus recruiting program. Furthermore, the nature of the recruiting system will vary, with some systems utilizing an employer selection-based system and others applying a candidate-based point or bidding system for requesting interviews. Because of the variability and complexity of on-campus recruiting systems, no single software package for placement services would be applicable to all career centers. Some career centers have acquired nationally marketed, computer-based applications to recruiting services and have applied these systems to their recruiting services. Other career centers have developed their own computer-based applications to drive their on-campus recruiting system. Regardless of the scope, complexity, or nature of the recruiting system (large or small, centralized or decentralized, or preselection, first-come, first-served, and/or candidate bidding), the process common to all recruiting services is that they attempt to match candidates with employers to maximize the mutual values of both in an on-campus interview. Following a match, the interview is scheduled by the career center. Clearly, any matching and scheduling system can be supported by computer-based applications. Presently, some career centers drive their recruiting systems primarily through the exchange of paper with minimal computerization, and others have developed paperless computerized matching and scheduling systems while many career centers are in a transition phase using some form of computerization to exchange information. A thorough review of software applicable to the range of on-campus recruiting systems offered by career centers is beyond the scope of this chapter, particularly in light of the rapid evolution and application of computer technology to recruiting.

Before reviewing more comprehensive examples of computer-based, on-campus interview systems, it should be noted that certain procedures common to virtually all recruiting systems, for example, candidate registration, may benefit from technical applications. For example, some colleges and universities issue student identification cards used for procedures such as checking out library materials or gaining access to dining halls. Such a system could be utilized by career centers for registration and access to on-campus interviews; that is, students could simply present a student identification card that would be read by the career center to create a database of recruiting registrant information. Furthermore, a paper-based interview request form, such as the example shown in Chapter 5, could be loaded into a software system and made accessible to students through a word processing package in university computer laboratories to facilitate the production, adaptation, and revisions of the request form. Furthermore, Connexion plans to develop a candidate information system and database that are compatible with the UNICORE system used by many career centers in support of their on-campus recruiting program.

The University of Nebraska (Routh, 1989) reported making a transition from a paper-driven to computer-based centralized on-campus recruiting system over a six-month period. At the university, student résumés are entered into local and national databases. These résumés are then used for referrals to on-campus interviews. Students bid for interviews on terminals and schedule times without visiting the career center. Nebraska reported that the use of a nationally based candidate database, Resume Expert, was central to initiating a computerized system. This process places the responsibility on the student for developing the computerized résumé. The database of student résumés is loaded into the career center system. In addition, students have three methods to obtain interviews: (1) a bidding system, (2) employer preselection, and (3) open sign-ups.

The Universal College Recruiting System (UNICORE) is a comprehensive database management and office automation package designed specifically for career centers providing placement and on-campus recruiting services. One of the advantages of UNICORE is that it includes a range of system configuration options that allow for the specialization of various parameters unique to the career center recruiting system. System flexibility includes the options for academic programs specific to the college or university, use of bidding or preselection systems, and standard scheduling times used by the career center. UNICORE includes a calendar system for scheduling employer visits. Also, UNICORE may be used in support of a bidding system for interview selection, and four types of interview bidding systems are built into the program. A first-come, first-served sign-up system is available, and the preselection of candidates and student records can be searched on subject areas (major and minor), grade point average (subject and cumulative), graduation date, citizenship, and degree level. Lists of students, as well as résumés, may be printed by any preselection criteria. The system also includes a computerized interview scheduling system. For example, student interviewing time preferences are stored in a student file for use during scheduling so that optimum scheduling can be performed without entering new time preferences with every request. A second advantage of UNICORE is its module design, which enables career centers evolving toward computerization initially to use only a portion of UNICORE's system in establishing a database of employer schedules and candidate information. At a future point, the career center may use these records to position itself for UNICORE use in driving its recruiting system for matching and scheduling interviews.

Other computer-based interview scheduling systems include Sign-Up, developed by the Placement Office at the University of Minnesota, and PC Automated Senior Recruitment, developed by the Career Services Office at Brooklyn College.

COMPUTER-ASSISTED CAREER GUIDANCE SYSTEMS

One of the most common uses of technology in the college or university career center is computer-assisted career guidance systems (CACGS). For example, the CPC computer/technology survey (1991) found that CACGS were among the top three computerized functions reported by college career centers, the others being word processing and employer databases. Johnston, Buescher, and Heppner (1988) noted that "computerized career information and guidance programs are flourishing and most career centers have at least one interactive system" (p. 39). This section of the chapter reviews systems commonly used in college and university career centers—DISCOVER for Colleges and Adults (American College Testing, 1988) and SIGI PLUS (Educational Testing Service, 1987). Also, the application of CACGS within the career center is reviewed. Sample CACG field evaluations and research are identified, and issues regarding CACGS use are discussed. For a more comprehensive review of CACG issues, the reader is referred to the following literature:

Rayman, J. R. (1990). Computers and career counseling. In W. B. Walsh & S. H. Osipow (Eds.), *Career counseling: Contemporary topics in vocational psychology* (Chap. 7). Hillsdale, NJ: Lawrence Erlbaum Associates.
Computer-assisted counseling. (1983). *Counseling Psychologist, 11*(4).
Computers in counseling and development. (1984, November). *Journal of Counseling and Development, 63*(3).
A special issue on computers and career development. (1985). *Journal of Career Development, 12.*

Furthermore, the Center for the Study of Technology in Counseling and Career Development at Florida State University includes a unit that serves as a clearinghouse for computer-assisted guidance systems. A sample of the CACG materials available through this clearinghouse includes:

Sampson J. P., & Reardon, R. C. (1991). *Computer-assisted guidance: General issues bibliography.* Tallahassee, FL: Center for the Study of Technology in Counseling and Career Development.
Sampson, J. P. (1991). *Computer-assisted career guidance: Ethical issues bibliography.* Tallahassee, FL: Center for the Study of Technology in Counseling and Career Development.

Sampson, J. P., Reardon, R. C., & Ryan-Jones, R. E. (1991). *Computer-assisted career guidance: DISCOVER bibliography*. Tallahassee, FL: Center for the Study of Technology in Counseling and Career Development.

Sampson, J. P., Reardon, R. C., & Ryan-Jones, R. E. (1991). *Computer-assisted career guidance: SIGI PLUS and SIGI bibliography*. Tallahassee FL: Center for the Study of Technology in Counseling and Career Development.

Sampson, J. P., Shahnasarian, M., & Reardon, R. C. (1985). *A national survey of the use of DISCOVER and SIGI: Technical report No. 1*. Tallahassee, FL: Clearinghouse for Computer-Assisted Guidance Systems, Project LEARN.

Review of Computer-Assisted Career Guidance Systems

As noted earlier, use of CACGS is one of the most common applications of technology by college career centers, and two systems that enjoy widespread use are DISCOVER and SIGI PLUS. Essentially, both systems are stand-alone, interactive programs in which users may select from several parts or modules for addressing career-planning and decision-making issues, completing self-assessments of career-related attributes, and/or gathering educational and career information. The systems may be used for several sessions over a period of time, and both systems maintain user records that may be built upon through subsequent use. The systems may be used only to gather career information or may be used in a more interactive manner for engaging in the career-planning process. Rayman (1990) provides a thorough comparison of the contents and advantages of each system. A brief outline of system content for DISCOVER for Colleges and Adults and SIGI PLUS follows.

DISCOVER for Colleges and Adults provides clients with assistance in the following general areas:

1. Learning about internal or self information that contributes to informed career choices, including interests, values, skills, and experiences
2. Providing career information for over 400 occupations
3. Learning about how to make informed decisions related to educational and career planning
4. Providing information concerning two-year colleges, four-year colleges, and graduate schools.

Completion of the entire system would span approximately four to five hours. However, clients may select the use of certain parts of this system or may go directly to career information files. A diagnostic instrument, the Career Journey, is included in Part 1, and users may opt to complete this exercise to receive feedback concerning career issues and related DISCOVER parts that would be of particular benefit. Most DISCOVER screens may be printed by the user. DISCOVER is organized into nine parts:

PART 1: THE CAREER JOURNEY: Assesses user development and needs in the career-planning process.

PART 2: LEARNING ABOUT THE WORLD OF WORK: Uses the World-of-Work Map; allows for the exploration of majors, programs of study, occupations, and military programs.

PART 3: LEARNING ABOUT YOURSELF: Provides the opportunity for self-assessment in four areas: interests, abilities, experiences, and values; the system integrates this information to help the user in achieving greater self-understanding.

PART 4: FINDING OCCUPATIONS: Provides a list of occupations related to interests, abilities, values, and/or experiences; also searches for occupations by specific job characteristics or by selecting occupations from the User's Guide.

PART 5: LEARNING ABOUT OCCUPATIONS: Gives detailed information about more than 450 occupations; each occupation listed enables the user to select up to 14 topics for further information, including work tasks, training programs, salary range, and employment outlook.

PART 6: MAKING OCCUPATIONAL CHOICES: Provides assistance in choosing a path of training for future occupations; majors or programs of study related to occupational interest are also displayed.

PART 7: PLANNING NEXT STEPS: Helps to improve job-seeking skills and create a cover letter, résumé, or job application; provides information about two- and four-year colleges, graduate schools, financial aid, and military programs.

PART 8: PLANNING YOUR CAREER: Provides a definition of "career," enables the drawing of a "Career Rainbow" concerning the future and the roles that the user would like to play, and plans action steps toward a future career.

PART 9: MAKING TRANSITIONS: Provides understanding of the transition process; assists the user in viewing life and career as a series of transitions; determines "temperature" of anticipated transitions and how to weather a transition with a minimum amount of stress.

SIGI PLUS provides clients with assistance in the following general areas:

1. Learning about internal or self information that contributes to informed career choices, including values, interests, and skills.

2. Providing career information for over 220 occupations.

3. Providing information on typical preparation paths to any occupation listed in the system.

4. Learning about informed decision making related to educational and career paths.

Completion of all SIGI PLUS parts takes approximately four to five hours, and users may choose to complete any part of the system. Section 1 provides an overview of SIGI PLUS and recommends desirable pathways through the system. Following completion of this section, users may choose to complete any part of the system. Only certain SIGI PLUS screens are designated and available for printing by the user.

SIGI PLUS is organized into nine sections:

1. INTRODUCTION: Includes an overview of SIGI PLUS and recommends a pathway through the system based on the present user situation; the user then chooses which section to use next.

2. SELF-ASSESSMENT: Considers user interest and skills; assists the user in looking at work-related values, main interest fields for use at work, and ratings of activities associated with interests and skills.

3. SEARCH: Assists user in gathering information concerning occupations of interest; the user may choose features of interest in work (from self-assessments and/or levels of education required) and features to avoid in work, for example, writing, mathematics, outdoor work; provides a list of occupations matching user responses.

4. INFORMATION: Enables the user to choose one or two occupations at a time and ask questions, such as what skills each occupation requires, possibilities for advancement in the field, potential income, and educational requirements.

5. SKILLS: Outlines specific skills required for any occupation listed in the system; also includes information on special skills and work style needed for management; enables the user to complete a self-rating of skills.

6. PREPARING: Informs the user of typical training or college education needed for any occupation in the system and estimates user likelihood of completing preparation by considering four factors: finding time, finding money, handling the difficulty, and staying motivated.

7. COPING: Informs the user how to get practical help with issues related to career preparation, such as finding time and money and arranging care for others; a special feature in coping allows the user to receive specific suggestions and engage in exercises for time management.

8. DECIDING: User may look at three occupations at a time and ask questions such as: Will I enjoy this occupation?, What are my chances?, All things considered, would this be a good choice for me?

9. NEXT STEPS: Assists the user in moving toward career goals by planning short-term goals, such as acquiring more education or training, developing new skills, building a network of contacts, and writing a résumé.

Use of CACGS Within the Career Center

CACGS may be used by career centers in three ways: (1) as stand-alone interventions for providing career information or facilitating the career-planning process, (2) in support of other career center services, and (3) as a vehicle to promote career center services and facilitate client understanding of the career-planning process.

Additional research is reviewed in the following section, but it should be noted that early studies of DISCOVER and SIGI (Sampson and Stripling, 1979; Garis

& Bowlsbey, 1984) have shown the systems to be effective in facilitating client progress in educational/career planning without counselor or other career center interventions. These studies have also shown that CACG use often serves as a catalyst for further user involvement in career counseling or in seeking additional career center services. CACGS as stand-alone interventions enable the career center to offer an additional "treatment modality" that is current, provides consistent interventions, and maintains a basic level of quality. Users can benefit from the career information available through CACGS with minimal screening or involvement in other career center services. However, it is particularly important for the career center to screen clients wishing to use CACG for educational/career planning. For example, Garis and Bowlsbey found that clients using DISCOVER over a five-week period demonstrated significantly more career-planning progress than a wait-listed control group. However, in this study clients were screened carefully regarding their level of personal and academic adjustment prior to assignment to CACG use. Furthermore, a group assigned to both DISCOVER and individual counseling demonstrated even further career-planning progress than the CACG use–only group. In light of such data, it is recommended that career centers using CACG as a stand-alone treatment for career planning require client screening prior to system use. Client screening for CACG use can easily be accomplished using a brief walk-in intake counseling system, as discussed in Chapter 5. Consideration should be given to the following issues in screening clients for CACG use as stand-alone interventions:

1. Current level of emotional and social adjustment
2. Past and present academic performance
3. Timing or urgency associated with the academic/career-planning process.
4. Expectations regarding system effectiveness and client ability to integrate CACG information into the career decision-making process
5. Possible use of CACG with career counseling or other career center services
6. CACG as an appropriate intervention for client presenting issues, questions, or concerns

In addition to providing an intake screening system for CACG use, career centers should provide staff support for users. For example, a clerical staff member, career librarian, paraprofessional, or student assistant should be trained regarding CACG content and use and be available to help students in initially using CACGS, to answer questions, and to monitor software/hardware performance. Support staff would also be available to refer CACG users to additional career center services. CACGS should be located close to staff available to support the system, and the location should provide some measure of client privacy and confidentiality. CACGS are commonly located in the career library with a section designated for computer use to ensure staff support and a relatively quiet and controlled environment.

Often CACGS are integrated into other career services. In addition to CACGS use alone, the *DISCOVER Professional Manual* addresses system integration in the following ways:

1. One-to-one counseling and DISCOVER
2. Group counseling/guidance/workshops and DISCOVER
3. Curriculum and DISCOVER

As noted earlier, studies such as that of Garis and Bowlsbey (1984) suggested that stronger effects on career-planning progress were achieved through a combination of the computer and individual counseling. However, although CACGS are commonly integrated into group career counseling programs, workshops, or credit courses, data in support of their additive effects on group-based programs are inconclusive. Sampson, Shahnasarian, and Reardon (1987) have suggested that integrating traditional interventions (individual, group, and curriculum approaches) with computer-assisted interventions has several advantages, such as reducing the likelihood of viewing the computer as a magical answer to decision making and providing opportunities for prescreening and follow-up activities. However, Garis and Niles (1990) found that the inclusion of SIGI PLUS or DISCOVER within career-planning courses did not demonstrate gains on career-planning measures over career-planning courses with CACGS. This finding appears consistent with Hollands, Magoon, and Spokane's (1981) observations that adding similar or diverse career interventions often fails to produce greater effects. This is not to suggest that CACGS should never be embedded in career-planning groups, workshops, or courses. CACGS integration may not be intended to add to the programs' effects on general career-planning progress. Rather, CACG use with group-based programs may (1) help educate clients in the career-planning process and its components, (2) bring clients into the career center, and (3) be used in a very circumscribed fashion, that is, require completion of only one or a specific series of system parts.

When CACG is used in conjunction with individual counseling, similar consideration should be given to the referral by the counselor. Questions for consideration are: What is the intended outcome for CACG use?, Which CACG parts are most appropriate for the client?, How will the client report back to the counselor regarding CACG use?, and How will CACG information be integrated into the counseling process? Regardless of supporting individual counseling or group-based programs, when used with other assessments, consideration should be given to the rationale and fit of CACG use within the assessment package. An obvious, yet important, difference between CACGS and many traditional assessments such as the Strong Interest Inventory is that due to their interactive nature, ability as stand-alone interventions, and comprehensive nature, client use of CACGS and the integration of this information may not be as controlled by career center staff. Traditional assessment, however, is more focused on a particular career-planning attribute and almost always requires referral and interpretation by a professional.

In addition to CACGS as a stand-alone treatment or its use in conjunction with other career center services, CACGS have further utilization for the career center.

Perhaps more than any other career center intervention. CACG represents a synthesis of almost all of the ingredients of the career-planning process. As a result, they provide a compact and powerful vehicle for educating and involving clients in the career-planning process. As noted earlier, CACG users tend to seek individual career counseling, and CACG use has been shown to stimulate client information-seeking behavior in the career library (Garis & Bowlsbey, 1984). Through publicizing and offering CACGS, the career center may develop a strong referral network and attract more clients to its office. Therefore, in addition to serving as a stand-alone intervention and a support service to other career center interventions, CACG may serve a vital role in facilitating client awareness and use of the career center. Although not always desirable, because of their comprehensive nature, visibility in providing concrete interventions, and the expectancy effect achieved through computerization, CACGS, when well publicized, may serve as a focal point of career center services. If career centers choose to view and use CACG in this light, it is even more incumbent that screening, support by well-trained staff, and referral systems be provided to ensure user sophistication regarding CACG use.

Additional CACG Research and Summary of Issues

Research has suggested that DISCOVER and SIGI PLUS are effective in facilitating student career development (Rayman, Bryson, & Bowlsbey, 1978; Sampson & Stripling, 1979; Garis and Bowlsbey, 1984; Kapes, Borman, & Frazier, 1986; Fukuyama, Probert, Neimeyer, Nevill, & Metzler, 1988; Peterson, Ryan-Jones, Sampson, Reardon, & Shahnasarian, 1988; Garis & Niles, 1990). Garis and Niles (1990) investigated the effects of DISCOVER and SIGI PLUS when used alone or in conjunction with career-planning courses at Penn State University and the University of Virginia. Measures of career-planning progress included the Survey of Career Development (1977), self-assessment of confidence and progress in educational/career planning, and the Career Decision Scale (Osipow, Carney, Winer, Yanico & Koschier, 1976). Results indicated that:

1. Both DISCOVER and SIGI PLUS were equally more effective than controls in facilitating career-planning progress.

2. Credit courses were effective in facilitating career-planning progress, but, in conditions where CACGS were included in career-planning courses, they did not add to the career-planning progress of students.

Garis and Bowlsbey (1984) randomly assigned subjects to four groups: (1) a DISCOVER use–only group, (2) an individual counseling group, (3) a DISCOVER and individual counseling group, and (4) a wait-list control group. The Survey of Career Development (Rayman, 1977), a ten-item confidence and progress in educational/career-planning questionnaire, a behavior log and the Career Development Inventory (Super, Thompson, Lindeman, Jordaan, & Myers,

1981) were all used as outcome measures. The results of the study yielded the following conclusions:

1. All treatment groups showed positive effects in self-rated educational/career-planning progress on all scales of the Survey of Career Development and on the Career Planning and Career Exploration scales of the Career Development Inventory.
2. DISCOVER use alone and individual career counseling alone were equivalent in exerting a positive influence on subjects' self-rated progress in educational/career planning.
3. The combined DISCOVER/counseling treatment produced stronger effects on career-planning progress than either of its components used separately.

When considered collectively, research has supported CACGS as an effective career-planning intervention. However, as discussed earlier, research has been quite inconclusive regarding CACGS use and effectiveness in conjunction with other career center services. Furthermore, Johnston et al. (1988) noted that CACG has not been evaluated carefully regarding psychometric qualities and suggested that we ought to inspect CACG system contents more carefully. They further observed that although computer-assisted guidance systems are enjoying widespread use, they may not be used appropriately as completely unstructured, stand-alone interventions. They noted that because most major CACG systems contain assessment components, it is relevant to examine these components in the same way paper-and-pencil measures have been assessed for years.

Therefore, it can be concluded that CACGS are very visible interventions and enjoy widespread use within college career centers. DISCOVER and SIGI PLUS are capable of facilitating client career-planning progress. However, college career centers should carefully consider the following questions when including CACGS among their services:

1. How are clients screened before using CACGS?
2. Where are CACGS located? Do they provide some measure of privacy and confidentiality of records?
3. What staff support is available to clients during CACGS use?
4. How are users informed of the meaning of CACG information? Are they aware of limited reliability and validity data for the assessment packages embedded within CACGS?
5. Are clients referred to CACGS for use as a global treatment package? When are they referred to particular system parts?
6. When used in conjunction with individual counseling, at what point are CACGS most beneficial, that is, prior to, during, or following individual meetings with counselors?
7. How are CACGS used with other career center services, that is, groups, outreach programs, and courses?
8. How are CACGS used with other assessments?
9. What are the goals and expected outcomes for CACGS within the career center?

10. What types of clients may benefit most from CACGS use? What types of clients may experience difficulty with CACGS?

11. How are career center staff trained regarding CACG content and applications?

12. How are schedules and records for CACGS maintained, and how are the systems evaluated?

COMPUTER-BASED INTEREST AND PERSONALITY ASSESSMENT

Currently, software packages are available for most assessments used in support of career-planning services that enable the measures to be administered and scored on-site. The advantages of on-site administration and scoring of assessments are rather clear. They reduce turnaround time to receive profiles, control the testing environment, and, when administered in large quantities, reduce career center testing costs. Although research has not been completed to support such claims, it would be expected that most users enjoy inserting their responses in a computer rather than completing a paper-and-pencil measure. Despite the advantages of computer-based assessment, career centers should be aware of potential limitations in using assessment software. For example, start-up costs can be high for purchasing or leasing software and acquiring appropriate hardware. The relative ease of providing on-site scoring of assessments could contribute to their widespread and, occasionally, inappropriate use by staff. Furthermore, care must be exercised by the career center to ensure appropriate testing conditions and confidentiality of records. Because computer-based assessments are so accessible, it is important that clients be scheduled for assessment only through staff referrals, and scored assessments should be returned to the professional for interpretation with clients. Computer-based assessments could be located with CACGS in a designated computer section of the career library to ensure a professional testing environment and to provide adequate staff support.

Software for assessment frequently used in support of career-planning services is available through the following publishers:

Consulting Psychologists Press, Inc.

Strong Interest Inventory (SII). E. K. Strong, Jr., J. C. Hansen, and D. C. Campbell

Myers Briggs Type Indicator (MBTI). I. B. Myers and K. C. Briggs

California Psychological Inventory (CPI). H. G. Gough

National Computer Systems

Career Assessment Inventory - Enhanced and Vocational Versions. C. B. Johansson

Psychological Assessment Resources, Inc.

Self-Directed Search (SDS) Form R: Computer Version. J. L. Holland

The Psychological Corporation

Differential Aptitude Tests (DAT): Computerized Adaptive Edition (with Career Planning Program). G. K. Bennett, H. G. Seashore, and A. G. Wesman.

ADDITIONAL TECHNOLOGICAL APPLICATIONS

In addition to computers, other technology has been developed and made affordable to career centers over the past decade, including fax machines, video cameras, and phone communication systems. Fax machines enjoy widespread use in exchanging information with employers in support of on-campus recruiting programs and in receiving position vacancies from employers. Video cameras and videocassette recorders (VCRs) have enabled career centers to offer role-played videotaped interviews. Further application of video, communications, and computer technology is enabling career centers to begin to offer live video employment interviews. For example, Penn State's Career Development and Placement Services provides employers recruiting at its University Park Campus with the opportunity to interview additional candidates off-site, located at geographically dispersed branch campuses, through a live video-audio communication system. Phone systems and voice mail applications are being developed rapidly that enable career centers to offer call-in services for employment information or for candidates using an on-campus recruitment system.

SUMMARY

It should be noted that the computer-based programs reviewed in this chapter were provided as examples of technical applications that are available to the career center, and their inclusion was not meant to imply endorsement by the authors. The application of computers is evolving rapidly and creates one of the most challenging issues for career center management. Simply becoming informed of currently available software applications to a range of career center services is very difficult. Indeed, in contacting software developers marketing services in recent publications, it was found that some had already gone out of business. Furthermore, the ability to identify and adopt computer-based applications marketed nationally to complex localized career center services, such as on-campus recruiting, can present challenges. CACG perhaps enjoys most widespread utilization of technology in the career center, but its application with other career-planning services is not well understood.

There is no doubt that computer applications to almost all career center services hold promise. As a result, it is incumbent on career center staff to become aware of the range of computer applications available to support respective services and plan for their application. Many career center computerized systems are currently in place, and many others will follow. It is important to maintain perspective concerning the primary mission common to all career centers—providing student services. As computerization continues to evolve, it will be important that career centers use technical applications in an informed, planful, and sophisticated manner to ensure effectiveness and efficiency in service delivery.

REFERENCES

American College Testing. (1988). *DISCOVER for colleges and adults*. Iowa City, IA: Author.

College Placement Council, Inc. (1991). *Computerization sourcebook*. Bethlehem, PA: Author.

Drake, Beam, & Morin, Inc. (1987). *Career Navigator Manual: The computer powered job search system*. New York: Author.

Educational Testing Service. (1987). *SIGI PLUS*. Princeton, NJ: Author.

Fukuyama, M. A., Probert, B. S., Neimeyer, G. S., Nevill, D. D., & Metzler, A. E. (1988). Effects of DISCOVER on career self-efficacy and decision making of undergraduates. *Career Development Quarterly, 37*, 56–62.

Garis, J. W., & Bowlsbey, J. H. (1984, December). DISCOVER and the counselor: Their effects upon college student career planning progress. *ACT Research Report* (No. 85).

Garis, J. W., & Hess, H. R. (1989). Comparing the effects of Navigator and a credit course on college student job search progress. *Career Development Quarterly, 38*, 65–74.

Garis, J. W., & Niles, S. G. (1990). The separate and combined effects of SIGI and DISCOVER and a career planning course on undecided university students. *Career Development Quarterly, 38*, 261–274.

Holland, J. C., Magoon, T. M., & Spokane, A. R. (1981). Counseling psychology: Career interventions, research and theory. *Annual Review of Psychology, 32*, 279–305.

Johnston, J. A., Buescher, K. L., & Heppner, M. J. (1988). Computerized career information and guidance systems: Caveat emptor. *Journal of Counseling and Development, 67*, 39–41.

Kapes, J. T., Borman, C. A., & Frazier, N. (1986, December). *Comparing SIGI and DISCOVER: Student and counselor outcomes*. Paper presented at the annual meeting of the American Association for Counseling and Development, Chicago.

Osipow, S. H., Carney, C. G., Winer, J. L., Yanico, B., & Koschier, M. (1976). *The career decision scale* (3rd rev.). Odessa, FL: Psychological Assessment Resources.

Peterson, G. W., Ryan-Jones, R. E., Sampson, J. P., Reardon, R. C., & Shahnasarian, M. (1988, April). *A comparison of the effectiveness of three computer-assisted career guidance systems: DISCOVER, SIGI and SIGI PLUS*. Paper presented at the annual meeting of the American Educational Research Association, New Orleans.

Rayman, J. R. (1977). *The survey of career development*. University Park, PA: Career Development & Placement Services.

Rayman, J. R. (1990). Computers and career counseling. In W. B. Walsh & S. H. Osipow (Eds.), *Career counseling: Contemporary topics in vocational psychology* (pp. 225–262). Hillsdale, NJ: Lawrence Erlbaum Associates.

Rayman, J. R., Bryson, D. L., & Bowlsbey, J. H. (1978). The field trial of DISCOVER: A new computerized interactive guidance system. *Vocational Guidance Quarterly, 26*, 349–360.

Routh, L. (1989, May). *Changing from paper to computers in six months*. Paper presented at the National Meeting of the College Placement Council, San Antonio, TX.

Sampson, J. P., Shahnasarian, M., & Reardon, R. C. (1987). Computer-assisted career guidance: A national perspective on the use of DISCOVER and SIGI. *Journal of Counseling and Development, 65*, 416–419.

Sampson, J. P., & Stripling, R. O. (1979). Strategies for counselor intervention with a computer-assisted career guidance system. *Vocational Guidance Quarterly, 27*, 230–238.

Smith, E. (1983). Career Key: A career library management system. *Vocational Guidance Quarterly, 29,* 150–158.

Super, D. E., Thompson, A. S., Lindeman, R. H., Jordaan, J. P., & Myers, R. W. (1981). *The career development inventory.* Palo Alto, CA: Consulting Psychologists Press.

Appendix 7.1

Information Regarding Software Used in Support of Career Development and Placement Services

Alumni Information System
TSM Associates
P.O. Box 171
Granite Springs, NY 10527

CaLANdar 1.29
Microsystems Software, Inc.
600 Worchester Rd.
Framingham, MA, 01701

Connexion
Peterson's
202 Carnegie Center
P.O. Box 2123
Princeton, NJ 08543-2123

The Coordinator II
Action Technologies, Inc.
1145 Atlantic Ave.
Alameda, CA 94501

Front Desk
Peachtree Software
3445 Peachtree Rd., NE
Atlanta, GA 30326

Job Quest
Leo Charette
Director of Career Planning
Hartwick College
Oneonta, NY 13820

JOBLINK
JOBLINK, Inc.
P.O. Box 5306
Garden Grove, CA 92645

kiNexus, Inc.
Computer Learning Center
160 E. Route 4
Paramus, NJ 07652

Meeting Maker 1.0
On Technology, Inc.
155 Second St.
Cambridge, MA 02141

Appendix 7.1 (continued)

The Micro Job Search Tool Kit
Career Development Software, Inc.
P.O. Box 5379
Vancouver, WA 98668

Network Scheduler II
PowerCore, Inc.
1 Diversatech Dr.
Manteno, IL 60950

PC Automated Alumni Career Mentor Records
Gregory A. Kuhlman
Director, Career Services
Brooklyn College
1303 James Hall, Campus Rd. and Bedford Ave.
Brooklyn, NY 11210

PC Automated Appointment Scheduling
Gregory A. Kuhlman
Director, Career Services
Brooklyn College
1303 James Hall, Campus Rd. and Bedford Ave.
Brooklyn, NY 11210

PC Automated Career Library Records
Gregory A. Kuhlman
Director, Career Services
Brooklyn College
1303 James Hall, Campus Rd. and Bedford Ave.
Brooklyn, NY 11210

PC-File III
Jim Button
ButtonWare
P.O. Box 5786
Bellevue, WA 98006

The Perfect Resume Computer Kit
Permax Systems, Inc.
5008 Garden Ave. #2, Box 6455
Madison, WI 53716

Resumes by Ralph
Resume-Link
P.O. Box 218
Hilliard, OH 43026

Resume Expert
Professional Resource Center
1575 Universal Ave., Suite 200
Kansas City, MO 64120

Appendix 7.1 (continued)

Resume Express
Permax Systems, Inc.
5008 Garden Ave. #2, Box 6455
Madison, WI 53716

Resume Link
P.O. Box 218
Hilliard, OH 43026

Resume Writer
Bootware Software Company, Inc.
28024 Dorothy Dr.
Agoura Hills, CA 91301

ResumeMaker
Kane and Associates
654 Bair Island Rd., Suite 100
Redwood City, CA 94063

Schedule + 1.00a
Microsoft Corp.
1 Microsoft Way
Redmond, WA 98052

Signup
Herb Harmison
Placement Director
University of Minnesota
500 Lind Hall, 207 Church St., SE
Minneapolis, MN 55455

SkillSearch Corporation
102 Woodmont Blvd.
Suite 500
Nashville, TN 37205

UNICORE
5930 Crestone St.
Golden, CO 80403-1018

The Winning Approach to Interviewing
Professional Resource Centers
1575 Universal Ave., Suite 200
Kansas City, MO 64120

8

Working with Corporate, Governmental, and Nonprofit Employers

The relationship the career center maintains with its employer constituency is critical. While most large universities have a director of corporate relations working out of the development office, that person devotes most of his or her effort to cultivating relationships with employers in the interest of securing grants, gifts, and other contributions to the university. Only in rare cases do directors of corporate relations contribute in any significant way to the mission or goals of the career center's placment function. That being the case, the responsibility for cultivating and maintaining a solid employer clientele for the purpose of providing employment opportunities for graduates and alumni rests squarely with the career center, in particular, with those staff having the responsibility for the placement function. In our judgement, the fundamental premise that must underlie a corporate relations program is that the employer is the customer, and the success of the enterprise depends on meeting the needs of the customer. In this chapter we discuss the following aspects of working with employers: employer development, its purpose and nature; employer relations—maintaining and enhancing long-term relationships with employers; communications; the coordination of employer visit; facility needs as they relate to employers; the sharing of expectations with employers; and the actual interview process itself.

EMPLOYER DEVELOPMENT

The establishment of solid relationships with a broad range of employers from business, industry, and government is the lifeblood of the placement function. Cultivating these relationships is a complicated and time-consuming business that begins with a contact initiated either by an employer or by a staff member from the career center. Generally the term *employer development* implies that career center staff are making the initial contact, with the hope of expanding employment options for university graduates. The initiatives and resources devoted to the employer development function range from substantial at most Ivy League and other elite, principally private institutions, to little or nothing at some public colleges and universities.

There are several reasons for the enormous range in resources devoted to the employer development function by various institutions. First, the placement of graduates is significantly affected by geography in much the same way as choice of college. In brief, most graduates seek employment within a few hours' drive of their home. The degree to which graduates of a university conduct a truly national search for employment relates positively and directly to whether the university has a national reputation, whether it attracts students regionally or nationally, and the nature of its predominant disciplines. For example, an Ivy League university like the University of Pennsylvania attracts undergraduate students from a much broader geographic area (nationally) than a land-grant university like Penn State, which attracts the vast majority of its undergraduates from Pennsylvania and neighboring Middle Atlantic states. Similarly, the graduates of the University of Pennsylvania are more likely to seek and secure employment nationally while the majority of Penn State graduates will secure employment in Pennsylvania and the Middle Atlantic region. These realities of geography have significant implications for employer development. In brief, the career services staff at the University of Pennsylvania spends considerable money in support of travel, time, and resources to cultivate employers from coast to coast. Penn State, on the other hand, spends comparatively little on employer development and concentrates that effort regionally. Of course, the curriculum of the two institutions also has a bearing on this issue. A large percentage of the undergraduate student body at the University of Pennsylvania is enrolled in the College of Arts and Sciences and preprofessional programs, while the majority of students at Penn State are enrolled in the colleges of engineering, science, business administration, and agriculture. Clearly, the reputation, mission, and nature of the university's academic programs will dictate its employer development strategy.

Once a relationship has been established with an employer, no matter what the geographic location or employer type, it is important to maintain and enhance that relationship through an ongoing employer relations program. The keys to quality employer relations are simple: (1) the employer is the customer, and the customer is (almost!) always right and (2) the placement services provided to employers must be the very best, the most courteous, and the timeliest that can be afforded. The remaining portion of this chapter is devoted to identifying and describing the elements of a quality employer relations program.

EMPLOYER RELATIONS

From the placement perspective, the cornerstone of a quality employer relations program is the on-campus recruitment program. If employers participate successfully in on-campus recruitment, good relations will almost surely exist between that employer and the educational institution. All other interactions between the institution and the employer, while they may contribute to the success of the relationship, are of secondary importance. If an employer consistently conducts on-campus interviews, consistently makes employment offers, and consistently hires students from a given institution and if those students hired are consistently successful with that organization, quality employer relations will almost certainly exist. Despite the importance we attach to on-campus recruitment, it is only one element of employer relations. In this section we describe the on-campus recruitment relationship, as well as a range of other relationships and interactions that exist or occur between employers and institutions, and comment on each in turn.

On-Campus Recruitment

Most universities have large on-campus recruitment operations (some conducting as many as 30,000 individual interviews per year). Smaller institutions normally have smaller on-campus recruitment programs, but even the smallest usually conduct some on-campus interviews. Clearly all colleges and universities endeavor to persuade companies and organizations to visit their campuses for the purpose of conducting job interviews with prospective graduates. The actual physical presence of employers on the campus communicates powerfully to students that their college or university has strong ties to business, industry, and government and that there is a light at the end of the tunnel—that employment is available after graduation.

The purpose of on-campus recruitment is to assure the orderly and systematic flow of graduates into the labor force. The process varies enormously from one campus to the next, with some being totally centralized and others being widely decentralized to the point that individual academic departments may conduct their own on-campus interviewing operations. Despite the variation in how on-campus recruitment is organized from one campus to the next, the goals of the process remain remarkably similar—getting the right student in the right room at the right time with the right employer. On-campus recruitment is the most tangible and most visible service offered in the career center. It is at the heart of the relationship between employers and the academy, and it must be carried out with maximum attention to quality and consistency.

Career Fairs

Career fairs are an increasingly popular form of employer relations. Indeed, some large campuses sponsor as many as ten such fairs each academic year. Career fairs have become so popular that the College Placement Council now publishes a *Career and Job Fair Finder* (College Placement Council [CPC], 1991), which contains data on more than 1,700 career days, job fairs, and consortium activities nationwide. Such events take many forms, but the essential elements of career fairs that have made them so popular are as follows:

1. They create opportunities for students, faculty, and staff to interact directly with employer representatives and shift the financial burden for doing so to the employer. A note of caution here: some career centers and academic departments have used career fairs as a means of generating revenue to support other programs. We believe this is both inappropriate and unethical. We have often heard employers speak resentfully about the rising fees associated with career fairs. Career fair fees should be kept as low as possible and should never be regarded as a means of generating revenue for purposes other than covering the costs of the fair itself. Excessive fees and fee abuses have the potential to destroy the viability of the career fair concept.

2. They provide students (freshmen through graduate students) with an opportunity to interact with employers and secure information on a broad range of topics, including full-time employment opportunities, summer work, internships, cooperative education, scholarship and grant opportunities, and general information about various employers, and all at low risk.

3. They provide students with an opportunity to convey their credentials (résumés) directly to employer representatives and to receive feedback about their employability.

4. They create a carnival-type atmosphere with lots of giveaways that generates high student participation and interaction.

5. They provide the option of targeting fairs to certain types of students, for example, minority students, international students, engineering students, business students, liberal arts students.

6. From the employer's perspective, they provide a legitimate forum to enhance the company image on campus—to fly the corporate flag—without making any commitments to hire. This may be a particularly attractive feature for organizations that are not in the hiring mode but want to maintain a presence on campus.

7. They provide employers with the opportunity to "source" or prescreen students for later interviews through the on-campus recruitment process or through direct contact.

8. They provide employers with the opportunity to engage in "early identification" of undergraduates who have excellent potential. This technique is particularly helpful in identifying women and minorities for potential employment.

9. They provide interested faculty members with the opportunity to interact with company representatives without leaving the "security" of the ivory tower.

In summary, career fairs have become an important element of career center employer relations. They represent a vital link between employers and the student body. The credibility of employers adds greatly to information available from career center staff and faculty. Even though the information provided by employers at career fairs rarely goes beyond that available in the placement library, student acceptance will be greater because of this credibility (Shingleton & Fitzpatrick, 1985). Only on-campus recruitment plays a more critical role in successful employer relations with students.

Campus Faculty Visitations

It is often extremely beneficial for corporate representatives to visit the campus for the express purpose of interacting with key faculty members and conveying to them the nature of their company's employment opportunities and personnel needs. Faculty can and do exercise considerable sway over student opinion regarding which are the "best" employers. It is therefore important that employers make an effort to convey as accurately as possible their corporate culture to faculty. Not only do faculty affect the career decision making of students with their explicit comments about companies as being either good or bad employers, but the examples they use in case studies and class discussion often subtly affect student perceptions of companies. Leaving faculty perceptions of the corporate culture to chance is clearly not in the best interest of the recruiting organization. Companies that have a strong record of hiring the best and brightest from given academic programs almost universally have well-established and active campus faculty visitation programs. Through such programs employers can not only assure the flow of quality graduates to their organization but also shape the curriculum with their suggestions in ways that enhance the value and relevance of the education being delivered.

Class Presentations

A related but slightly different twist on faculty visitations is a program that provides classroom presentations and lectures by key corporate officials. Some companies have formal lecture programs that are advertised directly to appropriate academic departments, while others take a less formal, less structured approach. Whatever the approach, corporate-sponsored class presentations and lectures are an excellent means of enhancing employer relations. The key to the success of such programs is the establishment of "common ground" on which corporate officials can relate directly with faculty and students. For example, the subject of a lecture might be the use of total quality management (TQM) within the industrial engineering department of a major corporation. Such a lecture has the potential to (1) show students the relevance of the classroom experience to real life situations, (2) convey to faculty members the importance of including certain subjects in the curriculum to enhance the marketability of students, (3) convey to students the quality and sincerity of a potential employer by direct exposure to a current employee, and (4) help the employer to identify highly motivated potential employees from among the class members. Employer class presentations are a powerful tool in the establishment of quality employer relations.

Career Center Staff Visits to Employers

Though much of the interaction between employers and the academy takes place on campus, career center staff visits to employer facilities can be a valuable component of an employer relations program. Such visits should be planned well in advance and should take employer convenience into consideration. Most employers will welcome the opportunity to host a career center staff visitation if it is scheduled at their convenience and the goals are made clear to them well in advance (Zibelli, 1987).

Class Visitations to Plants

Another way to enhance employer-institutional relations is through employer-sponsored class visitations to company plants. Class plant visitations have the added advantage of getting students into the work environment where they can actually see and feel the corporate culture. Often employers are more than willing to cover the cost of such visits. There is no more powerful way for employers to advertise their employment opportunities and enhance their image on campus than through "word of mouth" from a busload of enthusiastic students who have just returned from being treated to an impressive plant visit.

Participation in Regional and National Conferences

While most large universities need not rely on conference participation to ensure quality employer relations, such conferences can be critical to the employer relations strategy of smaller institutions and those institutions that do not have large technical or business schools. Indeed, regional placement association conferences continue to provide considerable return for the cost to institutions wanting to strengthen their relationships with employers.

Finally, it is important to note that the type of employer being sought will also have an impact on the nature of the employer relations program. Relations with nonprofit and government employers differ from those with corporate employers in several ways. First, corporate employers tend to pursue relationships with colleges and universities in a much more aggressive and consistent fashion than do nonprofit employers and governmental agencies. Most corporations assign a representative the responsibility of coordinating college relations with a specific institution. That assignment is typically a multi-year assignment, with significant time being spent to assure that the channels of communication are open and that the relationship is strong and positive. In contrast, most governmental agencies and nonprofit organizations spend a minimum of time relating to career centers. They are in and out of the market as their personnel needs dictate, but they often do little to maintain a sustained relationship with the career center or other institutional representatives. In short, they tend to come to campus on their terms and do not expend the energy necessary to develop a solid and sustained relationship. These tendencies have an obvious impact on the image that many students hold of employment in the nonprofit and governmental sectors of the economy. Despite this disadvantageous image, government and nonprofit agencies continue to be major employers of college and university graduates. In recognition of this fact, career centers must work extra hard to maintain quality relations with them.

COMMUNICATIONS

Communications with employers should be direct, honest, and consistent, with a view to the establishment of long-term relationships. Communications used to be simple. They took three basic forms: direct person-to-person contact (on campus, at the employer's location, or at a neutral location like a conference), phone communication, and written communication (mail). Computers, fax machines, video phone interviews, voice mail, and other technological innovations have ushered in a new era of employer communications. While these innovations have speeded up the process, for the most part they have done little to alter the basic nature of employer-career center communications. In this section we describe the key types of communication that support the on-campus recruiting function and provide examples of various forms and informational pieces used by various career centers. We also comment briefly about the impact of technology on communications in the career center and end with some general observations regarding employer-career center communications.

Communications Involving On-Campus Recruiting

While there is considerable variability from one campus to the next, most employer recruiting visits are preceded by a sequence of critical communications that goes something like this:

1. Initial contact by employer inquiring about how to become involved in the on-campus interview process
2. Response from the placement office providing general information about employer services as well as specific informational pieces
3. The booking of a recruitment date approximately 6–12 months in advance of the visit
4. Mailing of placement office recruiting information forms to the employer
5. Return by the employer of placement office recruiting information forms
6. Announcement to students that the employer will be conducting on-campus interviews, with an invitation that students engage in the interview process
7. Some method of generating a list of students to be interviewed (first come, first served sign-up system, preselect system, bidding system, or some variation on these)
8. Conduct of the actual on-campus interviews

Each of these key steps in the recruiting process has associated with it various formal and/or informal forms of communication, which are described and discussed here.

1. Initial employer inquiry. Employer inquiries about on-campus recruitment are usually quite informal and most often consist of a brief telephone contact or a letter of inquiry.

2. Career center response. The career center response to an employer inquiry about on-campus recruiting should be immediate and should include a cover letter from the director (or person in charge of on-campus recruiting) that urges the employer to book a recruiting date as soon as possible and includes a brochure that briefly outlines the services available to employers and offers additional information and assistance upon request. An example of a typical employer brochure is presented in Appendix 8.1.

3. Booking of a recruitment date. Once the employer has decided to become involved in on-campus recruiting, a call is placed to the placement office to reserve the appropriate number of interview rooms on the desired date(s). This is normally a routine communication, but one that changes the relationship from a casual information exchange to a formal contractual agreement.

4. Career center response. The career center response consists of a packet of materials containing the following items:

A. A cover letter from the placement director or person in charge of coordinating on-campus recruiting. Such letters usually thank the employer for his or her interest and describe the contents of the packet. An example of a typical cover letter appears in Appendix 8.2.

B. A campus recruiting information form, which must be completed by the employer and returned. An example of such a form used at the University of Notre Dame is included in Appendix 8.3.

C. A series of handouts or a recruiter handbook describing the many "ins and outs" of on-campus recruiting, including sections addressing such issues as the recruiting calendar, parking arrangements, the university calendar, hotel accommodations, directions and a map to the career center, and reference materials about the institution, including an institutional profile, degrees granted, majors available, geographical distribution of graduates, directory of faculty, staff, and administrators, directory of career-related student organizations and advisers, college catalog, and so on.

The University of Notre Dame produces one of the best recruiter handbooks we have seen, entitled, *Recruiting at the University of Notre Dame* (Career and Placement Services, 1991). It is a 32-page compendium of information for recruiters that is both comprehensive and concise. Rather than a handbook, some institutions supply employers with a packet of individually produced informational materials that are less integrated but often equally effective. Whatever the approach, this mailing should include as much relevant information as possible, organized efficiently and tailored carefully to meet the specific needs of the employer.

5. Return of campus recruiting information form. Once the employer has received the recruiting information form, it should be completed carefully in accordance with the instructions from the career center and returned at the earliest possible date to ensure prompt processing. Since these forms vary from institution to institution and are usually an integral part of the individual career center process, it is imperative that employers complete the form carefully and not substitute their own forms or formats. Finally, most career centers specify a return deadline, and most are rather adamant that the deadline be met.

6. Announcement of the employer's recruitment visit to students. Once the campus recruiting information form is received by the career center, it is the responsibility of the career center effectively to promote the employer visit to all qualified students and secure credentials (résumés or standardized interview request forms) from those students who are both qualified and interested in interviewing with the company. A key link in this communications chain is often a placement manual, which not only describes office services, policies, and procedures but also provides a list of employers interviewing on campus, together with the dates of those visits. The employer also has responsibilities here, which include providing employer literature (both permanent and giveaway), advertising in the campus newspaper and/or other means, and perhaps even conducting on-campus prerecruiting informational sessions or direct mail campaigns. This process varies considerably from campus to campus and employer to employer but ultimately leads to the generation of interview schedules.

7. Generation of interview schedules. Based on the information provided to them by the career center and the employer, students engage in the scheduling process, which may be a preselection system, a first-come, first-served system, a computer bidding system, or some combination, depending on the institution. Once the schedules are set, all that remains is for the employer to arrive on campus to complete the process by conducting interviews.

8. Conduct of interviews. The final and most important step in the sequence of communications is the direct communication that takes place as recruiters interact one-on-one with students in actual on-campus interviews (Appendix 8.4). Most career centers provide recruiters with a carefully prepared on-campus interview folio that includes explicit information about the operation of the interview center, a transcript release form, an evaluation form, and the résumés of those students to be interviewed.

Changing Modes of Communication with Employers

With the advent of computers, fax machines, voice mail, and other technologies, the mode of communications between employers and career centers has changed dramatically. There is increasing pressure to standardize student résumés and transmit them electronically rather than in hard copy form. Private vendors are promoting electronic résumé banks like kiNexus (1992), Connexion (1992), and Resume Expert (1992), and placement professionals are encouraging standardization to ensure compatibility between on-campus computer systems and those in corporations—the major effort in this regard being DASIS (DAta Sheet Interchange Standard, 1992). While we believe it is necessary for career center staff to stay abreast of technological change (and we have devoted a chapter to computerization), we also believe that the medium is not the message and that computerization and standardization are not the keys to better communications. Indeed, in some ways they represent a potential threat to the placement profession, which has traditionally relied heavily on quality interpersonal relationships and has placed a high value on individuality and diversity.

Still another technological trend is that of video telephone interviews, which have the potential to supplement and perhaps ultimately replace on-campus interviewing (DeShong, Davis, Peterson, & Rayman, 1990). While the technology is still improving, early indications are that this medium has tremendous potential and may be of particular benefit to small campuses that do not traditionally attract large numbers of employers.

In summary, we are impressed by the speed and potential of technology, but not necessarily by its current effectiveness in our unique, interpersonally dependent profession. We must endeavor to tap its potential without losing sight of the fact that ours is a profession that was founded on, and continues to be dependent on, direct interpersonal contact.

Finally, we believe that honesty, directness, and consistency are the keys to quality communications between employers and career centers. There should never be any hesitancy on the part of either employer or career center staff to interact informally by phone to supplement formal communications. Frequent informal phone contact not only is necessary to resolve issues that inevitably arise during the conduct of business, but often serves as a basis for the development of long-term trust and mutual respect.

COORDINATION OF EMPLOYER VISITS

While the most commonly understood employer visit is the visit to conduct on-campus employment interviews with students, employer representatives engage in campus visits for a broad range of different reasons. In general, we believe it is desirable for employers at least to touch base with the career center staff, no matter what the purpose of the visit. A number of different types of visitation are listed here, together with a rationale for why involvement of the career center staff is desirable.

Campus Faculty Visits

Occasionally, employers wish to visit campus for the purpose of interacting with faculty members from key departments. Such visits may involve a discussion of students for possible employment, suggestions regarding the curriculum, possible grants or scholarships for a given department, or even research collaboration between the company employees and certain faculty members. It is quite beneficial for staff of career services to be aware of these visits even if career services involvement is minimal. Many times career center staff can direct employers to particularly responsive faculty or faculty who have a particular project or research interest that is similar to those of the employer. Often career center staff are happy to make the necessary local arrangements to put employers in touch with key faculty, such as arranging the itinerary, including transportation and lodging. Being involved in such interactions also benefits career center staff by making them more aware of the nature of the employee needs of certain employers.

An added benefit to career center staff is the opportunity to tour facilities and meet faculty from one's own institution as a participant in the employer visit. In our experience, many career center staff rarely get the opportunity to ask questions of faculty or tour labs and other academic facilities within their own institution, particularly in large universities. Career center staff participation in employer visits to academic departments provides that opportunity while placing no additional burden on faculty.

Campus Administrator Visits

Increasingly, companies are reducing the number of institutions at which they recruit and targeting the institutions they do visit more carefully. There is an attempt to establish ties not only with career center staff and key faculty but also with high-level college and university administrators as well. Thus, companies that may have recruited at several hundred institutions five years ago may now recruit at only 30 to 40 institutions. Companies often refer to these select target schools as "focus schools," and they make a real effort to cultivate long-term relationships with a broad range of university officials right up to the president. A common approach involves the visitation of a team of corporate representatives, including several from human resources, several line managers, and one key executive whose responsibility is to establish a relationship with top university administrators. Thus a certain parallelism develops between the two organizations: human resources staff from the corporation interact with career center staff; plant/office managers, research scientists, and engineers interact with faculty; and corporate vice presidents and chief executive officers (CEOs) interact with university deans, vice presidents, and presidents. Such relationships, if they continue over a period of years, lead to very strong personal and professional ties and a broad range of productive collaborations that go well beyond placement.

Informational Sessions for Students

Often employers conduct informational sessions the evening before recruitment interviews in an attempt to convey essential company information to students in a group. This allows recruiters to utilize valuable interview time to focus on the student's qualifications rather than on delivering canned company publicity as a part of the interview. It is vitally important that the career center be made aware of these informational sessions and that career center staff be invited to participate when possible and appropriate. Confusion invariably results when employers conduct informational sessions without notifying the career center. Often students stop by the career center to ask questions about employer informational sessions. If the staff of the career center is unaware of such sessions, everyone's credibility suffers. In general the career center should play an active role in coordinating employer-sponsored informational sessions for students, and, at the very least, employers should notify career center staff of their intention to conduct such informational sessions.

Career Fairs

It seems unlikely that a career fair could be held on a small campus without the knowledge and cooperation of the career center, but on large university campuses, career fairs are sometimes sponsored by individual colleges or even departments, and sometimes the career center staff is not even aware that a career fair is in process. It is important for career center staff to "keep their antennae up" and to do what is necessary politically and organizationally to stay in the "communications loop" regarding all forms of career programming throughout the campus. On most campuses the career center is, and should be regarded as, the primary source of information regarding campuswide career programs. Employers, faculty, administrators, and students can all help by relating to the career center as a sort of clearinghouse for all career-related programs.

Prerecruitment Visits

Often employer representatives wish to visit campus prior to on-campus interviews for the purpose of "sourcing" appropriate interviewees through a variety of means. It is extremely useful if such visits are coordinated through the career center. Employers must realize that their unannounced visits to campus, while always welcome, are often disruptive, sometimes inconvenient, and nearly always better if prearranged! Career center staff everywhere will appreciate not only being made aware of, but also being involved in, all employer prerecruitment visits.

INTERVIEW FACILITIES

In addition to the careful coordination of employer visits, certain physical facilities are necessary to assure the success and efficiency of on-campus recruitment. In this section we describe what we regard as essential interview facilities and comment on various issues that frequently attend their use.

Parking

Parking is probably the single greatest source of complaint by employers about on-campus recruitment. Our view is that employers are our customers. They are buying the only product we have to sell—quality graduates who will become their employees. They should be treated as valued customers and guests, and that treatment certainly should extend to parking privileges. Yet, most college and university administrators, especially those vested with authority over parking facilities, are not prepared to provide employers with adequate, convenient parking. Succinctly put, parking for employers should be within a block's distance of the interview center. It should be convenient and reasonably priced, but not necessarily free. Parking arrangements that fall short of these criteria are likely to be a continuing source of friction between employers and the institution.

On the other hand, some employers have very unrealistic expectations about the privileges they feel entitled to in conjunction with their campus visit. The parking situation on a college or university campus is no different than that in any city or town—parking is always in short supply, and it is always governed by well-posted policies and regulations. Employers who violate those policies and regulations are subject to the same fines as anyone else, and the career center staff cannot and should not "fix" employer parking tickets.

Interview Rooms

It is a temptation to relegate recruiters to cubicle-type rooms with poor lighting, ventilation, and acoustical characteristics on the premise that they are on campus for only a short period of time anyway, so they ought to be able to make do. We think this is a very shortsighted approach. The conduct of employment interviews is a very demanding and strenuous process, which can be made immeasurably more pleasant for employers and students alike if proper attention is given to the environment. With this in mind, we recommend the establishment of minimum standards for interview rooms as follows:

Size: All interview rooms should be at least 100 square feet in size.

Confidentiality: Rooms should have floor-to-ceiling walls and should be reasonably soundproof.

Clocks: All rooms should have clocks that are readily visible to both the employer and the student.

Carpeting: All rooms should be carpeted to muffle sound and create an appropriate atmosphere.

Furniture: All rooms should be equipped with a comfortable swivel chair for employers, a table, desk or other writing surface, one or two comfortable visitors' chairs for students, a coatrack, and wastebasket.

Optional: A phone in every interview room is a very desirable option but also one that few career centers can afford.

Lighting and Ventilation: All rooms should be well lighted and ventilated with adequate temperature and humidity controls.

Wall Decor: Walls should be suitably decorated with pictures, paintings, or wall hangings so as to create a professional environment.

Recruiter Lounge. An interview center should include an adequate recruiter lounge that contains the following amenities: comfortable chairs, worktables, coffee, tea, and a soda vending machine, telephones, copy machine, and an information rack containing the following basic resources: road atlas; college or university catalogs; placement manuals; brochures and informational pieces about local restaurants, lodging, and entertainment opportunities; and admissions and other general institutional informational pieces.

Catering Service. Many employers like to provide snacks at informational meetings they sponsor in conjunction with on-campus recruiting. We recommend that career center staff stay out of this business and simply refer employers to local area caterers. In our experience, catering arrangements become hopelessly complex and detract career center staff from more important functions. Of course, if the budget allows and the career center has sufficient staff, coordinating catering service for employers is a much appreciated service.

Copy Service. We believe that career centers should provide quality, free copy service to employers who visit campus for the purpose of conducting on-campus interviews. To discourage abuse, we do, however, recommend that an upper limit be placed on the free copies an employer can make.

Phones. Phones should be set up so that employers can make credit card and 800-number long-distance calls and free local calls only. If regular long-distance capability is available, it will be abused by a small number of employers, but even a small number of abusers can run up a substantial bill.

Group Rooms. It is very desirable for any placement facility to have at least one large room that can be used for group sessions. A small percentage of employers like to interact with up to 20 students at a time for the purpose of exchanging information. Such employers are not really conducting interviews; they are simply sharing information with potential employees. Typical examples of employers using this technique are the Peace Corps, various graduate and professional schools, and certain other governmental agencies. The availability of a group room may also be useful to large corporations as a base of operations in cases where they send ten or more recruiters to campus on a single day. In emergency situations a group room can be subdivided to provide supplementary interview rooms.

Audiovisual Equipment. The modern-day career center should be in a position to provide employers with a range of audiovisual (AV) equipment upon request. The most commonly used pieces of equipment are overhead transparency projectors, video playback machines, and slide projectors. Large career centers (those with more than 20 interview rooms) will probably find it advantageous and cost-effective to own their own such equipment for employer use, while smaller centers will probably rely on institutional AV services.

On-Site Staff and Clerical. Members of the professional staff should be on hand to greet employers each morning and provide them with a brief office orientation. At least one clerical staff member should be available throughout the day to provide message service and other basic clerical support to employers, though in no case should employers expect full clerical support. In our experience, employers will "exact" as much clerical support as the career center is prepared to provide. Ground rules regarding the nature and extent of clerical support to employers should be made explicit in center-provided recruiter informational packets so that employer expectations do not exceed available clerical staff time.

Placement Library. Every career center maintains a placement library where permanent employer literature is kept on file. At a minimum each employer file should contain a current annual report and several supplementary informational pieces. Often employers provide a videotape as well. Importantly, employers should be strongly encouraged to review the contents of their employer file to assure its accuracy and timeliness at each campus visit. This expectation should also be made explicit in the on-campus recruiting information packet.

Luncheon Arrangements. Some career centers arrange rather formal luncheons for employers, including the opportunity to dine with a faculty member from a department of the employer's choice. We believe this is a very nice touch and something that can be easily done on small campuses with limited numbers of employer visits. However, at large universities where it is not uncommon for 50 or more employers to be on campus each day, such luncheon arrangements can be prohibitively costly. It is also the case that many employers would rather have their lunch hour free to "do their own thing" since the rest of their day is so structured and demanding.

SHARING OF EXPECTATIONS

Expectations on the part of employers and placement staff vary widely from company to company and institution to institution. Our experience suggests that there are about ten really key issues where a meeting of the minds is essential for successful on-campus recruitment and employer relations. These key issues are discussed below.

Criteria for Who Interviews on Campus. While most colleges and universities would like to attract a broad base of bonafide employers to campus, it is necessary to establish certain standards, or the integrity of the placement service can be jeopardized. Here are some common standards. Employers wishing to utilize placement service facilities must:

1. Provide the placement office with a copy of their affirmative action/equal opportunity statement. This statement will be kept on file.
2. Provide the placement office with the name, address, and phone number of a representative who can be readily contacted regarding both routine matters and problems or issues that may arise.
3. Provide assurance that their organization is a reputable employer of college graduates offering bonafide employment on a salaried basis.
4. Provide the placement office with sufficient company information so that students have a basis for judging the company as a potential employer.
5. Agree to abide by the placement office policies and procedures for on-campus recruiting.
6. Agree to abide by *The Principles for Professional Conduct* as established by the College Placement Council (1990).

Interactions with University Officials. Employers often express uncertainty about whether or not it is necessary to contact the placement director before directly contacting other university officials, including faculty, administrators, staff, and students. On large campuses this is usually more problematic than on small ones, but, in general, no matter what size the institution, it is extremely helpful if career center staff are at least made aware of the fact that employers are carrying out initiatives directly with certain faculty or staff. Similarly, in the case of large corporations where there is a college recruitment coordinator, placement staff should keep corporate representatives apprised of individual initiatives that may be under way with corporate regional or divisional staff or offices. While it is mostly a matter of courtesy, in a small number of cases informing the central corporate office of career center initiatives can help the center to deal with corporate political realities of which the center staff may be unaware.

Testing on Campus. Increasingly, employers are pressuring career services staff to allow various types of on-campus testing as a part of the interviewing process. There are several compelling reasons most career centers are reluctant to permit such testing. First, when testing is done on career center premises, the career center has the legal responsibility to ensure that the test reliably measures some human variable that is a valid predictor of job performance. Few career centers have either the time or expertise necessary to evaluate the reliability and validity of the many different testing instruments that employers propose to use. In general, legal counsel has advised against allowing employment testing on career center premises. We strongly concur with this position.

A second related issue concerns whether or not various tests may discriminate differentially across racial, ethnic, gender, and other lines. Here again, career center staff are unlikely to have either the expertise or time necessary to make appropriate determinations on these issues.

Third, we have had experience with employers who wish to use a variety of aptitude and general ability measures that are frankly an affront to students who are about to graduate with degrees in rigorous departments from accredited institutions of higher learning. Such inappropriate testing is both an insult and a waste of student time.

Finally, most career centers have limited interview space and are therefore reluctant to allow employers to utilize scarce interview rooms for testing. In brief, we believe employer testing is best done on the employer's premises as a part of the secondary interview process.

Affirmative Action. With only rare exceptions, most colleges and universities have carefully developed affirmative action statements that guide their behavior in relation to a range of possible discriminatory actions. Career services offices must keep an up-to-date file of employer affirmative action statements, and, in turn, they should be willing to provide to employers upon request the assurance of their own policy with respect to affirmative action. Here is an example of a typical affirmative action policy for a college or university: ''XYZ University is committed to the policy that all persons shall have equal access to programs, facilities, admission, and employment without regard to personal characteristics not related to ability, performance, or qualifications as determined by university policy or by state or federal authorities. The XYZ University does not discriminate against any person because of age, ancestry, color, disability or handicap, national origin, race, religious creed, sex, sexual orientation, or veteran status.'' As we have previously indicated, employers who fail to provide an affirmative action statement should not be allowed to utilize career services.

Ethical Standards. Both employers and career service offices must operate in accordance with a strict set of ethical standards. These standards are spelled out in *Principles for Professional Conduct for Career Services and Employment Professionals* (CPC, 1990). A copy of these principles is presented in Appendix 4.2, with the permission of the College Placement Council. If either an employer or a career services staff member feels that a breach of ethics has taken place, action should be taken as expeditiously as possible to resolve the issue. The College Placement Council provides an advisory opinion service and offers suggested problem-solving procedures for those who seek assistance in the resolution of ethical issues. Brief descriptions of these two CPC services are also described in Appendix 4.2.

Open/Closed Schedules. A frequent area of conflict between employers and career services staff involves so-called open versus closed interview schedules. In brief, an open schedule is one in which the employer does not have the final say about which candidates will receive interviews. Career centers may use a first come, first served sign-up procedure, a bidding system, or any number of other techniques to build the interview schedule, but, however the schedule is built, the employer does not have the option of making the final selections. A closed schedule, on the other hand, is one in which the employer has the final say in who gets interviews. Such a system is sometimes referred to as a ''preselection'' system, meaning that employers are provided with the résumés of all the candidates who have expressed an interest. The employer then picks and chooses only those students with whom he or she wants an interview.

Career Center Staff Recommendations. It is our experience that employers still seek placement staff recommendations regarding individual students. We believe this request is a vestige of a bygone era when many career center directors knew all their graduating seniors personally and before the on-campus recruiting process had become professionalized. In the modern era we believe it is inappropriate for career center staff either to offer or to provide recommendations about individual students unless those students have worked for the career center, in which case the recommendation would be like any other employer reference. Career center staff must set an example to faculty and other administrators in this area. It is important to discourage ''good-old-boy'' networking and special favors to pet students.

Being on Time. On-campus interviewing is a complex process that requires cooperation and good faith on the part of all the participants. On large campuses it is not uncommon for as many as 500 interviews to be scheduled on a single day. This high level of activity requires discipline on the part of the recruiter, the career center staff, and the students. Being on time for these interviews and operating on time throughout the course of the day is absolutely essential if success is to be achieved. In our experience, the most common breakdown in this system occurs when recruiters fail to arrive on time or are habitually late in conducting their interview schedule. Ensuring that recruiters understand the consequences of such behavior and creating an environment where "being on time" is a way of life are the responsibility of the career center staff.

Employer Adherence to Career Center Deadlines and Policies. While the on-campus interview is typically a simple half-hour interaction, an elaborate and complex set of interactions and procedures lead up to successfully getting the right student in the right room at the right time with the right employer. This complex set of interactions is a very fragile system that breaks down quickly unless all parties play by the same set of rules. In particular, employers must be sensitive to the deadlines established by career centers and make every effort to meet those deadlines. Examples of critical employer deadlines are deadlines for booking interview rooms, for completing and returning the on-campus recruiting forms that every career center requires, for shipping employer literature for use by students prior to their interviews, and for screening student credentials and providing a list of those students selected for interviews (for those using a prescreening approach). Most career centers will "go the extra mile" to be flexible, but established policies and procedures allow them to conduct thousands of interviews with very modest resources. Without the cooperation of employers, the system breaks down and chaos results.

Getting Information to Those Who Actually Come to Campus. One frequent cause of confusion between career center staff and corporate recruiters is the fact that most of the telephone and mail communication between the career center and the employer is handled by a recruitment coordinator at the company who may have never visited the campus. Thus, even though detailed instructions are sent to the recruitment coordinator about parking, hotel accommodations, food service, and the like, this information often never gets to the actual recruiters who visit the campus. Thus, recruiters arrive without the necessary information to assure the efficient conduct of their business. They are uncertain about parking. They think that the interviews are one hour in length instead of a half hour. They don't know where the interview center is located, and so on. Unfortunately, this type of misunderstanding is often the rule rather than the exception.

ACTUAL INTERVIEWS

Once the employer has arrived on campus, the bulk of the organizational work has been completed. The actual interviews are the culmination of nearly a yearlong cycle of events, and the content of those interviews is largely and appropriately controlled by the employer. Nevertheless, there are certain details of the on-campus interviewing process that require career center involvement and cooperation. In this section we describe and discuss some of the many issues that must be considered to assure the smooth operation of the on-campus interviewing process.

Timing

A key question is when the day should start and end. The length of the interview day will depend on the availability of space, travel arrangements, and the wishes of the employer. Most career centers would prefer that interviews start early (8:00 or 8:30) and run late (at least until 4:30) so that interview opportunities for students can be maximized. In the end, however, the final decision must rest with the employer.

Length of Interviews. Most career centers are quite flexible about interview length, preferring that employers elect the interview length that best suits their needs. In general, most employers seeking bachelor's-level candidates conduct half-hour interviews while those seeking master's- or doctoral-level graduates may prefer 45-minute or one-hour interviews. The important thing is for employers to indicate clearly their intentions regarding interview length on the recruitment information form. Often recruiters complain about the length of the interviews scheduled by career center staff only to find that their own recruitment coordinator specified the length of interview.

Provision of "Carry-away" Literature. Many employers ship brochures and annual reports to campus prior to their visit and request that career center staff distribute these materials to those students with whom they have scheduled interviews. While this task seems simple enough, it can become burdensome, and some large university career centers have discontinued this service. At one large university we visited, the career center received an average of five UPS shipments of employer information each day during the recruiting season, totaling several tons annually. The provision of employer "carry-away" literature can be a useful service to students, but career center staff must monitor this practice on a continuing basis to assure that the costs do not outweigh the benefits.

Provision of Permanent Literature. All career centers maintain a placement library that contains employer literature, including annual reports, periodical employer newsletters, corporate histories, and miscellaneous promotional pieces designed to be a resource to students in researching potential employers. A placement library is an essential service, which must be carefully maintained and updated through a cooperative arrangement between placement library staff and visiting employers. Large centers will want to establish a computerized database of employer literature so that periodic inventories can be run and requests generated for updated information. Employers should be encouraged to review their permanent literature each time they visit campus to assure that they are being represented by their latest informational pieces.

Provision of Video Materials. Increasingly, employers find it beneficial to provide videotapes to career centers as a means of visually conveying information about their organization to students. The quality and utility of such videotapes vary widely, but employer videos have clearly become an important medium for the delivery of employer information. Many employers require that students selected for on-campus interviews view their company videotape prior to the interview.

The use of videotapes has exploded in the last five years. Several large career centers we have contacted have employer video libraries of more than 300 tapes, while ten years ago employer videotapes were nonexistent.

Application Forms. Many employers request that students complete and submit an official "application for employment" at the time of the on-campus interview. While this should be a rather routine matter, it is important that employers communicate their intent regarding application forms well in advance of the interview data and make arrangements with the career center to ensure that students have adequate lead time to complete the forms. A great deal of confusion regarding application forms can be avoided if application form policies and expectations are made explicit.

Transcripts. Many career centers provide employers with transcript release forms. These forms allow employers to secure written permission from those students interviewed so that the process of securing official transcripts can be expedited. In the near future some career centers are likely to be in a position to provide computer-generated transcripts right in the interview center so that employers will be able to pick up their transcripts at the end of the interview day and leave campus with everything they need to make an informed decision about the day's interviewees.

Tracking Results of Employers. In our experience few employers provide a comprehensive accounting (or tracking) of their on-campus interview activity to college or university career centers. This is ironic since employers frequently seek salary data and other employment-related data from the career center. Apparently employers do not realize that the data career centers provide are derived from employer reports. In short, the quality of the salary data that career centers provide employers and the quality of the CPC salary survey can be no better than that provided by each individual employer to the career center.

We strongly encourage all employers conscientiously to report the disposition of their on-campus recruiting activity to all the college and university career centers at which they recruit. In an effort to encourage more employers to report the disposition of their recruiting efforts, we provide in Appendix 8.5 an example of a reporting form that is used by Babcock & Wilcox. The immediate feedback provided by this form is supplemented later with copies of all letters sent to the students interviewed. We have found the format of this report to have excellent utility, and we would encourage all employers to adopt some similar reporting strategy.

SUMMARY

The key to working effectively with employers is a strong commitment on the part of both career center staff and employer representatives to understanding and working within the separate cultures of higher education, on one hand, and business, industry, and government, on the other. Employer relations looks very different from the two sides of the table, and even more different from one employer to the next and one college or university to the next. Both employers and placement staff must learn to understand and appreciate the vagaries and differences of each individual relationship. In the end, consistency, continuity, and commitment are the keys to establishing and maintaining a productive working relationship.

REFERENCES

Career and Placement Services. (1991). *Recruiting at the University of Notre Dame*. Notre Dame, IN: Notre Dame University.

College Placement Council. (1990). *Principles for professional conduct for career services and employment professionals*. Bethlehem, PA: Author.

College Placement Council. (1991 - Updated annually in June). *CPC career and job fair finder*. Bethlehem, PA: Author.

DASIS. (1992). DAta Sheet Interchange Standard. National Center for Computer Standards in Recruitment and Placement, 50 Lind Hall, 207 Church Street SE, Minneapolis, MN 55455.

DeShong, R. L., Davis, D. L., Peterson, M. B., & Rayman, J. R. (1990). Video interviewing: An effective alternative for the multi-campus school? *Journal of Career Planning & Employment, 50*(3), p. 23–25.

kiNexus. (1992). Information Kinetics, 640 North LaSalle Street, Suite 560, Chicago, IL 60610.

Peterson Guides. (1992). *Connexion*. Princeton, NJ: Author.

Resume Expert Systems. (1992). *Resume Expert*. Overland Park, KS: Author.

Shingleton, J. D., & Fitzpatrick, E. B. (1985). *Dynamics of placement*. Bethlehem, PA: College Placement Council Foundation.

Zibelli, R. J. (1987). Do recruiters appreciate "get acquainted" visits to their offices by placement directors? *Journal of Career Planning and Employment, XLVII* 25–26.

Appendix 8.1
Penn State Placement Services

Comprehensive Career Development and Placement Services for Students

Individual Career Counseling

Multiple Session Counseling Groups

Computer-based Guidance System

Weekly Seminars (Resume Preparation and Interview Skills)

Career Information Center

Placement Library

Education Career Services

On-Campus Recruitment Program

Programming for Special Interest Groups

Career Speakers Bureau

Alumni Career Services

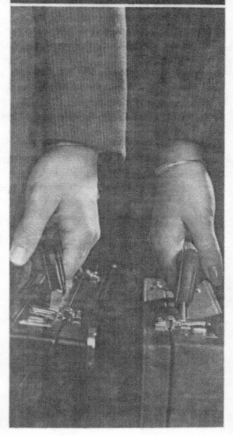

Appendix 8.2
Recruiting Coordinator Letter

PENNSTATE

(814) 863-0225   FAX (814) 863-0226

Recruitment/Scheduling Office
Career Development and Placement Services

407 Boucke Building
The Pennsylvania State University
University Park, PA 16802

Dear Recruiting Coordinator:

Enclosed are materials that will help you complete the planning for your recruiting visit to Penn State.

CONDUCTING A SUCCESSFUL RECRUITING VISIT

I want to assure you that we are very interested in providing the support necessary for you to have a successful recruiting visit with us. To assist us in obtaining this goal, it is very important for you to adhere to the deadlines established for efficient handling of your requirements. With this in mind, please extend immediate attention to the following items:

1. <u>Type and return</u> the enclosed CAMPUS INTERVIEW NOTICE by the due date specified on the form.
2. <u>Mail</u> a quantity of your HAND-OUT RECRUITING LITERATURE to us in sufficient quantity to accommodate the number of students you expect to interview.

PROMOTING YOUR VISIT

Information on your organization, opportunities, and college relations activities can be presented to the students you recruit through the **Placement Manual**--our primary Career Search Guide for students. Your employer image and information are contained in a special Employer Reference Section of this publication used by all seniors. To be included in this publication, please contact Petra Thedos, CRS Publications, 67 Walnut Ave., Suite 207, CLark, NJ 07066, 201/382-9600.

PARKING INFORMATION

All interviews are conducted in the Interview Center, located in McAllister Building. Parking spaces are at a premium so you should plan to arrive at least 30 minutes prior to your first interview. Report to the attendant at the entrance to the visitors' parking lot indicated on the enclosed map. The attendant will then give you further instructions on where you will park for the day. **NOTE: VISITOR PARKING LOTS ARE EQUIPPED WITH PARKING METERS.** There is a charge for parking of 25 cents for 40 minutes. Change will be available from the lot attendant. Meters are 12 hour maximum.

CAMPUS MAP

To facilitate your movement throughout the campus, please refer to the enclosed map depicting building locations. Specific instructions are included as part of the map.

I am very appreciative of your interest in visiting PENN STATE for the purpose of meeting your human resource needs. I believe that you will find your trip to be both productive and rewarding. We look forward to being of assistance to you.

Sincerely,

Ralph L. DeShong
Associate Director

Enclosures

An Equal Opportunity University

281

Appendix 8.3
Campus Recruiting Information Form

CAMPUS RECRUITING INFORMATION FORM
Career and Placement Services
Theodore M. Hesburgh Library
University of Notre Dame
Notre Dame, Indiana 46556
(219) 239-5200
FAX (219) 239-7700

PLEASE TYPE INFORMATION AND RETURN

FOR OFFICE USE

1991-92

EMPLOYER / DIVISION		CONTACT PERSON
ADDRESS	PRINCIPAL PRODUCTS / SERVICES	TITLE
		PHONE ( )
		FAX ( )

DATE _____ (AND) DATE _____
NO. OF OPEN SCHEDULES _____ NO. OF OPEN SCHEDULES _____
NO. OF INVITATIONAL SCHEDULES _____ NO. OF INVITATIONAL SCHEDULES _____

POSITION TITLE(S) AND DUTIES (Attach Job Description if available)	MAJORS REQUESTED BY POSITION (Refer to reverse side)	Bach.	Mast.	Ph.D.

INTERVIEWING FOR FOLLOWING LOCATIONS (Please indicate by position)

WILL INTERVIEW:
☐ December Graduates
☐ May Graduates
☐ August Graduates
☐ All of the above

CHECK ALL APPLICABLE: ♦
_____ Equal Employment Opportunity Employer
_____ Any qualified candidate, regardless of visa status.
(This includes practical training authorization.)
_____ Anyone with authorization to work full-time in the U.S.
(This does not include practical training authorization.)
_____ U.S. Citizen only. (Your organization must be one of the following. Please check one.)
☐ Defense Contractor   ☐ U.S. Government Agency

SPECIAL INSTRUCTIONS FOR STUDENTS AND PLACEMENT OFFICE

SIGNATURE   DATE

282

PENNSTATE

Interview Center

Welcome to the Penn State Interview Center

Penn State has long recognized that for both the student and the prospective employer, the process of evaluation and selection is vitally important.

For most students, the on-campus interview is their first professional interview—a bridge between their long years of education and their venture into careers.

For participating companies and organizations, the interviews are a prime opportunity to screen graduates for the qualifications and specializations essential to their ongoing work.

To this end, we are pleased to have you use this outstanding facility and look forward to having you visit again in the very near future.

The Staff of the Career Development and Placement Services

Appendix 8.5
Babcock & Wilcox Interview Record

GO 9118-79-1
BW 149 (R6/84)

MEMO FOR:

Babcock & Wilcox
a McDermott company

_____ DATE

_____, Placement Officer at _____

Listed below are names of the students we interviewed during our visit. The action taken is indicated. We will advise each student the result of their interview.

Page _____ of _____

Copies of all letters which we write to
these students will be sent to you.

Recruiters:

Address all correspondence to:

**COLLEGE RECRUITING DEPARTMENT
THE BABCOCK & WILCOX COMPANY
P. O. BOX 61038
NEW ORLEANS, LOUISIANA 70161**

No. 1 _____

No. 2 _____

No. 3 _____

No. 4 _____

	NAME		DEGREE	RECRUITER NUMBER	ADVISING 'NO INTEREST'	INVITING TO VISIT US	REFERRING RECORD FOR CONSIDERATION	APPLICABLE JOB DESCRIPTION NUMBER	MINORITY CODE "(See Below)"
	LAST	FIRST							
1			BS/ms	2			✓	RDA-m-2	
2			BS	1	✓				
3			BS				✓	NTD-m-15	
4			BS				✓	NTD-M-14	
5			BS		✓				
6			BS				✓	NTD-m-10	
7			BS				✓	NTD-E-1	
8			BS				✓	NTD-m-3	
9			BS				✓	DP-m-3	
10			BS				✓	NDT-m-7; NDT-m-1	
11			BS				✓	NUD-E-3	
12			AS/BS				✓	NTD-e-4	4
13									
14									
15									
16									
17									
18									
19									
20									
21									
22									
23									
24									
25									

ACTION TAKEN

WERE ANY MINORITY CANDIDATES INTERVIEWED? ☒ YES ☐ NO

* 2 - BLACK   3 - HISPANIC   4 - ASIAN   5 - AMERICAN INDIAN   6 - FEMALE

9

Coordination of Graduate Assistants, Interns, and Peer Counselors

College and university career centers may choose to include graduate students and paraprofessionals in their staffing patterns for three reasons. First, career centers may, in part, shoulder responsibility for representing and advancing the career development field on their campus. In doing so, career centers provide education and training of students pursuing career development professions. For example, in functioning through a management-by-objective system, one of Penn State's Career Development and Placement Services broad mission statements is to "assist other professionals or paraprofessionals in developing knowledge and skills in the delivery of career services and develop a cooperative relationship with those academic departments preparing professionals or paraprofessionals in areas related to career development."

When assuming an education and training function in career development, it is important for the career center to establish and maintain linkages with academic departments involved in the career preparation of students pursuing degrees related to counseling and career development. Career centers providing education and training to those interested in the delivery of career services would provide graduate assistantships or offer internships at the undergraduate, as well as graduate, level.

A second reason for the use of graduate students or paraprofessionals in its staffing pattern is to increase the amount of human resources available to assist the career center in offering services. Graduate assistants and interns benefit from education and training in the delivery of career services but also make a contribution in providing services on behalf of the career center. In addition to full-time staff, graduate students, and interns, other paraprofessionals can be recruited and trained for the delivery of career center services. Such students include undergraduate peer counselors, student advisory board members, or work-study students. Indeed, at many colleges and universities, non–full-time staff may represent a significant proportion of the career center's human resources available for delivery of its services. When carefully trained and supervised, graduate assistants and paraprofessionals are capable of providing significant and cost-effective services.

A third benefit of graduate students and paraprofessionals is that, by nature, such staff change roles more than full-time professionals. While the training of temporary staff may present a challenge, graduate students, interns, and peer counselors offer energy, enthusiasm, and freshness to the career center. Such temporary staff may offer feedback to the career center based on a more external, less biased perspective than full-time professionals. Undergraduate peer counselors and student advisory board members may be valuable sources of feedback regarding the perceptions of the career center and its services by the student body. Furthermore, graduate students and interns who are counselors in training may help to keep the career center staff abreast of current research and trends in the career development field. Graduate assistants and interns are frequently interested in conducting research for theses or course projects. As a result, they may be interested in conducting field research in career development issues that may be helpful to the career center for program evaluation.

This chapter reviews the inclusion of the following types of students in career center staffing:

1. Graduate assistants
2. Interns (graduate and undergraduate)
3. Peer counselors
4. Other student assistants, that is, practicum students, student advisory board members, and work-study students

It should be noted that the above categories of part-time professionals or paraprofessions are not mutually exclusive. For example, an undergraduate student could conceivably be a member of the student advisory board, participate as a peer counselor, and receive credit for the experience through an internship. In addition to reviewing the use of graduate assistants, interns, or peer counselors in the career center, this chapter addresses the recruitment, training, and supervision of student assistants.

GRADUATE ASSISTANTS

Career centers within universities offering graduate degree programs in counselor education or counseling psychology may find it helpful to acquire funds for providing graduate assistantships sponsored by the career center. Monetary issues are always a concern for career centers. However, in light of the temporary nature of assistantships and the lack of required benefits, funding for graduate assistantships may be a more realistic and cost-effective option than soliciting financial support for adding full-time positions. In some cases, the career center may solicit funds for graduate assistantships from other academic units. For example, when a credit course in career planning is sponsored by a particular academic unit, it may be reasonable to request funds in support of a graduate assistantship to teach or assist in teaching the course. After receiving training and being provided with sufficient supervision, doctoral-level graduate assistants may be capable of providing services at the same level of quality as other career center full-time staff. Often, doctoral students have acquired significant counseling experience prior to returning to a graduate program. All graduate assistants will require an orientation to the career center. In cases when doctoral graduate assistants have acquired general counseling experience without focused experience in career development, training and supervision will be necessary in adapting counseling techniques and experience to career issues. When graduate students are not familiar with the university structure, training will be required regarding referral resources and the range of academic programs. Doctoral-level graduate assistants may be capable of providing a variety of career center services, including counseling, program delivery, and teaching career education courses. Because they are involved in doctoral-level training in counseling, graduate assistants are often particularly interested in obtaining further counseling experience with supporting supervision or gaining experience as course instructors. Furthermore, as doctoral-level graduate assistants obtain career center experience, some may be interested in conducting thesis research within the office. Doctoral-level research can be a powerful tool in serving as a catalyst for empirically based approaches to field evaluation of career center programs and services.

Therefore, doctoral-student graduate assistants may be capable of assuming levels of responsibility comparable to those of full-time professionals. For example, they may provide counseling services to the same client pool as full-time staff, offer outreach programs, or teach career education courses. Obviously, however, the primary role of graduate assistants within the university is that of student and not professional. As a result, while challenging and fully utilizing graduate assistants, career centers should exercise caution in not over-extending the limits of the assistantship in order to allow time for course work and study.

Master's-level graduate assistants are not as common as doctoral-level assistants. However, when master's-level assistantship funds are acquired, the use of these students within the career center may be more measured and less comprehensive than is true of doctoral-level students. Most often, unlike doctoral students, master's students would be regarded as "counselors in training." Therefore, their use in counseling would be more limited and often would require screening and differentiation in the client caseload to ensure quality counseling services. Furthermore, master's-level graduate assistants may not have the experience or knowledge to shoulder sole responsibility for delivering more sophisticated career center services such as teaching courses for credit. Often, master's-level graduate assistants may be used effectively and in a more controlled fashion in assuming responsibility for coordinating a particular career center service or project. Master's-level graduate assistants could be trained to coordinate career days or to develop and deliver well-defined outreach programs to particular student groups. In certain instances, it may be feasible for the career center to obtain funding and develop a master's-level assistantship through a proposal to provide services to special student groups. For example, many colleges and universities have educational opportunity planning committees (EOPC) that consider proposals for programs and services to facilitate the recruitment and retention of minority students. Career centers could propose, through the receipt of EOPC funds, to provide master's-level graduate assistantships for the development and delivery of career services to special populations. Programs could include offering a minority career day, coordination of special outreach programs to minority student organizations, coordination of a minority internship program, and/or conducting a needs assessment concerning career services of interest to a particular population, such as Hispanic students.

When career centers offer graduate assistantships, it is important that a cooperative relationship be developed with academic departments preparing professionals for careers in counseling and career development. Greater attention is paid later in this chapter to graduate student recruitment and supervision. However, when qualified, it is desirable for career center staff to hold affiliate faculty rank in graduate departments of counselor education or counseling psychology. Involvement of career center staff in graduate programs would facilitate communication and understanding regarding career center assistantships by faculty and students in the department. This relationship would help the career center in recruiting graduate students and would assist the academic department in the admissions process and financial aid planning for its students. Furthermore, affiliate faculty status of career center staff would contribute to their understanding of the academic environment of graduate assistants while, in turn, graduate department faculty might better understand career center functions through exposure to affiliate faculty.

CAREER CENTER INTERNSHIPS

Graduate-Level Interns

Career centers offer internships for all of the reasons noted in this chapter's introduction, that is, to provide a training function in assisting students in the acquisition of knowledge and skills in delivering career services, to enhance career center staffing, and to receive fresh ideas as well as stimulate research/evaluation activity. For the purposes of this chapter, we define internship, unlike assistantships, as an academic requirement for credit that may include pay. Therefore, an internship, in some measure, is directly related to the student's academic program. As a result, the career center will typically need to provide feedback to the academic department regarding intern performance. Career center internships are quite varied. They could be provided to doctoral, master's, or undergraduate students. Some may involve substantial amounts of time, (e.g., 20 hours per week within the career center) while others may require only a few hours of career center involvement per week. Some internships may have wide-ranging responsibilities, and others may be very focused or project-specific.

Certain graduate-level internships may resemble assistantships and differ only in terms of the student's receiving credit rather than pay. In such cases, the graduate student may seek a career center internship in order to receive added career counseling experience or to receive a thorough orientation to the delivery of career services. Other graduate-level internships may be more specific in nature and focused on research and evaluation of a career center–related issue or service. For example, the Career Planning and Placement office at Lafayette College offers focused and specialized internships. One communications internship (editorial and graphics) involves the development and editing of a newsletter, as well as other publicity. A second communications internship (video products) is focused on the coordination of videotaped interviews with alumni, as well as the production of other video-based materials used in support of career center services.

Occasionally, career centers may develop a relationship with a counselor education or counseling psychology graduate program to develop a systematic approach to career center internships. For example, an agreement could be struck in which all graduate students interested in a career internship would complete a one-credit course offered by the career center to orient students to career development and placement issues and services. Following completion of the orientation course, interested graduate students could apply for a more in-depth internship with the career center. Another graduate-level internship model could include counseling psychology doctoral students completing a required, one-year, full-time internship in a college or university counseling center. When such internships are completed within counseling centers that do not provide career services, students may be offered a "rotation experience" within the career centers as part of their experience. For example, counseling psychology students completing their American Psychology Association (APA)–approved internship at Penn State's Counseling and Psychological Services are offered, depending on experience and interest, a rotational experience within the local hospital psychiatric center or through the university's Career Development and Placement Services.

Undergraduate Interns

Most career center internships that carry credit would be offered to graduate-level counselors in training. However, limited undergraduate internships may be offered by the career center. For example, some undergraduates in a career center peer counseling or advising program may wish to receive internship credit through the field experience. Occasionally, an undergraduate may have a research interest associated with career center activity. For example, some undergraduate honors or scholars programs require an undergraduate honors thesis. Psychology majors may wish to complete honors thesis research concerning a particular career center activity such as evaluating the effectiveness of a peer advising or mock interview program. Business majors may be interested in placement-related research such as investigation of the screening criteria used by employers in the interview process or tracking recruiting activity for certain majors.

Therefore, a sample of career center internships that could be completed by students includes:

1. A general orientation to the career center for a relatively small amount of credit and time; direct service delivery would be limited and under careful supervision

2. In-depth experience in the career center, including direct service delivery such as counseling and programming for relatively large amounts of credit and time; essentially the intern functions as a part-time staff member, and usually such internships are offered to doctoral-level students or advanced master's students

3. A focused or project-specific graduate internship; areas of interest could include assisting in career education course instruction, assisting in revising or developing on-campus recruiting systems, development and delivery of career education outreach programs to particular student populations, development and implementation of a career day, development of promotional or media-based information, or coordinating a mock interview program

4. A research-evaluation–based internship addressing a particular career-related issue or career center service; often such internships are associated with completion of doctoral or master's theses

5. An undergraduate internship focused on evaluation and research required for a course project or for an honors thesis

6. An undergraduate internship associated with direct service delivery such as by a peer counselor, student assistant, or mock interviewer

PEER COUNSELORS

Use of students in paraprofessional roles is common in college and university career centers. A survey conducted by the American College Personnel Association (ACPA) (McKenzie & Manoogian-O'Dell, 1988) found that 163 career centers reported the use of a paraprofessional program. Predictably, more smaller colleges reported the use of paraprofessionals in career services; that is, approximately one-half of the private four-year institutions use paraprofessionals whereas approximately one in five institutions with graduate-level programs utilizes paraprofessionals in the career center.

Although this chapter section is headed "Peer Counselors," the use of students in career centers aside from assistantships and internships might be better labeled as "Paraprofessionals." Ender (1983) defines the use of students in the career center as follows: "Paraprofessionals are students who have been selected and trained to offer educational services to their peers. These services are intentionally designed to assist in the adjustment, satisfaction, and persistence of students toward attainment of their educational goals. Students performing in paraprofessional roles are compensated for their services and supervised by qualified professionals'' (p. 324).

The Career Center at Florida State University uses students as paraprofessionals and refers to them as career advisers (Peterson, Sampson, & Reardon, 1991). The rationale for this title is that it does not connote a professional counselor certification; "adviser" is the title often used in university student services and relates to a variety of staff backgrounds. It should be noted that career advisers at Florida State serve as the primary contact and resource person for clients using its Curricular-Career Information Services (CCIS). Staff serving as career advisers are not limited to paraprofessionals but may include professional counselors on permanent staff and career counselor trainees completing internships, as well as doctoral-level graduate students.

McKenzie and Manoogian-O'Dell (1988) summarize some of the following benefits of utilizing students in career center paraprofessional roles as follows:

1. *Benefits to the center*. Added services and programs without increased costs of time and money; assistance in publicizing and advertising services to other students; assistance in internship and job development; renewed interest and enthusiasm; input and feedback from the student's perspectives.

2. *Benefits to the student body*. Provide an opportunity to capitalize on the impact that students have on one another through constructive use of role modeling; peer counselors may be equally or, in some cases, more effective in providing certain services (Zunker & Brown, 1966; Delworth, Sherwood, & Casaburri, 1974; Ender & McFadden, 1980); provides a forum for the development of leadership skills.

3. *Benefits to the student worker*. Exposure to a variety of situations that enhance personal growth and development; development of skills that have lifelong application.

4. *Benefits to the program coordinator*. Professionals are freed to perform services and tasks that require higher levels of knowledge and skill; increase job satisfaction of professional staff; opportunities to serve as mentor and role model to student staff.

While use of peer counselors holds a number of advantages to the career center, their responsibilities should be carefully defined and circumscribed. Furthermore, the training program and ongoing supervision necessary to ensure a quality paraprofessional program will require a significant amount of staff time. The authors do not suggest that paraprofessionals be selected and trained to provide broad career center services such as general career counseling or to offer a range of outreach programs to varied student groups. However, paraprofessionals may be trained in a specific facet of some of these services. For example, paraprofessionals trained to conduct mock interviews may be viewed as offering a specific type of career counseling, or paraprofessionals trained to conduct orientations to career center services or résumé preparation workshops may support outreach program efforts.

Paraprofessionals' programs will vary in the scope of responsibilities given to student assistants. For example, at Penn State's Career Development and Placement

Services, the peer counseling program is limited to conducting videotaped mock interviews. Other colleges and universities may include a wide range of responsibilities in their job descriptions for paraprofessionals. For example, career assistants named Student Associate and Relations Team (START) at the University of Texas at Austin have different job descriptions but may include some of the following responsibilities:

- Critique résumés and cover letters
- Teach or co-teach workshops/classes
- Perform intake counseling
- Coordinate and host receptions and panels
- Host visiting employers
- Interact with employers or alumni to develop recruitment visits, summer jobs, and internships
- Interact with professionals or alumni to develop career consultants, externship sponsors
- Complete administrative/clerical tasks
- Design fliers and other marketing devices
- Lead library and facility tours
- Deliver outreach programs and services
- Develop educational materials

At the University of Illinois, Urbana-Champaign, paraprofessional career consultants share the same job description, including the the following responsibilities:

- Critique résumés and cover letters
- Teach or coteach workshops/classes
- Perform intake counseling
- Coordinate and host receptions and panels
- Interact with employers or alumni to develop recruitment visits, summer jobs, and internships .
- Host visiting employers
- Complete administrative/clerical tasks
- Design fliers and other marketing devices
- Offer computer assistance guidance
- Lead library and facility tours
- Maintain satellite facilities
- Deliver outreach programs and services
- Participate in research projects
- Develop educational materials
- Recruit and interview new members

The ACPA survey concerning the use of students in career services that was previously discussed found that the following elements of student staff members' job descriptions were among those reported by 163 paraprofessional program coordinators:

- Design fliers
- Perform clerical tasks
- Lead tours
- Critique résumés
- Teach workshops
- Conduct outreach programs
- Assist with student use of computer
- Perform intake counseling
- Coordinate panels
- Prepare materials
- Provide research assistance
- Perform career counseling
- Develop recruiters
- Host employers
- Conduct video mock interviews
- Complete special projects
- Develop alumni sponsors
- Interpret tests
- Maintain satellite facilities

As noted earlier, the categories of students involved in career center services are not mutually exclusive. For example, students participating in a paraprofessional program may also be completing internships. At Penn State, peer counselors participating in the video mock interview programs are on a volunteer basis, but the option is also provided to undergraduate students who wish to enroll for internship credits through a psychology course. Compensation or incentives for participation in a paraprofessional program will vary. In some cases, peer counselors will be paid, others will be voluntary, and many paraprofessionals' programs involve academic credit. The University of Illinois at Urbana-Champaign provides credit hours through an educational psychology course.

The ACPA survey of student use in career centers found that of the 163 paraprofessional program coordinators contacted, 64 percent of the student assistant programs involved hourly wages, 25 percent were voluntary, 21 percent included credit, 9 percent received a stipend, and 2 percent received tuition waivers.

Regardless of the nature of the experience, breadth of responsibility, or type of compensation, all students (doctoral-level graduate assistants, graduate or undergraduate interns, peer counselors, or work-study students) must receive adequate training and supervision to ensure ethical and effective service delivery.

OTHER STUDENT INVOLVEMENT IN THE CAREER CENTER

Additional involvement of students in the career center could include (1) graduate student counselors-in-training completing practicums, (2) student advisory boards, and (3) students approved for work-study funds.

Almost all graduate programs related to career counseling require some sort of practical experience. Often, graduate departments of counselor education maintain a counseling center to provide students with laboratory experience under faculty supervision. However, it may be desirable for the career center to cultivate a relationship with a counselor education graduate department in order to serve as a practicum site. In doing so, the career center provides clients and a counseling system with supervision shared with faculty. For example, at Penn State's Career Development and Placement Services, plans are being developed for the Career Center to serve as a required practicum site for all first-year doctoral students pursuing the Ph.D. program in counseling psychology. The Career Center would provide clients and space as well as share practicum supervision with the faculty. A similar practicum model could be developed at other universities to provide master's-level field experience.

In addition to offering internships or peer counseling programs, career centers may wish to establish a student advisory board. The principal mission of a student advisory board would be to serve as a vehicle for the career center to receive feedback from students and continue to be responsive to student career-related needs. A further mission of a student advisory board could be to serve in an advocacy role for the career center in promoting its services to students or in representing the career center in functions such as career days. Student advisory boards should include a representative sample of the student population stratified by semester standing, undergraduate and graduate status, gender, ethnicity, age, and college or degree program. As noted earlier, student advisory board members may wish to serve in an advocacy role for the career center, but this should be secondary to assisting the center in its responsiveness to meeting student career issues and needs. Evaluation models were discussed in Chapter 4, and most career centers routinely evaluate their services. However, many evaluation programs address the responses of clients who are currently involved in the career center or have received services. A student advisory board could serve as a catalyst for conducting a needs survey among the general student population who have not developed a relationship with the career center. A needs survey such as the example shown in Figure 9.1 could be developed and administered by student advisory board members to students in their respective academic units. Furthermore, student advisory board members could staff tables in high traffic areas such as a student union or graduate center to disseminate survey forms. Student advisory board members could also participate in career center committees in planning for program evaluations, planning new services, and developing publicity for particular services.

Frequently, career centers will serve as employment sites for students receiving work-study funds. In such cases, work-study students may not share the same investment in the career center as interns or peer counselors, and, as a result, their job descriptions may be more specialized or clerical in nature. However, work-study student employment may offer advantages similar to those of graduate assistants described earlier in this chapter. In many cases, work-study students may be trained to staff career center public areas such as the career library or reception area to greet clients and answer initial questions. Care must be taken not to view work-study students similarly or provide them with the same range of responsibilities as student interns or peer counselors. Nonetheless, work-study students should be provided with training and supervision to ensure quality in representing the career center in a clerical or support staff role. Often work-study students can be included as support staff with responsibilities that relate to their skills or academic program. For example, a computer science major may assist the career center in a project that involves computerization familiarity and skill.

RECRUITMENT, TRAINING, AND SUPERVISION OF STUDENT ASSISTANTS

In recruiting graduate students for assistantships and internships, it is vital that the career center develop linkages with appropriate graduate departments, such as counselor education, counseling psychology, and higher education administration. The development of a liaison between the career center and graduate departments involved in career counselor training is mutually beneficial: the graduate department may provide qualified career center staff with affiliate faculty rank and benefit from using the career center as a field setting to provide its graduate students with counseling experience while the career center benefits from the human resources available through graduate students. When career center staff hold affiliate faculty rank, they can become involved in the recruitment and admissions process of graduate students. For example, when graduate student candidates visit the college or university for admission interviews, they may be provided with tours of the career center and receive information regarding potential assistantships or internship opportunities. Announcements of assistantships similar to the example provided in Figure 9.2 could be distributed to appropriate graduate departments.

A systematic procedure should be developed for informing and recruiting graduate students concerning internships. Once again, the internship would represent a partnership between the career center and graduate department. Announcements of career center internships such as the example shown in Figure 9.3 could be distributed within the graduate academic department. Graduate faculty serving as intern coordinators should be informed of the career center and its internships in order to refer students to the field experience.

Figure 9.1
Student Needs Survey

Thank you for agreeing to complete this survey. Your input is valuable in helping us to serve all Penn State students in the most helpful ways possible.

1. Have you heard of Career Development and Placement Services and the services we offer?

    _____ Yes   _____ No

    If yes, how did you hear?

    _____Collegian   _____Residence Hall
    _____College/Department   _____Flyer/Poster
    _____Other University Office   _____Class
    _____Orientation   _____Friend
    _____Student Organization   _____Other _____
                                                           (Please indicate)

FOR THE FOLLOWING QUESTIONS, PLEASE INDICATE WHETHER YOU WERE AWARE OF, HAVE EVER USED, OR THINK YOU WOULD USE OUR SERVICES:

		Was aware of this service	Have used this service	Would use in the future
2.	INTAKE COUNSELING (walk-in service for brief assistance with resumes and vitas, cover letters, and interview request forms, general questions, and scheduling of counseling services)	_____	_____	_____
3.	INDIVIDUAL CAREER COUNSELING (one-hour sessions to explore career-related issues, including choosing a major or career, and individual job search planning for all majors)	_____	_____	_____
4.	COMPUTERIZED CAREER GUIDANCE SYSTEMS: DISCOVER OF SIGI PLUS	_____	_____	_____
5.	CAREER PLANNING COURSES (job search and professional development in various career fields)	_____	_____	_____
6.	OUTREACH PROGRAMMING (seminars on career issues and programs by request of student groups)	_____	_____	_____
7.	CAREER INFORMATION CENTER (houses reference materials such as books and files on careers, undergraduate majors and graduate programs at PSU, Grad School information, placement data on PSU graduates, internship postings, employer directories, videos on companies and job search, and job search guides)	_____	_____	_____
8.	INTERVIEW TRAINING CENTER (videotaped practice interviews)	_____	_____	_____
9.	ON-CAMPUS RECRUITING (corporations and government agencies which recruit students to fill both permanent and summer/internship positions)	_____	_____	_____

Figure 9.1 (continued)

	Was aware of this service	Have used this service	Would use in the future
10. PLACEMENT LIBRARY (listings of job openings by college, government employment opportunities, nationwide computerized job listing service, information on companies and government agencies which participate in on-campus recruiting)	_____	_____	_____
11. EDUCATION CAREER SERVICES (weekly vacancy listing, credentials service and assistance with job search in public and private elementary and secondary education, and higher education and nursing	_____	_____	_____

PLEASE TAKE A FEW MOMENTS TO SHARE SOME OF YOUR IDEAS:

12. Do you have any ideas for improving any of our existing services?

13. What services would you like to see us provide that we currently do not offer?

14. Please note any career-related concerns you believe are especially important to students like yourself (undergraduate, graduate, college, program, special population, etc.)

15. Do you have any ideas of how we can better inform students like yourself about our services?

16. PLEASE LET US KNOW A LITTLE ABOUT YOURSELF: (circle one)

    College: AG A&A BA COMM ED EMSC ENGR HHD LA SC DUS

    Major: _____

    Sex: M   F

    Standing: Fr So Jr Sr Grad

If you are interested in any of our services, please stop by the Intake Office in 412 Boucke! Thank you for your time.

Figure 9.2
Graduate Assistantship Announcement and Description

THE PENNSYLVANIA STATE UNIVERSITY

CAREER DEVELOPMENT AND PLACEMENT SERVICES

POSITION VACANCY
Graduate Assistantships (Counselors)

Primary Functions

Offer direct individual and group counseling services to college
students.

Duties and Responsibilities

Provide students with assistance in a range of career development issues
including the exploration, confirmation, and implementation of
educational/career plans. Also, assist in the delivery of the Office's
career education and outreach programs.

Qualifications

A master's degree in counseling psychology, counselor education, student
personnel, or equivalent, is the minimum. Applicant must be able to
counsel students in both individual and group settings.

Supervision

Graduate Assistant Counselors are provided with individual supervision
by a licensed psychologist on a weekly basis. Group case reviews and
counseling staff meetings are held bi-weekly.

Terms of Employment

Assistantships are half time; 20 hours per week. Appointment is for two
consecutive semesters beginning Fall and continuing through Spring
Semester.

Application Procedure

Direct a letter of application and resume as well as three letters of
recommendation to the Associate Director of Counseling, Career
Development and Placement Services, 404 Boucke Building, University
Park, PA 16802.

All materials must be received by April 3, 1992.

CAREER DEVELOPMENT AND PLACEMENT SERVICES
A unit of the Division of Counseling Services and Program Assessment
Office of the Vice President for Student Services
An Affirmative Action/Equal Opportunity Employer

Figure 9.2 (continued)

GRADUATE ASSISTANTSHIPS IN CAREER DEVELOPMENT AND PLACEMENT SERVICES

Career Development and Placement Services offers a career counseling assistantship experience. Graduate Assistants involve themselves intensively in the office's counseling and activities and may elect a less-in-depth experience in a broad range of office activities. Following is a listing of the major activities carried out by the Office.

-Career counseling with approximately 6,000 students per year. Counseling is provided through intake, individual appointments, small group services, and credit courses. Career counseling activities include values clarification, interest assessment, computer-assisted guidance, the teaching of decision making skills, resume and cover letter preparation, interview skill building, the provision of occupational and career information and other topics as dictated by the client.

-The sponsorship and delivery of more than 300 workshops/ seminars/group sessions per year on the following topics:

        Getting into Graduate and Professional School
        Interview Skills for International Students
        Job Search for Blacks
        Career Issues for Women
        Job Search Techniques
        Interview Skills
        Looking for a Major
        Resume Preparation
        Dual Career Couples
        Career Planning

-The organization and supervision of approximately 22,000 student/ employer interviews per academic year and associated placement activities. Most of these interviews are conducted during the Fall and early Spring Semester.

-The maintenance of a library of information on over 1,000 companies which regularly recruit on the PSU campus.

-The delivery of computerized career assistance DISCOVER.

-The design and teaching of career courses for several of the colleges including: Liberal Arts, Business Administration, Education, Agriculture, Human Development.

299

Figure 9.3
Internship Announcement and Description

INTERNSHIP IN CAREER DEVELOPMENT AND PLACEMENT SERVICES

Career Development and Placement Services offers a diverse internship experience. Interns may involve themselves intensively in a few office activities in which they have particular interest or they may elect a less in-depth experience in a broad range of office activities. Following is a listing of the major activities carried out by the office:

- Individual career counseling with approximately 4,000 students per year. These sessions include values clarification, interest assessment, the teaching of decision making skills, resume and cover letter preparation, interview skill building, the provision of occupational and career information, and other topics as dictated by the client.

- The sponsorship and delivery of workshops/seminars/group sessions on the following topics:

Getting into Graduate and Professional School	Interview Skills
Interview Skills for International Students	Choosing a Major
Career Issues for Women	Resume Preparation
Job Search for African-Americans	Dual Career Couples
Other topics upon request or as the need arises	

Approximately 300 of these sessions are conducted each year.

- The organization and supervision of approximately 25,000 student/employer interviews per academic year and associated activities. Most of these interviews are conducted during the fall and early spring semesters.

- The maintenance of a library of information on over 1,000 companies which regularly recruit on the PSU campus.

- The maintenance of a career resource center to assist students in their personal career development.

- The delivery of computerized career guidance (DISCOVER, SIGI PLUS).

- The development of quality handouts on timely career-related topics.

- The administration of Alumni Career Services (ACS) to assist alumni of PSU in finding employment after graduation.

- The organization and dissemination of job listings brought to our office by employers in business, government, and industry.

- Follow-up studies and manpower studies initiated and conducted by our office and for other University offices.

- The delivery of Education Career Services (ECS) including credential services, the publication of vacancy notices, and the organization of on-campus job interviews.

- The publication of a tabloid entitled <u>Career Planning News</u> in the fall.

- The design and teaching of career courses for several of the Colleges including: Liberal Arts, Business Administration, Education, Agriculture, Human Development.

- Involvement in employer relations.

- Management of the office budget, personnel, and staffing.

<u>Purpose of Internship</u>

1. To acquire knowledge in the area of Career Development and Placement Services.

2. To practically apply knowledge of Career Development and Placement Services, thereby providing training for the student and service to CDPS.

300

Figure 9.3 (continued)

<u>Requirements</u>

1. Candidate must be currently enrolled in a related graduate program at PSU.

2. Candidate must exhibit a strong student service commitment.

3. All applicants will be screened by the Director of CDPS or a coordinating staff member, and the decision to offer an internship will be based upon the mutuality of the needs of the student and CDPS.

4. The internship will be conducted in accordance with the guidelines specified in the Division of Counseling and Educational Psychology publication entitled, "Field Experience and Practicum Syllabus for Student Personnel Option."

5. It is preferred that all candidates complete the one-credit Counselor Education Course 596 (individual Studies in Career Development).

6. The internship may be taken for 1 to 3 credits with the expectation that 4 to 5 hours of work will be required for each hour of credit.

<u>Procedures</u>

1. Interested students should submit a letter of application together with a resume to the Director of CDPS at least five weeks prior to the semester they desire to start their internship experience. The letter should provide pertinent information concerning related past experiences and what the student hopes to achieve through the internship.

2. Once selected for an internship, the student will be assigned to a coordinating staff member. The student will then develop a contract with his/her coordinating staff member specifying objectives to be accomplished, activities and evaluation criteria to be employed.

<u>Training</u>

A. <u>General</u>

1. Training will include an introduction and overview of the total service provided by CDPS. It is expected that the intern will become familiar with our outreach programs, publicity functions, manpower information, recruiting and placement procedures, career resource center, testing, counseling, etc.

B. <u>Specific</u>

1. Specific training will be provided by a CDPS staff member in the conduction and critique of videotaped role-played interviews (Mock Interviews) for graduating seniors and graduate students.

2. The intern will also have the responsibility of presenting outreach programs as part of the Seminar Series (i.e., Resume Preparation, Preparing for Interviews, or Completing Interview Request Forms).

3. An opportunity for co-counseling with professional staff may be provided <u>for those who have supervised counseling experience</u>.

C. Interns will choose one area that is agreed upon by them and the coordinator to study in depth, and the intern will be required to submit a project in this area by the end of his or her internship experience.

<u>Evaluation</u>

1. The internship will be evaluated by the student, his/her coordinator, and the Director.

2. A letter grade will then be submitted by the Director of Career Development and Placement Services.

mr2.4 (WP)
9/2/92

Undergraduate internships and paraprofessional programs would also involve cooperative efforts with appropriate undergraduate departments. For example, the career center may wish to develop a relationship with faculty teaching advanced undergraduate courses in industrial psychology or human resource management to recruit students who may be interested in participating in a mock interview peer counseling program. Further, most colleges have offices for student involvement or leadership housed within their student activities function. Career centers could provide job descriptions of paraprofessional programs to such offices, and, when student involvement or leadership fairs are held at a college or university, the career center should be represented to recruit students for their experiences.

There is a range of traditional forms by which to advertise assistantships, internships, or paraprofessional programs, like fliers, ads in the campus newspaper, and announcements in outreach programs. However, the referral of students to such experiences is facilitated through developing a systematic and cooperative approach with other key offices, such as academic departments and student activities units.

A thorough discussion of selection criteria for involving students in the career center is beyond the scope of this chapter. However, the ACPA survey of career center use of student staff members found that the following criteria were frequently considered by career centers in selecting students for paraprofessional programs:

- Faculty/staff recommendations
- Previous leadership experience
- Written application
- Grade point average
- Academic major
- Résumé
- Previous counseling experience
- Peer ratings
- Training performance

Obviously, the nature and extent of training and supervision will vary with respect to the type of student involvement in the career center. Training and supervision of advanced doctoral students engaged in career counseling will be quite different from the training and supervision of work-study assistants engaged in clerical or reception functions. Regardless of type of student involvement, training and supervision should be provided that are consistent with the CAS standards discussed in Chapter 3.

Graduate students engaged in career counseling through assistantships, internships, or practicums would be provided with initial orientation to all career center services and observe programs provided by experienced career center staff. It is particularly helpful to require new graduate student counselors to observe intake to become familiar with the diversity of career center clients, hear their presenting concerns, and observe interventions and referral strategies. Since many graduate student counselors are relatively new to the college or university, it is important that they visit and become informed of other student services that are available as referral sources. Other training activities would include orientation to the career information center and its resources, review of traditional and computer-assisted assessments, and review of the counseling, scheduling, and record-keeping systems. Following an initial training program, graduate student counselors may begin to carry a limited caseload with individual and group supervision.

A common supervisory model to support graduate student counselors would include career counseling staff meetings held, at least, biweekly and small group counseling team meetings, as well as weekly individual supervision. Meetings involving all career counseling staff and including graduate assistants and interns would address a range of topics and issues, such as (1) case reviews, (2) guest speakers from within the college or university reviewing their academic programs or student services or addressing special client issues, (3) in-service training for particular career counseling skills, such as providing career information or addressing multicultural counseling issues, (4) discussion of career counseling issues with particular populations, that is, women, returning adults, lesbian and gay clients, disabled clients, or culturally diverse clients, and (5) team-building exercises or informal review of staff backgrounds to facilitate collegiality. Clearly, a review of counselor training and supervision models for graduate student counselors is not realistic for this chapter. There are a number of excellent resources, including specific volumes of *Counseling Psychologist* (Fretz, 1990; Whitely, 1982), that have been devoted to counselor training and supervision. However, in general, an outline of a training and supervision system to support graduate student counselors within a career center would include:

Training

1. Orientation to the career center
   a. Meeting with staff and review of responsibilities
   b. Review of career center services
2. Review of career counseling procedures, scheduling, and record-keeping systems
3. Observation of career center services and programs
   a. Intake counseling
   b. Small group counseling
   c. Outreach programs
   d. Career library
   e. Placement/recruiting services
4. Visitation and orientation to other student services and referral sources within the college or university

Supervision (Individual and Group)

1. Review of client issues in career counseling through counseling staff meetings, team supervision, and individual meetings
2. Review of career counseling intervention issues
   a. Client relationship and process issues
   b. Assessment
   c. Career information
3. Case reviews
   a. Question-and-answer sessions with the supervisor regarding a case
   b. Information requirements for selected cases
   c. Intervention strategies
   d. Counselor-client process issues within cases

As seen in the above outline, training of graduate student career counselors should proceed from initial information and orientation to observation for training purposes and, then, to supervision in support of limited career counseling. Individual supervision would also evolve from initial information-based questions to a review of interventions appropriate to related cases, and eventually supervision would address more subtle and dynamic counseling process issues.

Often, internships include more structured training and supervision than can be provided through a credit course required prior to or during the field experience. As noted earlier, internships represent a cooperative effort between the career center and the academic department providing credit. As a result, supervision may be shared between a field supervisor in the career center and a faculty intern coordinator from the academic department. Training and supervision models for internships are quite varied; however, regardless of training system, to ensure a quality experience, the internship responsibilities, supervision, and evaluation process should be clearly defined and understood by the student, the career center, and the academic department. An example of a contract and final report outline for a master's-level internship is provided in Figure 9.4

Clearly, the training and supervision provided to undergraduate student paraprofessionals who are less experienced than graduate assistants or interns are at the heart of such programs' ability to make a meaningful contribution to the career center and its clients. McKenzie and Manoogian-O'Dell (1988) state, "It has been the experience of these authors, that consistent and caring supervision of student staff provides the most important link to success (p. 14)."

Since undergraduate paraprofessionals are relatively inexperienced, it is important that a training and supervision program be as defined and structured as possible. Also, areas of paraprofessional responsibilities should be well defined and circumscribed. Supervision and evaluation of peer counselors should include little ambiguity and be provided by a staff member designated as a paraprofessional program coordinator. In their survey of student use in career centers, McKenzie and Manoogian-O'Dell (1988) have reported that paraprofessionals are often not adequately trained. They indicate that approximately 45 percent of the career centers surveyed reported providing ten hours or less of preservice training.

Delworth and Yarris (1978, p. 4) outline the following procedures for the development and implementation of a paraprofessional training program:

1. Identify the kinds of competence and expertise that are necessary for adequate performance of each task or role.
2. Identify the cognitions, affect, and skills needed for each kind of competence and state these requisites as specific behavioral objectives.
3. Assess the trainees' current knowledge and abilities.
4. Decide the overall format and sequence of training.
5. Determine the particular techniques to be used in training.
6. Plan ongoing supervision/consultation processes.
7. Design evaluation procedures.
8. Design processes to train cotrainers (if any).
9. Implement and evaluate the training program.
10. Redesign the program as indicated by the evaluation.

Delworth and Yarris (1978, p. 22) recommend that paraprofessional training, when it is devoted to teaching specific skills, should consider the following:

1. Translate the skill into specific objectives.
2. Develop training procedures that sequentially explain the effective use of the skills, model the skill being effectively practiced, and provide practice with performance feedback for trainees until the minimum acceptance competence is attained.
3. Provide supervised practice with "real life" situations.
4. Provide learning situations (such as reading, presentations, discussions) in which the important theoretical and practical literature may be studied and integrated with skills.

The content of the paraprofessional training programs identified by the McKenzie and Manoogian-O'Dell (1988) survey of 163 career centers included the following topics in rank order:

- Communication/counseling skills
- Campus resources
- Job search skills
- Career-planning strategies
- Career development theory
- Office procedures

Figure 9.4
Internship Contract Proposal and Final Report Form

THE PENNSYLVANIA STATE UNIVERSITY

Department of Counselor Education, Counseling Psychology,
and Rehabilitation Services Education

STUDENT PERSONNEL SERVICES INTERNSHIP CONTRACT PROPOSAL

DATE:

TO: Internship Coordinator

FROM: _____: On Site Internship Supervisor

        _____: Prospective Intern

1. Preparation for the Internship.

    A. Present skills and experience (competencies):

    B. Student Personnel experience and coursework:

2. Reason(s) for selecting this particular Internship
    site.

3. Objectives for the Internship:

    A. Selected area(s) of concentration:

    B. Objectives:

    C. Methodology for achieving objectives:

    D. Internship product:

4. Agreements (hours, compensation, etc.)

Approved: _____
                On-site Internship Supervisor

          _____
                        Intern

          _____
                    Field Supervisor

cc: Intern
     On-site Supervisor
     Field Supervisor
     File

SBLDOC11/90

306

Figure 9.4 (continued)

<u>SUPERVISOR'S FINAL REPORT</u>

<u>Student Personnel Option Internship</u>

Name of Intern_____

Name of Supervisor_____

Location of Site_____

Date of Final Evaluation_____

Number of Credits of Internship_____

Degree to which internship objectives outlined in the contract were
met. Evaluate intern in terms of each specific objective noting
additional activities or esponsibilities undertaken.

Comment on the nature of the intern's professional attitudes and
behavior, the relationship established with other co-workers, new
skills acquired, the ability to work with decreasing amounts of
supervision.

Answer only if applicable. Indicate whether or not the agreed upon
intern-prepared product was completed. Evaluate how well it meets
the criterion on adequately reflecting all or a major part of the
internship responsibilities.

Additional comments:

_____
     Signature of Supervisor

_____   _____
     Signature of Intern   Date

_____
          Grade Recommended
(Negotiated between intern and supervisor)

Send to: Coordinator, Student Personnel Option
           The Pennsylvania State University
           327 CEDAR Building
           University Park, PA   16802

SBLDOC11/90

307

- Leading workshops
- Values clarification
- Business writing
- Goal setting
- Appreciation of differences
- Leadership skills
- Time management
- Student development theory
- Team building
- Computer programs
- Decision making
- Marketing skills
- Testing

Occasionally, training programs are packaged through a credit course required prior to involvement in a career center paraprofessional program. For example, the University of Illinois at Urbana-Champaign offers a course—Educational Psychology 199—that enables paraprofessional career consultants to (1) learn basic microcounseling techniques, (2) develop general counseling skills using role plays, (3) assess interests, values, and skills, (4) become familiar with career-planning and occupational information resources, (5) become familiar with career-planning instruments and exercises, and (6) learn basic job search skills, such as cover letter and résumé design, that could be shared with others.

Peterson et al. (1991) reported that the Career Center at Florida State University has developed an extensive career adviser in-service training program for staff working in the Curricular-Career Information Service (CCIS) that includes the following four phases:

1. Orientation, a two-hour overview of the CCIS system.
2. Introduction (first 5 weeks), a 50- to 75-hour sequence including familiarization with resources, equipment operation, direct observation of services, staff meetings, and completion of selected module activities.
3. Trial (weeks 6-15), a 100-hour sequence where the trainee begins to assist some clients with less complex concerns, working under the close supervision of senior career advisers.
4. Career adviser (16 weeks plus), a continuing phase in which the individual refines specialized helping skills, using more complex interventions for special populations.

The paraprofessional program at the University of Texas at Austin includes 26 to 40 hours of preservice training and 10 to 45 hours of on-the-job training. Follow-up supervision includes 2 hours per week of group supervision and at least 10 hours of weekly individual supervision. Topics covered in the training program include:

- Communication and counseling skills
- Effective leadership skills
- Goal setting and assessment
- Career development theory
- Business writing and etiquette
- Appreciation of differences
- Time management
- Leading effective workshops and meetings
- Values clarification
- Campus resources and referral techniques
- Job search skills and strategies
- Career and life planning
- Assertiveness skills
- Giving feedback/evaluating process

In considering the training programs outlined above, it is apparent that career centers choosing to include paraprofessionals in their staffing patterns have made a commitment to providing specific and thorough training to program participants to ensure ethical and professional service delivery. While the advantages of increased staffing in the career center through the inclusion of students are clear, career centers choosing this option also must make an investment of substantial staff time for the development of initial training programs and providing subsequent supervision and evaluation of student assistants.

SUMMARY

The use of graduate and undergraduate students within the staff adds to the career center's human resources, expands its mission to training other professionals and paraprofessionals in the delivery of career services, and serves as a catalyst for strengthening career center linkages with academic departments. Care must be exercised in defining the various roles that students may play in career center staffing. For example, it is possible that a large comprehensive career center in a university setting could involve all of the following types of student staff within a single semester:

- Doctoral-level graduate assistant counselors enrolled in counselor education or counseling psychology programs
- Doctoral-level students completing required practicum rotations in the career center

- Doctoral-level interns involved in field research within the career center
- Master's-level students in counselor education (student personnel administration option) completing internships
- An undergraduate psychology major completing an honors thesis related to a career center service
- Undergraduate students providing peer career counseling services
- Undergraduate and graduate students serving as student advisory board members
- Work-study students providing clerical and staff support functions
- Doctoral students from other universities involved in APA-approved counseling psychology internships completing a rotation experience in the career center

Obviously, the various roles and job responsibilities in the career center must be defined clearly and understood by students and staff. Differential training and supervision patterns appropriate to each student role must be developed and implemented by career center staff. If these expectations are not met, involvement of student assistants in the career center can be fraught with unmet expectations and frustration by students and career center staff. Most importantly, lack of adequate job descriptions and the systematic training and supervision of student assistants would erode career center quality in its service delivery to clients. When the above expectations are met in involving students in the delivery of services, the career center benefits from the energy, commitment, and freshness that student assistants offer, thereby enhancing the career center's responsiveness in addressing the career-related needs of its clients.

REFERENCES

Delworth, U., Sherwood, G., & Casaburri, N. (1974). *Student paraprofessionals: A working model for higher education*. Washington, DC: American Personnel and Guidance Association.

Delworth, U., & Yarris, E. (1978). Concepts and process for the new training role. In U. Delworth (Ed.), *Training competent staff* (pp. 1–15). San Francisco: Jossey-Bass.

Ender, S. C. (1983). Students as paraprofessionals. In T. K. Miller, R. B. Winston, Jr., & W. R. Mendenhall (Eds.), *Administration and leadership in student affairs: Actualizing student development in higher education*. (pp. 323–339). Muncie, ID: Accelerated Development.

Ender, S. C., & McFadden, R. B. (1980). Training the student professional helper. In F. B. Newton & K. L. Ender (Eds.), *Student development practices: Strategies for making a difference* (pp. 127–142). Springfield, IL: Charles C. Thomas.

Fretz, B. R. (Ed.). (1990). Systematic training. *Counseling Psychologist, 18*(3).

McKenzie, I. L., & Manoogian-O'Dell, M. (1988). Expanding the use of students in career services: Current programs and resources. *American College Personnel Association Media Publication*, No. 45.

Peterson, G. W., Sampson, J. P., & Reardon, R. C. (1991). *Career development and services: A cognitive approach*. Pacific Grove, CA: Brooks/Cole.

Whiteley, J. M. (Ed.). (1982). Supervision in counseling. *Counseling Psychologist, 10*(1).
Zunker, V. G., & Brown, W. F. (1966). Comparative effectiveness of student and professional counselors. *Personnel and Guidance Journal 44*(7). 738–743.

10

Epilogue

REPRISE

Handbook for the College and University Career Center has attempted to establish several fundamental premises. One of them is that career centers in institutions of higher education are still an evolving organizational form. Their shape, location, scope, and content are intimately linked to the institutional history and purposes that they execute. But within such a context, it is also obvious that career centers are institutional forms that connect elements of the past, the present, and the future in service to college students, adolescents, adults, and other constituent groups.

College and university career centers are contemporary organizations that combine the historic commitment to placement of graduates as an institutional priority with the more recent concern with helping students with their career development needs as they proceed from entry to college, to choice of a major, to preparation for placement. As college and university career centers have become increasingly comprehensive in their purposes, constituencies, and services, the need for planning and for enlarged visions of their contributions to the campus community as a whole has intensified.

A second major and overriding premise of this reference is that career centers must be planned; they are far too important, for too many college students, to their total education and their transition from college to the next educational, career, or social step to be allowed to arise spontaneously and grow amorphously. Without planning, they are inefficient and possibly wasters of precious resources; without planning, their utility for their constituents may be far less than it might or should be. Once attributed to Albert Einstein was the remark: "I never think of the future. It comes soon enough." Whether or not this remark is apocryphal, those engaged in providing career services in colleges and universities cannot afford the luxury of ignoring the future. To assume that the future will be a replication of the past is folly. To avoid such folly requires planning skills plus the management of whatever plan for the career center emerges in order to ensure the wisest use of resources and the fullest set of responses possible to the needs that are present within the student populations of specific institutions.

Planning, as portrayed in this reference, has accented the importance of understanding the character and diversity of college student career needs as major input to the planning process for career centers. As subsets of this issue, emphasis has been given to the diverse career needs experienced by traditional-age college students, minority students, returning adults, international students, and other segments of the student population. While there are universal needs and concerns shared in some measure by all college students regardless of age or gender, it is also true that some student needs are different in kind from student group to student group. Examples of these unique needs have been provided throughout the book.

Planning is intended to foresee the needs for the intervention delivery systems that will originate in, and are tailored to, the characteristics of specific career centers. While resources, needs, and other institutional factors will dictate the precise elements to be included, the trend in career centers is to become more comprehensive in the services they provide. Many illustrations of such techniques and programs have been cited in this book, including individual and group counseling, career courses and workshops, building and maintaining a career library, using technology in the career center, matching students and potential employers, working directly with recruiters, and engaging in a variety of forms of outreach to academic departments and other campus units.

Career centers, whether centralized or decentralized in their organizational structure within a particular college or university, are fascinating entities because, by purpose or mission, they must bridge two rather unique cultures. Career centers, while housed in academic institutions and tied to their philosophical and financial priorities, must, to be effective, also be credible to employers. As representatives of the colleges or universities whose students, alumni, and faculty are their "customers," career center staff must also consider recruiters from school systems, government agencies, businesses, and industries as their "customers." Thus, career center staff must speak the language and observe the customs and procedures that characterize "academe" while also speaking the language and respecting the different organizational cultures that are reflected in the employers, recruiters, or interviewers who come to the campus to find graduates who have the skills they need.

As pointed out at several places in the chapters on planning and management, while career centers must portray a favorable fit with the academic context in which they are found—for example, have staff members who hold affiliate or joint appointments in academic departments, do research, provide graduate assistantships or employment to some students of the college or university where they are located, offer intern experiences—they are frequently judged by criteria that are more likely to be found in the corporate world than in the academic world—for example, number of student placements in jobs, salaries received, cost-benefit ratios of staff costs to placements, number of employers recruiting at the campus in a given year, amounts of money contributed to the career center by corporate sponsors.

As career centers bridge two "customer" cultures, most of them have dualistic missions: one is the development of students' readiness for placement, and the second is the "brokering" of students in a modern industrial or advanced technological society where the quality of human capital, knowledge, ideas, and advanced academic skills have replaced experience, raw material, and physical assets as the major ingredients by which employers maintain a competitive edge. The combined emphases on the development of student skills that are prerequisite to successful placement and the more specific events that occur at the point of placement suggest the reality that career centers must view placements as a process of student career development that unfolds incrementally in parallel with the academic maturity that students are accruing through the total college experience. Both the academic and the career development skills of students ultimately must be "packaged" and brokered at the culmination of the placement process: the placement event.

In their developmental and educational missions and in their placement missions, contemporary career centers have a large array of interventions, training models, and placement procedures from which to select. These have been discussed throughout this reference. However, to be somewhat redundant in this closing summary, there are inventories of these possibilities that may be useful. For example, colleges and universities typically have used four major approaches to deliver career service to students: (1) courses, workshops, and seminars that offer structured group experiences in career planning, job access skills, decision making, and related topics; (2) group counseling activities; (3) individual counseling; and (4) placement programs or procedures (Herr & Cramer, 1992). In a fuller sense, however, discussions of each of these approaches can be expanded to address whether or not they use technology (e.g., computer-assisted career guidance programs for exploration of possible majors or jobs, computer-assisted scheduling of employers with students who are graduating from academic majors and with technical skills sought by such employers); what kinds of informational support system they require (e.g., a career resource center, a section in the library, a collection of general career material augmented by trade or industry directories, annual reports of corporations recruiting students); whether or not career services will be general in nature and available for all students or tailored to specific student subpopulations (e.g., international students, athletes, returning adult students, alumni, university or college staff); and whether "customers" of the career center will come to one physical location to receive services or obtain them from decentralized locations, have access to computerized information available throughout a campus, or receive career services through different types of outreach programs in dormitories, fraternities and sororities, or other settings. As each of these possibilities is considered, it is likely to lead to other planning questions. For example, if a decision is taken to create a career library to support the other programs of the career center, then issues emerge as to where information will be housed, the scope of the information that will be required, the form in which information will be provided (e.g., hard copy, video, audio, computerized), the management and staffing of the information, and the types and times of student access to information.

A further matter that career center staff need to appreciate and address is the center's role as a training ground for students and, particularly, for graduate students who are interested in a potential professional role as a career counselor or in the management of such services. In one sense, this issue is a subset of a larger one relating to how students will be employed within the career center. Will they serve as peer counselors, generalist student helpers, graduate assistants, or interns? The use of students in the career center provides an excellent mechanism for cooperation with academic programs, particularly those in counselor education, counseling psychology, college student personnel services, or human services that need to find graduate assistantships for their students that have relevance to their degree or employment goals. But, as career centers become more fully staffed with professionally trained and credentialed counselors or psychologists and more comprehensive in the services they provide, they also have the potential to offer internships to graduate students from institutions other than the college or university in which they are located, in response to the requirements of various professional associations (e.g., the American Psychological Association) for one-half or full-time internships that are paid and supervised. Regardless, of which of these student roles is included in the career center, a major planning issue is who will do the supervision, how formal and intense it will be, and what professional guidelines will be used to shape the nature of such supervisory relationships. As the nature of the career needs of college students is more fully understood by colleges and universities, the opportunities for employment in career centers are likely to increase, and the pressures of career centers to provide paid and unpaid, formal and informal training activities for students will likely intensify.

FUTURE TRENDS AND ISSUES

In the preceding section, we have reiterated many of the themes that have constituted this reference's content. Many of these themes embody enduring issues for the planning, shaping, and implementing of career centers in small colleges or in large universities. Thus, in very general terms, any career center must consider its scope and objectives, staffing, resources, use of technology, and other essential questions. However, how these questions are answered in specific, not general, terms, will likely be dependent on whether a particular institution is public or private, large or small, in a state with a healthy economy or one that is in financial crisis, with a student body that is relatively homogeneous or quite heterogeneous with regard to age and cultural diversity, and in an institution that is primarily undergraduate or that encompasses all of the elements of a multi-versity.

In myriad ways, the variables just identified will continue to interact in complex ways for each institution and for its career center into the foreseeable future. In this sense, it is not really possible to speak of the status or health or directions for career centers except as one considers individual centers in individual institutions. Although in this section we discuss some of the trends likely to be of increasing importance in the future, they are likely to be of more or less significance from one institution to another. For these reasons, in its discussion of planning, Chapter 3 differentiated between long-term strategic planning factors and those that are short-term.

Depending upon how far into the future one wishes to project, both long-term factors and short-term factors are important considerations. But the long-term factors (behavioral expectations, career development theory, professional development standards, position of career services within the university structure, institutional goals and mission) tend to be more stable than short-term factors. The latter include the economy, changing student demographics, staff strengths and weaknesses, current social and political issues of the day, and administrative directives. These short-term factors constitute much of the substance of future trends and issues as they are now unfolding.

The Economy

As a short-term planning factor, the economy is both a trend and an issue. As a trend, federal and state budgets are now recovering from the effects of an economic recession, bearing the costs of the Gulf War, and, perhaps, attempting to respond to too many special interest requests without the planning and priority setting necessitated by reduced revenues associated with rising unemployment rates, loss of world market shares in goods exported, the transfer of industries and jobs abroad, and other related factors. One consequence of these conditions, among many others, is the reality that in state after state, the level of economic support for higher education in relative terms is diminishing. Colleges and universities are closing programs and seeking other ways to reduce costs while also accenting their strengths.

When the availability and the adequacy of money to support an institution become a major concern, many issues that had been latent during times of economic affluence begin to surface and to be considered as part of the planning process. These issues range across a spectrum from, for example, the place and cost of intercollegiate athletics in the higher education environment, whether fees should be charged for services to students that had previously been included in student tuition, whether physical plant maintenance and landscaping can be reduced, the contributions made by student affairs programs and practitioners to the higher education mission, and the cost-benefit ratio of these services. Into this mix of issues invariably comes the question of the role and importance of the career center: are the outcomes achieved still relevant to the mission of the college or university? Can the services be provided more economically? Does the scope or comprehensiveness of these services need to be reduced? Are there economic outcomes associated with the services provided by the career center?

As Caple (1992) has suggested: "An answer is shaped by the way a question is framed, so directions taken by an institution may be defined by its statement of mission. To further the analogy, if a question is important, so is the way it is answered. If defining the mission is important, so is the way the institution achieves it" (p. 3). Economic constraints are reframing institutional questions about missions to be achieved, populations to be served, programs to be retained or enhanced. In a major sense, these questions are implicit value issues. They ask about importance, goals, priorities. They express a need to reassess whether the institution has been drawn into a competition to do too many things that are of unequal importance to the institution's basic mission, however that is defined. They ask about how quality can be preserved and what institutional strengths should be enhanced, given greater visibility, and provided scarce resources to expand or to become stronger.

In periods of economic austerity, processes of strategic planning or total quality management are advanced as responses to the need to ponder and reexamine the institutional pathways to be taken and those to be avoided. While career centers can be victims of such scrutiny, they can also be beneficiaries of it. Economic circumstances can stimulate an increased appreciation of the role of the career center as a mechanism that lives in both the academic and the corporate cultures and in so doing has direct ties to potential economic resources. As such, the career center offers opportunities to identify and feed back "market niches" for the college or university as represented by adult populations to be educated in special programs or consultative services to be rendered and as mechanisms to screen and map the social environment, the changing needs for students skills, and other areas in which the college or university can shape its behavior to take advantage of the economic opportunities that are emerging.

While it is typical for much of the professional literature and the popular press to view current economic conditions as troublesome and as constraints to progress in higher education, there are other ways to view the implications of economic circumstances as they relate to career centers. One of these is reflected in the dynamics of the global economy.

The Global Economy

Although it is a truism that international economic competition and the global economy are placing new demands on national economic resources to support industrial development, basic and higher education, and the acquisition and implementation of advanced technology in workplaces and classrooms, other ripple effects may be of major importance to the future roles of career centers. One is that the global economy has moved the locus of concern in nation after nation from primary emphases on availability of raw materials and state-of-the-art equipment to the quality of the work force. As the structure of the world's economy is undergoing rapid change, the political, social, and economic corollaries of such change are placing new demands upon human resources in virtually every nation. It is becoming increasingly clear in national development plans, strategic industrial goal setting, and various international forums that the key factor in a nation's ability to compete in the growing global economy is the quality of its work force as defined by the literacy, numeracy, flexibility, and teachability that characterize it. Many nations, particularly in East Asia, have understood this challenge clearly for several decades. They have set new standards for the unparalleled development of human resources as national priorities, and they have created technological systems necessary to support the maximization of the productivity of these human resources (Schlosstein, 1989, p. xiv).

To make a very long and complex story short, the dynamics of the global economy potentially affect career centers in colleges and universities in at least three ways. First, if career center staff understand such implications of the global economy as the absolute and unequivocal demand for high-quality technical and service-producing work forces in all nations engaged in international economic competition as well as the changes in skills and opportunities stimulated by the global economy, this information can be used to affirm the importance to the university and its various student and alumni constituencies of the diverse roles played by the career center. In this sense, career center staffs will need to broaden their understanding of the occupational structure to consider not only opportunities and employers available within a local, state, or national arena, but the options being created in cross-national or multinational terms.

Second, if the first implications of the global economy for the career center are essentially correct, then an additional implication is that career centers may need to alter the perspectives and resources they use to accommodate the changes in student skills and knowledge they advocate in individual counseling or in the content of career-planning courses and workshops designed to prepare students for placement. This does not mean that the global economy necessitates totally new models of career development. Instead, what seems to be apparent is that as international economic competition shapes the skill requirements and work environments of both domestic corporations and multinational ones, certain skills and perspectives become more important for workers at all levels.

The third implication of the emerging global economy for career centers has to do with the breadth and depth of content used in the information systems provided by the career center. For example, does the career center responsive to the implications of the global economy confine its information resources about jobs to those in the United States or broaden them to include jobs available within the nations of the North American Free Trade Agreement? If the latter, then information about jobs in Canada and in Mexico would also be appropriate. So would job information about multinational corporations originating in the United States but having offices or plants in nations within the European Economic

Community or in the Association of South East Asian Nations (ASEAN). Such perspectives are no longer exotic or fantasied. The world is now divided into three primary trading blocks comprised of clusters of nations among which many of the constraints to cross-national occupational mobility of workers have been removed within each of the clusters, not between them. In other word, workers from the United States can now work within Canada, or, in the near future, Mexico without many of the visa or work permit requirements previously in force. Canadians and, in all likelihood, Mexicans can move more freely into workplaces in the United States, Mexico, or Canada with less constraint than has been historically true. However, U.S., Canadian, or Mexican workers must still face significant barriers to working in the nations of the European Economic Community or the ASEAN (Association of South East Asian Nations).

The issue for the career center staff is what they will do to reflect in their consultations with academic departments and university administrators, in their interactions with students, or in their mission statement how they plan to accommodate the changing opportunity structure for students in the United States and abroad. What skills will they encourage students to acquire? What information sources and systems will they implement?

With respect to skills to be advocated, spatial limitations here preclude an expanded discussion of the matter, but selected examples can make the point. These are perspectives that career centers must share with academic departments and with individual counselors as they plan the content of their outreach and their interventions.

One of these is the need for technological and computer literacy. From a global perspective, technology becomes critical at every step of international trade, production, and communication as raw materials, labor forces, and ideas are integrated into world systems of commercial interaction. As such, the pervasive implementation of advanced technology has altered the mix of jobs available and the content of work in a ripple effect across national economies. It has given superordinate importance to work forces that are literate, flexible, adaptable and teachable. Lifelong learning is no longer relevant to only small segments of the working populations but has required much larger and growing segments of the work force to be comprised of knowledgeable workers. Advanced technology is basically a process of generating, analyzing, and applying information for different purposes and using different media in different settings. In the twentieth century, knowledge has rapidly become the economy's foundation and its true capital. Knowledge has replaced experience as the primary requisite for employability. Knowledge is transforming the organization of work, the skill requirements, and the psychology of work related to effectively integrating technologies into the workplace and helping persons interrelate with these technologies. These are challenges that career centers must help students anticipate and prepare to accommodate as they deal with such views as those of Weiner and Brown (1989), who state: "The relentless advance of technological development puts even highly educated persons at risk of becoming to some extent functionally illiterate" (p. 11).

Beyond the rapidly growing importance of technological and computer literacy, whether or not one is in a technology-intensive occupation, other skills will be increasingly important as a function of the emerging global economy. As a function of the growth of multinational corporations or mergers of firms across nations, persons in many domestic jobs will be involved in import-export relationships in which they may move to other nations on temporary or long-term bases or will have significant contact with nationals from other countries. In either case, workers who are bilingual or multilingual will be prized, and their careers will be enhanced by such skills. While English may have become the lingua franca of the commercial world, other nations in influential economic situations are reasserting the importance of their own language (e.g., Germany and France) or the significance of cultural-language interactions in many nations, which require a knowledge of the national language, even if English is the official commercial language, in order to understand the nuances of the transaction under way and the subtleties of meaning embedded in such transactions. Similarly, in a world where the emergence of the global economy signifies, among other matters, that nations throughout the world are in transition or transformation, attempting to modify their political systems while simultaneously attempting to retain their cultural identity as they integrate themselves into national collaboratives, knowledge of cultural differences, world history, political, and legal and economic systems will likely become as important for a growing number of jobs as are accounting procedures, machine skills, and other technical competencies. Given the variety of physical and social ecologies in which a global economy must be played out, the need will increase for persons who have skills in the legal and regulatory systems of other nations and the abilities to examine and plan in accordance with the environmental impact of construction projects and industrial processes so they are integrated within differential national environmental laws and circumstances. So, too, will the need increase for managerial and entrepreneurial skills related to the administration, organization, and stimulation of new, downsized, and decentralized organizations of work.

In more specific terms, there are sets of skills being identified as important to work life in a global economy that also recognize the potential ambiguity of many aspects of a global economy, as well as the pressures for coping with information overload or inadequacy, communications problems, or human conflict. One model of such essential skills in the career development of workers is that defined by the U.S. Congress's Office of Technology (1988, p. 243) as including:

Skills of Problem Recognition and Definition
- recognizing a problem that is not clearly presented
- defining the problem in a way that permits clear analysis and action
- tolerating ambiguity

Handling Evidence
- collecting and evaluating evidence
- working with insufficient information

- working with excessive information

Analytical skills
- brainstorming
- hypothesizing counterarguments
- using analogies

Skills of Implementation
- recognizing the limitation of available resources
- recognizing the feedback of a proposed solution to the system
- the ability to recover from mistakes

Human Relations
- negotiation and conflict resolution
- collaboration in problem solving

Learning Skills
- ability to identify the limits of one's own knowledge
- ability to ask pertinent questions
- ability to penetrate poor documentation
- ability to identify sources of information (documents and people)

Amundson (1989), a Canadian counseling psychologist, has described many of the skills that have global applicability from the perspective of competence. His view might well be a credo that career centers need to impart to their student clients. Amundson indicates that competence is not just a state of doing; it is a state of being that gives one the capacity or the power to deal adequately with emerging situations. Amundson suggests that there are eight components in his model of competence and that virtually every job demands some capability in each of these eight areas: a sense of purpose; self-, other-, and organizational under-standing; communication and problem-solving skills; theoretical knowledge and understanding of facts and procedures; practical experience; a supportive organizational context that at minimum has elements that allow people to achieve without wasting time and resources; a support network that allows competent people to give and to receive help as part of maintaining their competency, self-confidence, and acceptance of themselves; and the strength to learn from mistakes and persevere.

Aside from the implications of the global economy for some reemphasis of, or additions to, the skills ordinarily considered by career centers to constitute career development, there are also questions to be considered about information systems that may need to be created. At this point, speculation about possibilities is more likely than facts, but the general possibilities likely to emerge in the future are not too difficult to discern. For example, it is likely that new forms of comprehensive information will become available on educational and occupational opportunities across the various regional economic trading blocks with which workers or students of a particular nation are likely to interact. For example, a directory integrating the U.S. Department of Labor's *Occupational Outlook Handbook* with its Canadian and Mexican counterparts to create a *North American Occupational Outlook Handbook* is feasible and would be useful. Such a directory could be linked or cross-referenced with the directories of occupational opportunity now being compiled under the aegis of the European Community (Banks, Raban, & Watts, 1990). Computer databases about higher education and other training opportunities in Canada and Europe could be linked with American systems, as could occupational databases describing job opportunities in these nations as well as analyses of what educational or worker qualifications mean from one nation to another.

This brief discussion only highlights a trend that career centers will increasingly need to plan for and respond to. In a world of immense political and economic transition, a global economy rapidly changes both the metaphors and the realities of the contexts which the clients of career centers during the forthcoming decades will attempt to enter, maintain, retrain for, change career trajectories or forge new career patterns. The psychological dynamics, shifts in career possibilities, and modifications in educational and training requirements, as well as the realities of cultural differences in a global economy, will shape new paradigms of career counseling and career services in the career centers of the immediate future.

Diversity and Student Demographics

Beyond the multiple potential effects upon career centers in colleges and universities that arise from the constraints imposed as a function of limitations on economic resources available to higher education generally, a second major trend that will continue to affect career centers, as far as one can see into the future, is diversity of the student population. Diversity takes many forms: gender, sexual preference, race, ethnicity, age, religious background, geographic or regional origin within the United States, international, physical impairment, socioeconomic level, ability. Not all of these variables are ordinarily considered as factors in the diversity of the student population. Typically, the factors most visible are those of majority-minority status, as defined in racial or ethnic terms. Such variables are extremely important, but diversity issues are also implicit in gender balance, in the number and types of persons with physical impairment, in the spread or clusters of persons representing various socioeconomic levels, in the ratios and visibility of persons of different sexual preference, in the size and origin of the international student body, and in the proportions of traditional and nontraditional-aged college students. In many ways, each of these variables can be seen as defining cultures whose members may have somewhat different aspirations, needs, skills, and perspectives on careers than persons from other cultures. As the demographics of the American population continue to show more rapid proportional increases in its citizens from minority, rather than majority, group background, American higher education continues to be a magnet for international students from nations throughout the world, and U.S. policies and practices continue to provide support for the democratization of access to higher education for persons across socioeconomic, racial, and ethnic spectrums, and the career center will be significantly involved in planning for, removing barriers to, and fostering a multicultural organization and environment for its clients. To do so will undoubtedly require multidimensional responses.

Among the issues that career centers must plan for and implement are culturally diverse staffs and mission statements that must incorporate multicultural values and expectations and be tied to culturally sensitive services. Staff development must focus on implications of cultural diversity in both the sensitivity to, and the content of, interventions offered to clients. Attitudes in the staff and in the environment of the career center must reflect a celebration of cultural diversity in clients, not simply a toleration of such diversity. Displays of culturally relevant artifacts, artwork, and posters need to be visible manifestations of such organizational attitudes.

In addition to the climate of the career center toward cultural diversity, there is a need for a research presence in the center that attempts to assess the career development needs and aspirations of culturally diverse clients and the effects upon them of the services offered. Such research should not be focused only on culturally diverse constituents; it is necessary to know the degree to which other constituent groups need services or programs that enhance both their cross-cultural capabilities and their cultural identity. Thus, programs dealing with cross-cultural communications, conflict resolution, sexuality/gender issues, and other content may be warranted. Similarly, programs for international students dealing with models of, and expectations of, American work organizations represent bridges from one set of cultural phenomena related to work, its personal importance, and its ethos to a different set of cultural perspectives. Other programs dealing with American models of career development and decision making compared with those more typical of other nations provide contexts in which international and American students and staff can learn about these processes as alternative cultural constructions that are used differently across settings and organizations but that do not demean a differently defined process in another culture.

International students and other culturally different college students may share many similar career needs, but they are also likely to have separate needs. For example, in one comparison of the academic and career needs of international and U.S. college students (Leong & Sedlacek, 1989), it was found that the needs of international students were greater in each of these areas than were those of U.S. students. Part of the explanation is that international students place more emphasis than U.S. students on the academic and vocational aspects of a college education than on its social and curricular aspects. Unlike American students, international students tend to be less interested in exploring job opportunities and developing effective job-seeking skills (probably because these are United States-oriented) than in preparing for the career they are interested in, obtaining work experience in it, and seeing a career counselor about their plans. These career needs of international students are likely reinforced because most international students study in the technical and scientific areas, not in the social science and humanities areas. As some observers have suggested (Walter-Samli & Samli, 1979; MacArthur, 1980), they study in America for so many years that they may not be aware of job opportunities in their own home country. Such knowledge is more likely to be available to a student who is fully funded by his or her government than for a student who is paying for his or her own costs or is on a college or university financial aid package. In either case, international students may need to be helped periodically to assess whether what they are studying and the job opportunities available to them upon their return to their home country continue to be congruent. Thus, periodic reviews of progress and evaluations of their training to be sure that there are links to opportunities in their home countries seem essential.

Career centers can also create programs to help international students anticipate and prepare to deal with reverse culture shock. After a long period of study in the United States, international students may need assistance to consider the implications of how differences in life-style, equipment availability, and social and cultural expectations will affect them when they return home. The career center is, perhaps, uniquely able on most campuses to provide responses to these needs. As the number of international students coming to the United States continues to grow and to become even more Asian in proportion (Herr & Cramer, 1992), the career center on many campuses will need to address directly and systematically such career needs.

In contrast to the career needs of international students or many of the other culturally diverse groups, another student population increasing in number is the adult student. Many of these persons may be part-time students, precluding their access to the career center unless hours are available to them in the evening or on Saturday. Many of these persons also have family obligations, needs to work while going to school, and some skepticism about seeing career counselors who are younger than they. These persons frequently need help with the psychological transition from being a full-time worker to being a student; with issues of time and money management; with validation that their decision making has been appropriate as they make major career changes; and with assurance that they are in an appropriate curriculum to achieve the career outcomes they seek.

There are unique career concerns that affect other groups of culturally different students. For example, college students with disabilities are typically found to be concerned about their employment future, their qualifications for particular careers, resource problems, and the availability of appropriate support services that offer staff members who understand the needs of people with disabilities and encourage them to have confidence in their future (Schriner & Roessler, 1990). A population related to college students with physical disabilities is college students with learning disabilities (McGuire, Hall, & Litt, 1991). These students frequently demonstrate inadequate planning and organizational skills, insufficient goal setting, poor time management, and anxiety about career plans that can be addressed by the career center in specially defined programs. While found both in culturally different and in traditional populations, other groups of college students add to the diversity required in planning for student needs. One of these is student athletes. This group of students, many of whom are minority students, have been found, particularly in large universities, to experience several career development issues: lack of identification of academic and career plans, unrealistic goal setting, lack of self-confidence outside athletics, and the assumption that they will become professional athletes, even though only a small percentage of all college athletes ever achieve such a goal (Wilkes, Davis, & Dever, 1989). Again, this is a rather unique group of college students, living in a culture (the athletic environment) that sets them apart from other college students and requires of the career center planning and services that are tailored to the needs of such a population. While much more deserves to be said about diversity in the likely clients of the career center in the future, the examples provided intend to illustrate how changing student demographics, particularly the trends toward increasing proportions of culturally diverse students, must be acknowledged in the planning for, and services provided by, career centers.

Professionalism and the Comprehensiveness of Career Centers

In the trends just discussed—economic fiscal constraints, the challenges of the global economy relative to skill requirements and the organization of work, and the growing diversity of the college or university student population—there are many concerns and issues that have been addressed in more or less comprehensive ways in earlier chapters.

One of the issues for career centers is the continuing need for growing professionalism in career center staff. As the complexity of the services provided and the diversity of the clients being served grow, the needs for career center staff who are fully trained in counseling psychology, counselor education, and related areas become critical. Career centers are increasingly basing their planning and services on theoretical models of college student career development, and it is essential that their staff members understand and think in such terms. It is also likely that while career centers will continue to straddle or bridge both academic and corporate cultures, their professional staff members will need to carry the fullest possible academic credentials. Directors of career centers and other key staff members will likely need doctoral degrees and personal affiliations for teaching and research with academic departments in order to tighten the view of the career center as an academic entity, not an employment agency housed in an academic environment.

Increasingly symbolic as well as functional will be the needs in career center staff for persons who have attained status as licensed psychologists, professionally certified counselors, and other such professional designations. Such credentials are increasingly important in attracting graduate students as interns or graduate assistants from academic programs (e.g., counseling psychology and counselor education) that require formal supervision by appropriately trained and credentialed persons. These credentials are also important because they are recognized by those in academic departments as acknowledgments that the career center staff are professional peers who are expert in their domains of application. Support of academic departments for the purposes, functions, and personnel of career centers will increasingly be important matters as economic resources available in higher education become limited. The professional credibility of career center staff will provide more ready access to faculty members in academic departments. Such faculty members are sources of student referrals, promoters of programs in career centers, and users of resources from the career center to include career and related information in their own courses. As issues of professional credibility of career center staff and resources are dealt with effectively, the career center will want continuously to nurture such academic faculty-career center communications by finding other creative strategies to reach out to faculty. Possibilities include writing articles for faculty newsletters, appointing a faculty liaison to each academic department, or, in the case of multiversities, hosting coffee hours for department faculty, consulting or collaborating on projects of mutual interest (e.g., cooperative education placement), and providing opportunities for students of particular departments to identify regional graduate schools with programs of direct relevance to that academic department's content (Arthur & Menzel, 1990).

Finally, perhaps, the constant seeking of professional training, credentials, and credibility for career center staff members is also likely to heighten the probability that career centers will incorporate professional organizational guidelines and ethical statements into their planning and procedures. Membership of career center staff members in such organizations as the American Counseling Association, the American Psychological Association, the National Career Development Association, and the College Placement Council provides information about in-service training for various types of career development specialists, access to information on career interventions and trends, descriptions of, and training materials in, career counseling competencies, uses in career interventions of technology, professional guidelines related to the establishment and operation of career centers, and ethical standards and opportunities for credentialing in various professional specialties.

CONCLUSION

This epilogue has had two purposes. One has been to reassert several of the overarching premises that have been pervasive in the earlier nine chapters. The second has been briefly to discuss several of the short-term factors that will likely affect career centers for the foreseeable future. They include issues of economic constraints, changing employment opportunities fostered by a global economy, growing diversity within the demographics of college student populations, and a growing need to attend to the professional training and credibility within the academic and the corporate cultures of career center staff.

In many ways the comprehensive missions of contemporary career centers identified here are recent phenomena. Career centers with both a student career development and a placement goal are evolving in many organizational forms in American higher education. In truth, these forms and their evolution have not yet found professional maturity in many higher education institutions. We hope that the content of this handbook will be useful to institutions creating career centers and those in the process of redefining career centers. We believe careful attention to the recommendations and examples included will assist in the development of career centers that are responsive to the uniqueness of student career needs and to those of the employers who will ultimately provide them career opportunities, that are planful and comprehensive, and that are tailored to the institutional purposes that they serve with integrity and credibility.

REFERENCES

Amundson, N. E. (1989). *Competence: Components and development*. Unpublished manuscript, Department of Counselling Psychology, University of British Columbia, Vancouver, Canada.

Arthur, J. V., & Menzel, F. S. (1990). Faculty and career center collaboration. *Journal of College Student Development, 31*(6), 566–567.

Banks, J.A.G., Raban, A. S., & Watts, A. G. (1990). The single European market and its implications for educational and vocational guidance services. *International Journal for the Advancement of Counselling, 13*(4), 275–294.

Caple, R. B. (1992). A mission is the task assigned. *Journal of College Student Development, 33*(1), 3–4.

Herr, E. L., & Cramer, S. H. (1992). *Career guidance and counseling through the lifespan. Systematic approaches*. (4th ed.). New York: Harper Collins.

Leong, F. T., & Sedlacek, W. E. (1989). Academic and career needs of international and United States college students. *Journal of College Student Development, 30*(2), 106–111.

MacArthur, J. D. (1980). Career services for university international students. *Vocational Guidance Quarterly, 29*, 178–181.

McGuire, J. M., Hall, D., & Litt, A. V. (1991). A field-based study of the direct service needs of college students with learning disabilities. *Journal of College Student Development, 32*(2), 101–108.

Office of Technology Assessment, U.S. Congress. (1988). *Technology and the American economic transition. Choices for the future*. Washington, DC: Author.

Schlosstein, S. (1989). *The end of the American century*. New York: Congdon & Weed.

Schriner, K. F., & Roessler, R. T. (1990). Employment concerns of college students with disabilities: Toward an agenda for policy and practice. *Journal of College Student Development, 31*(4), 307–312.

Walter-Samli, J. H., & Samli, A. C. (1979). A model of career counseling for international students. *Vocational Guidance Quarterly, 28*(1), 48–55.

Weiner, E., & Brown, A. (1989). Human factors: The gap between humans and machines. *Futurist, 23*(3), 9–11.

Wilkes, S. B., Davis, L., & Dever, L. (1989). Fostering career development in student athletes. *Journal of College Student Development, 30*(6), 567–568.

Selected Bibliography

Bjorkquist, P. M. (1987). Career development for the liberal arts student. *Journal of College Student Development, 28,* 377.

Broch, S. B., & Davis, E. M. (1987). Adapting career services for the adult student. *Journal of College Student Personnel, 28,* 87.

Brown, R. D. (1988). *Performance appraisal as a tool for staff development.* San Francisco: Jossey-Bass.

College Placement Council. (1990). *Principles for professional conduct for career services and employment professionals.* Bethlehem, PA: Author.

College Placement Council. (1991a). *Computerization sourcebook.* Bethlehem, PA: Author.

College Placement Council. (1991b). 1991 Career Planning & Placement Survey. Bethlehem, Pa: Author.

Council for the Advancement of Standards. (1986). *CAS standards and guidelines for student services/development programs.* Iowa City, IA: American College Testing Program.

Healy, C. C., & Reilly, K. C. (1989). Career needs of community college students: Implications for services and theory. *Journal of College Student Development, 30*(6), 541–545.

Herr, E. L., & Cramer, S. H. (1988). *Career guidance and counseling through the life span* (3rd ed.). Glenview, IL: Scott, Foresman.

Gelatt, H. B. (1962). Decision-making. A conceptual frame of reference for counseling. *Journal of Counseling Psychology, 9,* 240–245.

Gelatt, H. B. (1989). Positive uncertainty: A new decision-making framework for counseling. *Journal of Counseling Psychology, 36*(2), 252–256.

Herr, E. L., & Cramer, S. H. (1992). *Career guidance and counseling through the life span. Systematic approaches* (4th ed.). New York: Harper Collins.

Keller, G. (1983). *Academic strategy: The management revolution in American higher education.* Baltimore: Johns Hopkins University Press.

Keller, J. W., Piotrowski, C., & Rabold, F. L. (1990). Determinants of career selection in undergraduates. *Journal of College Student Development, 31*(3), 276–277.

Kroll, J., & Rentz, A. L. (1988). Career planning and placement. In A. L. Rentz & G. L. Saddlemire (Eds.), *Student affairs functions in higher education.* Springfield, IL: Charles C. Thomas.

Lent, R. W., & Hackett, G. (1987). Career self-efficacy: Empirical status and future directions. *Journal of Vocational Behavior, 30,* 347–382.

Leong, F. T., & Sedlacek, W. E. (1989). Academic and career needs of international and United States college students. *Journal of College Student Development, 30*(2), 106–111.

McKenzie, I. L., & Manoogian-O'Dell, M. (1988). Expanding the use of students in career services: Current programs and resources. *American College Personnel Association Media Association Publication,* No. 45.

Ouchi, W. (1981). *Theory Z.* Reading, MA: Addison-Wesley.

Peters, T. J., & Waterman, R. H. (1984). *In search of excellence.* New York: Warner Books.

Peterson, G. W., Sampson, J. P., & Reardon, R. C. (1991). *Career development and services: A cognitive approach.* Pacific Grove, CA: Brooks/Cole.

Rayman, J. R. (1990). Computers and career counseling. In W. B. Walsh & S. H. Osipow (Eds.), *Career counseling: Contemporary topics in vocational psychology* (pp. 225–262). Hillsdale, NJ: Lawrence Erlbaum Associates.

Sampson, J. P., Shahnasarian, M., & Reardon, R. C. (1987). Computer-assisted career guidance: A national perspective on the use of DISCOVER and SIGI. *Journal of Counseling and Development, 65,* 416–419.

Schriner, K. F., & Roessler, R. T. (1990). Employment concerns of college students with disabilities: Toward an agenda for policy and practice. *Journal of College Student Development, 31*(4), 307–312.

Shingleton, J. D., & Fitzpatrick, E. B. (1985). *Dynamics of placement. How to develop a successful planning and placement program.* Bethlehem, PA: CPC Foundation.

Walter-Samli, J. H., & Samli, A. C. (1979). A model of career counseling for international students. *Vocational Guidance Quarterly, 28,* 48–55.

Whiteley, S. M., Mahaffey, P. J., & Geer, C. A. (1987). The campus counseling center: A profile of staffing patterns and services. *Journal of College Student Personnel, 28,* 71–81.

Wilkes, S. B., Davis, L., & Dever, L. (1989). Fostering career development in student athletes. *Journal of College Student Development, 30*(6), 567–578.

Index

About the Authors

EDWIN L. HERR is Distinguished Professor of Education and Associate Dean for Academic Programs and Research at the College of Education, Pennsylvania State University. For 24 years he served as Director of the College of Education Counseling Service and as Head, Department of Counselor Education, Counseling Psychology and Rehabilitation Services Education at the same university. His many publications include *Career Guidance and Counseling Through The Lifespan, Counseling In A Dynamic Society: Opportunities and Challenges, and Controversies in the Mental Health Profession*. He is presently writing a book on the foundations of vocational education.

JACK R. RAYMAN is Affiliate Professor of Education and Counseling Psychology and Director, Career Development and Placement Services, Pennsylvania State University. His interests include counseling and career psychology, and the theory and practice of career development. He has written several book chapters, and his articles have appeared in publications such as *Journal of Business and Technical Communications* and the *Journal of Career Planning and Employment*.

JEFFREY W. GARIS was formerly the Associate Director, Career Development and Placement Services, and Affiliate Assistant Professor of Counselor Education at Pennsylvania State University. He now serves as Director, the Career Center, Florida State University. His articles have appeared in *Career Development Quarterly*, the *Journal of Career Development* and the *Journal of College Placement*.